ELECTRONIC

MEDIA

MANAGEMENT

FOURTH EDITION

ELECTRONIC

MEDIA

MANAGEMENT

FOURTH EDITION

PETER K. PRINGLE

MICHAEL F. STARR

WILLIAM E. McCAVITT

Focal Press

Boston • Oxford • Auckland • Johannesburg • Melbourne • New Delhi

Focal Press is an imprint of Elsevier Science.

∞ This book is printed on acid-free paper.

Library of Congress Cataloging-in-Publication Data
Pringle, Peter K.
    Electronic media management/ Peter K. Pringle, Michael F. Starr,
    William E. McCavitt. —4th ed.
      p.   cm.
    Includes bibliographical references and index.
    ISBN 0-240-80332-9 (pbk. : alk. paper)
    1.   Broadcasting—Management. 2. Television stations—Management.
    3. Radio stations—Management.   I. Starr, Michael F., 1940- .
    II. McCavitt, William E., 1932- .   III. Title.
    HE8689.6.M33   1999
    384.54'068—dc21   99-11797
                                      CIP

British Library Cataloguing-in-Publication Data
A catalogue record for this book is available from the British Library.

The publisher offers special discounts on bulk orders of this book.
For information, please contact:
Manager of Special Sales
Elsevier Science
200 Wheeler Road
Burlington, MA 01803
Tel: 781-313-4700
Fax: 781-313-4802

For information on all Focal Press publications available, contact our
World Wide Web homepage at http://www.focalpress.com

10 9 8 7 6 5
Printed in the United States of America

CONTENTS

FINANCIAL MANAGEMENT   31

HUMAN RESOURCE MANAGEMENT   71

BROADCAST PROMOTION AND MARKETING 213

BROADCAST REGULATIONS 245

MANAGING THE CABLE TELEVISION SYSTEM   281

PREFACE

The few years that have passed since the publication of the third edition of this book have been momentous. Two major broadcast networks — ABC and CBS — acquired new owners. One cable giant, Time Warner, purchased another, Turner Broadcasting System. The era of Webcasting began. The first major overhaul of telecommunications law in more than sixty years occurred.

The implications of these changes, and others, are examined in this new edition, which seeks to equip electronic media students for management in a new millenium — and for the unprecedented challenges that will assuredly accompany it.

Only one major change has been made to the book's organization. Instead of trying to predict the broad future in a closing chapter, the authors have added to each chapter a section that anticipates developments in the topic area covered.

All the remaining chapters have been updated, some extensively. New case studies accompany each. The glossary and the bibliography reflect, respectively, the new language and literature that characterize what has been termed the "Megamedia Age."

We thank the reviewers and users of the third edition for their observations and suggestions. We owe special thanks to the supportive staff at Focal Press and, especially, to our editor Terri Jadick. Her understanding and patience are without equal.

Acknowledgments

Arter & Hadden, Washington, D.C.

Blackburn & Company, Alexandria, Virginia

Dan Brown, President, Radio Chattanooga, Chattanooga, Tennessee

Duane Bryan, Promotions Director, WRCB-TV, Chattanooga, Tennessee

Don Checots, President, KPTS-TV, Wichita, Kansas

Corporation for Public Broadcasting, Washington, D.C.

Glenn B. Enoch, Director of Research and Data Services, ESPN, New York City

Fisher Wayland Cooper Leader & Zaragoza, Washington, D.C.

Ralph Flynn, Local Sales Manager, WRCB-TV, Chattanooga, Tennessee

Goodstarr Broadcasting, LLC, Wichita, Kansas

Media Services Group, Inc., Jacksonville, Florida

National Association of Broadcasters, Washington, D.C.

John B. Phillips, Jr., Miller & Martin, Chattanooga and Nashville, Tennessee and Atlanta, Georgia

Gene Shatlock, Area Vice President and General Manager, Comcast, Chattanooga, Tennessee

Southern Illinois University Broadcasting Service, Carbondale, Illinois

Tom Tolar, General Manager, WRCB-TV, Chattanooga, Tennessee

Joseph Vincenza, Program Director, KMUW-FM, Wichita, Kansas

Chuck Wilkins, General Sales Manager, Radio Chattanooga, Chattanooga, Tennessee

1 BROADCAST STATION MANAGEMENT

This chapter examines broadcast station management by

☐ defining management and tracing the roots of today's management thought and practice

☐ identifying the functions and roles of the broadcast station general manager and the skills necessary to carry them out

☐ discussing the major influences on the general manager's decisions and actions

When AT&T announced a voluntary early retirement program for its 52,000 managers in January 1998, it projected that about 10,000 of them would sign up. At the deadline five months later, more than 15,000 had accepted the offer. A decisive factor in their decision was the generous financial package — up to 20 percent more than their normal pension, an average of $300,000 for each departing manager. In a strong employment market, some of the retirees looked forward to finding another executive position.

However, concerns about the future may have been a compelling reason for many. One survey in 1998 found that more than 71 percent of executives believed their companies or industries would be threatened by mergers, downsizing, or restructuring in the following twelve months.[1] They feel "they can never be sure of their future, given the constant pace of change," said an official of the firm that conducted the survey.[2]

Change is a way of life for broadcast station managers, who have to contend routinely with a shifting public policy climate and accelerating technological innovation. But that is only one of the challenges they confront. Like any other business, the station must be operated profitably if it is to survive and satisfy the financial expectations of its owners. At the same time, it must respond to the interests of the community it is licensed to serve by the Federal Communications Commission (FCC). Balancing the private interests of owners and the public interest of listeners or viewers is a continuing challenge.

A broadcast station engages in many functions. It is an advertising medium, an entertainment medium, an information medium, and a service medium. To discharge those functions in a way that meets the interests of advertisers, audiences, and employees is an additional challenge. Another challenge grows out of the increasingly competitive environment in which broadcast stations operate.

A radio study revealed that overall listening nationwide fell 6 percent between 1997 and 1998, and that the decline affected most formats.[3] That followed a loss of about 9 points in the percentage of the population listening to radio in the average quarter-hour between 1989 and 1997.[4]

Managers of television stations affiliated with ABC, CBS, and NBC have seen a steady and continuing erosion of their audience in the face of competition, first from Fox affiliates, then, more recently, from those of The WB and UPN networks. For all stations, the greatest threat comes from cable, which recorded an increase of more than 7 million subscribers between 1993 and 1997 to reach more than 67 percent of all TV households.[5] In the same five-year period, its prime-time audience share grew by a dramatic 50 percent.[6] Add to the mix direct broadcast satellite (DBS) services with about 7 million subscribers,[7] videocassette recorders (VCRs) in 84 percent of American homes,[8] and the explosion in household Internet use, and it is easy to understand why managers conclude that they face unprecedented competition.

Responsibility for a station's operation is entrusted by the owners to a chief executive, usually called the general manager. This chapter will look at the roles and responsibilities of the general manager, or GM. First, however, it will be helpful to consider what management is, as well as the evolution of management thought and practice during the lifetime of broadcasting.

MANAGEMENT DEFINED

If you were to ask a group of people what management means, chances are that each would offer a different definition. That is not surprising, given the diversity and complexity of a manager's responsibilities.

Schoderbek, Cosier, and Aplin define it as "a process of achieving organizational goals through others."[9] Resource acquisition and coordination are emphasized by Pringle, Jennings, and Longenecker: "Management is the process of acquiring and combining human, financial, informational, and physical resources to attain the organization's primary goal of producing a product or service desired by some segment of society."[10] Others view it from the perspective of the functions that managers perform. For example, Carlisle speaks of "directing, coordinating, and influencing the operation of an organization so as to obtain desired results and enhance total performance."[11]

Mondy, Holmes, and Flippo expand those functions and underline the importance of people as well as materials: "Management may be defined as the process of planning, organizing, influencing, and controlling to accomplish organizational goals through the coordinated use of human and material resources."[12] That is the definition that will be used in this book.

EVOLUTION OF MANAGEMENT THOUGHT

It is tempting to think of management as a comparatively modern practice, necessitated by the emergence of large business organizations. However, as early as 6000 B.C., groups of people were organized to engage in undertakings of giant proportions. The Egyptians built huge pyramids. The Hebrews carried out an exodus from Egyptian bondage. The Romans constructed roads and aqueducts, and the Chinese built a 1,500-mile wall. It is difficult to believe that any of these tasks could have been accomplished without the application of many of today's management techniques.

To understand current management concepts and practices requires familiarity with the evolution of management thought. It traces its start to the dawn of the twentieth century, when the foundations of what later would be called *broadcasting* were being laid. Just as broadcasting has evolved, so has systematic analysis of management. The dominant traits of different managerial approaches have been identified and grouped into so-called schools. The first was the classical school of management.

The Classical School

Classical management thought embraces three separate but related approaches to management: (1) scientific management, (2) administrative management, and (3) bureaucratic management.

Scientific Management   At its origin, scientific management focused on increasing employee productivity and rested on four basic principles:

- systematic analysis of each job to find the most effective and efficient way of performing it (the "one best way")
- use of scientific methods to select employees best suited to do a particular job
- appropriate employee education, training, and development
- responsibility apportioned almost equally between managers and workers, with decision-making duties falling on the managers

The person associated most closely with this school is Frederick W. Taylor (1856–1915), a mechanical engineer, who questioned the traditional, rule-of-thumb approach to managing work and who earned the title "father of scientific management."

Taylor believed that economic incentives were the best motivators. Workers would cooperate if higher wages accompanied higher productivity, and management would be assured of higher productivity in return for paying higher wages. Not surprisingly, he was criticized for viewing people as machines.

However, his contributions were significant. Management scholar Peter Drucker attributes to Taylor "the tremendous surge of affluence . . . which has lifted the working masses in the developed countries well above any level recorded before."[13] Job analysis, methods of employee selection, and their training and development are examples of ways in which principles of scientific management are practiced today.

Administrative Management If Taylor was the father of scientific thought, the French mining and steel executive Henri Fayol (1841–1925) can lay claim to being the father of management thought. While Taylor looked at workers and ways of improving their productivity, Fayol considered the total organization with a view to making it more effective and efficient. In so doing, he developed a comprehensive theory of management and demonstrated its universal nature.

His major contributions to administrative theory came in a book, *General and Industrial Management*, in which he became the first person to set forth the functions of management or, as he called them, "managerial activities":

Planning: Contemplating the future and drawing up a plan to deal with it, which includes actions to be taken, methods to be used, stages to go through, and the results envisaged

Organizing: Acquiring and structuring the human and material resources necessary for the functioning of the organization

Commanding: Setting each unit of the organization into motion so that it can make its contribution toward the accomplishment of the plan

Coordinating: Unifying and harmonizing all activities to permit the organization to operate and succeed

Controlling: Monitoring the execution of the plan and taking actions to correct errors or weaknesses and to prevent their recurrence[14]

To assist managers in carrying out these functions, Fayol developed a list of fourteen principles (Figure 1.1). He did not suggest that the list was exhaustive, merely that the principles were those that he had needed to apply most

Figure 1.1 *Fayol's 14 principles of management. (Source: Henri Fayol,* General and Industrial Management. *Translated by Constance Storrs. London: Sir Isaac Pitman and Sons, 1965, pp. 19–42. The explanations have been paraphrased.)*

Principle	Explanation
1. Division of work	Specialization of work results in higher and better productivity.
2. Authority and responsibility	The right of the manager to give orders and to demand conformity, accompanied by appropriate responsibility.
3. Discipline	Obedience and respect for agreements between the firm and its employees.
4. Unity of command	An employee should receive orders from only one superior.
5. Unity of direction	Each group of activities having the same objective should have only one plan and one head.
6. Subordination of individual interest to general interest	The interest of one employee or group of employees should not prevail over that of the concern.
7. Remuneration of personnel	Payment should be fair and, as far as possible, satisfactory to both employer and employee.
8. Centralization	Each firm must find the optimum degree of centralization to permit maximum utilization of employee abilities.
9. Scalar chain	The line of authority, from top to bottom, through which all communications pass.
10. Order	Materials and employees in their appropriate places to facilitate the smooth running of the business.
11. Equity	Kindness, fairness, and justice in the treatment of employees.
12. Stability of tenure of personnel	Employees must be given time to get used to new work and to succeed in doing it well.
13. Initiative	The freedom and power to think out and execute a plan.
14. Esprit de corps	Establishing harmony and unity among the personnel.

frequently. He warned that such guidelines had to be flexible and adaptable to changing circumstances.

Fayol's contributions may appear to be merely common sense in today's business environment. However, the functions of planning, organizing, and controlling that he identified are still considered fundamental to management success. Many of his principles are incorporated in business organization charts and, in the case of equity, are enshrined in law.

Bureaucratic Management   At the same time that Taylor and Fayol were developing their thoughts, Max Weber (1864–1920), a German sociologist, was contemplating the kind of structure that would enable an organization to perform at the highest efficiency. He called the result a *bureaucracy* and listed several elements for its success. They included:

- division of labor
- a clearly defined hierarchy of authority
- selection of members on the basis of their technical qualifications
- promotion based on seniority or achievement
- strict and systematic discipline and control
- separation of ownership and management[15]

It is unfortunate that contemporary society associates the word bureaucracy with incompetence and inefficiency. For while it is true that a bureaucracy can become mired in rigid rules and procedures, Weber's ideas have proved useful to many large companies that need a rational organizational system to function effectively, and they have earned him a berth in the annals of management thought as "the father of organizational theory."

Contributors to the classical school of management concerned themselves with efforts to make employees and organizations more productive. Their work revealed several of their assumptions about the nature of human beings, among them the notion that workers are motivated chiefly by money and require a clear delineation of their job responsibilities and close supervision if work is to be accomplished satisfactorily. Such assumptions would not withstand the scrutiny of the school that followed.

The Behavioral School

The trend away from classical assumptions began with the human relations movement, which dominated during radio's heyday in the 1930s and 1940s. Among the greatest contributors to the movement were Mary Parker Follett (1868–1933) and Chester I. Barnard (1886–1961), both of whom rejected the view of the "economic man" held by the classical theorists.

Follett, a philosopher, argued in her writings that workers can reach their full potential only as members of a group, which she characterized as the foundation of an organization. In reality, managers and workers are members of the same group and, thus, share a common interest in the success of the enterprise.

Barnard, the president of New Jersey Bell Telephone Company, conceived of an organization as a "system of consciously coordinated activities or forces of two or more persons." As employees work toward the accomplishment of the organization's objectives, they have to be able to satisfy their own needs. Identifying ways of meeting those needs and, simultaneously, enhancing the effectiveness and efficiency of the organization, are the principal challenges facing managers.

However, the most far-reaching contributions to the human relations movement were made by Elton Mayo (1880–1949), a Harvard University psychologist. Between 1927 and 1932, Mayo and Fritz J. Roethlisberger (1898–1974) led a Harvard research team at Western Electric's Hawthorne plant in Illinois. The research focused on ways of improving worker efficiency by evaluating the factors that influence productivity. Its results redirected the course of management thought and practice.

What was observed in only one of the experiments gives a clue to the importance of the Hawthorne studies. To determine the effect on productivity of lighting levels, illumination remained constant among one group of workers (control group) and was systematically increased and decreased among another (experimental group). Contrary to expectations, productivity in both groups rose, even when the lighting in the experimental group was decreased.

The result of this and other experiments, combined with observation and interviews, convinced Mayo and his team that factors other than the purely physical have an effect on productivity. They realized that the one constant factor was the degree of attention paid to workers in the experimental groups. Thus was born the *Hawthorne Effect*, which states that when managers pay special attention to employees, productivity is likely to increase, despite a deterioration in working conditions.

The recognition that social as well as physical influences play a role in worker productivity marked an important milestone. Henceforth, greater attention would have to be paid to the needs of employees, who were now perceived as something other than mechanical, interchangeable parts in the organization.

The human relations movement evolved into the behavioral management school. It assumed dominance in the 1950s and 1960s, as the new medium of television was establishing its popularity in American households. Among this school's major contributions were new insights into the needs of individuals and their role in motivating workers.

In an attempt to formulate a positive theory of motivation, Abraham Maslow (1908–1970), a psychologist, asserted that human beings have certain basic needs and that each serves as a motivator. He identified five such needs and organized them in a hierarchy, starting with the most basic:

- *Physiological:* Food, water, sex, and other physiological satisfiers
- *Safety:* Protection from threat, danger, and illness; a safe, orderly, predictable, organized world
- *Love:* Affection and belongingness
- *Esteem:* Self-esteem and the esteem of others
- *Self-actualization:* Self-fulfillment; to become everything one is capable of becoming[16]

The physiological and safety needs are seen as primary needs, and the remainder, dealing with the psychological aspects of existence, as secondary. Maslow theorized that when one need is fairly well satisfied, it no longer serves as a motivator. Instead, attention turns to the next level on the hierarchy. However, he recognized that the order is not rigid, especially at the higher levels. For example, some people may value self-esteem more than love, and others may never aspire to self-actualization.

There is little empirical data available to support Maslow's theory.[17] Nonetheless, it led to the realization that satisfied needs might have little value in motivating employees and that different techniques might have to be used to motivate different people, according to their particular needs.

While Maslow considered all needs to be motivators, Frederick Herzberg (b. 1923), another psychologist, proposed that employee attitudes and behaviors are influenced by two different sets of considerations. He called them *hygiene factors* and *motivators*.[18]

Hygiene factors[19] are those associated with conditions that surround the doing of the job and include the following: supervision; interpersonal relations with superiors, peers, and subordinates; physical working conditions; salary; company policies and administrative practices; benefits; and job security.

Responding to employees' hygiene needs, concluded Herzberg, will eliminate dissatisfaction and poor job performance but will not lead to positive attitudes and more productive behaviors. Those are accomplished by meeting the second set of considerations, the motivators, or factors associated with the job content. They include achievement, recognition, the work itself, responsibility, and advancement.

Interestingly, there is a close relationship between Herzberg's hygiene factors and the lower-level needs identified by Maslow, and between the motivators and Maslow's self-esteem and self-actualization needs.

The implications of this two-factor theory of motivation are clear. Employees have certain expectations about elements in the environment in which they work. When they are satisfactory, workers are reassured that things are as they ought to be, even though those feelings may not encourage them to greater productivity. However, when environmental expectations are not met, dissatisfaction ensues. An employer must provide for both the hygiene needs and the motivators to achieve a motivated work force. The critical task, therefore, lies in satisfying employees' needs for self-actualization by giving them more responsibility, providing opportunities for advancement, and recognizing their achievement.

Studies appear to show that Herzberg's theory is applicable more to professional and managerial-level employees than to manual workers. Nonetheless, his contributions provided a better understanding of motivation and have had significant effects on job design.

Influenced by the theorists of self-actualization, and especially Maslow, Douglas McGregor (1906–1964), an industrial psychologist, underscored the importance of assumptions about human nature and their effects on motivational methods used by managers. He argued that, despite important advances in the management of human resources, most managers clung to traditional assumptions, which he labeled *Theory X* (Figure 1.2). Managers who saw their employees as having a dislike of work, lacking ambition, and requiring direction were likely to rely on coercion, control, and even threats as motivational tools.

McGregor offered *Theory Y* (Figure 1.2), which took an entirely different view of human nature. Managers who adopted these assumptions considered employees capable of seeking and accepting responsibility, and of exercising self-direction in furtherance of organizational goals — without control and the threat of punishment.

Figure 1.2 *Theory X and Theory Y. (Source: Douglas McGregor,* The Human Side of Enterprise. *New York: McGraw-Hill, 1960, pp. 33–34, 47–48.) Reprinted with permission of McGraw-Hill, Inc.*

Theory X

1. The average human being has an inherent dislike of work and will avoid it if he can.

2. Because of this human characteristic of dislike of work, most people must be coerced, controlled, directed, or threatened with punishment to get them to put forth adequate effort toward the achievement of organizational objectives.

3. The average human being prefers to be directed, wishes to avoid responsibility, has relatively little ambition, and wants security above all.

Theory Y

1. The expenditure of physical and mental effort in work is as natural as play or rest.

2. External control and the threat of punishment are not the only means for bringing about effort toward organizational objectives. Man will exercise self-direction and self-control in the service of objectives to which he is committed.

3. Commitment to objectives is a function of the rewards associated with their achievement.

4. The average human being learns, under proper conditions, not only to accept but to seek responsibility.

5. The capacity to exercise a relatively high degree of imagination, ingenuity, and creativity in the solution of organizational problems is widely, not narrowly, distributed in the population.

6. Under the conditions of modern industrial life, the intellectual potentialities of the average human being are only partially utilized.

McGregor summarized the difference between the two theories in this way:

The central principle of organization which derives from Theory X is that of direction and control through the exercise of authority — what has been called the "scalar principle." The central principle which derives from Theory Y is that of integration: the creation of conditions such that the members of the organization can achieve their own goals best by directing their efforts toward the success of the enterprise.[20]

While McGregor's Theory X and Theory Y are based on assumptions about human nature, William Ouchi (b. 1943) uses Theory A and Theory Z to refer to organizations. He characterizes most U.S. companies as type A and most Japanese companies as type Z, and suggests that the United States can learn much about managing people more effectively from the Japanese model.[21] However, his assertions have come under attack for their failure to recognize the cultural differences between the two nations and their impact on employee management practices.

By drawing attention to the key role played by employees in the attainment of organizational goals, and the importance of recognizing and striving to satisfy their needs, the behavioral school has had a lasting impact on management. In particular, it has resulted in greater attention to the work environment and on-the-job training for employees, and in a realization that people-management skills are a fundamental management attribute.

Management Science

This school of management thought had its origins during World War II and was known, in the beginning, as operations research. In some respects, it represented a reemergence of the quantitative approach favored by Taylor. However, advances in management technology, especially the computer, rendered it much more sophisticated.

Basically, management science involves construction of a mathematical model to simulate a situation. All variables bearing on the situation and their relationships are entered into a computer. By changing the values of the variables, the outcomes of different decisions can be projected.

By replacing descriptive analyses with quantitative data, this approach has been useful in management decision making on matters that can be quantified, such as financial planning. A major shortcoming is its inability to predict the behavior of an organization's human resources.

Modern Management Thought

By the 1960s, management theory incorporated elements of the classical, behavioral, and management science schools. However, theorists could not agree on a single body of knowledge that constituted the field of management. Indeed, one writer likened the situation to a jungle.[22]

Since then, steps have been taken toward clearing the jungle with the adoption of approaches aimed at integrating some of the divergent views of disciples of the earlier schools. Two contemporary perspectives are *systems theory* and *contingency theory*.

Systems Theory
According to the systems theory, an enterprise is seen as a system, "a set of objects with a given set of relationships between the objects and their attributes, connected or related to each other and to their environment in such a way as to form a whole or entirety."[23]

An organizational system is composed of people, money, materials, equipment, and data, all of which are combined in the accomplishment of some purpose. The subsystems typically are identified as divisions or departments whose activities aid the larger system in reaching its goals.

Certain elements are common to all organizational systems (Figure 1.3). They are *inputs* (e.g., labor, equipment, and capital) and *processes*, that is, methods whereby inputs are converted into *outputs* (e.g., goods and services). *Feedback* is information about the outputs or processes and serves as an input to help determine whether changes are necessary to attain the goals. Management's role is to coordinate the input, process, and output factors and to analyze and respond to feedback.

Figure 1.3 *Systems approach to organizational management.*

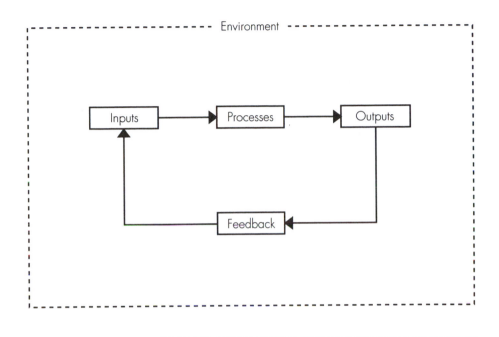

The systems approach emphasizes the relationship between the organization and its external environment. Environmental factors are outside the organization and beyond its control but have an impact on its operations. Accordingly, management must monitor environmental trends and events and make changes deemed necessary to ensure the organization's success.

Contingency Theory   The contingency, or situational, approach to management traces its current origins to systems theory and the desire to identify universal principles of management. It recognizes that principles advanced by earlier schools may be applicable in some situations, but not in others, and seeks an understanding of those circumstances in which certain managerial actions will bring about the desired results.

It is ironic that this line of thought did not emerge as a major force until the mid–1960s, since its significance in the study of leadership was recognized in the 1920s by Follett. She noted that "there are different types of leadership" and that "different situations require different kinds of knowledge, and the man possessing the knowledge demanded by a certain situation tends in the best managed businesses, other things being equal, to become the leader of the moment."[24]

The recent study of contingency principles has been relatively sparse, focusing mostly on organizational structure and decision making. Finally, however, this approach has attracted the attention of theorists to functions other than leadership and has impressed on the field the realization that management is much more complex than earlier theorists imagined.

It is this complexity that makes it impossible to suggest a style for all managers, including those who manage broadcast stations. What is appropriate for one manager in one circumstance with one group of employees may be quite inappropriate for another manager in another circumstance with a different group.

Management Thought in the 1990s Revolutionary developments in the world and in the workplace triggered changes in management thought and practice as the twentieth century drew to a close. The end of communism's dominance in the former Soviet Union and Eastern Europe created new opportunities in a world already characterized by the growing internationalization of business. An era of global interdependence was ushered in by the formation of a single trading bloc among European countries and by ratification of the North American Free Trade Agreement (NAFTA) by the United States, Canada, and Mexico. Technical innovation and the growing heterogeneity of the American work force rendered the organizational world of the 1990s strikingly different from that in which early theorists operated.

Accompanying these developments was a focus on customers' needs and, especially, on their expectations of quality in the products they purchase and the services they use. This gave rise to a new approach to management, *total quality management* (TQM). The approach may have been new in the United States, but its underpinnings were not. In fact, it drew elements from management science, scientific management, and the behavioral approach, and it may be characterized as another attempt to clear the jungle. Nor was its practice new. It was introduced in Japan in the aftermath of World War II by several Americans, the most prominent of whom was W. Edwards Deming (1900–1993), a statistician.

The foundation of Deming's approach to TQM is the conviction that uniform product quality can be ensured through statistical analysis and control of variables in the production process. As the philosophy evolved and technological change became commonplace, his insistence that employees be trained to understand statistical methods and their application and to master new skills assumed greater significance. So, too, did awareness that employees are an integral part of the quality revolution and that, without their total commitment to continuous product or service improvement, any attempt to practice this management philosophy will be doomed.

The success that Deming and other quality proponents achieved in Japan may be judged from that country's rebirth as a major economic power. Indeed, the introduction and growth of total quality management in the United States are due, in large measure, to the realization among many American companies that a similar approach was needed if they were to survive.

The contributions to management thought and practice described in this chapter provide some guidelines for the manager. However, pending the development of a set of universal management principles, the style of most managers probably is summarized best by business mogul T. Boone Pickens, Jr.: "A management style is an amalgamation of the best of other people you have known and respected, and eventually you develop your own style."[25]

MANAGEMENT LEVELS

It is often assumed that management is concentrated at the top of an organization. In reality, anyone who directs the efforts of others in the attainment of goals is a manager. In most companies, including broadcast stations, managers are found at three levels:

Lower: Managers at this level closely supervise the routine work of employees under their charge and are accountable to the next level of management. A radio station local sales manager who reports to the general sales manager, and a television production manager who answers to the program manager, are examples.

Middle: Managers who are responsible for carrying out particular activities in furtherance of the overall goals of the company are in this category. In broadcast stations, the heads of the sales, program, news, engineering, and business departments are middle managers.

Top: Managers who coordinate the company's activities and provide the overall direction for the accomplishment of its goals operate at this level. The general manager of a broadcast station is a top manager.

Even though the contents of the remainder of this chapter apply in varying degrees to all three levels, the focus will be on the top level, that occupied by the general manager.

MANAGEMENT FUNCTIONS

The general manager (GM) is responsible to the station's owners for coordinating human and physical resources in such a way that the station's objectives are accomplished. Accordingly, the GM is concerned with, and accountable for, every aspect of the station and its operation. In discharging the management responsibility, the GM carries out four basic functions: planning, organizing, influencing or directing, and controlling.

Planning

Planning involves the determination of the station's objectives and the plans or strategies by which those objectives are to be accomplished. Through the planning process, many objectives may be identified. Usually, they can be placed in one of the following categories:

Economic: Objectives related to the financial position of the station and focusing on revenues, expenses, and profits

Service: Programming that will appeal to audiences and be responsive to their interests and needs; the contribution of the station to the life of the community

Personal: Objectives of individuals employed by the station

A major purpose of objective-setting is to permit the coordination of departmental and individual activity with the station's objectives. Once the station's objectives have been formulated, the objectives of the different departments and employees within those departments can be developed. Individual objectives must contribute to the accomplishment of departmental objectives, which, in turn, must be compatible with those of other departments and of the station. In addition, all objectives must be attainable, measurable, set against deadlines, and controllable.

Once agreement on objectives has been reached, plans or strategies are developed to meet them. Planning provides directions for the future. However, it does not require the abandonment of plans that contribute to the achievement of the station's current objectives and that are likely to be instrumental in enabling the station to accomplish its future objectives.

Planning cannot anticipate or control future events. However, it has many benefits since it

- compels the GM to think about and prepare for the future
- provides a framework for decision making
- permits an orderly approach to problem solving
- encourages team effort
- provides a climate for individual career development and job satisfaction

Organizing

Organizing is the process whereby human and physical resources are arranged in a formal structure and responsibilities are assigned to specific units, positions, and personnel. It permits the concentration and coordination of activities and management control of efforts to attain the station's objectives.

In the typical broadcast station, organizing involves the division of work into specialties and the grouping of employees with specialized responsibilities into departments. The following departments are found most frequently in commercial broadcast stations.

Sales Department

The sale of time to advertisers is the principal source of revenue for commercial radio and television stations and is the responsibility of a sales department, headed by a sales manager. Many stations subdivide the department into national/regional sales and local sales. Sales to national and regional advertisers are entrusted to the station's sales representative company, or station rep. Local sales are the responsibility of the station's salespersons, typically called account executives.

Program Department

Under the direction of a program manager or director, the program department plans, selects, schedules, and, with the assistance of the production staff, produces programs.

News Department

In many stations, the information function is kept separate from the entertainment function and is supervised by a news director. The department is responsible for regularly scheduled newscasts, news and sports specials, and documentary and public affairs programs.

Engineering Department

This department is headed by a chief engineer or technical manager. It selects, operates, and maintains studio, control room, and transmitting equipment, and often oversees the computers. Engineering staff also are responsible for technical monitoring in accordance with the requirements of the Federal Communications Commission. In some stations, studio production personnel report to the head of this department.

Business Department

The business department carries out a variety of tasks necessary to the functioning of the station as a business. They include secretarial, billing, bookkeeping, payroll, and, in many stations, personnel responsibilities.

Broadcast stations engage in several other functions, which may be assigned to separate departments or subdepartments, or may be included in the duties of departments already identified. The following additional functions are among the most common.

Promotion and Marketing

This function involves both program and sales promotion. The former seeks to attract and maintain audiences, while the latter is aimed at attracting advertisers. Both functions may be the responsibility of a promotion and marketing department. Some stations assign program promotion to the program department and sales promotion to the sales department.

Traffic

Traffic often is carried out by a subdepartment of the sales department. It is called the traffic department and is headed by a traffic manager. The function includes the daily scheduling on a program log of all content to be aired by the station, the compilation of an availabilities sheet showing times available for purchase by advertisers, and the monitoring of all advertising content to ensure compliance with commercial contracts.

Continuity

Continuity is concerned chiefly with the writing of commercial copy and, in many stations, constitutes a subdepartment within the sales department. The continuity director supervises its activities and reports to the sales manager. In stations where the writing of program material and public service announcements are included, the continuity director may answer to the heads of both the sales and program departments.

The general manager's success in organizing rests heavily on the selection of employees. Of particular importance is the selection of department heads to whom the GM delegates responsibility for the conduct and accomplishments of the various departments.

The GM also must strive to ensure that the organizational structure enables the station to meet its objectives, and that problems arising from overlapping

Figure 1.4   *Organization of a commercial television station in a medium market.*

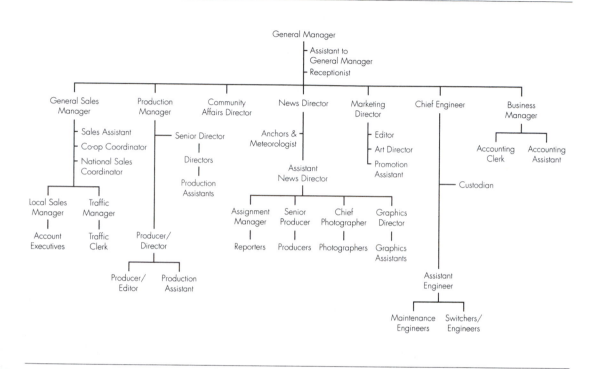

Figure 1.5   *Organization of three radio stations operating under the same owner and general manager.*

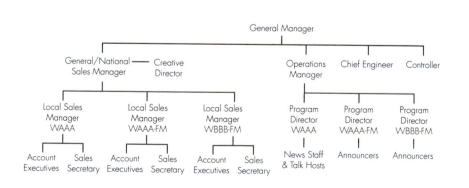

or nonexistent responsibility are corrected. The structure is influenced by many factors, among them the number of employees, the size of the market, and the preferences of the GM. As a result, there is no "typical" organization. Figure 1.4 contains an example of the structure of a medium-market television station. Figure 1.5 reflects the organization of three commonly-owned radio stations in a market of similar size.

Influencing or Directing

The influencing or directing function centers on the stimulation of employees to carry out their responsibilities with enthusiasm and effectiveness. It involves *motivation, communication, training,* and *personal influence.*

Motivation   The major theories of motivation were discussed earlier in this chapter. For the general manager, motivation is a practical issue, since the success of the station is tied closely to the degree to which employees are able to satisfy their needs. The greater their satisfaction, the more likely it is that they will contribute fully to the attainment of the station's objectives. Accordingly, the GM must be aware of the needs of individual employees and must create an environment in which they want to be productive.

Basic needs include adequate compensation and fringe benefit programs, safe and healthy working conditions, friendly colleagues, and competent and fair supervision. For most employees, such needs are met adequately and do not serve as powerful motivators.

Satisfaction of other needs may have a more significant impact on how employees feel about themselves and the station and on their efforts to contribute to the station's success. Included in these higher-level needs are factors such as job title and responsibility, praise and recognition for accomplishments, opportunities for promotion, and the challenge of the job. Once basic needs are satisfied, therefore, the GM must respond to those higher-level needs if motivation is to be successful.

Communication   Communication is vital to the effective discharge of the management function. It is the means by which employees are made aware of the station's objectives and plans and are encouraged to play a full and effective part in their attainment.

As a result, the general manager must communicate to employees information they need and want. They need information on what is expected of them. The job description sets forth general guidelines, but they must have specifics on their role in carrying out current plans. If they are to shoulder their duties willingly and effectively, they want to know about matters influencing their economic status and their authority to carry out responsibilities.

This downward flow of communication is important, but it must be accompanied by management's willingness to listen to and understand employees. Accordingly, it is necessary to provide mechanisms for an upward flow of communication from employees to supervisors, department heads, and the GM. Departmental or staff meetings, suggestion boxes, and an open-door policy by management permit such a flow.

Lateral flow, or communication among individuals on the same organizational level, also is important in coordinating the activities of the various departments in pursuit of the station's plans and objectives. A method used by many stations to ensure such a flow is the establishment of a management team that meets on a regular basis. Usually, it comprises the general manager and all department heads.

Training　Most employees are selected because they possess the background and skills necessary to carry out specific responsibilities. However, they may have to be trained in the use of new equipment or the application of new procedures. Occasionally, employees are hired with little experience and have to be trained on the job. Whenever training is necessary, the general manager must make certain that it is provided and that it is supervised by competent personnel.

One of the major benefits of training programs is the provision of opportunities for existing employees to prepare themselves for advancement in the station. As a result, employee morale is heightened, and the station enjoys the advantage of creating its own pool of qualified personnel.

Some stations encourage employees to advance their knowledge and skills by paying for their participation in workshops, seminars, and college courses, as well as their attendance at meetings of state and national broadcasting associations. In all such cases, the general manager should be sure that the experiences will contribute to the employee's ability to carry out responsibilities more effectively, thereby assisting the station in meeting its objectives.

Personal Influence　Stimulating employees to produce their best efforts requires that the general manager and others in managerial or supervisory positions command respect, loyalty, and cooperation. Among the factors that contribute to such a climate are management competence, fairness in dealings with employees, willingness to listen to and act on employee observations and complaints, honesty, integrity, and similar personal characteristics. In effect, personal influence includes all those behaviors and attitudes that contribute to employees' perceptions of their importance in the station's efforts and achievements and the worthiness of the enterprise of which they are a part.

Controlling

Through planning, the station establishes its objectives and plans for accomplishing them. The control process determines the degree to which objectives and plans are being realized by the station, departments, and employees.

Periodic evaluation of individuals and departments allows the general manager to compare actual performance to planned performance. If the two do not coincide, corrective action may be necessary.

To be effective, controlling must be based on measurable performance. The size and composition of the station's audience can be measured through ratings. If the audience attracted to the station or to certain programs does not match projections, the control process permits the recognition of that fact and leads to discussions about possible solutions. The result may be a change in the plan, such as a revision downward of expectations, or actions to try to attain the original objectives.

Similarly, sales revenues can be measured. An analysis may reveal that projected revenues were unrealistic and that an adjustment is necessary. On the other hand, if the projections are realizable, discussions may lead to a decision to hire additional account executives, make changes in the rate card, or adjust commission levels.

The costs of operation are measurable too. They are discussed in the next chapter, along with methods of controlling them.

MANAGEMENT ROLES

Management functions reflect the major responsibilities of the general manager. However, they provide little insight into the diverse and complex activities the general manager undertakes on a daily basis.

Henry Mintzberg found that managerial activity is characterized by brevity, variety, and fragmentation.[26] Managers spend short periods of time attending to different tasks and are interrupted frequently before a specific task is accomplished. Writing memoranda, reading and writing letters and electronic mail (E-mail) messages, receiving and making telephone calls, attending meetings, and visiting employees and persons outside the organization are examples of activities that consume a great deal of a manager's time and energy. There are others as well.

Mintzberg identified ten roles and grouped them in three categories: (1) interpersonal, (2) informational, and (3) decisional.[27]

Interpersonal Roles

As the symbolic head of the organization, the manager serves as a

Figurehead: The manager carries out duties of a legal or ceremonial nature. For the broadcast station general manager, this role is discharged through the signing of documents for submission to the Federal Communications Commission and by representing the station at community events, for instance.

Leader: Establishing the workplace atmosphere and guiding and motivating employees are examples of ways in which the general manager carries out the leadership role.

Liaison: The GM's interaction with peers and other individuals and groups outside the station links the organization with the environment. The GM's relationships with other general managers, with program suppliers, and with community groups reflect this role.

Informational Roles

The manager is the organization's "nerve center" and, as such, seeks and receives a large volume of internal and external information, both oral and written. In these roles, the manager acts as a

Monitor: Information permits the manager to understand what is happening in the organization and its environment. Receipt of the latest sales report or threats of a demonstration to protest the planned airing of a program enable the GM to exercise this role.

Disseminator: The manager distributes external information to members of the organization and internal information from one subordinate to another.

Spokesperson: In this role, the manager speaks on behalf of the organization. An example would be a news conference at which the GM reveals plans for a new broadcast facility.

Decisional Roles

These roles grow out of the manager's responsibility for the organization's strategy-making process and involve the manager as

Entrepreneur: The manager is the initiator and designer of controlled change. For example, the GM of a TV station may set in motion procedures aimed at attaining first place in local news ratings.

Disturbance handler: In this role, the manager deals with involuntary situations and change that is partially beyond his or her control. An example would be resolving a dispute between the program manager and the sales manager on the advisability of carrying a particular program.

Resource allocator: The manager determines priorities for the expenditure of money and employee effort.

Negotiator: The manager represents the organization in negotiating activity. Working out a contract with a program supplier or union would place the GM in this role.

MANAGEMENT SKILLS

To carry out their functions and roles effectively, managers require many skills. Robert L. Katz identifies three basic skills that every manager must have in varying degrees, according to the managerial level.[28] For the general manager of a broadcast station, all are important:

Technical: Knowledge, analytical ability, and facility in the use of the tools and techniques of a specific kind of activity. For the general manager, that activity is managing. While it does not demand the ability to perform all the tasks that characterize a broadcast station, it does require sufficient knowledge to ask pertinent questions and evaluate the worth of the responses. Accordingly, the GM should have knowledge of

- the objectives of the station's owners
- management and the management functions of planning, organizing, influencing or directing, and controlling
- business practices, especially sales and marketing, budgeting, cost controls, and public relations
- the market, including the interests and needs of the audience and the business potential afforded by area retail and service establishments

- competing media, the sources and amounts of their revenues
- broadcasting and allied professions, including advertising agencies, station representative companies, and program and news services
- the station and the activities of its departments and personnel
- broadcast laws, rules, and regulations, and other applicable laws, rules, and regulations
- contracts, particularly those dealing with network affiliation, station representation, programming, talent, music licensing, and labor unions

Human: The ability to work with people and to build a cooperative effort. The general manager should have the capacity to influence the behavior of employees toward the accomplishment of the station's objectives by motivating them, creating job satisfaction, and encouraging loyalty and mutual respect. An appreciation of the differing skills and aspirations of employees and departments also is essential if the station's activities are to be combined in a successful team effort.

Conceptual: The ability to see the enterprise as a whole and the dependence of one part on the others. To coordinate successfully the station's efforts, the GM must recognize the interdependence of programming and promotion, sales and programming, and production and engineering, for example. Equally important is the ability to comprehend the relationship of the station to the rest of the broadcast industry, to the community, and to prevailing economic, political, and social forces, all of which contribute to decisions on directions that the station will take and the subsequent formulation of objectives and policies.

To these skills, the successful general manager should add desirable personal qualities. They include

- *foresight,* the ability to anticipate events and make appropriate preparations;
- *wisdom* in choosing among alternative courses of action and *courage* in carrying out the selected action;
- *flexibility* in adapting to change;
- *honesty* and *integrity* in dealings with employees and persons outside the station; and, finally
- *responsiveness* and *responsibility* to the station's owners, employees, and advertisers.

The GM also must be responsive and display responsibility to the community by leading the station in its community relations endeavors and by setting an example for other employees to follow.

INFLUENCES ON MANAGEMENT

The degree to which the general manager possesses and uses the skills described will play an important part in determining the station's fortunes. But there are other forces that contribute to the GM's decisions and actions and that influence the effectiveness with which the management responsibility is discharged. The most significant influences are described in this section.

The Licensee

Ultimate responsibility for the operation of a radio or television station rests with the licensee, the person or persons who have made a financial investment in the enterprise and enjoy an ownership interest. Like all investors, they expect that they will reap annual profits from the station's operation and that the financial worth of their investment will increase in time. As a result, the general manager must seek to satisfy their expectations and weigh the financial impact of all actions.

The Competition

Radio and television stations compete against each other and against other media in the market for advertising dollars. That translates into competition for audiences. A station gains audience from, or loses audience to, other stations, and few significant management actions will pass without producing a reaction among competitors. Similarly, many of the general manager's actions will be influenced by those of competing stations.

The Government

As detailed in Chapter 7, "Broadcast Regulations," the federal government is a major force in broadcast station operation. It exerts its influence through its three branches — executive, legislative, and judicial — and through independent regulatory agencies, chiefly the Federal Communications Commission.

Executive Branch   Broadcast stations are affected by the actions of several executive branch departments, notably the Executive Office of the President, the Department of Justice, the Food and Drug Administration (FDA), and the National Telecommunications and Information Administration (NTIA).

Executive Office of the President   The President influences broadcast policy and regulation in numerous ways. He can recommend legislation; he nominates members for, and appoints the chairperson of, regulatory agencies whose policies, rules, and regulations apply to radio and television stations; and he can exert influence through the annual federal budget process.

Department of Justice   This department prosecutes violators of the Communications Act and of rules and regulations applicable to broadcast station operation. The department's antitrust division is concerned with station ownership and may take action when it believes that ownership or other circumstances are resulting in a restraint of trade.

Food and Drug Administration   A division of the Department of Health and Human Services, the FDA regulates mislabeling and misbranding of advertised products.

National Telecommunications and Information Administration

Part of the Department of Commerce, the NTIA advises the President on telecommunications policy issues.

Legislative Branch The House of Representatives and the Senate enact broadcast legislation and approve the budgets of the regulatory agencies. In addition, the Senate has the power of approval of presidential nominees for regulatory agencies. Both the Senate and the House may influence broadcast policy and regulation through congressional hearings on issues of controversy or concern.

Judicial Branch Federal courts try cases against violators of laws, rules, and regulations, and hear appeals against decisions and orders handed down by regulatory agencies.

Regulatory Agencies Federal regulatory agencies operate like a fourth branch of government and enjoy executive, legislative, and judicial powers. The agency with the greatest influence on broadcast operations is the Federal Communications Commission, whose role is described later. The commission regulates radio and television stations in accordance with the terms of the Communications Act of 1934, as amended. For the general manager, its most significant and awesome power is that of renewing or revoking the station's license to operate.

Other regulatory agencies that influence the broadcast media are the Federal Trade Commission (FTC), which polices unfair trade practices and false or deceptive advertising, and the Federal Aviation Administration (FAA), whose concerns include the placement and maintenance of broadcast towers.

Broadcasters are engaged in interstate commerce and, for the most part, are subject to federal authority. However, state and local governments may also affect stations through laws on matters such as business incorporation, taxes, advertising practices, individual rights, and zoning and safety ordinances.

The Labor Force

The number of people available for work, and their skills, have a direct impact on the success of all businesses, including broadcasting. The station's ability to hire and retain qualified and productive employees is a major determinant of the station's performance.

Labor Unions

The general manager of a station in which personnel are represented by one or more unions is required to abide by the terms of a union contract governing, among other things, wages and fringe benefits, job jurisdiction, and working conditions (for details, refer to Chapter 3, "Human Resource Management"). In nonunionized stations, the general manager must be attentive to the treatment of employees, not only for reasons of morale or competitiveness, but to guard against the threat of unionization.

The Public

To generate advertising revenue, the station must attract an audience for its programming. Accordingly, as noted in Chapter 4, "Broadcast Programming," the public is a major force in program decision making. Organized publics, also known as citizen or pressure groups, attempt to influence decisions on a wide range of actions. Among the causes undertaken by different groups have been improvement in employment opportunities for minorities, the elimination of violent and sexual content, and the promotion of programming for children.

Advertisers

The financial fate of commercial broadcast stations rests on their appeal to advertisers. Attracting audiences sought by advertisers and enabling advertisers to reach them at an acceptable cost are major factors in program and sales decisions.

Economic Activity

The state of the economy, locally and nationally, determines the amount of money people have to spend on advertised products and their spending priorities. When the economy is sluggish, businesses pay more attention than usual to their advertising expenditures and may be tempted to reduce them, thereby posing a challenge for broadcast stations and other advertiser-supported media.

The Broadcast Industry

Standards of professional performance and content are set forth in a station's policy book or employee handbook. The industry at large also is instrumental in establishing standards. Even though the radio and television codes of the National Association of Broadcasters have been abandoned, many stations continue to adhere to their provisions on program and advertising content, and individual employees subscribe to industrywide standards formulated by broadcast organizations or associations in which they hold membership.

Social Factors

Since broadcast stations must be responsive to the interests of their communities, social factors play an important role in program decisions. Stations must analyze, interpret, and respond to trends in the size and composition of the local population, employment practices, income, and spending habits.

Technology

Advances in technology resulted in the emergence of radio and television broadcasting and continue to play a major part in station practices. Today, the general manager experiences, and must respond to, the influence of new broadcast technologies, as well as those technologies that are being introduced into the home and that provide alternative leisure-time pursuits for the public.

WHAT'S AHEAD?

When broadcast station managers gaze into their crystal ball, they will be both cheered and concerned. The cheer arises from projections that total radio station advertising will reach $18.9 billion by 2001, an increase of 45 percent over 1996.[29] Advertising on local television stations will climb 25 percent, to $26.7 billion. This 5.2 percent annual revenue growth for TV is down from 7.7 percent in the previous five-year period,[30] but is quite respectable in light of the audience erosion stations continue to experience. The concern grows out of the realization that competition will intensify, without question for television and probably for radio.

A seventh broadcast television network has been launched and an eighth is a distinct possibility, with the result that, in larger markets, more affiliates will be fighting for a piece of the shrinking broadcast audience pie. But the impact of the newcomers will be barely noticeable compared to the apparently unstoppable onward march by cable, whose record prime-time audience share of 42 in 1997–98 was just 5 points short of the combined share of ABC, CBS, and NBC.[31] Even though cable's household penetration percentage is likely to decline slightly in the early years of the twenty-first century, the projected increase in the number of television channels available in the average home from 49 in 1997[32] to 165 in 2005[33] makes certain a further reduction in the size of broadcasting's audience.

Possibly adding to television broadcasters' woes, DBS subscriptions — fueled by more channels, a drop in the cost of a satellite dish purchase to as little as $149, and rising cable costs — are expected to more than double by 2004, to a TV household penetration of 18 percent.[34] However, the impact will depend, at least in part, on the outcome of Congressional efforts to permit satellite retransmission of local stations into the market, so-called "local-into-local" service.

Radio stations will not be spared additional competition. In 1997, the FCC awarded licenses to two companies for the construction and operation of satellite digital audio radio services (SDARS) to be beamed to vehicles. Several dozen channels of music and other programming are planned, posing a direct threat to the size of stations' mobile audiences.

At the same time, the possibility looms of competition from low-power radio stations transmitting at a power of from one watt to three kilowatts. Reacting to the FCC's 1998 invitation for comments on two low-power proposals, some broadcasters argued that implementation would jeopardize full-power broadcasters' ability to provide free, full-service, and interference-free programming.

Both radio and television general managers will be keeping a close eye on the effects of online household penetration, predicted to grow from just over 20 percent in 1997 to about 70 percent by 2005.[35] Earlier forecasts suggested that it could result in a reduction in the use of traditional media, especially television.[36] However, a study by Pew Research Center indicated that — at least when it comes to news — consumers are using the Internet as a supplement to, rather than as a replacement for, their customary media sources.[37]

Even so, the dramatic growth in the popularity and utilization of the online medium in the home dictates that managers determine their relationship with it. Several hundred radio stations are Webcasting their programming, and more than 4,000 radio and television stations have established a presence through a Website. But the challenge is to identify and pursue a business model that will enable them to capitalize on it financially.

Three models have been contemplated. A *marketing* model that primarily promotes the station and builds relationships with listeners and viewers. Many stations have adopted this model, despite its limited revenue potential. An *ad sales* model, being pursued by some stations, involves the station in the sale to advertisers of both air time and an Internet presence, and the design of campaigns incorporating elements appropriate to each medium. Here, the potential financial payoff is greater, but it assumes a commitment of time and the availability of expertise from the sales department. Finally, there is a *full-service* model, placing broadcasters in the advertising, connection, and hardware businesses. With this approach, the station would sell clients a Web presence, offer consumers dial-up accounts, and make available to businesses Web servers and high-speed Internet connections. This model offers the greatest opportunities for revenue enhancement, but carries with it a heavy investment in capital, staff, and time, and a degree of technical expertise not typically found in stations.

Of more immediate concern to most TV general managers is the FCC-mandated transition to digital transmission. The cost — an estimated $3 million to $6 million — is daunting, especially for stations in medium and small markets. The Consumer Electronics Manufacturers Association (CEMA) predicts that 10 million digital television (DTV) sets will be sold by 2004 and that market penetration will reach 30 percent two years later.[38] However, uncertainty surrounds the readiness of viewers to spend from $2,000 to $5,000 more than the cost of their comparably-sized analog receivers. Consumer response also will be influenced by the amount of digital programming available and could be hampered by lack of agreement among the four major networks on a single digital standard.

Stations, too, will have to decide how to use their expanded bandwidth. A decision in favor of high-definition television (HDTV) would replace the analog signal with one of superior visual and audio quality, but would not necessarily generate additional income to cover the investment. Multicasting, or delivering several programs as an alternative or complement to HDTV, would provide viewers with pictures only slightly better than analog but could open up more revenue streams through the sale of subscriptions or additional advertising slots. Since the FCC's digital allotment is free only to stations who do not use it to charge for services, managers will have to weigh increased revenue potential against fees that will be imposed.

Digital broadcasting is in the future of radio stations as well, with the promise of near-CD quality sound for FM stations and an AM sound closer to today's analog FM signal. Under the digital audio broadcasting (DAB) prototype in development, frequencies will stay the same, as will most transmission sites. Managers will have to defray the costs associated with the transition, but the challenge of meeting them will be nothing like that experienced by their television counterparts.

A much greater challenge to radio station general managers is a personal one, arising from the transformation in their responsibilities. The in-market consolidation of stations in the wake of the Telecommunications Act of 1996 led — in many markets — to the dismissal of several station managers and their replacement by just one, charged with the running of three or more stations. Not surprisingly, many of these new "cluster" managers are finding difficulty adjusting to their new position.

A study to determine the job skills required revealed that 77 percent of managers had a greater use for delegation, 75 percent for time management, and 61 percent for focus. Sixty-one percent indicated "all organizational skills."[39] Among the other skills mentioned by close to one-half of the managers surveyed were culture development, conflict management, and budgeting. Many felt that their general role was shifting from that of a broadcaster to a businessperson, reflecting the new emphasis by owners on increased profitability. The degree of success attained in responding to intensified financial pressures will determine the future of many in this new era of radio station management.

SUMMARY

Management is defined as the process of planning, organizing, influencing, and controlling to accomplish organizational goals through the coordinated use of human and material resources.

The current practice of management has been influenced by several schools. The first was the classical school, which focused on the productivity of organizations and their employees. It was followed by the behavioral school, which drew attention to the importance of satisfied employees to successful operation. Management science was characterized by an emphasis on quantifying the likely outcomes of different managerial decisions. Modern management thought attempts to integrate the various perspectives of earlier schools by concentrating on systems theory and contingency theory. Total quality management also reflects an integration through its focus on customer needs and expectations.

The general manager of a broadcast station has four major functions: (1) planning, or the determination of the station's objectives and the plans or strategies to accomplish them; (2) organizing personnel into a formal structure, usually departments, and assigning specialized duties to persons and units; (3) influencing or directing, that is, stimulating employees to carry out their responsibilities enthusiastically and effectively; and (4) controlling, or developing criteria to measure the performance of individuals, departments, and the station and taking corrective action when necessary.

On a day-to-day basis, the GM carries out several roles — interpersonal, informational, and decisional. Technical, human, and conceptual skills are required, together with personal attributes.

Among the significant influences on the GM's decisions and actions are the licensee, competing media, the government, the labor force and labor unions, the public, and advertisers. Economic activity, the broadcast industry, social factors, and technology also are influential.

The challenges the general manager faces include dealing with increased competition, harnessing the potential of the Internet, implementing the transition to digital transmission and, in radio, adjusting to a new role as manager of three or more stations.

CASE STUDY

You are general manager of two radio stations, a 100,000-watt FM with an adult contemporary format and a 5,000-watt AM whose format is news/talk.

You assumed your position three months ago, and brought to it more than ten years of experience as general sales manager of the stations. During that time, the FM has performed very well and places regularly among the top two stations (persons 12+) in the 18-station market. Sales revenues reflect the stations' strong appeal to advertisers.

The AM switched to its present format eight years ago. It has established a loyal audience and typically ranks sixth in the market. Its revenues compare favorably with those of stations with the same format in markets of similar size.

At the time of your appointment as general manager, your company was negotiating the purchase of two additional FM stations in the market. One broadcasts at 3,000 watts with a contemporary Christian format; the other at 6,000 watts with a news/talk format. Both stations place in the bottom third.

A program consultant recommends that — if the purchase is agreed — the format of the first station be changed to oldies. The second station would retain its news/talk format but target a younger demographic than your existing AM.

Your company president asks to meet with you. He advises that satisfactory terms have been reached and that the purchase will proceed. The consultant's recommendations will be adopted. In addition, he tells you that he has given a verbal assurance that he will retain as many account executives as possible from the two purchased stations. The same goes for the program hosts of the newly acquired news/talk station.

Exercises

1. How will you order your financial priorities so as to protect your two existing stations and, at the same time, seek to build the strength of the purchased stations?

2. If you pursue the president's assurances on staff retention, you will be employing account executives against whom your staff has been competing. What kind of challenges will you confront as you integrate the staffs and how will you strive to meet them?

3. Competition has been intense between your AM and the FM news/talk station you have acquired. Program hosts on both stations have traded insults and challenges on a regular basis. Should you allow such on-air rivalry to continue or terminate it? Why?

NOTES

1. *The Chattanooga Times*, April 20, 1998, p. B8.

2. *Ibid.*

3. John Merli, "Listening Down in '98," *Broadcasting & Cable*, June 29, 1998, p. 71.

4. John Merli, "APR Listening Trend Continues Downward," *Broadcasting & Cable*, January 5, 1998, p. 40.

5. *Cable Television Developments*, p. 2.

6. "Ups and Downs in Prime Time," *Broadcasting & Cable*, May 18, 1998, p. 4.

7. *Satellite Business News*, May 6, 1998, p. 1.

8. *1998 Report on Television*, p. 15.

9. Peter P. Schoderbek, Richard A. Cosier, and John C. Aplin, *Management*, p. 8.

10. Charles D. Pringle, Daniel F. Jennings, and Justin G. Longenecker, *Managing Organizations: Functions and Behaviors*, p. 4.

11. Howard M. Carlisle, *Management Essentials: Concepts for Productivity and Innovation*, p. 10.

12. R. Wayne Mondy, Robert E. Holmes, and Edwin B. Flippo, *Management: Concepts and Practices*, p. 6.

13. Peter F. Drucker, *Management: Tasks, Responsibilities. Practices*, p. 181.

14. Henri Fayol, *General and Industrial Management*, pp. 43–107. Explanations of the functions have been paraphrased.

15. Max Weber, *The Theory of Social and Economic Organization*, pp. 329–334.

16. A. H. Maslow, "A Theory of Human Motivation," *Psychological Review*, 50:4 (July, 1943), pp. 370–396.

17. For an example, see Geert H. Hofstede, "The Colors of Collars," *Columbia Journal of World Business* (September-October, 1972), pp. 72–80. After studying job-related goals of more than 18,000 employees of one company with offices in sixteen countries, Hofstede concluded that there was a high correlation with Maslow's theory. The goals of professionals related to the higher needs, of clerks to the middle-range needs, and of unskilled workers to the primary needs.

18. Frederick Herzberg, Bernard Mausner, and Barbara Bloch Snyderman, *The Motivation to Work*, pp. 113–119.

19. *Ibid.*, p. 113. Herzberg explained his use of the term *hygiene* as follows: "Hygiene operates to remove health hazards from the environment of man. It is not a curative; it is, rather, a preventive. . . . Similarly, when there are deleterious factors in the context of the job, they serve to bring about poor job attitudes. Improvement in these factors of hygiene will serve to remove the impediments to positive job attitudes."

20. Douglas McGregor, *The Human Side of Enterprise*, p. 49.

21. William G. Ouchi, *Theory Z: How American Business Can Meet the Japanese Challenge*, pp. 11–37.

22. Harold Koontz, "The Management Theory Jungle," *Academy of Management Journal*, 4:3 (December, 1961), pp. 174–186.

23. Peter P. Schoderbek, Charles D. Schoderbek, and Asterios G. Kefalas, *Management Systems: Conceptual Considerations*, p. 260.

24. Henry C. Metcalf and L. Urwick (eds.), *Dynamic Administration: The Collected Papers of Mary Parker Follett*, p. 277.

25. T. Boone Pickens, Jr., "Pickens on Leadership," *Hyatt Magazine*, Fall/Winter, 1988, p. 21.

26. Henry Mintzberg, *The Nature of Managerial Work*, pp. 31–35.

27. *Ibid.*, pp. 54–94.

28. Robert L. Katz, "Skills of an Effective Administrator," *Harvard Business Review*, 52:5 (September-October, 1974), pp. 90–102.

29. Steve McClellan, "2001, an $80 Billion Odyssey," *Broadcasting & Cable*, July 28, 1997, p. 16.

30. *Ibid.*, p. 17.

31. "Ups and Downs in Prime Time," *Broadcasting & Cable*, May 18, 1998, p. 4.

32. *1998 Report on Television*, p. 19.

33. *Cablevision Blue Book*, Vol. VII (Spring/Summer, 1998), p. 22.

34. *Ibid.*, p. 8.

35. *Ibid.*, p. 24.

36. A 1997 Nielsen Media Research study for America Online (AOL) showed that viewers in AOL households typically watch 15 percent less television in a day than the total U.S. average. (Richard Tedesco, "That's Intertainment," *Broadcasting & Cable*, June 2, 1997, p. 54.)

37. "Internet News Takes Off," <http://www.people-press.org/med98rpt.htm>.

38. "Consumers Want HDTV, CEMA Study Finds," *AV Video Multimedia Producer*, April, 1998, p. 22.

39. Elizabeth A. Rathbun, "Boning Up on Cluster Management," *Broadcasting & Cable*, April 8, 1998, p. 50.

ADDITIONAL READINGS

Brown, James A., and Ward L. Quaal. *Radio-Television-Cable Management*, 3rd ed. New York: McGraw-Hill, 1998.

Covington, William G., Jr. *Systems Theory Applied to Television Station Management in the Competitive Marketplace*. Lanham, MD: University Press of America, 1997.

Czech-Beckerman, Elizabeth Shimer. *Managing Electronic Media*. Boston: Focal Press, 1991.

Drucker, Peter F. *Managing in a Time of Great Change*. New York: Truman Talley Books/ Dutton, 1995.

Herzberg, Frederick. *Work and the Nature of Man*. Cleveland, OH: World Publishing, 1967.

Lacy, Stephen, Ardyth B. Sohn, and Jan LeBlanc Wicks. *Media Management: A Casebook Approach*. Hillsdale, NJ: Lawrence Erlbaum, 1993.

Marsteller, William A. *Creative Management*. Lincolnwood, IL: NTC Business Books, 1992.

Maslow, Abraham H. *Motivation and Personality*, 2nd ed. New York: Harper & Row, 1970.

Robbins, Stephen P., and Mary Coulter. *Management*, 5th ed. Upper Saddle River, NJ: Prentice Hall, 1996.

Sashkin, Marshall, and Kenneth J. Kiser. *Putting Total Quality Management to Work: What TQM Means, How to Use It and How to Sustain It Over the Long Run*. San Francisco: Berrett-Koehler, 1993.

Small Market Television Manager's Guide—II, The. Washington, DC: National Association of Broadcasters, 1992.

Strategic Planning Handbook for Broadcasters. Washington, DC: National Association of Broadcasters, 1994.

2 FINANCIAL MANAGEMENT

This chapter reviews the increasingly important area of financial management and examines

☐ the two major forms of financial statements used in the industry

☐ basic accounting terminology frequently employed by electronic media managers

☐ methods used to produce good financial performance and to monitor financial progress

For years, electronic media education has focused on the operating skills thought to be necessary for a successful career in the industry. Traditionally, the major topics studied have been sales, programming, production, and management. Massive changes triggered by the deregulatory climate of the 1980s catapulted another subject to prominence in the curriculum. That subject is financial management.

Deregulation brought financial speculators into the electronic media business. The prevailing wisdom of the mid-to-late 1980s was the "greater fool" theory. Under this concept, money was made by selling a broadcast license or cable franchise to another at a profit. Operational performance was de-emphasized in favor of appreciation potential.

All that changed around 1989. Prices had risen to the point that operations could no longer retire the massive debt run up by speculators. Numerous electronic media companies went into default, and prices dropped.

In the mid-1990s, broadcast stations and many cable systems were valued on a multiple of the cash flow they generate. Operational financial performance was the new coin of the realm.

Then, in 1996, everything changed again with passage of the Telecommunications Act. Gone were the national ownership limits on radio altogether and those for television were relaxed. In-market ownership combinations of up to eight radio stations were permitted, depending on market size.

The adoption of the new law set off another round of speculative buying and consolidation almost without regard to financial performance.

The radio consolidation was largely completed by late 1998 and now operators, once again, are going back to the basics of producing operating results and return on investments for public and private investors. Clearly, into the new century, operational financial performance will once again be the coin of the realm.

Pressure to acquire basic financing and accounting knowledge is coming from other sources, too. In the technology-driven decade of the 1990s, lines of distinction between traditional forms of electronic media became blurred or nonexistent. This development is spawning a need for a new breed of communication manager — one with both a traditional background and basic accounting and financial skills.[1]

It is not possible in the pages of this chapter to make anyone a financial expert. The goal here is to acquaint the student with financial terms and concepts and with the typical financial reports used. It is recommended strongly that today's electronic media student pursue a more detailed examination of these matters through finance or accounting courses.

THE ACCOUNTING FUNCTION

The accounting function in the electronic media today is performed using specialized computer software developed by various companies. The leading television traffic and accounting systems are provided by Columbine. Radio software companies include Computer Concepts, CBSI (Custom Business Systems, Inc.), DARTS (Data Accounts Receivable and Traffic System), and

The Traffic C.O.P. by Broadcast Data Consultants. Columbine also has a system for radio. Some of these software systems are integrated or interfaced with digital audio systems like Digilink by Arrakis or Audio Vault by Broadcast Electronics. Whether computerized or manual, and whatever the system utilized, certain accounting concepts and terminology are basic. Any person with serious management ambition must master them.

Effective financial management requires detailed planning and control. Planning expresses in dollar terms the plans and objectives of the enterprise. Control involves the comparison of projected and actual revenues and expenses. The basic planning and control mechanism is the *budget*.

To prepare the budget, management collects from department heads financial data and reviews and edits them. Most stations and systems use a form to display the information for the budget period, usually one year. Figure 2.1 is a twelve-month calendar summary form employed by a radio multiple station operator in an annual budget preparation.

Budgeting deals with the future. However, past experience suggests realistic revenue and expense amounts. Generally, a reserve account is maintained to cover emergencies. During the year, regular budget reports permit the general manager to compare planned and actual results and to make necessary adjustments.

Budgeting and cost controls, together with financial forecasting and planning, are among the major responsibilities of the business department. Other responsibilities include banking, billings to and collections from advertisers and advertising agencies, payroll administration, processing of insurance claims, tax payments, purchasing, and payments for services used.

Fundamental to the efficient discharge of the accounting function are the establishment and maintenance of an effective and informative accounting system that will protect assets and provide financial information for decision making and the preparation of financial statements and tax returns. Such a system is based on financial records. As noted above, most such records are produced for electronic media concerns via specialized computer software.

Planning Financial Records

No matter what the electronic media business is — radio, television, cable, or other — management requires certain basic information to function. This includes amounts and sources of revenues and expenditures, and levels of operational profitability on a monthly and annual basis.

Cable system operators are concerned about their main revenue source, subscribers, while broadcasters want details of advertising sales. On the expenditure side, both cable and broadcast managers require information on programming costs. Cable operators need figures on pole rent and contract labor. Broadcasters care about the cost of maintaining the transmission plant.

Whatever the particular need, the quest for management financial information must begin with the design of a record-keeping system that will produce the desired results. Every manager embarking on the task of setting up financial records is looking for guidance (i.e., what is a good model? or what has worked well for others?). Fortunately, excellent materials are available on financial records planning.

Figure 2.1   *Budget worksheet used by a multiple radio station operator.*

Goodstar Broadcasting
1998 Proposed Budget

Station _____

1998	JAN	FEB	MAR	APR	MAY	JUN	JUL	AUG	SEP	OCT	NOV	DEC	TOTAL
Income													
Local Spot Sales													
Other Local Sales													
Total Local Sales													
National Sales													
Regional Spot Sales													
Total Time Sales													
Non-Broadcast Rev. (Rental etc.)													
Total Gross Income													
Cost of Goods Sold													
Local Agency Comm. (15%)													
National Agency Comm. (15%)													
Regional Agency Comm (15%)													
Regional Rep. Comm (15%)													
National Rep. Comm (15%)													
Total COGS													
Gross Profit													
Engineering Expenses													
Payroll													
Outside Labor-Contract													
Repair & Maintenance													
Parts & Supplies													
Equipment Rental													
Freight on Equipment													
Auto Expenses													
Total Engineering Expenses													

Figure 2.1 *Continued*

Station _____

Goodstar Broadcasting
1998 Proposed Budget

1998	JAN	FEB	MAR	APR	MAY	JUN	JUL	AUG	SEP	OCT	NOV	DEC	TOTAL
Program Expense													
Payroll													
Payroll Taxes (12%)													
Talent Fees-Pd by Client													
Production Supplies													
Promotion/Prizes													
Advert & Promo													
Special Programs													
Supplies													
Program Expense-Other													
Total Program Expense													
Sales Expense													
Payroll													
Commissions													
Payroll Taxes (12%)													
Sales Promotions													
Telephone-Promotions													
Sales Promotions-Other													
Total Sales Expense													

Figure 2.1   *Continued*

Goodstar Broadcasting
1998 Proposed Budget

Station _____

1998	JAN	FEB	MAR	APR	MAY	JUN	JUL	AUG	SEP	OCT	NOV	DEC	TOTAL
General Administrative Expense													
Payroll													
Payroll Taxes (12%)													
Contract Labor													
Commissions													
Employee Benefits (Health etc.)													
Bonuses													
Employee Benefits-Other													
Tower Rent													
Rent													
Transmitter Monitoring													
Telephone													
Electricity													
Gas													
Water/Sewer													
Cablevision													
Trash Service													
Bldg Maintenance & Repair													
General Taxes													
Insurance													
Office Supplies													
Office Equipment Leases													
Office Equip Repair/Maint													
Office Equipment Purchase													
Computer Maintenance													

Figure 2.1 *Continued*

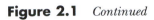

Station _____

Goodstar Broadcasting
1998 Proposed Budget

1998	JAN	FEB	MAR	APR	MAY	JUN	JUL	AUG	SEP	OCT	NOV	DEC	TOTAL
Computer Internet Service													
Postage													
Postage Meter Rental													
Postage-Other (FedEX etc.)													
FCC Fees													
BMI/ASCAP/SESAC Fees (3.9%)													
Memberships/Dues													
Subscriptions/Publications													
Printing													
Client Entertainment/Meals													
Personal Property Taxes													
Miscellaneous													
Legal													
Legal FCC													
Bank Service Charge													
Bad Debt W/O's													
Total General Admin. Expense													
Corporate/Expenses													
Administrative Allocation													
Total Corporate Expense													
Total Expenses													
Net Income													
Total Multistation Sales													

Figure 2.2   *Vendor proposal to design and install a traffic and accounting system for a group radio operation.*

CBSI CustomClassic System
12-Stations Centralized
Lease Terms

CBSI CUSTOMCLASSIC SYSTEM, Multi-Terminal, w/Windows

Includes: License of CBSI Radio Program Log
            License of CBSI Radio Accounts Receivable
            License of CBSI Radio Sales Analyzer
            License of CBSI Radio Co-op/Copywriter
            License of CBSI Radio Auto Weekly Scheduler
            License of CBSI Radio Daily Report
            License of CBSI Radio Operator Rights
            License of CBSI Radio Programmable Avails
            License of CBSI Radio Customer/Collection Letters
            License of CBSI Radio Satellite/Event
            License of CBSI Radio CustomReports
            License of CBSI Radio Agency Management
            License of CBSI Radio Power+PLUS
            CBSI Multi-Terminal Software — up to 8 Terminals
            Niakwa RT (8 Terminal/Windows/Novell)
            Pre-Loading of Station Data at CBSI
            20 Days On-Site Operator Training**

CBSI INTERACCT ACCOUNTING SYSTEM, Level One

Includes: General Ledger Accounts   Operator Rights
            Vendors Accounts   Import/Export
            Bank Reconciliation   Project Accounting
            15-84 Accounting Periods w/Detail Vendor Tables
            Full Security/Operator Audit Trail 1–12 Secondary Tables
            Notations   Report Sequence
            Password Security   Payroll
            Design Financial Reports
            2 Days On-Site Operator Training**

TOTAL SYSTEM TRAINING & INSTALLATION $16,402.00
MONTHLY SOFTWARE FEE $2,004.00/mo

The principal sources utilized to set up accounting records are specialized computer software companies that design and customize traffic and accounting systems for single and multiple station operators. Figure 2.2 presents a proposal submitted by CBSI to a multiple station radio operator for such a system. You will note that the proposal provides for the design and implementation of financial reports. Figure 2.3 depicts how a centralized traffic and accounting system might be configured.

Another such source is the National Association of Broadcasters (NAB), which publishes an accounting manual for radio stations. Included in the

Figure 2.3   *Proposal for a multistation centralized traffic and accounting system.*

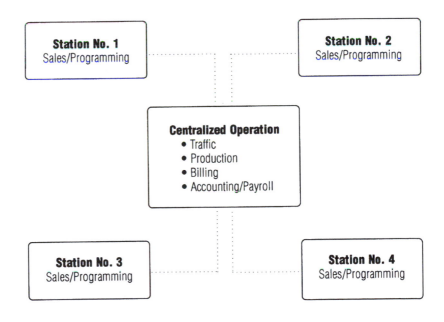

Centralization

Realizing your goals:
- Greater dominance in your market
- Better use of your talent
- Improved control
- Greater operational efficiency
- Increase your bottom line

Station No. 1
Sales/Programming

Station No. 2
Sales/Programming

Centralized Operation
- Traffic
- Production
- Billing
- Accounting/Payroll

Station No. 3
Sales/Programming

Station No. 4
Sales/Programming

Note: *All sales, programming and/or administration at individual station may be local or centralized*

publication are chapters on financial statements, accounting records, charts of accounts with explanations, and accounting system automation.[2]

Still another source of information is the Broadcast Cable Financial Management Association (BCFM). This organization, composed of industry members, concentrates on financial questions of import to its membership. It, too, publishes an accounting manual. The contents are principally detailed charts of accounts, with explanations, and model financial statement forms.[3]

Whether the system chosen is manual or computerized, it must be designed to deliver to management certain basic information and to render financial reports. It will consist of a number of journals and ledgers that record and summarize all financial transactions and events.

The records most commonly generated are the following:

Cash receipts journal shows all monies received, listed by revenue account number. It identifies the payer and, in the case of receipts for advertising, gross amounts, discounts, and agency commissions, and resulting net amounts. Journal entries cover a given period of time, at the end of which all amounts are totaled and posted to the general ledger. Individual client payments are credited to the appropriate account in the accounts receivable ledger (see Figure 2.4).

Cash disbursements journal records all monies paid out. Often, it is organized by major expense category and account number and lists the check number, date, amount, and the company or person to whom payment was made. Totals are posted to the general ledger (see Figure 2.4).

Figure 2.4   *Financial record-keeping process.*

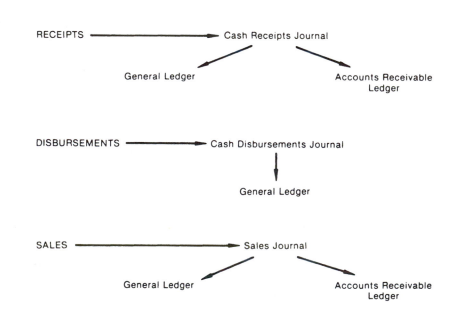

Sales journal lists all transactions after the commercial schedule has run and has been billed to the client. No entries are recorded until this happens. Entries are triggered by performance against the contract and not when the contract is signed. When made, sales journal entries include the client's name, invoice number, date, amount, and the name of the staff member who made the sale. If part of the cost results from the sale of talent or program materials and facilities, that information is entered. So, too, are details of tradeouts — the exchange of advertising time for goods or services. Entries for a given period are totaled and posted to the general ledger. Each gross billing figure is entered on the client's page in the accounts receivable ledger (see Figure 2.4).

General journal includes noncash transactions and adjustments, such as depreciation and amortization, and accrued bills not yet paid.

Accounts receivable ledger records money owed to the business by account. Using the ledger, the station or system prepares an aging sheet showing accounts that are current and those that are delinquent.

Accounts payable ledger lists monies owed by the business and includes the name of the creditor, invoice date and amount, and the account to be charged.

General ledger is the basic accounts book. It contains all transactions, posted from various journals of original entry to the appropriate account. The general ledger consists of two sections. One records figures for assets, liabilities, and capital, and the other the income and expense account figures.

Information from the general ledger is used to prepare two major financial records, the *balance sheet* and the *income statement*.

Balance Sheet   The balance sheet is a statement of the financial position of the station or system at a given time, and it comprises three parts:

- *assets*, or the value of what is owned
- *liabilities*, or what is owed
- *net worth* or *equity*, or the financial interest of the enterprise's ownership

The term "balance sheet" is derived from the fact that total assets should equal total liabilities plus net worth or equity. The two sides of the sheet are, therefore, in balance.

Assets   Assets are classified as follows:

Current assets are those assets expected to be sold, used, or converted into cash within one year. They typically include cash, marketable securities, notes, accounts receivable, inventories (including programming), and prepaid expenses.

Fixed assets are those assets that will be held or used for a long term, meaning more than one year. Land and improvements (e.g., a parking lot), buildings, the transmitter, tower, satellite uplinks and downlinks, antenna system, studio and mobile equipment, vehicles, office and studio furniture, and fixtures are among items considered fixed assets.

Fixed assets are tangible assets — things. They depreciate, which means that use over time reduces their value. Depreciation is a business expense. The amount of time over which a tangible asset may be reduced systematically in value is determined by Internal Revenue Service (IRS) guidelines. A more detailed discussion of depreciation occurs later in this chapter.

Other assets is a category that includes mainly intangible assets — those having no physical substance. Examples are the Federal Communications Commission license, organization costs, and goodwill. These assets are amortized, or written off, for financial statement reporting purposes.

Amortization, or write-off, of the goodwill amount means that the total amount is systematically reduced over a period of time by charging equal annual amounts to the profit and loss statement. Goodwill primarily represents the value of the broadcast license or cable franchise. For example, if a station were purchased for $6 million, and the value of its tangible assets were $3 million, then the goodwill amount would be $3 million. That amount would be charged to the station profit and loss account in equal annual amounts. For reasons discussed later in Chapter 10, "Entry into the Electronic Media Business," some intangible amounts, while deducted for financial statement reporting purposes, cannot be deducted for tax purposes.

An additional example of other assets is the network affiliation agreement of most television stations. In the mid-1980s, some stations began to write off for tax purposes these agreements. However, such attempts occasioned significant IRS controversy and litigation. Most of these disputes apparently have been resolved by the Omnibus Budget Reconciliation Act of 1993. The act provides that certain intangible or other assets may be amortized over a fifteen-year period. Under the new law, examples of permitted deductions are government licenses and permits, noncompete agreements, network affiliation agreements, franchises, trademarks, trade names, and goodwill. In the situation cited above, the acquired station had goodwill of $3 million. That amount would be amortized for tax purposes over fifteen years, at the rate of $200,000 per year.

Prepaid and deferred charges include all prepayments made. Insurance, taxes, and rents are examples.

Liabilities   Liabilities reflect short- and long-term debts. They are listed as follows:

Current liabilities include accounts, taxes, and commissions payable. Monies owed for supplies, real estate, personal property, social security and withholding taxes, music license fees, and sales commissions fall into this category. Current liabilities also include amounts due on program contracts payable within one year.

Long-term liabilities include those liabilities not expected to be paid within one year. Examples of such liabilities are bank debt, mortgages, and amounts due on program contracts beyond one year.

Net Worth   Net worth, or equity, records ownership's initial investment in the broadcast station or cable system, as increased by profits generated or reduced by losses suffered.

Preparing Financial Statements

Financial statement preparation begins with a chart of accounts, a list of account classifications. Each account is assigned a number. The following balance sheet chart of accounts is used by Goodstar Broadcasting L.L.C., a group radio station owner and operator.

Asset accounts are numbered 1000 to 1999. Liability accounts are numbered 2000 to 2999. Equity accounts are 3000 to 3900.

GOODSTAR BROADCASTING, L.L.C.
BALANCE SHEET
CHART OF ACCOUNTS

Account		Description	Acct. #
1000	Cash in Bank		1000
1000	Cash in Bank:1001 Corporate O		1001
1000	Cash in Bank:1002 Payroll Clear	Payroll Clearing Account	1002
1000	Cash in Bank:1010 KXXX/KQLS	KXXX/KQLS SUNFLOWER BANK	1010
1000	Cash in Bank:1011 KYUU/KSLS	KYUU/KSLS NATIONS BANK	1011
1000	Cash in Bank: 1012 KGNO/KOLS	KGNO/KOLS BANK OF SOUTHWEST	1012
1000	Cash in Bank: 1013 KGLS	KGLS FIRST NATL OF HUTCH	1013
1000	Cash in Bank: 1014 KWLS	KWLS THE PEOPLES BANK	1014
1000	Cash in Bank: 1015 KZLS	KZLS FARMERS BANK & TRUST	1015
1000	Cash in Bank: 1016 KFNF	KFNF FARMERS NATIONAL BANK	1016
1000	Cash in Bank: 1017 KILS	KILS SECURITY SAVINGS	1017
1000	Cash in Bank: 1018 KILS	KILS FIRST NATL HUTCHINSON	1018
1000	Cash in Bank: 1019 KNNS/KGTR	KNNS/KGTR 1ST NATL BANK TRUST	1019
1000	Cash in Bank: 1020 CD	CD PURCHASE-30 DAY	1020
1200	Accounts Rec-Advertisers		1200
1205	Accounts Rec-Trade		1205
1210	Accounts Rec-Other		1210
1215	Other Income-Not Billed	Other Income-Not Expected	1215
1499	Undeposited Funds		1499
1500	Prepaid Expenses		1500
1501	Prepaid License Fees/Adjs	Prepaid License Fees/Adjs	1501
1505	Prepaid FCC Fees	Prepaid FCC Fees-Regulatory	1505
1506	Natl Rep Comm Accr	Natl Rep Commission Accrual	1506
1510	Prepaid Insurance		1510
1600	Deposits-Utilities		1600

Account		Description	Acct. #
1601	Deposits-Offices	Deposits-Offices	1601
1800	Land		1800
1820	Building		1820
1825	Accum Depreciation-Bldg		1825
1830	Building Improvements		1830
1835	Accum Depreciation-BI		1835
1840	Furnishings & Fixtures	Furnishings & Equipment	1840
1841	Equipment	Equipment	1841
1842	Tower Construction	Tower Construction	1842
1843	Lease Hold Improvements	Lease Hold Improvements	1843
1845	Accum Depreciation		1845
1855	Accum Amortization		1855
1900	Escrow Account-Station Purchase		1900
1910	FCC License	FCC License	1910
1920	Call Letters	Call Letters	1920
1930	Goodwill	Goodwill	1930
2000	Accounts Payable		2000
2005	Accts Payable-Trade		2005
2010	Accts Payable-Other		2010
2200	Property Tax Payable	Property Tax Payable	2200
2100	Fed W/H Payable		2100
2110	FICA Tax Payable		2110
2115	KS-W/H Tax Payable		2115
2120	KS Unemployment Tax Payable		2120
2125	FUTA-Unemplymnt Tax Payable		2125
2130	Workers Comp Payable		2130
2135	Earned Income Cr Payable		2135
2140	Health Insurance Withholding		2140
2150	Life Insurance W/H		2150
2160	Dental Insurance W/H		2160
2170	Trade Obligations	Trade Obligations	2170
2180	Court Child Support Payable		2180
2190	Employee Advance	Employee Advance	2190
2195	Allowance for Doubtful Accounts	Allowance for Doubtful Accounts	2195
2600	Notes Payable		2600
3000	Opening Bal Equity		3000
3000	Opening Bal Equity: 3010 Class	Class A-Goodstar Inc.	3010
3000	Opening Bal Equity: 3020 Class	Class B-Holding	3020
3000	Opening Bal Equity: 3030 Capital	Capital Contribution-62nd St.	3030
3900	Retained Earnings		3900

It is from records of the kind detailed here that the balance sheet will be prepared (Figure 2.5).

Figure 2.5 *Example of a broadcast station's balance sheet.*

BALANCE SHEET

December 31, Year 1

Current Assets:	
Cash	$ 350,000
Accounts Receivable	1,000,000
Reserve for Bad Debt	(50,000)
Net Accounts Receivable	950,000
Prepaid Expenses	100,000
Total Current Assets	$2,400,000
Fixed Assets:	
Land	$ 400,000
Buildings	300,000
Equipment	200,000
Automobiles and Trucks	25,000
Office Furniture/Equipment	50,000
Leasehold Improvements	25,000
Total Fixed Assets	$1,000,000
Accumulated Depreciation	$ (100,000)
Net Fixed Assets	$ 900,000
Net Intangible Assets	3,700,000
Total Assets	$7,000,000
Current Liabilities:	
Accounts Payable	$ 300,000
Accrued Expenses	100,000
Current Notes Payable	600,000
Total Current Liabilities	$1,000,000
Long-Term Notes Payable	3,000,000
Shareholders' Equity:	
Common Stock	1,000,000
Retained Earnings Beginning	1,000,000
Retained Earnings Current Year	1,000,000
Retained Earnings Total	$2,000,000
Total Shareholders' Equity	$3,000,000
Total Liability and Equity	$7,000,000

The financial health of a company is often judged by examining two ratios computed from the balance sheet numbers. The first of these is *current ratio*, which is obtained by dividing total current liabilities into total current assets. A good current ratio is 1.5 to 1. The second is the *debt-to-equity ratio*. It is computed by dividing stockholders' equity by long-term debt. A satisfactory debt-to-equity ratio is considered to be 1 to 1.

Income Statement   The income statement also is known as the *operating* or *profit and loss (P and L) statement*. It summarizes financial transactions and events over a given period of time. The difference between revenues and expenses is the profit or loss for that period.

Revenues   A major source of revenue for all broadcast stations is the sale of time to local, regional, and national advertisers. Network compensation is an additional source for all network-affiliated television stations and some radio stations. Other broadcast revenues include the sale of programs and talent, and the rental of station facilities. Rents received for the use of station-owned towers or land, and interest and dividends are examples of non-broadcast revenues.

Revenue sources for cable systems are somewhat different. Most revenue is derived from subscribers. However, systems are developing their advertising revenue through the sale of local and national spots, principally in local availabilities in advertiser-supported cable satellite networks. Pay-per-view events and movies are becoming another significant growth area. Cable operators are required by law to set aside channel capacity for lease to third parties, and some receive revenue from such leases.

Expenses   Expenses are classified either as *direct* or as *operating and other*. Direct expenses are commissions paid to agencies for the sale of time. Operating and other expenses are listed according to the organizational structure. Usually, they reflect the costs of operating the major departments or areas of activity. In broadcast stations, they are technical (engineering), program, sales, promotion, news, and general and administrative.

Other expenses are cash and noncash expenses incurred in the operation of the business. Depreciation is an example of a noncash expense and results from the write-off of tangible assets, such as plant and equipment Typically, the asset is reduced by equal annual amounts over its life. The systematic annual reduction in the asset's value is an expense and is charged to the income statement.

The current U.S. tax laws divide tangible assets into 3-, 5-, 7-, 10-, 15-, 20-, and 41-year properties for purposes of calculating depreciation. Other noncash expenses may be amortized, the systematic reduction of an account over a period of time. As noted earlier, an example of an expense that is amortized is goodwill.

The term *amortization* is also frequently applied to program contracts, which are a cash expense item. Various methods for amortizing program contracts exist. One method is *straight line*, which permits a deduction of the total contract in equal annual amounts over the term of the contract. The alternate approach is called *accelerated amortization.* Under this method, larger amounts are written off in the early years of a contract, the theory being that the initial runs of a program have the most value. More detail on the specifics of these two approaches can be found in industry publications such as BCFM's *Accounting Manual for Broadcasters.* It should be noted that amortized program contracts are tax deductible and are usually charged to the program expense account, not to the "other" category.

Another common "other" expense is *interest.* Interest is the premium paid on amounts borrowed to finance acquisitions, purchases of equipment, or construction of a new facility.

Expenses are charged to the department incurring them. Those that are necessary for the overall functioning of the operation, such as utilities, generally are counted against general and administrative costs. Salaries and wages represent an expense in all departments. The following are examples of other broadcast department expenses:

Technical
- parts and supplies for equipment maintenance and repair
- rental of transmitter lines
- tubes for transmitter and studio equipment

Program
- program purchases
- rights to broadcast events (e.g., sports)
- recordings
- music licensing fees
- supplies (e.g., tapes)
- line charges for remote broadcasts

Sales
- commissions paid to staff
- commissions paid to station rep company
- trade advertising
- audience measurement
- travel and entertainment

Promotion
- sales promotion
- advertising and promotion of programs
- research
- merchandising

News
- videotape
- recordings, tapes, and transcripts
- raw film
- wire service
- photo supplies
- art supplies

General and Administrative
- maintenance and repair of buildings and office equipment
- utilities
- rents
- taxes and insurance
- professional services (e.g., legal, accounting)
- office supplies, postage, telephone and telegraph
- operation of station-owned vehicles
- subscriptions and dues
- contributions and donations
- travel and entertainment

Operating expenses are deducted from revenue to determine *profit* or *loss*. Profit is the amount by which revenue exceeds expenses. The profit resulting from the deduction of operating expenses from revenue is called *operating profit*. Such deductions do not include noncash expenses, such as the depreciation and amortization previously discussed. Once the operating profit has been determined, it is then further reduced by depreciation, amortization, and federal, state, and local taxes. Operating profit adjusted for other expenses and taxes is called *net profit*.

To operate effectively, electronic media managers must know how much cash their enterprise produces annually, not just how much profit. *Cash flow* is the term used to describe the cash generated. It is calculated by adding back to net profit the amounts charged to expenses for depreciation, amortization, interest, and taxes. It is the term cash flow that is used to determine the value of an electronic media property by applying multiples to it. For a more detailed treatment of these concepts, refer to the discussion of multiples and prices in Chapter 10, "Entry into the Electronic Media Business."

No income statement treatment can be complete without a discussion of trade-outs. A *trade-out* or *barter* transaction occurs when goods or services are provided in exchange for time. As direct transactions, they do not produce commissionable billings for advertising agencies and, depending upon individual station or system policy, may not result in commissions for account executives either. The transactions must be included on financial statements, with the major questions being the value to assign to them and when to record them.

The Broadcast Cable Financial Management Association recommends that the value of the transaction be equal to the cash saved as a result of the barter. On timing, the BCFM outlines three ways: (1) record income and expense in the same amount in the same period; (2) record income and expense in equal amounts over the term of the barter contract; or (3) record revenue as trade spots are run and expense as goods and services are used. One of these three methods must be selected and consistently applied.

Like the balance sheet, the income statement also begins with a chart of accounts. The sample here is the one used by Goodstar Broadcasting, L.L.C. All accounts have a four-digit number and a description. Revenue accounts are numbered 4000 to 4999 and agency and rep commissions 5000 to 5005. Expense accounts are items 6000 through 8920. Goodstar records the barter revenue and the resulting expense when the barter time airs. Goods and services received in trade or barter transactions normally replace what would otherwise be a cash expense for the company.

GOODSTAR BROADCASTING, L.L.C.
INCOME STATEMENT
CHART OF ACCOUNTS

Account		Description	Acct. #
4000	Broadcast Revenue		
4000	Broadcast Revenue: 4001	Local...Local Sales	4001
4000	Broadcast Revenue: 4002 Nation...	National Sales Revenue	4002
4000	Broadcast Revenue: 4003 Regio...	Regional Sales (CICTITP/KC)	4003
4000	Broadcast Revenue: 4004 Multi...	Multi State Received	4004
4000	Broadcast Revenue: 4005 Agricu	Agriculture Received	4005
4010	Broadcast Revenue: 4010 Speci...	Special Events-Promotions	4010
4000	Broadcast Revenue: 4015 Other I	Other Income	4015
4999	Uncategorized Income		4999
5000	Local Agency Commission		5000
5001	National Agency Commission		5001
5002	Regional Agency Commission		5002
5003	Agri-Net Agency Commission		5003
5004	National Rep Commission		5004
5005	Regional Rep Commission		5005
6000	Engineering Expenses		6000
6000	Engineering Expenses: 6001 Pay...	Payroll	6001
6000	Engineering Expenses: 6002 Pay...	Payroll Taxes	6002
6000	Engineering Expenses: 6005 Em...	Employee Benefits	6005
6000	Engineering Expenses: 6010 Out...	Outside Labor-Contract	6010

Account		Description	Acct. #
6000	Engineering Expenses: 6020 Re...	Repair & Maintenance	6020
6000	Engineering Expenses: 6025 Par...	Parts & Supplies	6025
6000	Engineering Expenses: 6050 Equ...	Equipment Rental	6050
6000	Engineering Expenses: 6060 Frei...	Freight on Equipment	6060
6000	Engineering Expenses: 6070 Aut...	Auto Expenses-Engineering	6070
6200	Program Expense		6200
6200	Program Expense: 6201 Payroll	Payroll	6201
6200	Program Expense: 6202 Payroll	Payroll Taxes	6202
6200	Program Expense: 6205 Employ...	Employee Benefits	6205
6200	Program Expense: 6210 Talent F...	Talent Fees-Pd by Client-Owed	6210
6200	Program Expense: 6215 Outside...	Outside Production-Talent	6215
6200	Program Expense: 6225 Producti...	Production Supplies	6225
6200	Program Expense: 6230 Promoti...	Promotions, Prizes	6230
6200	Program Expense: 6235 Advert &	Advert & Promo	6235
6200	Program Expense: 6240 Special	Special Programs	6240
6200	Program Expense: 6250 Supplies	Supplies	6250
6200	Program Expense: 6290 Ratings	Ratings	6290
6200	Program Expense: 6299 Other Pr...	Other Program Expense	6299
6400	Sales Expense		6400
6400	Sales Expense: 6401 Payroll	Payroll	6401
6400	Sales Expense: 6402 Payroll Tax...	Payroll Taxes	6402
6400	Sales Expense: 6403 Gen. Mgr's...	Gen. Mgr's Commission	6403
6400	Sales Expense: 6404 Commissio...	Commissions	6404
6400	Sales Expense: 6405 Employee ...	Employee Benefits	6405
6400	Sales Expense: 6406 Sales Bonus	Sales Bonus	6406
6400	Sales Expense: 6435 Sales Prom...	Sales Promotions	6435
6400	Sales Expense: 6435 Sales Prom...	Telephone-Promotions	6436
6400	Sales Expense: 6437 Other Sale...	Other Sales Promotions	6437
6400	Sales Expense: 6470 Sales Train...	Sales Training	6470
6600	General Administrative Exp		6600
6600	General Administrative Exp: 6601	Payroll	6601
6600	General Administrative Exp: 6602	Payroll Taxes	6602
6600	General Administrative Exp: 6603	Contract Labor	6603
6600	General Administrative Exp: 6604	Commissions	6604
6600	General Administrative Exp: 6605	Employee Benefits	6605
6600	General Administrative Exp: 6605	Coffee Supplies	6606
6600	General Administrative Exp: 6605	Continuing Education	6607
6600	General Administrative Exp: 6608	GM Overides	6608

Account		Description	Acct. #
6600	General Administrative Exp: 6610	Performance Bonus	6610
6600	General Administrative Exp: 6615	Insurance-Med/Dental/Life	6615
6600	General Administrative Exp: 6619	Tower Rent	6619
6600	General Administrative Exp: 6620	Rent	6620
6600	General Administrative Exp: 6621	Security	6621
6600	General Administrative Exp: 6625	Telephone	6625
6600	General Administrative Exp: 6630	Utilities	6630
6600	General Administrative Exp: 6630	Electricity	6631
6600	General Administrative Exp: 6630	Gas	6632
6600	General Administrative Exp: 6630	Water/Sewer	6633
6600	General Administrative Exp: 6630	Cablevision	6634
6600	General Administrative Exp: 6630	Trash Service	6635
6600	General Administrative Exp: 6636	Bldg Maintenance & Repair	6636
6600	General Administrative Exp: 6640	General Taxes	6640
6600	General Administrative Exp: 6645	Insurance	6645
6600	General Administrative Exp: 6650	Office Supplies	6650
6600	General Administrative Exp: 6651	Office Equipment Leases	6651
6600	General Administrative Exp: 6652	Office Equip Repair/Maint	6652
6600	General Administrative Exp: 6653	Office Equipment Purchases	6653
6600	General Administrative Exp: 6654	Computer Maintenance	6654
6600	General Administrative Exp: 6655	Computer Internet Service Chg	6655
6600	General Administrative Exp: 6660	Postage	6660
6600	General Administrative Exp: 6660	Postage Meter Rental	6661
6600	General Administrative Exp: 6662	Postage-Other (FedEX)	6662
6600	General Administrative Exp: 6665	Payroll Processing Fees	6665
6600	General Administrative Exp: 6670	FCC Fees	6670
6600	General Administrative Exp: 6671	BMI/ASCAP/SESAC Fees	6671
6600	General Administrative Exp: 6672	Membership/Dues	6672
6600	General Administrative Exp: 6673	ARB Fees	6673
6600	General Administrative Exp: 6674	Other Fees-Trademark/Copyright	6674
6600	General Administrative Exp: 6675	Subscriptions/Publications	6675
6600	General Administrative Exp: 6676	Goodstar Website	6676
6600	General Administrative Exp: 6679	Legal-FCC	6679
6600	General Administrative Exp: 6680	Legal Expenses	6680
6600	General Administrative Exp: 6681	Outside Accounting Services	6681
6600	General Administrative Exp: 6685	Printing	6685
6600	General Administrative Exp: 6687	Client Entertainment/Meals	6687
6600	General Administrative Exp: 6688	Personal Property Taxes	6688

Account		Description	Acct. #
6600	General Administrative Exp: 6690	Miscellaneous	6690
6600	General Administrative Exp: 6698	Bad Debt W/Qs	6698
6800	Miscellaneous Expenses		6800
6800	Miscellaneous Expenses: 6801 – P	Payroll	6801
6800	Miscellaneous Expenses: 6802 – P	Payroll Taxes	6802
6800	Miscellaneous Expenses: 6804 – C	Commissions/Bonus	6804
6800	Miscellaneous Expenses: 6805 – C	Car Allowance/Rental	6805
6600	Miscellaneous Expenses: 6807 – C	Cab fares/Parking/Tolls, etc.	6807
6800	Miscellaneous Expenses: 6810 – G	Gasoline/Oil/Repairs	6810
6800	Miscellaneous Expenses: 6811 – C	Car Mileage	6811
6800	Miscellaneous Expenses: 6815 – A	Air Travel	6815
6800	Miscellaneous Expenses: 6816 – T	Telephone-Long Distance	6816
6800	Miscellaneous Expenses: 6820 – M	Meals/Tips	6820
6800	Miscellaneous Expenses: 6825 – T	Travel Expenses-Hotel/Motel	6825
6800	Miscellaneous Expenses: 6826 – I	Incidentals/Misc.	6826
6800	Miscellaneous Expenses: 6850 – M	Moving Expenses	6850
6800	Miscellaneous Expenses: 6860 – S	Station Coverage Analysis	6860
6800	Miscellaneous Expenses: 6870 – P	Public Relations/Marketing	6870
6800	Miscellaneous Expenses: 6890 – B	Bank Service Charges	6890
6800	Miscellaneous Expenses: 6899 – I	Interest on Sale	6899
6999	Uncategorized Expenses		6999
8800	Other Income		8800
8950	Trade Revenue	Trade Revenue	8950
8910	Depreciation Expense	Depreciation Expense	8910
8920	Amortization Expense	Amortization Expense	8920

Figure 2.6 is an example of an income statement comparing the most recent month with the budget. Figure 2.7 provides comparative data on the accumulated year-to-date figures. Electronic media managers in this bottom-line world need at their disposal the kind of complete financial information depicted in order to succeed.

Different proportions of revenue are provided by each source to radio and television stations, and radio and television stations incur expenses differently. For example, local advertising provides most of the sales dollars generated by the typical radio station (Figure 2.8). The data are dated back to 1992, the year the NAB (National Association of Broadcasters) discontinued its Radio Financial Report. Industry consolidation has made data collection and comparison difficult, if not meaningless. For the typical network-affiliated television station, on the other hand, local advertising accounts for just over one-half of each sales dollar (Figure 2.9). Figuring for independent television revenue sources are no longer presented as they were in the previous edition

Figure 2.6 *Group radio consolidated profit and loss statement for one month compared with budget. (Source: Goodstar Broadcasting, Wichita, Kansas.)*

09/16/98

Goodstar Broadcasting, L.L.C.
P&L Budget Comparison
June 1998

	Jun '98	Budget	% of Budget
Ordinary Income/Expense			
Income			
4000 · Broadcast Revenue			
4001 · Local Sales	365,506.90	383,500.00	96.4%
4002 · National Sales Revenue	6,950.00	12,600.00	55.2%
4003 · Regional Sales (ICT/TP/KC)	3,030.80	6,500.00	46.6%
4004 · Multi State Received	18,544.32	18,900.00	98.1%
4005 · Agriculture Received	602.24	7,700.00	7.8%
4010 · Special Events-Promotions	2,368.00		
4015 · Other Income	8,978.11	9,875.00	90.9%
Total 4000 · Broadcast Revenue	409,980.37	439,075.00	93.4%
Total Income	409,980.37	439,075.00	93.4%
Cost of Goods Sold			
5000 · Local Agency Commission	8,097.00	7,358.00	110.0%
5001 · National Agency Commission	1,042.50	1,890.00	55.2%
5002 · Regional Agency Commission	96.78	488.00	19.8%
5003 · Agri-Net Agency Commission	90.34	1,155.00	7.8%
5004 · National Rep Commission	0.00	1,607.00	0.0%
Total COGS	9,326.62	12,498.00	74.6%
Gross Profit	400,653.75	426,577.00	93.9%
Expense			
6000 · Engineering Expenses			
6001 · Payroll	3,125.00	3,185.00	98.1%
6002 · Payroll Taxes	225.99		
6010 · Outside Labor-Contract	3,024.18	270.00	1,120.1%
6020 · Repair & Maintenance	1,411.51	480.00	294.1%
6025 · Parts & Supplies	1,948.89	605.00	322.1%
6050 · Equipment Rental	116.06	145.00	80.0%
6060 · Freight on Equipment	1,346.23	100.00	1,346.2%
6070 · Auto Expenses - Engineering	0.00	130.00	0.0%
Total 6000 · Engineering Expenses	11,197.86	4,915.00	227.8%
6200 · Program Expense			
6201 · Payroll	38,344.05	35,050.00	109.4%
6202 · Payroll Taxes	3,027.09	3,505.00	86.4%
6210 · Talent Fees-Pd By Client-Owed	0.00	215.00	0.0%
6225 · Production Supplies	0.00	285.00	0.0%
6230 · Promotions/Prizes	0.00	525.00	0.0%
6235 · Advert & Promo	178.18	0.00	100.0%
6240 · Special Programs	4,408.58	3,800.00	116.0%
6250 · Supplies	51.50	130.00	39.6%
6299 · Other Program Expense	0.00	130.00	0.0%
Total 6200 · Program Expense	46,009.40	43,640.00	105.4%
6400 · Sales Expense			

Figure 2.6   *Continued*

Goodstar Broadcasting, L.L.C.
P&L Budget Comparison
June 1998

09/16/98

	Jun '98	Budget	% of Budget
6401 · Payroll	35,226.41	50,000.00	70.5%
6402 · Payroll Taxes	4,602.49	7,867.00	58.5%
6403 · Gen. Mgr's Commission	12,129.61	4,278.00	283.5%
6404 · Commissions	25,935.48	24,390.00	106.3%
6406 · Sales Bonus	450.00		
6435 · Sales Promotions			
6436 · Telephone - Promotions	0.00	90.00	0.0%
6435 · Sales Promotions - Other	1,456.97	3,855.00	37.8%
Total 6435 · Sales Promotions	1,456.97	3,945.00	36.9%
6437 · Other Sales Promotions	0.00	70.00	0.0%
Total 6400 · Sales Expense	79,800.96	90,550.00	88.1%
6600 · General Administrative Exp			
6601 · Payroll	28,282.42	22,250.00	127.1%
6602 · Payroll Taxes	3,200.80	4,288.00	74.6%
6603 · Contract Labor	4,842.40	400.00	1,210.6%
6604 · Commissions	9.64		
6605 · Employee Benefits			
6606 · Coffee Supplies	16.73		
6605 · Employee Benefits - Other	174.15		
Total 6605 · Employee Benefits	190.88	0.00	100.0%
6608 · GM Overides	893.91	20,630.00	4.3%
6615 · Insurance-Med/Dental/Life	4,602.85	6,500.00	70.8%
6619 · Tower Rent	3,404.10	1,700.00	200.2%
6620 · Rent	4,049.00	3,550.00	114.1%
6621 · Security	186.00	0.00	100.0%
6625 · Telephone	15,821.56	7,400.00	213.8%
6630 · Utilities			
6631 · Electricity	15,887.01	11,500.00	138.1%
6632 · Gas	163.23	590.00	27.7%
6633 · Water/Sewer	25.35	285.00	8.9%
6634 · Cablevision	102.11	65.00	157.1%
6635 · Trash Service	120.17	130.00	92.4%
Total 6630 · Utilities	16,297.87	12,570.00	129.7%
6636 · Bldg Maintenace & Repair	2,256.27	340.00	663.6%
6640 · General Taxes	0.00	325.00	0.0%
6645 · Insurance	1,997.36	2,700.00	74.0%
6650 · Office Supplies	1,991.29	1,025.00	194.3%
6651 · Office Equipment Leases	222.27	225.00	98.8%
6652 · Office Equip Repair/Maintenance	464.74	285.00	163.1%
6653 · Office Equipment Purchases	0.00	85.00	0.0%
6654 · Computer Maintenance	0.00	255.00	0.0%
6655 · Computer Internet Service Chrgs	91.95	300.00	30.7%
6660 · Postage	1,515.00	1,150.00	131.7%
6662 · Postage-Other (Fed X)	115.00	130.00	88.5%
6670 · FCC Fees	0.00	1,350.00	0.0%

Figure 2.6 *Continued*

Goodstar Broadcasting, L.L.C.
P&L Budget Comparison
June 1998

09/16/98

	Jun '98	Budget	% of Budget
6671 · BMI/ASCAP/SESAC Fees	9,584.11	17,124.00	56.0%
6672 · Memberships/Dues	1,893.46	515.00	367.7%
6675 · Subscriptions/Publications	233.19	120.00	194.3%
6679 · Legal - FCC	0.00	325.00	0.0%
6680 · Legal Expenses	0.00	325.00	0.0%
6685 · Printing	3,507.32	240.00	1,461.4%
6687 · Client Entertainment/Meals	0.00	165.00	0.0%
6688 · Personal Property Taxes	2,235.48	1,400.00	159.7%
6690 · Miscellaneous	0.00	90.00	0.0%
6698 · Bad Debt W/O's	45,885.20	12,797.00	358.6%
Total 6600 · General Administrative Exp	153,774.07	120,559.00	127.6%
6800 · Miscellaneous Expenses			
6807 · Cab fares/Parking/Tolls etc	1.25		
6810 · Gasoline/Oil/Repairs	946.07		
6811 · Car Mileage	1,141.87		
6820 · Meals/Tips	530.68		
6825 · Travel Expenses-Hotel/Motel	380.00		
6890 · Bank Service Charges	0.00	100.00	0.0%
Total 6800 · Miscellaneous Expenses	3,499.87	100.00	3,499.9%
Total Expense	294,282.16	259,764.00	113.3%
Net Ordinary Income	106,371.59	166,813.00	63.8%
Net Income	106,371.59	166,813.00	63.8%

Figure 2.7 *Group radio year-to-date six-month consolidated profit and loss statement compared with budget. (Source: Goodstar Broadcasting, Wichita, Kansas.)*

09/16/98

Goodstar Broadcasting, L.L.C.
P&L Budget Comparison
January through June 1998

	Jan - Jun '98	Budget	% of Budget
Ordinary Income/Expense			
Income			
4000 · Broadcast Revenue			
4001 · Local Sales	1,797,330.61	2,114,000.00	85.0%
4002 · National Sales Revenue	93,796.80	49,300.00	190.3%
4003 · Regional Sales (ICT/TP/...	18,082.15	24,500.00	73.8%
4004 · Multi State Received	126,059.77	81,300.00	155.1%
4005 · Agriculture Received	4,439.70	31,200.00	14.2%
4010 · Special Events-Promoti...	49,205.72		
4015 · Other Income	53,189.65	59,250.00	89.8%
Total 4000 · Broadcast Revenue	2,142,104.40	2,359,550.00	90.8%
Total Income	2,142,104.40	2,359,550.00	90.8%
Cost of Goods Sold			
5000 · Local Agency Comm	43,009.78	40,727.00	105.6%
5001 · National Agency Commis...	14,646.22	7,395.00	198.1%
5002 · Regional Agency Commis...	1,508.99	1,840.00	82.0%
5003 · Agri-Net Agency Commis...	317.67	4,680.00	6.8%
5004 · National Rep Commission	9,875.11	6,287.00	157.1%
Total COGS	69,357.77	60,929.00	113.8%
Gross Profit	2,072,746.63	2,298,621.00	90.2%
Expense			
6000 · Engineering Expenses			
6001 · Payroll	16,916.72	19,110.00	88.5%
6002 · Payroll Taxes	1,351.56		
6010 · Outside Labor-Contract	8,245.70	1,620.00	509.0%
6020 · Repair & Maintenance	7,382.64	2,980.00	247.7%
6025 · Parts & Supplies	6,704.12	3,630.00	184.7%
6050 · Equipment Rental	3,158.46	790.00	399.8%
6060 · Freight on Equipment	1,684.93	570.00	295.6%
6070 · Auto Expenses - Engineer...	0.00	780.00	0.0%
Total 6000 · Engineering Expenses	45,444.13	29,480.00	154.2%
6200 · Program Expense			
6201 · Payroll	202,096.81	209,600.00	96.4%
6202 · Payroll Taxes	18,832.88	20,960.00	89.9%
6210 · Talent Fees-Pd By Client...	50.00	1,085.00	4.6%
6225 · Production Supplies	256.13	1,710.00	15.0%
6230 · Promotions/Prizes	3,802.79	1,850.00	205.6%
6235 · Advert & Promo	4,472.36	3,400.00	131.5%
6240 · Special Programs	29,046.51	22,800.00	127.4%
6250 · Supplies	506.76	780.00	65.0%
6299 · Other Program Expense	0.00	780.00	0.0%
Total 6200 · Program Expense	259,064.24	262,965.00	98.5%
6400 · Sales Expense			

ALL STATIONS

Figure 2.7 *Continued*

09/16/98

Goodstar Broadcasting, L.L.C.
P&L Budget Comparison
January through June 1998

	Jan - Jun '98	Budget	% of Budget
6401 · Payroll	262,115.11	300,000.00	87.4%
6402 · Payroll Taxes	31,250.27	44,144.00	70.8%
6403 · Gen. Mgr's Commission	45,963.14	17,667.00	260.2%
6404 · Commissions	133,367.19	123,767.00	107.8%
6406 · Sales Bonus	12,653.48		
6435 · Sales Promotions			
6436 · Telephone - Promotions	0.00	540.00	0.0%
6435 · Sales Promotions - Other	4,278.82	5,110.00	83.7%
Total 6435 · Sales Promotions	4,278.82	5,650.00	75.7%
6437 · Other Sales Promotions	0.00	420.00	0.0%
Total 6400 · Sales Expense	489,628.01	491,648.00	99.6%
6600 · General Administrative Exp			
6601 · Payroll	170,971.77	143,925.00	118.8%
6602 · Payroll Taxes	25,153.62	25,936.00	97.0%
6603 · Contract Labor	14,951.57	2,500.00	598.1%
6604 · Commissions	16,807.94		
6605 · Employee Benefits			
6606 · Coffee Supplies	178.31		
6607 · Continuing Education	112.80		
6605 · Employee Benefits - Oth...	329.28		
Total 6605 · Employee Benefits	620.39	0.00	100.0%
6608 · GM Overides	23,461.86	115,420.00	20.3%
6615 · Insurance-Med/Dental/Life	27,696.96	39,000.00	71.0%
6619 · Tower Rent	10,329.10	10,200.00	101.3%
6620 · Rent	20,444.00	21,900.00	93.4%
6621 · Security	1,749.00	2,700.00	64.8%
6625 · Telephone	76,829.39	44,400.00	173.0%
6630 · Utilities			
6631 · Electricity	101,371.59	69,000.00	146.9%
6632 · Gas	5,312.53	3,540.00	150.1%
6633 · Water/Sewer	201.36	1,710.00	11.8%
6634 · Cablevision	509.51	390.00	130.6%
6635 · Trash Service	731.19	780.00	93.7%
Total 6630 · Utilities	108,126.18	75,420.00	143.4%
6636 · Bldg Maintenace & Repair	5,886.64	2,040.00	288.6%
6640 · General Taxes	260.35	1,950.00	13.4%
6645 · Insurance	18,880.84	16,200.00	116.5%
6650 · Office Supplies	15,926.07	6,150.00	259.0%
6651 · Office Equipment Leases	1,932.49	1,350.00	143.1%
6652 · Office Equip Repair/Maint...	1,956.02	1,710.00	114.4%
6653 · Office Equipment Purcha...	26.61	510.00	5.2%
6654 · Computer Maintenance	81.00	1,530.00	5.3%
6655 · Computer Internet Servic...	603.65	1,800.00	33.5%
6660 · Postage			
6661 · Postage Meter Rental	373.61		

ALL STATIONS

Figure 2.7 *Continued*

09/16/98

Goodstar Broadcasting, L.L.C.
P&L Budget Comparison
January through June 1998

	Jan - Jun '98	Budget	% of Budget
6660 · Postage - Other	8,126.11	6,900.00	117.8%
Total 6660 · Postage	**7,752.50**	**6,900.00**	**112.4%**
6662 · Postage-Other (Fed X)	491.95	780.00	63.1%
6670 · FCC Fees	1,015.00	8,100.00	12.5%
6671 · BMI/ASCAP/SESAC Fees	65,127.64	92,023.00	70.8%
6672 · Memberships/Dues	11,192.25	2,990.00	374.3%
6675 · Subscriptions/Publications	1,534.24	720.00	213.1%
6679 · Legal - FCC	2,680.00	1,950.00	137.4%
6680 · Legal Expenses	187.31	1,950.00	9.6%
6685 · Printing	7,315.03	1,410.00	518.8%
6687 · Client Entertainment/Meals	326.02	990.00	32.9%
6688 · Personal Property Taxes	12,972.90	8,400.00	154.4%
6690 · Miscellaneous	0.00	540.00	0.0%
6698 · Bad Debt W/O's	160,304.11	68,959.00	232.5%
Total 6600 · General Administrativ...	**813,968.01**	**710,353.00**	**114.6%**
6800 · Miscellaneous Expenses			
6805 · Car Allowance/Rental	752.60		
6807 · Cab fares/Parking/Tolls etc	38.50		
6810 · Gasoline/Oil/Repairs	3,677.34		
6811 · Car Mileage	6,774.93		
6820 · Meals/Tips	3,017.43		
6825 · Travel Expenses-Hotel/Mo...	4,950.47		
6826 · Incidentals/Misc.	26.34		
6850 · Moving Expenses	594.82		
6890 · Bank Service Charges	0.00	600.00	0.0%
Total 6800 · Miscellaneous Expens...	**19,832.43**	**600.00**	**3,305.4%**
Total Expense	**1,627,936.82**	**1,495,046.00**	**108.9%**
Net Ordinary Income	**444,809.81**	**803,575.00**	**55.4%**
Net Income	**444,809.81**	**803,575.00**	**55.4%**

Figure 2.8 *Sources of a typical radio station's sales dollar. (Source:* 1992 NAB Radio Financial Report. *Used with permission of the National Association of Broadcasters.)*

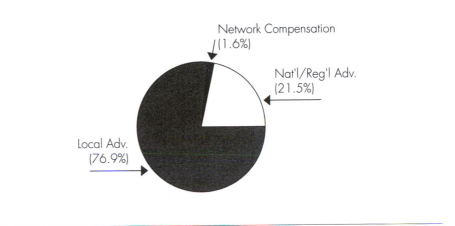

Figure 2.9 *Sources of a typical network-affiliated television station's sales dollar. (Source:* 1997 NAB/BCFM Television Financial Report. *Used with permission of the National Association of Broadcasters.)*

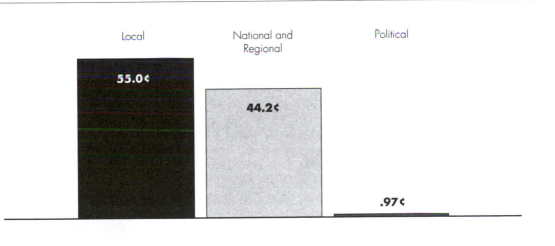

of this book. Most former independent stations are now associated with emerging commercial networks.

The typical radio station spends about 42 cents of each expense dollar on general and administrative costs and half of that amount on programming and production (Figure 2.10). Again, the data are from 1992. For the network-affiliated television station, however, the greatest single expense is the approximate 27 cents for programming (Figure 2.11).

Figure 2.10 *Allocation of a typical radio station's expense dollar. (Source:* 1992 NAB Radio Financial Report. *Used with permission of the National Association of Broadcasters.)*

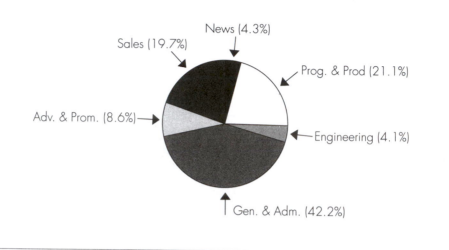

Figure 2.11 *Allocation of a typical network-affiliated television station's expense dollar. (Source:* 1997 NAB/BCFM Television Financial Report. *Used with permission of the National Association of Broadcasters.)*

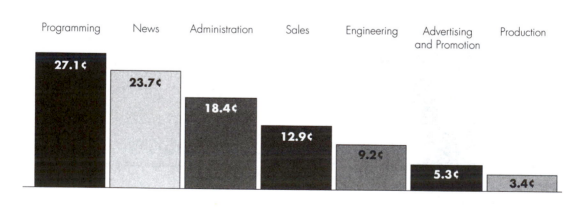

Eighty-six percent of the typical cable television system's revenue is derived from the sale of basic services (63 percent) and pay cable services (23 percent). Advertising sales account for 5 percent, and the remaining 9 percent comes from a variety of sources, including pay-per-view, home shopping, mini-pay, and digital audio. The allocation of expenses varies from system to system, and no reliable national averages are available.

COST CONTROLS

Radio, television, and cable have discovered the importance of cost controls only recently. For most of their history, all three enjoyed almost automatic and sizable annual revenue increases. In that climate, management increased profits primarily through such increases, not through reducing costs.

In the late 1980s, the equation changed for broadcast radio and television. The combination of general economic conditions, the rise of niche marketing due to cable, and the fragmentation of audience shares related to the FCC's liberal licensing policies all but eliminated the customary annual sales increases.

That tide was reversed with a booming economy in 1993 and has continued. Radio has increased its overall share of mass media advertising, and television is still growing in sales volume. However, its annual increase is at a lesser percentage than radio. Cable progress has been impacted by the emergence of DBS as a competitor. Cable rate regulation, introduced in 1992, was to expire in 1999 under the 1996 Telecommunications Act. However, continued subscriber rate increases have caused the Congress to contemplate possible reconsideration of that provision. Now that it passes almost 97 percent of the nation's 98 million TV households, cable must look to rate increases, new services and advertising for revenue growth.

In the new environment, albeit at different times, radio, television, and cable turned to cost controls. The most effective control technique capable of producing significant immediate results is personnel reduction. The 1996 act permitted expanded ownership consolidation, especially in local radio. That development has occasioned extensive reduction. Radio and television eagerly seized on this method, occasionally producing headlines with it. Increasing reliance on sophisticated automation for television, and automation plus utilization of satellite formats for radio, accelerated staff cutbacks.

When cable's moment of truth came, it focused initially on personnel adjustments, too. Cable also relied on automation technology to achieve some of its personnel goals. In addition, it turned to outside contractors to perform some of the functions formerly undertaken by staff. Cable uses independent contractors for installation, rebuilds, and other technical duties, and, in some instances, for the sale of local and spot advertising.

Once the immediate cost benefits of personnel reduction are realized, additional expense reduction is a lot more tedious and requires persistent management attention. Continuing vigilance and monitoring of certain expenditure categories historically have led to savings. Many of these items involve commonsense administration and are common to radio, television, and cable. They include the following:

1. Employee Performance

    A. Employees should be hired on the basis of their qualifications to carry out required tasks. If a staff member lacks the necessary skills, or has to be trained or assisted, performance will suffer and the station or system will not be receiving value for its salary or wage dollar.

B. Each employee's workload should be great enough to justify the position. Underemployment represents a waste of dollars and a drain on profits.

C. Employee efficiency is influenced by available resources. The company must provide the equipment and the space necessary to enable staff to produce quality work efficiently and economically.

D. The work environment must be conducive to productivity. Uncomfortable temperatures, noise, and interruptions detract from work, and may reduce accomplishments and profits.

E. Supervisory personnel should be conversant with the job description of each employee in their charge and, through example and direction, strive to ensure that each performs at maximum efficiency.

F. Clear policies should be established and enforced on employee working hours and privileges, such as the frequency and length of coffee or meal breaks. Abuse can result in lowered productivity. Similarly, policies should be set forth on personal use of the telephone and other facilities. An employee engaged in a personal telephone call or in personal use of a copying machine or computer may delay the completion of business. Further, the cost of long-distance telephone calls for personal reasons can be substantial.

G. Morale is an important element in the willingness of employees to assist in controlling costs. For that reason, management should not underestimate the significance of employer-employee relations and of other factors that contribute to morale.

2. Employee Compensation

Salaries and wages should be fair and competitive in the market. However, care must be taken with increases and overtime.

It is financially dangerous to lead employees to believe that they will receive automatic, periodic increases, unless that is company policy. Staff accustomed to receiving such increases will feel resentment if they are not granted or are discontinued. Instead, some employers prefer to grant bonuses, which are not viewed as a right and need not be given automatically or regularly.

Employees who regularly receive overtime pay regard it as part of their salary. When overtime is reduced or eliminated, they consider it a cut. If work cannot be completed in the normal work day, consideration should be given to adding part-time personnel at the regular rate of pay, thus avoiding the premium rates that have to be paid for overtime.

3. Professional Services

Some professional services are necessary, but their use should be reviewed periodically and controlled. The services used most by broadcast stations and cable systems are:

A. Accounting and auditing

The staff bookkeeper should be able to carry out most of the accounting. If not, an accounting firm will have to be used, and at a substantially higher cost. However, such a firm usually is engaged to file tax papers and conduct audits.

B. Legal

Most stations find it advisable to retain a Washington, D.C., attorney who is qualified to practice before the Federal Communications Commission. The attorney provides the station with timely information and advice, and is especially helpful in the preparation of license-renewal papers. The increasing burden and complexity of federal regulation also has led many cable systems to engage Washington counsel. Some systems are trying to minimize the expense by joining with others in a consortium. Engaging a local attorney in addition is not a wise expense for most stations or systems, since most of the help requested concerns the collection of overdue accounts. That is a service that can be rendered more economically by a collection agency.

C. Consulting

Stations often feel the need for outside advice on programming, news, sales, and promotion. Engaging consultants can be costly. A more economical approach is to try to include such assistance, if possible, among the services of the station rep company.

4. Facilities

A. Land and buildings

Even though the cost of purchasing land and buildings may be high, it is more advantageous for a station to own than to rent. This is true, particularly, of the land on which cable satellite downlinks or the broadcast transmitter tower and building are located. If the landowner demands an excessive amount of money to renew a lease, management faces a dilemma. It is especially acute for broadcasters, since the license to broadcast is granted on the present tower location. To move would involve costly engineering studies and attorney fees and would require FCC approval.

Rental of office and studio buildings poses fewer risks. However, it may be difficult or impossible to obtain the owner's approval to make structural changes aimed at increasing services or improving efficiency.

B. Equipment

All equipment should be purchased at the best price available and for its contribution to the quality, efficiency, or range of program or other services. If it will generate additional revenues or reduce costs, so much the better. The temptation to buy equipment for "prestige" should be avoided. The same is true of equipment that will not be used regularly. Renting rather than purchasing may make more sense. A similar approach should be taken with telephone equipment and services. They should be sufficient for the business's needs, but not extravagant.

5. Insurance

Insurance has become a major cost increase item. Some insurance requirements are mandated by state law. An example is workers' compensation. Loan agreements with the station's or system's lenders may require certain coverage, such as fire, automobile, title, or errors and omissions. Cost efficiencies on some types of insurance may be achievable through state or national broadcast or cable associations.

The major problem in recent years has been medical insurance. Premiums have escalated dramatically and are a major expense item. Employers constantly monitor such costs and pursue methods designed to limit the significant annual increases. Today, many companies require up to one or two years of service before an employee qualifies for employer-paid (or partially paid) medical insurance. Generally, deductibles have been increased and benefits have been capped or limited to contain costs. Employees have come to expect that medical insurance will be included in their compensation package. How it is administered is a definite morale factor.

6. Bad Debts

Failure to collect payment for time sold to advertisers is a problem that confronts many stations and a growing number of cable systems. Elimination of the problem is impossible, but it can be reduced through the statement and enforcement of a policy on billing and payment procedures. It may be necessary to terminate delinquent accounts to prevent additional losses and send a message to other advertisers.

7. Budget Control

Close control should be exercised over all expenditures. For purchases, this can be accomplished through purchase orders that require the general manager's signature. A control system should exist for other expenditures, including the following:

A. Travel and entertainment

A policy should be established for employees who incur work-related travel and entertainment costs, not only to control them but also to satisfy the requirements of the Internal Revenue Service. Before reimbursing employees, many companies require submission of an approval voucher signed by a supervisor or the general manager. Usually, it gives the date and purpose of the travel, locations, and details of and receipts for travel, food, accommodation, and other items, such as parking fees, tips, and tolls.

B. Dues

Management must determine those associations or organizations in which the station or system should hold membership. The National Association of Broadcasters (NAB) or the National Cable Television Association (NCTA) usually are high on the priority list. Affiliation with the state broadcast or cable association and the local chamber of commerce also may be considered advantageous. However, all memberships should be chosen with an eye to the benefits they provide.

Many companies believe that department heads and others should join appropriate local, state, or national organizations to advance their careers or the employer's interests. If the company has a policy of paying employee membership fees, it is important that each proposal for membership be considered on the basis of the benefits that will accrue to the individual and the company. If membership contributes little or nothing, monies spent will be wasted.

C. Subscriptions

Most employers subscribe to selected newspapers, magazines, and journals, and make them available to staff. Publications should be chosen for their contributions to the interests of the staff and the company. Costs can be reduced by eliminating those that are not read or are of marginal interest.

D. Contributions

All stations and systems confront requests from nonprofit organizations for financial contributions or air time. To control such expenditures, a policy should be implemented that permits the discharge of the "good corporate citizen" role and prevents resentment by those whose requests cannot be granted. Many companies put a dollar value on each public service announcement aired and mail an invoice to the organization indicating that the amount represents a contribution. Such records also provide useful documentation for license- or franchise-renewal purposes.

E. Communications

Broadcasting and cable always have been the home of deadlines and time demands. With today's emphasis on productivity and lean staffs, time pressures are intensified. Such an atmosphere produces an employee reliance on expedited means of communication, which almost always add to costs. Dependence on telephone, fax, photocopies, and express delivery services have become the rule, not the exception. Experienced management knows that even little numbers can grow quickly into larger ones, to the point of becoming unpleasant surprises.

Accordingly, managers must be alert to these expenditures and must develop methods of monitoring and control. For example, most communication systems today have electronic entry codes. They ensure that only authorized staff incur expenses. If employees exceed their authority or abuse their access, remedial action can be taken. The use of such codes has an immediate and dramatic effect on telephone, fax, and photocopy excesses. Abuse of costly overnight delivery services as a defense against almost-missed deadlines is not as easy to control and requires real management diligence.

MONITORING FINANCIAL PROGRESS

Management can monitor financial performance in a number of ways. The most obvious is to compare actual results for a month, quarter, or year with the budget and the comparable period for the prior year. A good financial statement, balance sheet, or income statement will give a manager all that information on one piece of paper (see Figure 2.6).

Another important monitoring technique is the comparison of the station's or system's financial progress with that of peers. One of the principal sources that provided comparison (the NAB's annual Radio Financial Report, cited in Figures 2.8 and 2.10) has been discontinued. However, its television report still will be available.

Figure 2.12 *NAB Television Financial Monitoring System Report order form. (Reprinted with permission of the National Association of Broadcasters.)*

**TELEVISION FINANCIAL MONITORING SYSTEM
REPORT ORDER FORM**

National Association of
NAB BROADCASTERS

STATION COMPARISON CRITERIA
To determine the parameters of your customized TVFMS report(s), please complete this form. You must return a separate completed order form for each report you wish to order.

Cost of single report . . . .   List Price: $400
                                                                   NAB Member Price: $200.00

Cost of each additional report, based on an alternate set of comparison criteria, (your order for additional reports must be received at the time we receive your original report request) . . . .   List Price: $200.00
                                                                   NAB Member Price: $100.00

Please select the option(s) in each of the following five criteria categories that best describes the television station(s) you wish to profile in your report. You must select an option in *each* of the five categories that follow or your request cannot be completed.

1) Type of Television Station — choose *one* category:
☐ VHF Affiliates   ☐ UHF Affiliates   ☐ All Affiliates
☐ VHF Independents   ☐ UHF Independents   ☐ All Independents
☐ All UHF   ☐ All UHF   ☐ All Stations

2) ADI Market (Arbitron Market Ranking) — choose a lower limit, upper limit or all markets.
Lower Limit (circle one):

| 1, | 6, | 11, | 16, | 21, | 26, | 31, | 36, | 41, | 46, | 51, | 56, | 61, | 66, | 71, | |
| 76, | 81, | 86, | 91, | 96, | 101, | 111, | 121, | 131, | 141, | 151, | 161, | 171, | 181, | 191, | 201 |

Upper Limit (circle one):

| 5, | 10, | 15, | 20, | 25, | 30, | 35, | 40, | 45, | 50, | 55, | 60, | 65, | 70, | 75, | |
| 80, | 85, | 90, | 95, | 100, | 110, | 120, | 130, | 140, | 150, | 160, | 170, | 180, | 190, | 200, | 215 |

3) Region — choose one region, any combination of regions, or all regions. (You may select more than one region).
☐ New England (CT, ME, MA, NH, RI, VT)
☐ Mid-Atlantic (NJ, NY, PA)
☐ South Atlantic (DE, DC, FL, GA, MD, NC, SC, VA, WV)
☐ East North Central (IL, IN, MI, OH, WI)
☐ East South Central (AL, KY, MS, TN)
☐ West North Central (IA, KS, MN, MO, NE, ND, SD)
☐ West South Central (AR, LA, OK, TX)
☐ Mountain (AZ, CO, ID, MT, NV, NM, UT, WY)
☐ Pacific (AK, CA, HI, OR, WA)
☐ All Regions

4) Year — choose beginning, intermediate and end year (you must specify all three).

Beginning	Intermediate	End
☐ 1983	☐ 1984	☐ 1985
☐ 1984	☐ 1985	☐ 1986

Note: Later years will be added annually as data becomes available.

5) Revenue and Expenses — choose *none, one* or *two* line items from those shown below. For each line item you select, you must choose an upper and lower dollar limit for that line item. All limits specified must be rounded off to the nearest half million.

Category	Lower Limits (Millions)	Upper Limits (Millions)
☐ Nat'l & Reg'l. Adv. Revenue	_____	_____
☐ Local Advertising Revenue	_____	_____
☐ Total Time Sales	_____	_____
☐ Total Net Revenue	_____	_____
☐ Prog. & Production Expenses	_____	_____
☐ News Expenditures	_____	_____
☐ Total Expenses	_____	_____
☐ No Revenue or Expense Limits Selected		

Note: Every effort will be made to accommodate the criteria you have selected to define your TVFMS report. However, certain restrictions are placed on the comparative station selection process to ensure confidentiality. A minimum of 10 stations must fit the specified criteria you have selected.

There are other sources for comparative information. One consists of newsletters and annual reports issued by Paul Kagan Associates, Inc., of Carmel, California.[4] Annual reports include the *Broadcast Financial Record* and the *Cable TV Financial Data Book*. Additional sources are available from the Radio Advertising Bureau (RAB),[5] the Television Bureau of Advertising (TVB),[6] and the Cabletelevision Advertising Bureau (CAB).[7] Revenue reports for some markets are compiled by Miller, Kaplan, Arase & Company.[8]

Another useful tool is the NAB's Television Financial Monitoring System, whose customized reports allow for the comparison of financial results of a particular station with those of similar stations. To use the system, it is necessary to send the NAB a special order form with details of the station for which comparative data are desired (see Figure 2.12).

Additionally, in some markets, stations report their revenue results to an accounting firm retained by all stations. Where available, this procedure provides a method of determining a station's revenue performance as a percentage of the total for the market. Since stations are no longer required to report their financial results to the FCC, this can be a valuable method of monitoring station and market performance.

Financial results are now the most important measurement of a manager's effectiveness. The electronic media manager must be knowledgeable about these important matters.

WHAT'S AHEAD?

No one can predict the future in a consolidating, technology-driven industry like electronic media with any accuracy. All we can do is spot trends.

One emerging trend is publicly-traded mega-companies that are vertically and horizontally integrated. Public companies are earnings-driven, and the market is unforgiving when profit forecasts are not fulfilled. As consolidation progresses, there will be more and more publicly-traded entities operating radio and television, even in small, unrated markets. These companies will be more budget- and performance-driven than even those of the late 1990s.

More than ever, financial management will be the measure of management success. Accordingly, it is vital that any aspiring broadcaster, cablecaster, or future electronic mediacaster of whatever comes along be well acquainted with financial terminology and concepts.

Electronic media students should include computer, business, accounting, and financial courses in their curriculum planning. The industry will become more centralized as to product and management. It will be more computer-driven, and the number of program staff will decline. What will be left largely will be financial, sales, and promotion personnel.

SUMMARY

Financial management demands an understanding of the accounting function, basic financial statements utilized by managers, methods of preparation, and the terminology employed.

The accounting function begins with the budget process, continues with the recording and reporting of transactions, and concludes with an analysis of financial results.

The budget is a planning and control document that plots the course of projected financial transactions (i.e., revenue, expense, profit, or loss). Actual daily results are recorded in journals and ledgers, and are transferred to financial statements by using charts of accounts. The two main financial reporting forms are the balance sheet and the income statement. The balance sheet reveals the condition of the business at a fixed point in time. It discloses total assets, liabilities, and capital of the operation. Ratios are then applied to balance sheet results to determine the relative strength or weakness of the company.

The income statement is another measure of financial health. It measures revenue and expenses, resulting in profit or loss for a given period of time.

After the results are reviewed and compared with the budget, cost control methods may be required. Even if financial results meet or exceed the budget, the electronic media manager might still be underperforming. Financial progress is also judged by a comparison of the results achieved with similar facilities inside or outside the market.

Once made, those additional comparisons may require management to effect further changes in station or system operations.

CASE STUDY

Sunflower Broadcasting is a Midwestern radio multiple owner and operator. The company has fourteen radio stations, nine FM and five AM, in eight communities. While the towns vary in size, none is a rated market. Sunflower acquired these stations from a large-market company that no longer wanted to operate in small markets. The Sunflower owner is a veteran broadcaster who wanted to invest but not operate. In turn, he has hired you to set up and operate a company and to manage these fourteen stations. The owner has invested some of his own money and has borrowed additional funds from a money center bank. The bank has a loan agreement with Sunflower that requires that financial results for each month be reported to the bank within fifteen calendar days of the end of each month. The stations have Arrakus hard disk drives for commercial spots and programs. Also in place are various computers of different shades of age, capacity, and operating condition. Nothing is new or standard. There is an accounting and traffic software system that dates back to 1983, and the manufacturer is out of business. The transfer of the station to Sunflower ownership will become final with the Federal Communications Commission in exactly forty days.

Exercises

1. As noted above, the bank requires information within fifteen days of the end of each month. Based on the information contained in this chapter, what two kinds of financial statements will the bank likely want to see? Please provide the names of the statements and describe briefly the purpose of each.

2. One of your immediate tasks will be to design the format for the statements the bank will require. What are your potential sources of assistance in the design and implementation of the system? What kind of system would you select to produce the required monthly data as quickly as possible? Please elaborate based on information and illustrations in this chapter.

3. One of the statements will disclose recognized ratios by financial analysts to gauge the health of the business. What is the name of the statement involved? Provide the formula for calculating the ratios.

NOTES

1. "1994 Career Guide," *U.S. News and World Report*, November 1, 1993, pp. 78–112.

2. Available through NAB Services, National Association of Broadcasters, 1771 N St., N.W., Washington, DC 20036.

3. Available through Broadcast Cable Financial Management Association, 701 Lee St., Suite 1010, Des Plaines, IL 60016.

4. Paul Kagan Associates, Inc., 126 Clock Tower Pl., Carmel, CA 93923-8734.

5. Radio Advertising Bureau, 304 Park Ave. South, New York, NY 10010.

6. Television Bureau of Advertising, 850 Third Ave., New York, NY 10022-6222.

7. Cabletelevision Advertising Bureau, 2757 Third Ave., New York, NY 10017.

8. Miller, Kaplan, Arase & Company, 10911 Riverside Dr., North Hollywood, CA 91602.

ADDITIONAL READINGS

Accounting Manual for Broadcasters. Des Plaines, IL: Broadcast Financial Management Association, 1981.

Accounting Manual for Radio Stations. Washington, DC: National Association of Broadcasters, 1981.

Estes, Ralph. *Dictionary of Accounting*. Cambridge, MA: MIT Press, 1986.

Financial Manager for the Media Professional. Des Plaines, IL: Broadcast Cable Financial Management Association (published bimonthly).

NAB Television Financial Report. Washington, DC: National Association of Broadcasters (published once every year).

Radio Business Report. Springfield, VA.: Radio Business Report (published weekly).

3 HUMAN RESOURCE MANAGEMENT

This chapter looks at the management of human resources and examines

☐ **the chief functions of human resource management**

☐ **the management of unionized workers**

☐ **selected laws and regulations governing the hiring and treatment of employees**

Broadcast stations in the same market, with comparable facilities and staffs of similar size, often achieve different levels of success. Some attain their objectives regularly, while others fare poorly. Why?

The reasons may be complex. Often, however, the difference may be traced to the way in which each station manages its personnel. The station that attracts qualified employees, compensates them fairly, recognizes and responds to their individual needs, and provides them with a pleasant working environment is rewarded with the amount and quality of work that lead to success. The station that pays more attention to the return on its financial investment than to its staff is plagued by low morale, constant turnover, and a continuing struggle in the competitive broadcast marketplace.

It has been observed that "No other element of the broadcasting enterprise can deliver as great a return on investment as its human resources."[1] Recognizing this, many large stations have established a human resources department, headed by a manager or director. Working with the general manager and other department heads, the department is involved in the following functions: (1) staffing, including staff planning and the recruitment, selection, and dismissal of employees; (2) employee orientation, training, and development; (3) employee compensation; (4) employee safety and health; (5) employee relations; (6) trade union relations, if staff members belong to a trade union; and (7) compliance with employment laws and regulations.

In most stations, however, these functions are handled by a number of different people. Typically, department heads are largely responsible for the management of employees in their respective departments. They recommend to the general manager departmental staffing levels, the hiring and dismissal of staff, and salaries and raises. They approve vacation and leave requests, supervise staff training and development, and ensure departmental compliance with legal and regulatory requirements. Similarly, if their staff is unionized, they carry out the terms of the union contract.

The general manager approves staffing priorities, hiring and dismissal, and salaries and raises for employees in all departments. The general manager monitors, also, the station's compliance with all applicable laws and regulations and with trade union agreements. The business manager is charged with maintaining employee records and processing the payroll.

THE FUNCTIONS OF HUMAN RESOURCE MANAGEMENT

Staffing

Planning   To meet its objectives, a broadcast station must have an adequate number of employees with appropriate skills, both in the station as a whole and in each department. Ensuring that enough qualified staff are available requires the projection of future needs and the development of plans to meet those needs. Together, these activities are known as *personnel planning*, which consists of five components:

> *Job analysis* identifies the responsibilities of the job, usually through consideration of the job's purpose and the duties that must be carried out in order to fulfill that purpose.

Job description results from the job analysis and includes purpose and responsibilities.

Job specifications grow out of the job description and set forth the minimum qualifications necessary to function effectively. Typically, they include a certain level of education and experience in similar work. Other specifications vary with the job.

Workload analysis is an estimate of the type and amount of work that must be performed if the station's objectives are to be met.

Workforce analysis involves consideration of the skills of current employees to determine if any of them have the qualifications to handle the job. If the analysis shows that some do, a selection may be made among them. If not, the station probably will seek a qualified candidate outside.[2]

To illustrate the personnel planning procedure, assume that a television station intends to expand its early-evening newscast from thirty minutes to an hour. The workload analysis indicates, among other things, that a co-anchor must be added. The work force analysis finds that none of the existing news staff is qualified. The job analysis concludes that the chief responsibility is to co-anchor the newscast and that additional responsibilities include writing and reporting for both the early and late newscasts. The job description lists the position title and the responsibilities it carries. The job specifications call for a degree in broadcasting or journalism and experience in TV news anchoring, writing, and reporting.

Recruitment Recruitment is the process of seeking out candidates for positions in the station, and, if necessary, encouraging them to apply. Many stations have a policy of filling vacant jobs with current employees, whenever possible. Such a policy can help build morale among all employees, since it shows management's concern for the individual and suggests that everyone will have an opportunity for advancement. From the station's standpoint, the practice is advantageous because management knows its employees and their abilities. In addition, the employee is accustomed to working with other station staff and is familiar with the station's operation. Stations that are part of a group usually post the opening with other stations in the group. Similar advantages apply.

When recruitment takes place outside the station or group, the particular vacancy will suggest the most likely sources of applicants. A common practice is to advertise the job in newspapers. In some communities, the local newspaper is a popular vehicle for clerical and technical vacancies. Many stations place advertisements in newspapers in nearby cities and even in all newspapers published in the state or region.

When the job requires skills or experience that may be in short supply in the community, or when the station wants to attract a bigger pool of applicants than would result from local, state, or regional advertising, advertisements often are placed in national trade publications. One of the most widely used publications is *Broadcasting & Cable* magazine, which carries help-wanted advertisements for a variety of radio and television personnel in management, sales, research, marketing, promotion, technical, financial and accounting, creative services, news, programming, and production.

A station may prefer, in addition or as an alternative, a publication directed particularly toward the kind of employee sought. For example, *Broadcast Engineering* magazine could be used to advertise a vacancy in the engineering department. Vacancies may be announced, also, in the publications of trade and professional organizations and of state broadcasting associations.

Increasingly, job seekers are adding on-line sources to the traditional print publications. Accordingly, stations should consider using their own Website and the sites of relevant publications and organizations to publicize their needs. Web-only job sites are an additional option. They include Radio-Online (www.radio-online.com) for radio openings, Broadcast Employment Services (www.tvjobs.com) for television, and Interscape Radio Pages (www.allstarradio.com/jobs/) for both media. All three sites offer postings at no charge to stations.

Station consultants may be helpful in suggesting candidates for positions, since they are familiar with employees in other markets.

Following equal employment opportunity practices, stations list job openings with the local office of the state employment service, private employment agencies, and local organizations of women and minorities.

A good source of applicants, particularly for entry-level positions, is the two-year college or university, especially if it has a broadcasting or communication department. Many stations in college and university towns conduct internship programs with such institutions and are able to identify potential employees during the internship. In the absence of an internship program, a call to the institution's placement office will bring the vacancy to the attention of students. Most placement offices keep files on recent graduates and will alert those with appropriate qualifications. If the office distributes a regular listing of positions to interested alumni, an even larger number of potential applicants will be reached.

Word of actual or anticipated vacancies spreads quickly through most stations. It is common, therefore, for employees to carry out informal recruiting by notifying friends and acquaintances. Additionally, many stations ask employees to suggest people who may be interested.

Most radio and television stations keep a file of inquiries about possible jobs. Persons visiting the station to ask about openings often are invited to complete an application for employment, even if no vacancy exists. The application may be filed for possible use later. A similar practice is followed with letters of inquiry. Obviously, the value of the file diminishes with the passage of time as those making the inquiry find other employment, and many stations remove from the file applications that are more than six months old. However, it may be a useful starting point.

Selection   When recruitment has been completed, the station moves to the selection process. This involves the identification of qualified applicants and the elimination of those who are not. Ultimately, it leads to a job offer to the person deemed most likely to perform in a way that will assist the station in meeting its objectives.

Many stations require applicants to complete an employment application form. Generally, it asks for personal information, such as name, address, and telephone number, as well as details of the position sought, education and work experience, and the names and addresses of references. An example of an application for employment form is shown in Figure 3.1. It calls for other

Figure 3.1 *Sample of application for employment in a broadcast station.*

Application for Employment

It is the policy of _____ not to discriminate unlawfully in its employment and personnel practices because of a person's race, color, religion, sex, national origin, disability, or age. Discriminatory employment practices are specifically prohibited by the Federal Communications Commission. If you believe your equal employment rights have been violated, you may contact the FCC, 1919 M Street, N.W., Washington, DC 20554, or other appropriate federal, state or local agency.

Instructions: 1. Type or print in ink. 2. Answer each question fully and accurately; use an additional sheet, if necessary.

Name (Last-First-Middle)	Previous Name*	Social Security No.	Date of Application
Address (Street and Number, City, State, Zip Code)		Area Code & Phone No.	Birth Date (Answer if you are less than 21 years of age.)
Position(s) sought		Date available to begin work	Have you ever worked for this Company?_____ If yes, when & where?

Are you prevented from lawfully becoming employed in this country because of visa or immigration status? _____
(Proof of citizenship or immigration status will be required upon employment.)

		Dates Attended*	Years Completed	Major Areas of Study	Degree Obtained	Date of Degree*
School	Name & Location	From To				
High						
College						
Military						
Other - Special Schools, Education & Training						

*For reference checking purposes only.

(Cont'd.)

Rev. 5/92

Figure 3.1 *Continued*

-2-
EMPLOYMENT HISTORY
(List positions in chronological order starting with current or most recent position.)

Company Name & Address	Employment Dates*	Base Pay
Employer	Hired	Start
Street Address	Separated	End
City and State	Name and Title of Immediate Supervisor	

Position Held and Description of Duties:

Reason for Leaving _____

Company Name & Address	Employment Dates*	Base Pay
Employer	Hired	Start
Street Address	Separated	End
City and State	Name and Title of Immediate Supervisor	

Position Held and Description of Duties:

Reason for Leaving _____

Company Name & Address	Employment Dates*	Base Pay
Employer	Hired	Start
Street Address	Separated	End
City and State	Name and Title of Immediate Supervisor	

Position Held and Description of Duties:

Reason for Leaving _____

Company Name & Address	Employment Dates*	Base Pay
Employer	Hired	Start
Street Address	Separated	End
City and State	Name and Title of Immediate Supervisor	

Position Held and Description of Duties:

Reason for Leaving _____

*For reference checking purposes only.   (Cont'd.)

Figure 3.1 *Continued*

-3-

May we contact your present employer? _____ If no, why? _____

U.S. MILITARY HISTORY

Present Selective Service Classification	Date Entered*	Date Discharged*	Initial Rank	Final Rank

Briefly describe your military duties.

_____

THE FOLLOWING PERTAINS TO ALL APPLICANTS. (Use an additional sheet if necessary.)
Note: Supply the following information if it is not in your resume. If the job you are seeking requires that you operate cameras, machines, computers, typewriters, etc., please indicate the specific ones you are skilled at operating, as well as software familiarity.

_____
_____
_____
_____
_____
_____
_____
_____

List any additional skills, qualifications or experiences which might support your application.	List hobbies and special interests.
Are there certain days of the week or hours in a day when you are not available to work?** Explain.	Are you able to perform the essential functions of the job for which you are applying subject to any duty of reasonable accommodation?

* For reference checking purposes only.
** All reasonable steps will be taken to accommodate religious preferences.

(Cont'd.)

Figure 3.1 *Continued*

-4-

Have you ever pled guilty to or been convicted of any crime?* (Omit minor traffic violations unless you are applying for a job which requires the operation of a motor vehicle.) If yes, state the crime(s), date(s), location(s), court(s) and sentence(s).

Are there any civil actions (other than contract actions) or criminal charges now pending against you? If yes, state the nature of the action(s) or charge(s), name and location(s) of court(s) and current status.*

If presently employed, why do you desire a job change? _____

I applied for this position because of:
_____ Advertisement in the _____ publication;
_____ Radio or television advertisement on _____ station;
_____ Recommendation of current employee named _____ ;
_____ Recruitment efforts at the _____ educational institution;
_____ Referral by_____ employment agency;
_____ Other. Please specify _____

PERSONAL REFERENCES (not former employers or relatives)

Name	Occupation	Street Address City, State (Zip Code)	Telephone No.

PLEASE READ CAREFULLY

I hereby authorize the investigation of all statements contained in this application. I certify that the information given on this application is true and complete, and **I understand and agree that false statements, misrepresentations or omissions of requested facts is sufficient cause for dismissal from employment.** I authorize the references listed above to give you any and all information concerning my previous employment and any pertinent information they may have, personal or otherwise, and release all parties from all liability for any damages that may result from furnishing same to you.

I understand and agree that if I am employed by   the employment relationship will be terminable at will at any time with or without cause by either party, notwithstanding any other oral or written statements by the Company prior to, at, or following date of employment, unless set out in writing, dated and executed by both parties.

I understand also that this application will be considered active for a period of six (6) months only.

Signature of applicant _____

*Guilty pleas, convictions or pending criminal charge(s) are not automatic bars to employment. Neither are pending civil actions. All circumstances will be considered.

information that the station may use in the selection, such as visa or immigration status and any criminal record or pending criminal or civil charges. In addition, it states the station's policy on nondiscrimination in employment, which will be discussed later in the chapter.

The station may ask applicants to take a test to prove that they have the skills claimed on the form. Candidates for a clerical position, for example, may have to demonstrate speed and accuracy on a word-processing test. Some stations use writing tests for entry-level positions in the newsroom.

Applicants for many positions prefer to provide the station with a résumé, in addition to, or instead of, a completed application form. The résumé permits the person seeking employment to emphasize qualifications and to provide more details than most application forms can accommodate.

For on-air positions, the station usually asks applicants for a tape containing examples of their work. In radio, the aim is to identify persons whose voice and style match station format, or whose news delivery commands credibility. In addition to considering voice, the television station is interested in physical appearance and manner of presentation.

Using the employment application form or résumé and, if appropriate, test results and the tape, the station can reduce the list of applicants to those who match most closely the job qualifications. The process of elimination usually continues until only a few names remain.

At this point, interviews may be arranged with those whose applications will be pursued. However, many stations prefer to carry out background and reference checks before proceeding, and with good reason.

Applicants seek to present their education, experience, and skills in the most favorable light. Most list accomplishments of which they are proud and ignore their shortcomings. Some even stretch the truth and give themselves job titles they never held or claim to be proficient in tasks for which they have only rudimentary ability. Furthermore, listed references are likely to be persons who are disposed favorably to the applicant.

Checking on the education of applicants usually is not difficult. A telephone call or letter to a school, college, or university can produce the required information.

The work experience check sometimes presents problems, especially if the applicant has held jobs with several stations over a number of years. However, the stations' personnel files should contain records of the candidate's job titles and responsibilities, employment dates, and salary.

Many stations try to obtain from previous employers details of the applicant's quality of work, ability to get along with colleagues and superiors, strengths and weaknesses, and the reason for leaving. It is not unusual to discover that managers under whom applicants have worked at other jobs have moved in the meantime. When this happens, perseverance is required to track down the manager and, in the event of failure, to find others who remember the applicant and are willing to respond to questions.

Obtaining responses is difficult for another reason: the increasing incidence of legal actions by persons receiving negative recommendations. For that reason, it is not unusual for employers to provide only confirmation of a former employee's dates of employment, job title, and responsibilities.

If the applicant has a job, questions may be posed to the current employer. But stations usually do so only with the approval of the applicant. Permission of the applicant is required, also, if the station plans to carry out a credit check. This practice is not widespread, but many stations conduct such a check on prospective employees whose job will entail the handling of money.

Checks with the references listed by the applicant usually concentrate on the circumstances through which the reference and the applicant are acquainted, and on personal and, whenever appropriate, professional strengths and weaknesses about which the reference can provide information.

If the background and reference checks support the station's preliminary conclusions about the applicant's qualifications, an interview will be scheduled. Of all the steps involved in the selection process, none is more important than the interview. The station will use the results to make a hiring decision. A good choice of candidate will add to the station's competitive strength. A poor choice may lead to a decision to dismiss the chosen candidate after only a short period of employment, leading to yet another search with its attendant expenditures of time, money, and effort.

Interviews are time-consuming for station employees who will be involved and may be costly for the station if the interviewees live in distant cities and the station meets the expenses of travel, meals, and accommodation. However, while application forms, tests, résumés, tapes, and background and reference checks yield a lot of information about applicants and their qualifications, only a face-to-face interview can provide insights into those personal characteristics that often make the difference between success and failure on the job.

The interview gives the station the opportunity to make a determination about the applicant's suitability based on observation of factors such as appearance, manners, personality, motivation, and communication abilities. The applicant's awareness of commercial broadcasting's philosophy, practices, and problems, and his or her attitudes toward them also may be gleaned from responses to questions. In addition, conclusions may be drawn about the applicant's ability to fit into the station.

Interviewing procedures vary. Some stations prefer an unstructured, freewheeling approach, while others follow a structured and formal method. The general manager may take part or merely approve or disapprove the hiring recommendation. In some stations, only the head of the department in which the vacancy exists participates; in others, the heads of all departments may be involved. Some stations include staff in the interviewing.

Whatever procedure is followed, the principal objective of the interview should be the same: an assessment of the candidate's suitability for the position. Of course, the interview may be used to obtain from the applicant additional details about qualifications or clarification of information contained on the application form or résumé. The interviewer may wish to provide the applicant with specific information about the station and the job to be filled. But such exchanges of information should be used only as a means of satisfying the principal objective, and not merely to fill the allotted time.

Those involved in conducting the interview can take certain actions to try to ensure that the objective is achieved:

Before the Interview

1. Become fully familiar with the responsibilities of the position to be filled and the education, experience, and skills necessary to carry them out. This will permit an understanding of what will be required of the new employee, and of the relative importance of education, experience, and skills.

2. Review the candidate's application form or résumé and, if appropriate, test results and tape. This will help to assess the candidate's qualifications and suggest possible questions for the interview.

3. Confirm the date and time of the interview and ensure that enough time has been allowed for it.

4. Give instructions that the interview must not be interrupted by other staff or by telephone calls.

During the Interview

1. Establish a friendly climate to put the interviewee at ease. This can be accomplished by a warm handshake, a smile, and some small talk.

2. Ask only job-related questions. Questions that do not lead to an assessment of qualifications for the position are wasted. They also may be dangerous if they suggest discrimination based on age, sex, or religion, for example.

3. Give the interviewee an opportunity to speak at some length and to answer questions fully. One method of doing this is to pose open-ended questions. If necessary, press the candidate with follow-up questions to obtain additional information.

4. Listen to the responses to the questions. Some interviewers prefer to make written notes during the interview, though this can be disturbing for an interviewee who is required to look at the top of someone's head during what should be a face-to-face exchange.

5. Give additional information about the job and the station to ensure that the candidate has a full understanding of them. Details of the full range of responsibilities, working hours, salary, and fringe benefits, and of the station's organization, goals, and role in the community are among the items that could be covered.

6. Allow time for the candidate to ask questions. In giving details of the job and the station, many interviewers assume that they are providing all the information a candidate requires. However, the interviewee may also be interested in considerations that are not job-related, such as the cost of housing, the quality of the public schools, and employment opportunities in the community for a spouse.

7. Pace the interview so that all planned questions are covered. Omission of questions and the responses may make a hiring decision difficult.

8. Terminate the interview politely. One way to end is to advise the candidate when a decision on filling the position will be made.

9. Ensure that the candidate is shown to the next appointment on the schedule. If the interview is the final appointment, arrange for the candidate to be accompanied to the exit.

After the Interview Record the results of the interview immediately. Some stations use an evaluation form that lists the qualifications for the job and permits the interviewer to grade each candidate on a scale from "poor" to "outstanding" on each. Other stations ask the interviewer to prepare a written memorandum assessing the candidate's strengths and weaknesses. When interviews with all candidates have been completed, the memoranda are used in making a recommendation.

Oral evaluations are not satisfactory, since they leave a gap in the station's employment records. This leads to problems if questions about hiring practices are raised by an unsuccessful candidate or the Federal Communications Commission.

As soon as the decision has been taken to hire one of the interviewed candidates, a job offer should be made promptly. A telephone call will establish if the candidate is still available and interested, and if the offer is acceptable.

To ensure that the station's records are complete, and to avoid misunderstandings, a written offer of employment should be mailed, with a copy. Among other information, it should include the title and responsibilities of the position, salary, fringe benefits, and the starting date and time. If it is acceptable, it should be signed and dated by the new employee and returned to the station, where it will become part of the employee's personnel file. The copy should be retained by the employee.

A letter should be mailed to the unsuccessful candidates, also, advising them of the outcome. They may not welcome the news, but they will appreciate the action, and the station's image may be enhanced as a result.

The station should keep records of all recruitment and selection activities, including the reasons for the selection of one candidate over others. The documentation may be useful in identifying effective procedures, and it may be necessary to satisfy inquires about, or challenges to, the station's employment practices.

Dismissals Staff turnover is a normal experience for all broadcast stations. It is a continuing problem for stations in small markets, where many employees believe that a move to a larger market is the only measure of career progress.

Stations in markets of all sizes are familiar with the situation in which a staff member moves on for personal advancement. In such circumstances, the parting usually takes place without hard feelings on the part of either management or employee.

Another kind of staff turnover is more difficult to handle. It results from a station's decision to dismiss an employee, an action that may send panic waves through the station. If it involves a member of the sales staff, it may also bring reactions from clients. If an on-air personality is involved, the station may hear from the audience.

Of course, some dismissals do not reflect ill on affected employees. Changes in station ownership, the format of a radio station, or locally produced programming at a television station may result in the termination of some employees. Economic considerations, such as those occasioned by in-market radio station consolidation, often lead to reductions in staff.

The majority of dismissals, however, stem from an employee's work or behavior. No station can tolerate very long a staff member who fails to carry out assigned responsibilities satisfactorily. Nor can a station continue to employ someone who is lazy, unreliable, uncooperative, unwilling to accept or follow instructions, or whose work is adversely affected by reliance on abuse of alcohol or drugs.

This is not to suggest that management should stand by idly while an employee moves inevitably toward dismissal. Several steps may be taken to avoid such an outcome. For example, a department head should point out unsatisfactory work immediately and suggest ways to improve. The employee should be warned in writing that failure to improve could lead to dismissal. A copy of the warning should be placed in the employee's file.

Similarly, the supervisor's awareness of the employee's inability or unwillingness to act in accordance with station policies should be brought to the attention of the noncomplying staff member. Action should be taken when the behavior is observed or reported, since tolerating it may suggest that it is acceptable. If the station has a written policy against the behavior, it should be sufficient to draw the employee's attention to it. Again, it would be wise to write an appropriate memorandum to the employee and to place a copy in the employee's file. The memorandum should indicate clearly that continuation of the behavior may result in dismissal.

Management actions of this kind may not lead to improvement or correction, but they will eliminate the element of surprise from a dismissal decision, and they will show that the station has taken reasonable steps to deal fairly with the employee.

If an employee is to be dismissed, the way in which the decision is reached is important. So, too, is the way in which it is carried out, since it is certain to produce a reaction from other employees. The most important reason for caution, however, is federal and state legislation.

Attorney John B. Phillips, Jr., has prepared a set of guidelines for management to follow before discharging an employee.[3] First, he recommends a review of the employee handbook to make sure that the station management has complied with all procedures identified therein. That review should be followed by a review of the employee's personnel file to determine if the documentation contained in it is sufficient to warrant the termination. It should show, for example, that the employee has been advised of the possibility of dismissal and has had ample opportunity to correct any problems or failures to perform as required.

Next, managers should evaluate the possibility of a discrimination or wrongful discharge claim. (Major federal laws on discrimination are described later in the chapter.) The following are among the questions that should be considered:

- How old is the employee?
- Is the employee pregnant?
- How many minority employees remain with the station?
- Does the employee have a disability?
- Who will replace the employee?
- How long has the employee been with the station?
- Does the documentation in the file support termination?
- Was the employee hired away from a long-time employer?

- Has the employee recently filed a workers' compensation claim or any other type of claim with a federal or state agency?
- Has the reason for termination been used to terminate employees in the past?

Phillips lists other questions that may have legal implications but that are primarily practical in nature:

- If the termination is challenged, can the station afford adverse publicity?
- To what extent has the station failed the employee?
- Assuming that the employee is not terminated and the problem is not removed, can the station tolerate its continuation?
- Is the employee the kind of person who is likely to "fight back" or file suit?
- What impact would termination have on employee morale and employer credibility? What about failure to terminate?
- Has the immediate supervisor had problems with other employees in the department?
- Does the employee have potential for success in a different department?
- Are there non-work-related problems that have created or added to the employee's problems at work?
- Has the employee tried to improve?
- Even if the termination is legally defensible, is it a wise decision?

Having reached a tentative decision to terminate, a manager may wish to let a noninterested party evaluate the decision before acting. However, this should not be viewed as a substitute for seeking legal advice if problems are anticipated.

If it is determined that dismissal is appropriate, Phillips suggests a termination conference with the employee. He offers the following guidelines:

1. Two station representatives should be present in most cases.
2. Within the first few minutes, tell the employee that he or she is being terminated.
3. Explain the decision briefly and clearly. Do not engage in argument or counseling, and do not fail to explain the termination.
4. Explain fully any benefits that the employee is entitled to receive and when they will be received. If the employee is not going to receive certain benefits, explain why.
5. Let the employee have an opportunity to speak, and pay close attention to what is said.
6. Be careful about what you say, since anything said during the termination conference can become part of the basis of a subsequent employee claim or lawsuit. In other words, do not make reference to the employee's sex, age, race, religion, or disability or to anything else that could be considered discriminatory.
7. Review the employment history briefly, commenting on specific problems that have occurred and the station's attempts to correct them.
8. Try to obtain the employee's agreement that he or she has had problems on the job or that job performance has not been satisfactory.

9. Take notes.

10. Be as courteous to the employee as possible.

11. Remember that you are not trying to win a lawsuit; you are trying to prevent one.[4]

What the employee was told and what the employee said should be included in the documentation of the conference, and it should be signed by all employer representatives in attendance.

Orientation, Training, and Development

All newly employed staff are new even if they have already worked in a radio or television station. They are with new people in a new operation. Accordingly, they should be introduced to other employees and to the station, a process known as *orientation*.

The introduction to other staff members may be accomplished through visits to the various departments, accompanied by a superior or department head. Such visits permit the new employee to meet and speak with colleagues and to develop an understanding of who does what. Some stations go further and require newcomers to spend several hours or days observing the work of personnel in each department.

An employee handbook designed for all staff often is used to introduce the new employee to the station. Typically, it includes information on the station's organization, its policies, procedures, and rules, and details of employee benefit programs and opportunities for advancement. Among the items usually covered in the section on policies, procedures, and rules are the following: office hours, absenteeism, personal appearance, salary increases, overtime, pay schedule, leaves of absence, outside employment, and discipline and grievance procedures. Information on employee benefits might include details of insurance and pension programs, holidays and vacations, profit-sharing plans, stock purchase options, and reimbursement for educational expenses.

One of the major purposes of an employee handbook is to ensure that all staff are familiar with the responsibilities and rewards of employment, thereby reducing the risk of misunderstandings that could lead to discipline or dismissal. It is important, therefore, that the employee read it and have an opportunity to seek clarification or additional details.

Training is necessary for a new employee who has limited or no experience. Often, it is necessary for an existing employee who moves to a different job in the station. Training is also required when new equipment or procedures are introduced.

Closely allied to training is employee *development*. Many stations believe that the existing staff is the best source of personnel to fill vacated positions. However, it will be a good source only if employees are given an opportunity to gain the knowledge and skills required to carry out the job.

A successful development program results in more proficient employees and, in turn, a more competitive station. Workshops and seminars are frequent vehicles for employee development. Many stations encourage attendance at professional meetings and conventions, as well as enrollment in college courses.

However, probably the most fundamental part of a development program is a regular appraisal session during which the department head reviews the employee's performance. The following are among the functions that may be evaluated:

- dependability in fulfilling job assignments
- knowledge of present job
- judgment
- attitude toward job, supervisor, other employees, and department
- amount of effort employee applies to job
- conduct on the job
- quality of work produced by the employee
- creativity and initiative
- overall evaluation of job performance[5]

Many stations use a performance review form with a grading scale. After grading all factors, the department head invites the employee to sign the form and indicate agreement or disagreement. In the event of disagreement, the employee may appeal the evaluation to the general manager. One copy of the form is retained by the employee and a second is placed in the employee's personnel file.

Performance reviews should enable employer and employee to exchange job-related information candidly and regularly. In addition to providing an opportunity to identify employee strengths, they also permit the department head to discuss weaknesses and ways in which they may be corrected, and to assess candidates for merit pay increases and promotion. At the same time, they may result in a demotion or dismissal.

A more comprehensive approach to employee development is afforded by the practice known as *management by objectives* (MBO), enunciated by Peter Drucker in *The Practice of Management*. Designed as a means of translating an organization's goals into individual objectives, it involves departmental managers and subordinates, jointly, in the establishment of specific objectives for the subordinate and in periodic review of the degree of success attained. At the end of each review session, objectives are set for the next period, which may run for several months or an entire year.

The MBO approach offers many advantages. It can lead to improved planning and coordination through the clarification of each individual's role and responsibility, and the integration of employees' goals with those of the department and the station. Communication can be enhanced as a result of interaction between managers and subordinates. In addition, it can aid the motivation and commitment of employees by involving them in the formulation of their objectives.

However, if the practice is to be successful, objectives must be attainable, quantifiable, placed in priority order, and address results rather than activities. Furthermore, rewards must be tied to performance. If they are not, cynicism probably will result and the worth of the endeavor will be diminished.

Compensation

The word *compensation* suggests financial rewards for work accomplished, but staff members seek other kinds of rewards, too. Approval, respect, and recognition are expectations of most employees. So, too, are working conditions that permit them to perform their job effectively and efficiently. The station that recognizes and rewards individual employee contributions and achievements will make employees feel good about themselves and the station. Their positive feelings will be enhanced if the station provides a pleasant work environment that facilitates the fulfillment of assigned responsibilities.

Salary   The Fair Labor Standards Act sets forth requirements for minimum wage and overtime compensation. It stipulates that employees must be paid at least the federal minimum wage. Stations in states with a rate higher than the federal minimum must pay at least the state minimum.

The act exempts from minimum wage and overtime regulations executive, administrative, and professional employees and outside salespeople, or those who sell away from the station. Small market stations also may exempt from overtime regulations announcers, news editors, and chief engineers.

As the major part of employees' compensation package, salaries must be fair and competitive. They must recognize each employee's worth and must not fall behind those paid by other employers for similar work in the same community. A perception of unfairness or lack of competitiveness may lead to staff morale problems and turnover.

Many stations pay bonuses to all employees. A Christmas bonus is common. Some stations provide employees with a cash incentive bonus, based on the station's financial results. Both kinds of bonus can generate good will and contribute to the employee's feelings of being rewarded.

Financial compensation for sales personnel differs from that of other staff and will be discussed in Chapter 5, "Broadcast Sales."

Benefits   Fringe benefits provide an additional form of financial compensation. Benefit programs vary from station to station and market to market. Some benefits cover employees only, while others include dependents. The cost of benefits may be borne totally by the station or by both the station and the employee.

The National Association of Broadcasters conducts an annual survey of television employee compensation and fringe benefits. It lists the following benefit programs:

Health benefits: Hospitalization, surgical, and major medical insurance coverage for both employees and their dependents. Most stations share the cost with the employee.

HMO: Employee and dependent participation in a health maintenance organization. Again, the cost typically is shared.

Dental: Available to employees and dependents on a cost-sharing basis.

Vision: Offered to employees and their dependents, with a sharing of cost.

Accidental death: Most stations provide it only for employees and meet the cost in full.

Group life insurance: Mostly provided for employees only and fully paid for by the employer.

Disability: Restricted to employees and covers both short- and long-term disability. Generally paid in full by the employer.

Pension plan: Contributions usually are made by the employer.

401-K plan: An employee may defer taxation on income by diverting a portion of income into a retirement plan. In most stations offering the plan, contributions are made by both the employer and the employee.

Education/career development: Some stations encourage employees to develop their knowledge and skills through courses of study, workshops, seminars, and so on. They offer tuition reimbursements for courses completed, and many cover the cost of participation in workshops and seminars.

Paid vacation and sick leave: The amounts usually are determined by length of service.

Paid holidays: These include federal, state, and, occasionally, local holidays.[6]

This list is not exhaustive. Among other benefit programs offered by stations are

Profit sharing: Part of the station's profit is paid out to employees through a profit-sharing plan. The amount of the payment usually is determined by the employee's length of service and current salary.

Employee stock option plan: This benefit offers an opportunity for an employee to purchase an ownership interest in the station through payroll deductions or payroll deductions matched by the employer. Some employers give stock as a bonus.

Thrift plan: The station pays into an employee's thrift plan (savings) account in some proportion to payments made by the employee.

Legal services: The employer usually pays the full cost for services resulting from job-related legal actions.

Jury duty: To ensure that employees on jury duty do not suffer financially, stations make up the difference between the amount paid for jury service and regular salary.

Paid leave: Some stations grant paid leave to employees attending funerals of close family members or performing short-term military service commitments, for example.

Good working conditions and a fair, competitive salary and fringe benefits program contribute much to an employee's attitude toward work and the employer. However, a pleasant working environment will not substitute for a salary below the market rate. Likewise, a good salary may be perceived as a poor reward for having to tolerate unreliable or antiquated equipment or a superior who is quick to criticize and slow to praise. In addition, fringe benefits will not be enough to make up for a station's failure to provide satisfactory working conditions or salaries.

Safety and Health

The workplace *should* be pleasant, but it *must* be safe and healthy. If it is not, the result may be employee accidents and illnesses, both of which deprive the station of the services of personnel and cause inconvenience and possibly added costs for the employer.

There is another important reason for protecting the safety and health of staff. Under the terms of the Occupational Safety and Health Act of 1970, an employer is responsible for ensuring that the workplace is free from recognized hazards that are causing, or are likely to cause, death or serious physical harm to employees. Many states have similar requirements. The act established the Occupational Safety and Health Administration (OSHA), which has produced a large body of guidelines and regulations. Many deal with specific professions, but a significant number apply to business and industry in general, including broadcasting.

Among general OSHA requirements imposed on all employers are the following:

- to provide potable water and adequate toilet facilities
- to maintain in a dry condition, so far as practicable, every workroom
- to keep free from protruding nails, splinters, loose boards, and unnecessary holes and openings every floor, working place, and passageway
- to remove garbage in such a manner as to avoid creating a menace to health, and as often as necessary or appropriate to maintain the place of employment in a sanitary condition
- to provide sufficient exits to permit the prompt escape of occupants in case of fire or other emergency

Some requirements are designed to protect employees who work closely with electrical power, heavy equipment, and tall structures, such as transmitter towers.

Even conscientious adherence to OSHA regulations does not guarantee an accident-free workplace. If an employee dies as a result of a work-related incident, or if three or more employees have to be hospitalized, OSHA requires that the employer report the fatality or hospitalization within eight hours to its nearest area office.

Obviously, the station cannot accept total responsibility for the safety and health of staff. Employees have an obligation to take care of themselves, and the 1970 act requires them to comply with safety and health standards and regulations. However, the station should take the lead in satisfying appropriate guidelines and regulations, requiring staff to do likewise, and in setting an example of prudent safety and health practices for employees to follow.

Employee Relations

Employees differ in their aspirations. Some may be content in their current job, while others may be striving for new responsibilities through promotion in their departments or transfer to another area of station activity. Still others may be using their present position as a stepping-stone to a job with another station.

But most employees share the need to feel that they are important, that they are making a valuable contribution to the station, and that their efforts are appreciated. Accordingly, the relationship between management and staff is important.

Good employee relations are characterized by mutual understanding and respect between employer and employee. They grow out of management's manifest concern for the needs of individual staff members and the existence of channels through which that concern may be communicated.

Much of the daily communication among staff is carried out informally in casual conversations in hallways, the lounge, or the lunchroom. Its informality should not belie its potential, for either good or ill. More rumors probably have started over a cup of coffee than anywhere else.

Managers should use the informality offered by a chance encounter with an employee to display those human traits of interest and caring that help set the tone for employer-employee relations. A smile, a friendly greeting, and an inquiry about a matter unrelated to work can do much to convince staff of management's concern. In addition, they can help establish an atmosphere of cooperation and build the kind of morale necessary if the station is to obtain from all employees their best efforts.

Informal communication is important, but limited. To guarantee continuing communication with staff, managers rely heavily on the printed word. A letter to an employee offering congratulations on an accomplishment, or a memorandum posted on the bulletin board thanking the entire staff for a successful ratings book, are examples.

Many stations communicate on a regular basis through a newsletter or magazine. Such publications often are a combination of what employees want to know and what management believes they need to know. They want to know about their colleagues. Anniversaries, marriages, births, hobbies, travels, and achievements find their way into most newsletters. Employees also are interested in station plans that may affect them.

Often, employee information needs are not recognized by management until they have become wants. Managers who are in close communication with employees recognize the desirability of keeping them advised on a wide range of station activities. The newsletter is a useful mechanism for telling staff members what they need to know by not only announcing but explaining policies and procedures, reporting on progress toward station objectives, and clarifying any changes in plans to meet them. Rumor and speculation may not be eliminated, but this kind of open communication should reduce both.

Bulletin boards are used in many stations to provide information on a variety of topics, from job openings to awards won by individuals and the station. Some stations permit staff to use the boards for personal reasons, to advertise a car for sale or to seek a baby-sitter, for example.

To a large extent, memoranda, newsletters, and bulletin boards reflect management's perceptions of employee information wants and needs. The ideas and concerns of nonmanagement staff are more likely to be expressed orally, to colleagues and superiors. Regular departmental meetings provide a means of airing employee attitudes.

When concerns are of a private nature, most employees are reluctant to raise them in front of their colleagues. Recognizing this, many department heads and general managers have an open-door policy so that staff may have immediate access to a sensitive and confidential ear.

The perceptions of employees often are valuable, not only in enabling management to be apprised of their feelings, but in bringing about desirable changes. Suggestions should be solicited from staff. Some stations go further and install suggestion boxes, awarding prizes for ideas that the station implements.

Because of the interdependence of employees and the need for teamwork, many stations encourage a cooperative atmosphere through recreational and social programs. Station sports teams, staff and family outings to concerts, plays, sports events, picnics, and parties—all are examples of activities that can help develop and maintain a united commitment to the station and its objectives.

HUMAN RESOURCE MANAGEMENT AND TRADE UNIONS

Relations between management and employees in many stations, particularly in large markets, are influenced by employee membership in a trade union. Among the major unions that represent broadcast personnel are the following:

UNION	EXAMPLES OF EMPLOYEES REPRESENTED
American Federation of Musicians of the United States and Canada (AFM)	Musicians in live or recorded performance in radio and television
American Federation of Television and Radio Artists (AFTRA)	Performers in radio and television programs and in taped radio and television commercials
Directors Guild of America (DGA)	Associate directors in radio; television directors, associate directors, stage managers, and program assistants
International Alliance of Theatrical Stage Employees, Technicians, Artists and Allied Crafts of the United States and Canada (IATSE)	Radio engineers and audio operators; television technicians, stage hands, camera operators, grips, and electricians
International Brotherhood of Electrical Workers (IBEW)	Radio and television technicians; television floor directors, film editors, announcers, camera operators, news writers, clerical and maintenance personnel
National Association of Broadcast Employees and Technicians (NABET)	Radio: continuity writers; traffic personnel; secretaries; board operators; disc jockeys; announcers and news anchors; producers; news and sports writers; and reporters.
	Television: continuity writers; traffic personnel; secretaries; videotape and audio operators; projectionists; switchers; transmitter, camera, and character generator operators; floor directors; directors and lighting directors; news and sports anchors; writers and reporters; news photographers; assignment editors and producers; and weather anchors.
Screen Actors Guild (SAG)	Actors in television series and in filmed television commercials
Writers Guild of America, East (WGAE)	Radio and television news writers, editors, researchers, and desk assistants; television promotion and continuity writers and graphic artists
Writers Guild of America, West (WGAW)	Writers of radio and television programs

The basic unit of a national or international union is the "local" union, which represents employees in a common job in a station or limited geographic area.

Like all employees, union members seek approval, respect, and recognition, and expect a safe and healthy workplace. They have similar concerns about salaries, fringe benefits, and job security.

However, management's treatment of unionized employees differs from that in nonunion stations. Take, for example, the matter of complaints. A nonunion employee generally presents the complaint directly to the supervisor or department head and, if necessary, to the general manager. If the employee is a member of a union, the complaint usually will be presented to management by a job steward. This procedure is one of many detailed in the document that governs management-union employee relations: the *union agreement* or *contract*.

The Union Contract

The union contract covers a wide range of content and reflects the interests and needs of the employees covered by it. Creative personnel may be concerned about their creative control and the way in which they are recognized in program credits. Technical staff, on the other hand, may be much more interested in the possibility of layoffs resulting from new equipment or the use of nontechnical personnel in traditionally technical tasks.

Most contracts contain two major categories of clauses: *economic* and *work and relationship*.

In the economic category, provisions on wages and fringe benefits dominate. The contract will set forth hourly rates of pay, premium rates for overtime and holiday work and, in some cases, cost-of-living adjustments. Among the fringe benefits generally covered are paid vacations and sick leave, insurance, pension, severance pay, and paid leave for activities such as jury duty.

The work and relationship section usually contains some or all of the following provisions:

Union recognition: The station recognizes the union as the bargaining unit for employees who are members of the union and agrees to deal exclusively with it on matters affecting employees in the unit.

Union security: The union may require, and the station may agree, that all existing employees in the bargaining unit become and remain members of the union and that new employees join the union within a specified period. Such a requirement is not permitted in so-called "right-to-work" states.

Union checkoff: The station agrees to deduct from the wages of union members all union dues, initiation fees, or other assessments, and to remit them promptly to the local union.

Grievance procedure and arbitration: This is a description of the procedure whereby employees may present or have grievances presented to their supervisors and, if necessary, the general manager. If the grievance is not withdrawn or settled, the contract may provide for its presentation to an arbitrator, whose decision will be final and binding on the station, union, and employee during the term of the contract.

No strike, no lockout: Contracts in which the grievance procedure requires the use of an arbitrator to settle grievances usually contain a clause forbidding strikes, work stoppages, or slowdowns by employees, and lockouts by management.

Seniority: Most unions insist on the use of seniority in management decisions on matters such as promotions, layoffs, and recalls. Preference in promotion is given to employees with the longest service to the station, provided that the employee has the qualifications or skills to perform the work. In the same way, senior employees will be the last to be affected by layoffs and the first to be recalled after a layoff.

Management rights: The contract recognizes the responsibility of station management to operate the station in an orderly, efficient, and economic way. Accordingly, the station retains the right to make and carry out decisions on personnel, equipment, and other matters consistent with its responsibility.

Many other provisions may be contained in the contract, including clauses on procedures for suspension or discharge of employees, the length and frequency of meal breaks, reimbursement to employees for expenses incurred in carrying out their work, and safety conditions in the station and in company vehicles. Many contracts also contain clauses permitting the station to engage nonstation employees to carry out work for which employees do not have the skill, and jurisdictional provisions stating which employees are permitted to carry out specific tasks.

Union Negotiations

The contract between a broadcast station and a labor union represents a mutually acceptable agreement and is the result of bargaining or negotiations between the two parties. To ensure that it serves the best interests of the station and its employees, management should take certain actions before and during the negotiations, and after the contract is signed.

Before the Negotiations

1. Assemble the negotiating team. The team should include someone familiar with the station's operation, usually the general manager. Familiarity with labor law or labor relations is desirable, and for that reason an attorney often is part of the team. If an attorney is not included, the station should obtain legal advice on applicable federal, state, and local requirements pertaining to bargaining methods and content.

2. Designate a chief negotiator to speak for the station. The person selected should have good communication skills, tact, and patience.

3. Ensure that members of the negotiating team are familiar with the existing contract and with clauses that the station wishes to modify or delete, and the reasons. They should also be aware of the union's feelings about the current contract and any changes it is likely to seek.

4. Determine the issues to be raised by the station and those likely to be raised by the union.

5. Establish the station's objectives on economic as well as work and relationship matters.

6. Anticipate the union's objectives.

7. Determine the station's positions and prepare detailed documentation to support them. In most cases, the station will identify provisions it must have and others on which it is willing to compromise.

During the Negotiations

1. Take the initiative. One method is to put the union in the position of bargaining up from the station's proposals. For example, the station may prepare a draft of a written contract for the negotiations, thereby placing on the union the burden of showing the reasons to change it.

2. Listen carefully to union requests and ask for clarification or explanation so that they may be understood fully. This will permit the station's team to prepare counterproposals or indicate parts of the proposed contract that meet the union's concerns or needs.

3. Keep an open mind. Refrain from rejecting union requests out of hand. Remember that, like the station, the union starts by asking for more than it expects to obtain and that the final contract will reflect compromises by both parties.

4. Be firm. An open mind and flexibility should not lead the union to believe that the station team is weak and can be pushed around. The station's chief negotiator should exhibit firmness when necessary, and support the station's arguments with a rationale and documentation.

5. Avoid lengthy bargaining sessions, since a tired and weary negotiating team may agree to provisions that prove to be unwise later.

6. Ensure that the language of the contract is clear and unambiguous. A document that is open to misunderstanding or misinterpretation will be troublesome to station management.

After the Contract is Signed

1. Follow the contract diligently and expect the union to do the same.

2. Ensure that all department heads and other supervisory personnel are familiar with the contract. If they are not, and they fail to adhere to it, trouble could result.

Reasons for Joining a Union

Broadcast union members are found most often in large-market radio and television stations. However, that does not mean that stations in smaller markets are immune to attempts to organize employees. In addition, such organizing often results not from the strength of a union but from management's insensitivity to employee interests and needs.

Management that values its staff and treats them fairly may never experience a threat of unionization. Management that fails to do so may confront an attempt due to one or more of the following factors:

1. Economic

A. Salaries that fall behind those of the competition in the market

B. Pay rates that are not based on differences in skills or the work required

C. Fringe benefits that do not match those of competing stations in the market

2. Working Conditions

A. Absence of guidelines or policies on matters such as promotions, merit pay increases, and job responsibilities

B. A workplace characterized by dirty offices; poor lighting, heating, and ventilation; unreliable equipment; and safety or health hazards

3. Management Attitudes and Behavior

A. Noncommunicative management, which leads, inevitably, to speculation, gossip, and rumor. This is particularly dangerous when changes are made without explanation in personnel, equipment, or operating practices.

B. Unresponsiveness to employee concerns. Employee questions that go unanswered often become major problems, especially if employees believe that management is trying to conceal information on actions that may affect their status or job security.

C. Favoritism. If management treats, or is perceived as treating, some employees differently from others, resentment may occur.

D. Discrimination. Even though discrimination is illegal, management actions may be interpreted by some employees as being discriminatory and based on considerations of race, color, religion, national origin, sex, age, or disability.

E. Ignoring seniority. Many employees believe that seniority and dedication to a station over a long period should be recognized by management in decisions on matters such as promotions. Union organizers will promise to obtain management recognition of seniority.

F. Us vs. them. Management that encourages its department heads and other supervisors to put a distance between themselves and their staff and to establish a combative rather than a cooperative environment will meet with resentment and distrust from most employees.

4. The Troublemaker

Most stations are familiar with the complainer, the person who finds fault with most things or, failing to find a problem, invents one. In some cases, the complainer goes further and becomes an agitator, claiming that a union would meet every employee concern and solve every problem. Often, the arguments sound so persuasive that other employees go along and the likelihood of unionization becomes real.

5. Competing Station

Union organization of staff at a competing station may result in an attempt at unionization, particularly if it succeeds in obtaining better salaries, fringe benefits, and terms and conditions of employment at that station.

Working with Unions

If, despite efforts to prevent it, a union is organized, management should view it not as a threat but as an opportunity to work cooperatively toward identified goals. That may be easier in theory than practice, but most union members recognize that their job satisfaction depends largely on the degree of success the station attains.

To help in any adjustment to the presence of a union, the following pointers are suggested:

1. Unionism is an accepted fact. Management must recognize that unions generally have reached a point of very high efficiency in bargaining and maintaining strength. Learn to live and work with them when necessary.

2. Management should take a realistic view of all mutual agreements and be very careful about altering, modifying, or making concessions in the established contractual arrangement.

3. Remember that rights or responsibilities that have been relinquished are hard to regain at the bargaining table. Similarly, granting concessions on grievances that have not been properly ironed out can cause future trouble, and rarely brings good will or satisfaction to the parties concerned.

4. Supervisors should be vigorously backed up. This does not imply that errors should be defended, but supervisors need support to maintain morale and company strength.

5. Dual loyalty is possible. In pursuing a positive approach, management must realize that in a well-run company the majority of clear-thinking union members know that a strong and progressive management is their best guarantee of security.

6. In employee communications, honesty is the best policy, even in the face of mistrust and disinterest. Candid communication of information about the company, its business outlook, and projected changes can help ensure the acceptance of its policies and principles.

7. Management should establish a working rapport with union officers and recognize the natural leadership they frequently display. Mutual respect should be reflected in efficient administration of all matters concerning management and the union.

8. A realistic effort should always be made to avoid either overantagonism or overcooperation. Either can be self-defeating and lead to an erosion of rights. Mature judgment is a must in preventing hasty or ill-considered decisions by union or management.

9. Management must manage. It can and should be fair and just in all its labor relations, but it should live up to all obligations and expect the union to do the same. A contract should never be a club for either to wield, but rather an agreement to be respected and obeyed.[7]

HUMAN RESOURCE MANAGEMENT AND THE LAW

Like other employers, broadcasters are required to comply with a large number of laws dealing with the hiring and treatment of employees. Among the most important federal laws are the following:

Civil Rights Act of 1964, as amended, makes it unlawful for an employer to discriminate in hiring, firing, compensation, terms, conditions, or privileges of employment on the basis of race, color, religion, sex, or national origin.

Age Discrimination in Employment Act of 1967, as amended, forbids employers with twenty or more employees from discriminating against persons forty years of age or older with respect to any term, condition, or privilege of employment, including, but not limited to, hiring, firing, promotion, lay-off, compensation, benefits, job assignments, and training.

Equal Pay Act of 1963, as amended, prohibits wage discrimination between male and female employees when the work requires substantially equal skill, effort, and responsibility, and is performed under similar working conditions.

Pregnancy Discrimination Act of 1978, an amendment to the 1964 Civil Rights Act, forbids discrimination based on pregnancy, childbirth, or related medical conditions. The act seeks to guarantee that women affected by pregnancy or related conditions are treated in the same manner as other job applicants or employees with similar abilities or limitations.

Americans with Disabilities Act of 1990 prohibits employers with fifteen or more employees from discriminating against qualified individuals with disabilities in job application procedures, hiring, firing, advancement, compensation, job training, and other terms, conditions and privileges of employment. Individuals are considered to have a "disability" if they have a physical or mental impairment that substantially limits one or more major life activities, have a record of such an impairment, or are regarded as having such an impairment.[8]

Family and Medical Leave Act of 1993 requires employers with fifty or more employees to make available to them up to twelve weeks of unpaid leave during any twelve-month period for one or more of the following reasons: for the birth or placement of a child for adoption or foster care; to care for an immediate family member (spouse, child, or parent) with a serious health condition; or to take medical leave when the employee is unable to work because of a serious health condition. Upon return from leave, employees must be restored to their original job, or to an equivalent job with equivalent pay, benefits, and other employment terms and conditions.

Equal Employment Opportunity

The Equal Employment Opportunity Commission (EEOC) is primarily responsible for ensuring compliance with federal laws prohibiting discrimination in employment practices. However, the Federal Communications Commission has enacted equal employment opportunities rules to which broadcasters must also adhere.[9]

The rules require that broadcast stations (1) afford equal opportunity in employment to all qualified persons and not discriminate because of race, color, religion, national origin, or sex; and (2) establish, maintain, and carry out a positive continuing program of specific practices designed to ensure equal opportunity in every aspect of station employment policy and practice. Under the terms of its program, a station must

- define the responsibility of each level of management to ensure a positive application and vigorous enforcement of its policy of equal opportunity, and establish a procedure to review and control managerial and supervisory performance

- inform its employees and recognized employee organizations of the positive equal opportunity policy and program and enlist their cooperation

- communicate its equal employment opportunity policy and program and its employment needs to sources of qualified applicants without regard to race, color, religion, national origin, or sex, and solicit their recruitment assistance on a continuing basis

- conduct a continuing campaign to exclude all unlawful forms of prejudice or discrimination based upon race, color, religion, national origin, or sex from its personnel policies and practices and working conditions

- conduct a continuing review of job structure and employment practices and adopt positive recruitment, job design, and other measures needed to ensure genuine equality of opportunity to participate fully in all organizational units, occupations, and levels of responsibility[10]

In carrying out its equal employment program, a station is required to engage in five activities directed chiefly at two categories of persons — (1) women and (2) minorities, specifically blacks (not of Hispanic origin), Hispanics, American Indians and Alaskan natives, Asians, and Pacific Islanders. A station should

- disseminate its equal opportunity program to job applicants and employees

- use minority organizations, organizations for women, media, educational institutions, and other potential sources of minority and female applicants to supply referrals whenever job vacancies are available in its operation

- evaluate its employment profile and job turnover against the availability of minorities and women in its recruitment area

- undertake to offer promotions of qualified minorities and women in a nondiscriminatory fashion to positions of greater responsibility

- analyze its efforts to recruit, hire, and promote minorities and women and address any difficulties encountered in implementing its equal employment opportunity program[11]

For each requirement, the FCC provides suggested actions that would demonstrate a good-faith effort to comply with its rules.

Late in 1998, the commission suspended its employment reporting requirements. The decision came in the wake of an appeals court ruling that held unconstitutional the rules requiring affirmative action in the hiring of minorities. FCC Chairman William Kennard pledged to design new rules that would pass muster with the court. What follows are details of the commission's procedures before the suspension was announced.

The commission monitors compliance through a station's Annual Employment Report (FCC 395-B) and through the Equal Employment Opportunity Program Report (FCC 396), which a station must file when seeking renewal of its license.

Form 395-B (Figure 3.2) requires a station with five or more full-time employees (those working thirty or more hours a week) to provide employment statistics for both full- and part-time paid employees by race, national origin, and sex in nine job classifications: officials and managers, professionals, technicians, sales workers, office and clerical, craft workers (skilled), operatives (semiskilled), laborers (unskilled), and service workers. A station with fewer than five full-time employees is not required to report such data.

Form 396 (Figure 3.3) requires a renewal applicant with five or more full-time employees to report activities undertaken in the preceding twelve months to execute the various elements of its equal employment opportunity (EEO) program. The form calls for information in eight categories:

Responsibility for implementation: The name and title of the person responsible for carrying out the program.

Policy dissemination: Practices used to disseminate the EEO policy to management, staff, and prospective employees.

Recruitment: Actions taken to attract qualified minority and women applicants for all types of jobs whenever vacancies occur.

Job hires: Total number of persons hired in the preceding twelve months, and the number of women and minorities in that total. Similar details are requested for hires in the upper-four job categories: officials and managers, professionals, technicians, and sales workers.

Promotions: Data on promotions, with the same breakdown as for job hires.

Available labor force: Evaluation of the station's employment profile and job turnover against the availability of minorities and women in the relevant labor market. The FCC uses labor force data for the Metropolitan Statistical Area (MSA) in which the station is located or county data if it is not in an MSA.

Complaints: Description of complaints filed against the station alleging unlawful discrimination in employment practices.

Other information: Optional information the station believes will assist the commission in evaluating its EEO efforts, such as training programs for minorities and women, and problems in attracting qualified minority and women candidates for employment or promotion.

A station with fewer than five full-time employees is not required to provide details of equal employment opportunity activities. Further, if minority group representation in the available labor force is less than 5 percent, a station may report only information on an EEO program directed toward women.

In reviewing a station's EEO compliance, the FCC follows a two-step procedure. First, the commission's staff makes an evaluation of a licensee's efforts based on the "full range of information available." That includes the Annual Employment Report, the EEO Program Report, and any adjudicated findings of discrimination. If, on the basis of this information, the commission concludes that the station has complied with its rules, no further action is taken.

However, if it is determined that the station's efforts have been less than satisfactory, the commission moves to the second step: a request for additional details in those areas of the EEO program that appear to be deficient.

Figure 3.2 *Broadcast Station Annual Employment Report (FCC 395-B).*

Federal Communications Commission
Washington, D. C. 20554

Approved by OMB
3060-0390
Expires 12/31/99

BROADCAST STATION
ANNUAL EMPLOYMENT REPORT

Facility Identification Number

SECTION I

A. Name of Licensee or Permittee

B. Address

SECTION II

A. TYPE OF RESPONDENT (check ONLY one)

COMMERCIAL BROADCAST STATION		NONCOMMERCIAL BROADCAST STATION	HEADQUARTERS

AM ☐ AM　　　　TV ☐ TV　　　　ER ☐ Educational AM or FM Radio　　HQ ☐

FM ☐ FM　　　　LP ☐ Low Power TV　　ET ☐ Educational TV

AF ☐ Combined AM & FM in same area (must file a combined report)　　IN ☐ International

B. List call letters and location(s) of included stations. AM station is to be listed first in a combined report. Provide former call letters for each station if changed since last 395-B report.

CURRENT CALL LETTERS	LOCATION(S)	FORMER CALL LETTERS

SECTION III

A. PAYROLL PERIOD COVERED BY THIS REPORT (DATE) _____

B. CHECK APPLICABLE BOX

☐ Fewer than five full-time employees during the selected payroll period (Complete page one only and certification statement and return to FCC)

☐ Five or more full-time employees during selected payroll period (Complete all sections of form and certification statement and return to FCC)

SECTION IV   CERTIFICATION

This report must be certified, as follows: (a) By licensee, if an individual; (b) By a partner, if a partnership (general partner, if a limited partnership); (c) By an officer, if a corporation or an association; or (d) By an attorney of the licensee, in case of physical disability or absence from the United States of the licensee.

WILLFUL FALSE STATEMENTS MADE ON THIS FORM ARE PUNISHABLE BY FINE AND/OR IMPRISONMENT (U.S. CODE TITLE 18, SECTION 1001), AND/OR REVOCATION OF ANY STATION LICENSE OR CONSTRUCTION PERMIT (U.S. CODE, TITLE 47, SECTION 312(a)(1)), AND/OR FORFEITURE (U.S. CODE, TITLE 47, SECTION 503).

I certify to the best of my knowledge, information and belief, all statements contained in this report are true and correct.

Signed _____　Title _____

Print Name _____　Date _____ Telephone No. (____) _____

FCC 395-B
February 1997

1

Figure 3.2 *Continued*

SECTION V - EMPLOYEE DATA

A. FULL-TIME PAID EMPLOYEE DATA		MALE					FEMALE				
JOB CATEGORIES	TOTAL	WHITE (NOT HISPANIC)	BLACK (NOT HISPANIC)	HISPANIC	ASIAN OR PACIFIC ISLANDER	AMERICAN INDIAN, ALASKAN NATIVE	WHITE (NOT HISPANIC)	BLACK (NOT HISPANIC)	HISPANIC	ASIAN OR PACIFIC ISLANDER	AMERICAN INDIAN, ALASKAN NATIVE
	(a-j)	(a)	(b)	(c)	(d)	(e)	(f)	(g)	(h)	(i)	(j)
OFFICIALS & MANAGERS											
PROFESSIONALS											
TECHNICIANS											
SALES WORKERS											
OFFICE & CLERICAL											
CRAFT WORKERS (SKILLED)											
OPERATIVES (SEMI-SKILLED)											
LABORERS (UNSKILLED)											
SERVICE WORKERS											
TOTAL											

A. PART-TIME PAID EMPLOYEE DATA		MALE					FEMALE				
JOB CATEGORIES	TOTAL	WHITE (NOT HISPANIC)	BLACK (NOT HISPANIC)	HISPANIC	ASIAN OR PACIFIC ISLANDER	AMERICAN INDIAN, ALASKAN NATIVE	WHITE (NOT HISPANIC)	BLACK (NOT HISPANIC)	HISPANIC	ASIAN OR PACIFIC ISLANDER	AMERICAN INDIAN, ALASKAN NATIVE
	(a-j)	(a)	(b)	(c)	(d)	(e)	(f)	(g)	(h)	(i)	(j)
OFFICIALS & MANAGERS											
PROFESSIONALS											
TECHNICIANS											
SALES WORKERS											
OFFICE & CLERICAL											
CRAFT WORKERS (SKILLED)											
OPERATIVES (SEMI-SKILLED)											
LABORERS (UNSKILLED)											
SERVICE WORKERS											
TOTAL											

FCC 395-B (Page 2)
February 1997

Figure 3.3 *Excerpt from Broadcast Equal Employment Opportunity Program Report (FCC 396).*

The purpose of this document is to remind broadcast station licensees of their equal employment opportunity responsibilities and to provide the licensee, the FCC and the public with information about whether the station is meeting these requirements.

GENERAL POLICY

A broadcast station must provide equal employment opportunity to all qualified individuals without regard to their race, color, religion, national origin or sex in all personnel actions including recruitment, evaluation, selection, promotion, compensation, training and termination.

A broadcast station must also encourage applications from qualified minorities and women for hiring and promotion to all types of jobs at the station.

I. RESPONSIBILITY FOR IMPLEMENTATION

A broadcast station must asign a particular official overall responsibility for equal employment opportunity at the station. That official's name and title are:

NAME _____   TITLE _____

It is also the responsibility of all persons at a broadcast station making employment decisions with respect to recruitment, evaluation, selection, promotion, compensation, training and termination of employees to ensure that no person is discriminated against in employment because of race, color, religion, national origin or sex.

II. POLICY DISSEMINATION

A broadcast station must make effective efforts to make management, staff, and prospective employees aware that it offers equal employment opportunity. The Commission considers the efforts listed below to be generally effective. Indicate each practice that your station follows. You also may list any other efforts that you have undertaken.

☐   Notices are posted informing applicants and employees that the station is an Equal Opportunity Employer and that they have the right to notify an appropriate local, State, or Federal agency if they believe they have been the victims of discrimination.

☐   Our station's employment application form contains a notice informing prospective employees that discrimination because of race, color, religion, national origin or sex is prohibited and that they may notify the appropriate local, State, or Federal agency if they believe they have been the victims of discrimination.

☐   We seek the cooperation of the unions represented at the station to help implement our EEO program and all union contracts contain a nondiscrimination clause.

☐   Other (specify)

III. RECRUITMENT

A broadcast station must make efforts to attract qualified minority and women applicants for all types of jobs at the station whenever vacancies occur.

Indicate each practice that your station follows and, where appropriate, list sources and numbers of referrals.

☐   When we place employment advertisements with media some of such advertisements are placed with media which have significant circulation or viewership, or are of particular interest to minorities and women in the recruitment area. Examples of media utilized during the past 12 months and the number of minority and/or women referrals are:

	Number of Referrals	
	Minority	Women
_____	_____	_____
_____	_____	_____

FCC 396 (Page 3)
November 1990

Figure 3.3   *Continued*

☐ Recruit prospective employees from educational institutions, including area schools and colleges with minority and women enrollments. Educational institutions contacted for recruitment purposes during the past 12 months and the number of minority and/or women referrals are:

Educational Institution	Number of Referrals	
	Minority	Women
_____	_____	_____
_____	_____	_____

☐ Contact a variety of minority and women's organizations to encourage the referral of qualified minority and women applicants whenever job vacancies occur. Examples of such organizations contacted during the past 12 months are:

Organization	Number of Referrals	
	Minority	Women
_____	_____	_____
_____	_____	_____
_____	_____	_____
_____	_____	_____

☐ We encourage present employees to refer qualified minority and women candidates for job openings. The number of minority and/or women referrals are:

Minority	Women
_____	_____

☐ Other (specify) and the number of minority and/or women referrals are:

Minority	Women
_____	_____

IV. JOB HIRES

A broadcast station must consider applicants for job openings on a nondiscriminatory basis. Further, to assure that qualified minorities and women are given due consideration for available positions, it must make efforts to encourage them to apply for job openings.

During the twelve-month period prior to filing this application beginning (Month-Day-Year) _____ and ending (Month-Day-Year), _____ we hired:

Total hires _____   Minorities _____   Women _____

During this period, for positions in the upper four job categories, we hired:

Total hires, upper _____   Minorities _____   Women _____
four categories

V. PROMOTIONS

A broadcast station must promote individuals on a nondiscriminatory basis. Further, to assure that qualified minorities and women are given due consideration for promotional opportunities, it must make efforts to encourage them to qualify and apply for advancement.

During the twelve-month period prior to filing this application beginning (Month-Day-Year) _____ and ending (Month-Day-Year) _____, we promoted:

Total promotions _____   Minorities _____   Women _____

During this period, in the upper four job categories, we promoted:

Total promotions, upper _____   Minorities _____   Women _____
four categories

VI. AVAILABLE LABOR FORCE

A broadcast station must evaluate its employment profile and job turnover against the availability of minorities and women in the relevant labor market. The FCC will use labor force data for the MSA in which your station is located, or county data if the station is not located in an MSA, to evaluate your station's equal employment efforts. If you use these data in your evaluation, you need not submit them to the FCC.

Figure 3.3 *Continued*

This section is optional.

As an alternative to MSA or county labor force data, you may use other data that more accurately reflect the percentages of women and minorities in the labor force available to your station. If such alternative data are used, that data must be submitted on the table below and an explanation attached as to why they are more appropriate.

Percentage in the Labor Force	Women	Blacks not of Hispanic Origin	Asian or Pacific Islanders	American Indians or Alaskan Natives	Hispanics

The above information is for: ☐ M.S.A.   ☐ City   ☐ County

☐ Other (specify)

VII. COMPLAINTS

You must provide here a brief description of any complaint which has been filed before any body having competent jurisdiction under Federal, State, territorial or local law, alleging unlawful discrimination in the employment practices of the station including the persons involved, the date of filing, the court or agency, the file number (if any), and the disposition or current status of the matter. Examples of such jurisdiction may include the Equal Employment Opportunity Commission, state and local equal opportunity commissions, or other appropriate agencies.

VIII. OTHER INFORMATION

You may also describe other information that you believe would allow the FCC to evaluate more completely your efforts in providing equal opportunity in employment at your station. Submission of such information is optional. Among the additional information you may choose to provide are:

Any training programs the station has undertaken that are designed to enable minorities and women to compete in the broadcast employment market including, but not necessarily limited to, on-the-job training and assistance to students, schools or colleges.

Any problems the station has experienced in assuring equal employment opportunity, or attracting qualified minority and women candidates for employment or promotion.

Any efforts the station has undertaken or will undertake to promote equal opportunity in its employment and to encourage applications from minorities and women.

Despite significant deregulation of the broadcast industry in recent years, equal employment opportunity has not been deregulated. Indeed, the FCC expanded its rules in 1993 to comply with the terms of the Cable Television Consumer Protection and Competition Act of 1992. The commission now conducts a review of the employment practices of television stations at the midpoint of their license period. Those stations whose employment profiles fall below the FCC's criteria receive a letter noting necessary improvements identified as a result of the review.

The commission may be reluctant to deny a station's license renewal application because of a deficient EEO program, but it can take other punitive actions. It may subject the station to hearings, for example, or grant a short-term renewal with a stipulation that the deficiencies be addressed within a specified period.

Managers can take steps to prevent such eventualities. At the least, they should

- demonstrate a serious attempt to comply with the rules
- establish and pursue on a continuing basis practices designed to ensure equal employment opportunity and the absence of discrimination in the recruitment, evaluation, selection, promotion, compensation, training, and termination of employees
- adhere strictly to the requirements aimed at recruiting, hiring, and promoting minorities and women, and employ as many of the activities suggested by the FCC as appropriate
- engage in a continuing assessment of the station's employment profile and evaluate regularly the effectiveness of recruitment efforts
- maintain thorough documentation of all personnel activities, especially steps taken to carry out the EEO program
- refrain from exaggeration, particularly in characterizing the role and responsibilities of minority and women employees

Sexual Harassment

One form of discrimination to which managers are paying more attention today is sex discrimination resulting from sexual harassment in the workplace. Nationwide attention was drawn to the problem in the 1990s in the wake of allegations against several high-profile public figures, including President Clinton, and a record sexual harassment lawsuit settlement.

The 1991 harassment charges leveled by Professor Anita Hill against Supreme Court nominee Clarence Thomas had a dramatic effect on the filing of complaints. In the year that followed, the Equal Employment Opportunity Commission announced a 53 percent increase in complaints, signifying an apparent greater willingness to report such incidents. Certainly, the problem was not new. In fact, the National Association of Working Women estimated *before* the Hill accusations that between 70 and 90 percent of women experience some form of sexual harassment during their careers.

Men, too, are victims. However, it was women — more than 300 of them — who brought a successful suit against Mitsubishi claiming that they had been mistreated at its auto plant in Normal, Illinois. In 1998, the company agreed to pay $34 million to settle the case, triple the previous record amount. The magnitude of the settlement provided strong evidence that sexual harassment is a serious issue.

Pressure on managers to treat the issue seriously was reinforced by four Supreme Court decisions during the decade. In 1993, the court agreed unanimously that employers can be forced to pay monetary damages even when employees suffer no psychological harm. In 1998, in another unanimous ruling, it determined for the first time that unlawful sexual harassment in the workplace extends to incidents involving employees of the same sex.

Later in the year, in two 7–2 decisions, justices held that an employee who resists a superior's advances need not have suffered a tangible job detriment in order to pursue a lawsuit against an employer. But the court said such a suit cannot succeed if the employer has an anti-harassment policy with an effective complaint procedure in place and the employee unreasonably fails to use it.

In the two latter decisions, the court established that

- employers are responsible for harassment engaged in by their supervisory employees.

- when the harassment results in "a tangible employment action, such as discharge, demotion, or undesirable reassignment," the employer's liability is absolute.

- when there has been no tangible action, an employer can defend itself if it can prove two things: first, that it has taken "reasonable care to prevent and correct promptly any sexually harassing behavior," such as by adopting an effective policy with a complaint procedure; and second, that the employee "unreasonably failed to take advantage of any preventive or corrective opportunities" provided.

Harassment may take many forms. Under guidelines issued by the Equal Employment Opportunity Commission, unwelcome sexual advances, requests for sexual favors, and other verbal or physical conduct of a sexual nature constitute sexual harassment when (1) submission to such conduct is made either explicitly or implicitly a term or condition of an individual's employment; (2) submission to or rejection of such conduct by an individual is used as the basis for employment decisions affecting such individual; or (3) such conduct has the purpose or effect of unreasonably interfering with an individual's work performance or creating an intimidating, hostile, or offensive working environment.[12]

The licensee is held responsible for acts of sexual harassment committed by its "agents" and supervisory employees, even if it has forbidden them. If the conduct takes place between fellow employees, again, the licensee is responsible when it knew, or should have known, of the conduct, unless it can show that it took immediate and appropriate corrective action. [13]

To guard against the employee absenteeism and turnover that often accompany sexual harassment, the adverse impact on productivity and morale, and the filing of charges and lawsuits, managers should take the following actions:

1. Develop a written policy that defines sexual harassment and states explicitly that it is a violation of law.

2. Make sure that all employees are aware of the policy and understand it.

3. Train employees, especially supervisory personnel, to recognize harassment so that they may take action if they suspect it and, thus, prevent potentially more serious consequences if the behavior goes unchecked.

4. Establish a procedure that encourages victims to come forward and assures them that their complaints will be handled promptly and professionally.

5. Investigate all complaints immediately and thoroughly and advise the parties of the outcome, even if the allegations are not substantiated.

6. Document all complaints and their disposition. Complete records will be useful if legal action is initiated.

Computer Use

Productivity loss and the potential for sexual harassment and other lawsuits also may result from unrestricted employee use of station computers.

To guard against such eventualities, some companies have installed software tools to monitor individual computer activity. The expectation is that staff members will be wary of spending large amounts of time on personal E-mail or Web surfing if they know that checks may be made on how they spend their "working" hours.

Of no less concern to managers is the fear that employee-originated E-mail or online chat room messages or the downloading of some Internet content may expose the station to an array of lawsuits. In addition to sexual harassment, the risks include defamation, discrimination, the dissemination of trade secrets, and copyright and trademark infringement.

Stations that reject monitoring because of its "big brother" aura may opt for filtering software to limit access to the Internet. However, that will not necessarily remove the possibility of inappropriate E-mail or chat room activity and legal liability.

Managers are advised to develop and enforce an "Acceptable Use Policy" (AUP) for computers. The following are among the provisions that should be considered for inclusion:

- Computers, software, and Internet and E-mail accounts are the property of the company and should be used for business purposes only.

- Internet and E-mail accounts cannot be used for an employee's personal interests.

- Downloading copyrighted software is prohibited.

- Accessing or sending sexually explicit material is forbidden.

- Participation in any online chat room or discussion group must be approved in advance and must not include statements about the company or its competitors.

- E-mail cannot be used to communicate trade secrets or other confidential information without prior written permission.

- Encryption is required for sensitive E-mail messages and accompanying files.

- Sending offensive or improper messages, such as those involving racial or sexual slurs or jokes, is prohibited.

- Employee access to a coworker's E-mail files must be authorized in advance.
- E-mail messages and Internet activity will be monitored from time to time by the employer.
- Violation of the policy will result in disciplinary action, up to and including dismissal.

In time, other problems may arise and require modifications or additions to the AUP.

To ensure that all staff members are familiar with the policy, a copy should be placed in the employee handbook. However, given the potential gravity of abuse of the company's computers, it may be advisable to conduct a training session on appropriate use and to require employees to sign an acknowledgment that they have received and understand the policy.

WHAT'S AHEAD?

Many challenges confront staff members who are responsible for human resource management. Among the most important are those posed by an increasingly diverse work force, changing employee values, the implications of possible downsizing, and the ever-present threat of incidents of sexual harassment.

Work Force Diversity

Today's work force is the most diverse in American history. The first wave of baby boomers, most of them white and male, is retiring but is not being replaced by employees of like color and gender. In fact, white males comprise a much smaller percentage of new hires than in earlier years.

Women now constitute the majority of new job entrants. Some are recent school or college graduates. Other are older and are reentering the job market after an absence of some years to raise children.

Many new employees are members of minority groups, chiefly African American and Hispanic, and, in some parts of the country, Asian.

Managing diversity will not be easy for those who are unaccustomed to its challenges. Nonetheless, managers must recognize and respond to this new reality in their recruiting, selection, orientation, and training activities.

If they are to succeed, managers must demonstrate an understanding of, and sensitivity to, the varied backgrounds, experiences, and ambitions of new staff and strive to ensure that other employees demonstrate similar traits.

Certainly, there is much work to be done. While total broadcast employment has shown a modest rise in recent years, the percentage of full-time minority employees has remained steady at about 20 percent. Similarly, the percentage of women has changed little and continues at about 41 percent. In the top-four job categories, the same picture emerges — little change.

Managers will also have to realize that women have particular responsibilities to family as well as job. That may require a greater degree of flexibility than has been customary in areas such as working hours and job sharing. However, it will be necessary if many new employees are to find an acceptable balance between the demands of work and home.

Employee Values

Accompanying the changes in the composition of the work force are differences between the values of new employees and of those they are replacing.

Dedication to work, striving for career advancement and economic security, and loyalty to employer are characteristics associated with members of the retiring and soon-to-retire baby boom generation. Many of today's new employees, "Generation Xers," bring to their jobs a new set of perceptions about society, life, and work, fashioned by their experiences as children of often-absent working parents.

A study of the values and aspirations of more than 4,000 "boomer babies" found a deterioration in their confidence in institutions, a realization that many of life's previous "guarantees" no longer hold true, and a belief that, given a chance, most businesses will take advantage of them. Forty percent of them do not expect pleasure from work and consider it just something to do for a living. For many Gen Xers, the study concluded, the relationship with work can be summed up in three words: "Just Pay Me."[14]

Motivating these employees and encouraging them to view themselves as part of a team striving for mutually beneficial goals will be difficult for managers. But they must seek to reconcile the values of new employees with the more traditional values of employers if both are to find satisfaction and success in their endeavors.

Downsizing

Changing employee values are not confined to those who are twenty-something and constitute Generation X. They are also evident among long-time employees who witnessed the termination of colleagues, relatives, and friends in the downsizing that characterized corporate America in the 1990s.

Broadcasting was not immune to the trend, as evidenced by the layoffs that resulted from in-market consolidation of radio stations. As competition for audiences and advertisers increases and pressures to improve the bottom line intensify, others may face a similar fate.

Managers must be equipped to deal with that possibility. They must understand that stress, frustration, and anger are not unreasonable reactions from those affected. Even workplace violence is a possibility. They must also understand that layoffs produce repercussions among employees who are spared.

To reduce the human suffering and to protect the station against adverse economic consequences, managers must provide relevant information promptly to those whose employment will be terminated. That would include details of the reasons for the company's decision, policies on severance pay and other benefits, and procedures for their distribution. An offer of assistance in locating another position would demonstrate a measure of caring in an apparently heartless situation. Similarly, they must relay to those who remain information on the effects of the dismissals on the range of their responsibilities and rewards.

Sexual Harassment

The confusion that characterized sexual harassment as a form of discrimination in the workplace has been largely swept away by the series of Supreme

Court decisions described earlier. Now it is obvious that the courts will take a stern view of transgressions and will place upon employers responsibility for ensuring that their supervisors and employees abide by the law.

Managers will have to recognize that the potential for harassment is always present and that passivity or ignorance will be worthless weapons in the event of litigation. They must continue to be vigilant and to take continuous efforts to educate all employees on the company's harassment policies and impress on them the serious consequences, both for victims and the station, of failure to comply with them.

SUMMARY

No asset is more important to a broadcast station than its human resources. In many large stations, human resource management is the responsibility of a human resources department, whose head reports directly to the general manager. However, in the majority of stations, personnel matters are the responsibility of several people, including the general manager and the heads of the various departments, including the business manager.

The basic functions of human resource management are staffing; orientation, training, and development; compensation; safety and health; and employee relations.

Staffing involves staff planning and the recruitment, selection, and dismissal of employees. Orientation seeks to introduce employees to their colleagues and the station, while training and development are attempts to develop employee talents and skills. Compensation includes financial rewards as well as approval, respect, and recognition. Safety and health involve the provision of a safe and healthy workplace. Employee relations are characterized by mutual understanding and respect between management and staff.

In many stations, the responsibilities and rewards of employment are described in an employee handbook. A union contract sets forth the relationship between management and trade union employees.

Broadcasters must adhere to laws dealing with the hiring and treatment of personnel. Among the most important federal laws are the Civil Rights Act of 1964, the Age Discrimination in Employment Act of 1967, the Equal Pay Act of 1963, The Pregnancy Discrimination Act of 1978, the Americans with Disabilities Act of 1990, and the Family and Medical Leave Act of 1993. In addition, they must comply with the Federal Communications Commission's equal employment opportunity rules and with rules governing sexual harassment in the workplace. Managers must also be attentive to the possibility that a variety of laws could be broken by unrestricted employee access to company computers.

Human resource managers confront challenges posed by unprecedented diversity of the work force, changing employee values, the increasing frequency of downsizing, and the constant threat of sexual harassment lawsuits.

CASE STUDY

A female receptionist complains to the station manager that a male reporter has been harassing her. According to the receptionist, the reporter has made crude references to certain parts of her body, has asked her if she ever has sexual fantasies, and has offered to take her out for a "long lunch."

He has also called her at home after hours and asked if he could come over to her apartment. And on the very morning she finally decided to report all of this to the station manager, the reporter walked up behind her and began rubbing her neck and back.

The station manager tells the receptionist to "lighten up a little." He explains to her that this particular reporter is very flirtatious, that he means nothing by what he says, and that if she'll simply tell him to "cool it," he'll eventually leave her alone.

Exercises

1. Did the station manager handle this appropriately? If not, what should have been done differently?

2. Can the station be held liable for sexual harassment in light of the reporter's conduct and the station manager's handling of the situation? Can the male reporter be held personally liable for this conduct? Can the station manager be held personally liable if the harassment continues?

3. What if the receptionist had failed to complain to anyone about the reporter's conduct. Would the station be off the hook with respect to a sexual harassment claim?

4. What if the reporter had only done one of the things mentioned above? Would this have amounted to sexual harassment? What if the reporter had only done two of the things mentioned above? How many incidents must happen before sexual harassment occurs?[15]

CASE STUDY

A news reporter is diagnosed with the HIV virus. He tells the news director of his diagnosis, explaining that he is taking medication and that the medication seems to be adequately dealing with the symptoms he had been experiencing.

Coworkers also learn of the reporter's condition. They tell the news director that they are nervous about working with the HIV-infected reporter and request that he be terminated or reassigned — or something.

People in the community also learn of the reporter's condition, and some of them call the station manager, expressing concern about dealing directly with the reporter. They ask that another reporter be assigned to cover events in which they are involved.

Exercises

1. Does the reporter have a disability under the Americans with Disabilities Act (ADA)? Does the reporter have to contract full-blown AIDS before he is protected by the ADA?

2. Can coworkers cause an HIV-infected employee to be terminated or reassigned? If coworkers threaten to resign, does this give the station more latitude?

3. Can the station avoid liability under the ADA if third parties (like community representatives) begin to complain about contact they are forced to have with a news reporter? What if advertisers threaten to pull their business if the station continues to employ an HIV-infected person as a reporter?

4. What if the reporter's condition worsens, he begins to lose weight, and his physical appearance takes a noticeable turn for the worse? Can the station remove the reporter at this point?

NOTES

1. James A. Brown and Ward L. Quaal, *Radio-Television-Cable Management*, p. 111.

2. R. Wayne Mondy, Robert E. Holmes, and Edwin B. Flippo, *Management: Concepts and Practices*, pp. 276–277, 280.

3. John B. Phillips, Jr., *Employment Law Desk Book*, pp. 239–240.

4. *Ibid.*, pp. 241–242.

5. *Personnel/Human Resources Forms Guideline for Broadcasters.*

6. *1997 Television Employee Compensation and Fringe Benefits Report.*

7. J. Leonard Reinsch and E. I. Ellis, *Radio Station Management*, p. 266. Reprinted by permission.

8. The act defines a "qualified" individual as a person who has the skill, experience, education, or other requirements to perform the essential functions of the position, with or without reasonable accommodation. Such accommodation is any modification or adjustment to a job or the work environment. It includes making existing facilities readily accessible to and usable by a person with a disability, restructuring a job, modifying work schedules, acquiring or modifying equipment, and providing qualified readers or interpreters. However, it does not require the employer to make an accommodation if it would impose an "undue hardship," that is, an "action requiring significant difficulty or expense" in light of the employer's size, resources, nature, and structure.

9. 47 *CFR* 73.2080.

10. *Ibid.*, (b).

11. *Ibid.*, (c).

12. 29 *CFR* 1604.11(a).

13. 29 *CFR* 1604.11(d).

14. "Understanding Generation X," *Knight-Ridder News*, Winter, 1996, p. 5.

15. This case study and the one that follows were prepared by John B. Phillips, Jr., of Miller and Martin, which has offices in Chattanooga and Nashville, TN and Atlanta, GA.

ADDITIONAL READINGS

Adler, Seymour. "Verifying a Job Candidate's Background: The State of Practice in a Vital Human Resource Activity," *Review of Business*, Winter, 1993, pp. 3–8.

Americans with Disabilities Act, The. Washington, DC: U.S. Equal Employment Opportunity Commission and U.S. Department of Justice Civil Rights Division, 1992.

Berg, Thomas R. "The Phenomenon of Employee Turnover: How Television Station General Managers and Department Heads Cope with Transition," *Broadcast Cable Financial Journal*, July-August, 1990, pp. 32–34, 36–38.

Dipboye, Robert L. *Selection Interviews: Process Perspectives.* Cincinnati, OH: South-Western, 1992.

Drucker, Peter F. *The Practice of Management.* New York: Harper & Row, 1954.

Equal Employment Opportunity Guidebook: How to Comply with the Requirements of the Federal Communications Commission. Washington, DC: National Association of Broadcasters, 1991.

Equal Employment Opportunity Trend Report. Washington, DC: Federal Communications Commission, published annually.

Guide to Disability Rights Laws, A. Washington, DC: U.S. Department of Justice Civil Rights Division, 1996.

Kochan, Thomas A. "Toward a Mutual Gains Paradigm for Labor-Management Relations," *Labor Law Journal*, August, 1993, pp. 454–464.

Kohl, John P., and Alan N. Miller. "U.S. Organizations' Response to AIDS in the Workplace: A Review and Suggestions for Managers," *Management Decision*, July, 1994, pp. 43–51.

Lacy, Stephen, Ardyth B. Sohn, and Jan LeBlanc Wicks. *Media Management: A Casebook Approach.* Hillsdale, NJ: Lawrence Erlbaum, 1993.

Liden, Robert C., Christopher L. Martin, and Charles K. Parsons. "Interviewer and Applicant Behavior in Employment Interviews," *Academy of Management Journal*, April, 1993, pp. 372–386.

Nelton, Sharon. "Sexual Harassment: Reducing the Risks," *Nation's Business*, March, 1995, pp. 24–26.

Ripley, David E. "How to Determine Future Workforce Needs," *Personnel Journal*, January, 1995, pp. 83–89.

Thacker, Rebecca A. "Innovative Steps to Take in Sexual Harassment Prevention," *Business Horizons*, January-February, 1994, pp. 29–32.

Vance, Kim, and Richard Lowe. "A Broadcaster's Guide to the Americans with Disabilities Act: Programming Your Station to Meet the Challenge," *Broadcast Cable Financial Journal*, September-October, 1991, pp. 20–22, 24, 26–28.

Wage and Hour Guide for Broadcasters, 2nd ed. Washington, DC: National Association of Broadcasters, 1991.

4 BROADCAST PROGRAMMING

This chapter treats the programming of radio and television stations and examines the

☐ role of the program department and the responsibilities of the program manager and other departmental staff

☐ types and sources of broadcast programs, and the strategies employed to air them with maximum effect

☐ major differences between programming a television station affiliated with one of the "Big Three" networks and programming an independent or a station affiliated with Fox or an emerging network

Commercial radio and television stations air thousands of hours of programs each year. Individual programs may be produced by the station itself or obtained from another source. They may be designed chiefly to entertain, inform, or educate. They may be sponsored or sustaining. They may attract audiences numbering a few hundred or many thousands.

Despite the differences among programs, the programming of all stations is determined by four influences:

The audience, which seeks out a station for its programs. Listeners or viewers may be exposed to other content, such as commercials and public service and promotional announcements, but their principal goal is to hear or view program content that satisfies their need at a particular time. Programs that fail to attract listeners or viewers, or fail to satisfy their needs, are imperiled. So are the financial fortunes of the station.

The broadcaster, who is responsible for operating the station profitably for its owners. The greater the audience, the greater the likelihood that a profit can be realized. Accordingly, the broadcaster selects and schedules programs to attract as many people as possible among the targeted audience.

The advertiser, whose principal interest in using a radio or television station is to bring a product or service to the attention of those most likely to use it. Programs that attract potential customers stand the best chance of attracting advertising dollars, especially if the number of people is large and the cost of delivering the commercial to them is competitive.

The regulator, or government and several of its agencies, notably the Federal Communications Commission. Its goal is to ensure that the station is operated in a way that serves the public interest. Since passage of the Radio Act of 1927, the regulator has taken actions aimed at compelling or encouraging broadcasters to engage in certain programming practices to satisfy that goal.

Much is said and written about broadcast programming. However, it would be unwise to identify any one influence for praise or condemnation. The programming we hear and see results from the interaction of all four forces. In this chapter, we will examine the audience and the broadcaster. The advertiser and the regulator will be treated later.

THE AUDIENCE

More than 98 percent of U.S. households have radio and television receivers. The programs they carry attract males and females of all ages and from all socioeconomic categories and ethnic groups.

The pervasiveness and appeal of radio are indicated by the following facts:

- Radio reaches more than 95 percent of persons aged 12 and over each week.
- Radio reaches 99 percent of teenagers (ages 12 to 17) weekly.
- Four out of five adults are reached by car radio each week.
- The average listener spends more than 22 hours per week listening to radio.[1]

The reach of television and the extent of its use are no less significant:

- 67 percent of U.S. households own two or more receivers.
- 63 percent of TV households receive 30 or more channels.
- Television is the main news source for 70 percent of the U.S. public.
- The average household views an estimated 7 hours and 12 minutes daily.[2]

The size and composition of the audience for the two media fluctuate. The weekday radio listenership peaks at 7:00 A.M. It holds fairly steady from 9:00 A.M. to 4:00 P.M., then begins to drop. On weekends, listenership is at its highest between 9:00 A.M. and 3:00 P.M.[3] Men listen more than women, with men aged 25 to 34 listening most. They are followed by men 35 to 44 and 45 to 49.[4]

The television audience grows throughout the day and reaches a peak between 9:00 and 9:30 P.M. People spend more time viewing during the winter than the summer. Sunday evening attracts the largest number of viewers, and Friday evening the smallest.[5] Women watch TV more than men, and older men and women more than younger adults. Teenagers and children aged 2 to 11 watch least.[6] Larger households and those with children view more than smaller households and those without children. There is more use of television in pay cable households than in those with basic cable or no cable at all. Differences among income classifications are not great, but households with an annual income of less than $30,000 view more than those with income exceeding that amount.[7]

THE PROGRAM DEPARTMENT

Of all the factors that determine the financial success of a radio or television station, none is more important than programming. It is programming that brings listeners or viewers to the station. If the number of listeners or viewers is large, and if they possess the characteristics sought by advertisers, the station will attract advertising dollars. Accordingly, the station's revenues and potential profits are influenced largely by its programming. Responsibility for programming is entrusted to a program department.

Functions

The major functions of the program department are

- the production or acquisition of content that will appeal to targeted audiences
- the scheduling of programs to attract the desired audience
- the production of public service and promotional announcements and of local commercials
- the production or acquisition of other programs to satisfy the public interest
- the generation of a profit for the station's owners

Organization

The program department is headed by a *program manager* or *program director* who reports directly to the general manager. In some stations, programming and production are combined in one department under an *operations manager*.

The number of people who report to the program manager, their titles, and their responsibilities vary. In addition, the titles and responsibilities of the program personnel in a radio station differ from those in a television station. We shall examine the two media separately.

Radio   The program department staff in a radio station with a music format generally includes the following:

Music Director   The music director is responsible for

- additions to and deletions from the station's playlist of music
- preparation of the playlist and supervision of its execution
- auditioning of new recordings
- consultation with the program manager on music rotation
- liaison with representatives of recording companies to obtain new releases
- contact with music stores on sales of compact discs and cassettes
- cataloguing and filing of compact discs (in large markets, this responsibility may be handled by a music librarian)
- in small markets, an air shift and some local production

Production Director   Among the chief responsibilities of the production director are

- production of local commercials
- production of other content, for example, public service and promotional announcements
- control of the station's sound quality

Announcers   Announcers frequently are called *disc jockeys* or *deejays*. Their major responsibility is an air shift, which includes

- introduction of recordings and programs
- reading of live commercials and promotional, public service, and station identification announcements
- delivery of time and weather checks and traffic reports
- operation of control room equipment

   In addition, announcers may

- produce commercials and other announcements
- serve as talent for commercials and other announcements
- double as music director or production director

In many stations, *continuity* or *creative services* and *traffic staff* report to the sales manager. In others, their activities are supervised jointly by the program manager and the head of the sales department. Continuity writers often are responsible for a variety of copy, including commercials and public service and promotional announcements. They also check copy for compliance with the station's program and advertising standards. Traffic personnel place on the schedule details of all program and commercial content to be aired.

News programming may be entrusted to the program manager or to a separate department. In each case, personnel usually include the following:

News Director   The news director's responsibilities may cover

- determination and execution of policies for news, sports, and public affairs programs
- supervision of the newsroom staff
- decisions on what to cover and how to cover it
- reporting and newscasting
- selection of topics and guests for public affairs programs
- hosting interview programs

Reporters   Reporters' duties usually include the gathering, writing, and reporting of local news and, on occasion, the reading of the news.

Sports may be assigned to a member of the news staff or to a sports director. The person responsible reports sports news and may conduct interview programs with local coaches and handle play-by-play in broadcasts of local school or college sports events.

At news-format stations, the program manager is, in essence, a news director. The staff consists of editors, anchors, reporters, writers, and desk assistants.

The staff of news/talk stations comprises personnel responsible for news, such as anchors and reporters, and for talk, including producers, hosts, and telephone screeners.

Television   In many television stations, the program department includes production and two subdepartments, film or film and videotape, and art. Usually, the two subdepartments are headed by a director.

The principal personnel are as follows:

Production Manager   The production manager reports directly to the program manager and has many responsibilities, among them

- monitoring of all content aired, whatever its source
- scheduling of live and videotaped productions
- production of local programs, commercials, and public service and promotional announcements
- supervision of all performing talent and all production personnel

Production Staff   The staff includes directors, producers, film and videotape editors, camera operators, staging and lighting personnel, floor managers, and others involved in studio production.

Film or Film and Videotape Director   This staff member usually reports to the production manager and is responsible for

- receiving and shipping films and videotapes and maintaining appropriate records
- screening films and videotapes for quality and adherence to the station's program and advertising standards
- marking films for commercial and other breaks

Art Director   The art director also reports to the production manager and handles the

- design and construction of sets
- production of graphics for programs and commercials, promotional, public service, and station identification announcements, and for advertising and promotional materials for use in other visual media

Many stations assign public service activities to a member of the program department staff and, with those activities, the title of *director of public service* or *community affairs*. The job carries the responsibility for the writing and production of public service announcements and the production of public affairs programs.

Continuity and traffic are handled in much the same way as in radio.

News Staff   News may be assigned to the program department or, more typically, to a separate department. The staff includes the following:

- *News director* determines and executes policy and supervises the newsroom staff.
- *Assignment editors* assign reporters and camera crews to cover stories.
- *Producers* determine newscast content and its order, and the time devoted to each story and segment.
- *Anchors* present the news, weather, and sports content. Often they combine the roles of anchor and reporter, preparing the content and presenting it live on the set.
- *Reporters* gather, write, and report the news. Usually, they edit their own videotape and prepare the story in a package.
- *Photographers* shoot videotape and work with reporters in compiling stories. In many stations, they serve as their own sound recordists.

THE PROGRAM MANAGER

Responsibilities

Program managers handle a wide variety of tasks. Those in small and medium markets are involved in a broader range of activities than their counterparts in large markets. Obviously, there are differences between programming a radio station and a television station. In addition, in television the amount of time spent on programming responsibilities is influenced greatly by the station's status as a network affiliate or independent. However, all program managers engage in four basic tasks: the *planning, acquisition, execution,* and *control* of programs.

Program Planning   Program planning involves the development of short-, medium-, and long-range plans to permit the station to attain its programming and financial objectives.

As we shall see later in the chapter, the principal focus in radio is on the selection of a format and other program content to attract and satisfy the needs of particular demographics. Planning also includes the hiring of announcers whose personality and style are compatible with the station's format.

In television, planning is directed toward the selection and scheduling of programs to appeal to the largest number of people among the available audience. Affiliated stations also must consider which network programs they will broadcast and which they will reject or delay.

Since programming is the essential ingredient in attracting audiences, and since some audiences are sought more than others by advertisers, planning usually is done by the program manager in consultation with the head of the sales department and the general manager.

Program Acquisition   The program manager implements program plans by having programs produced by the station itself or by obtaining them from other sources. The major sources of radio and television programs are described later in the chapter. Again, the head of the sales department and the general manager are involved.

Program Execution   Execution involves the airing of programs in accordance with the plans. The strategies of both radio and television program execution are described later.

The program manager coordinates the scheduling of content with traffic personnel, and its promotion with the promotion and marketing director. If news is handled by a separate department, coordination is necessary on coverage of special events and breaking stories.

Program Control   The program manager often is called the "protector" of the station's license because of the responsibility for ensuring that the station's programming complies with the terms of its license.

As protector, the program manager

- develops the station's program standards
- supervises all program content for adherence to the station's standards, the FCC's Rules and Regulations, and other applicable regulations and laws
- maintains records of programs broadcast

The program manager also controls

- the direction and supervision of departmental staff and their activities
- the station's compliance with certain contracts, such as those with a network, program suppliers, and music licensing organizations
- program costs, to ensure that they do not exceed budgeted amounts

Qualities

The program manager should be *knowledgeable* and should possess administrative and professional *skills* and certain *personal qualities*.

Knowledge   The program manager should have knowledge of

Station ownership and management: Their goals and the role of programming in achieving them.

The station and staff: Programming strengths and shortcomings, the relationship of the program department to other station departments, and the skills and limitations of departmental employees.

The market: Its size, demographic composition, economy, and the work and leisure patterns of the population as a whole and its various demographic groups; the community's problems and needs; for radio, the music and information tastes of the community and, for television, program preferences.

The competition: Current programming of competing stations, their successes and failures, and their program plans.

Program management: The duties of the program manager and how to discharge them. This includes knowledge of the sources and availability of program content; production process and costs; salability of programming and methods of projecting revenues and expenses; sources and uses of program and audience research; programming trends and developments in broadcast technology; laws and regulations pertaining to programming.

Content and audiences: Formats, programs, and other content; their demographic appeal; and the listening or viewing practices of the audience.

Skills   The program manager must possess a variety of administrative and professional skills, among them the ability to

- develop program plans through consideration of need, alternative strategies, and budget
- evaluate ideas for local programming and coordinate the activities of departmental staff in program production
- analyze and interpret ratings and other audience research, and assess the potential for the success of locally produced programs and those available from other sources

- select and schedule content to maximize availability and appeal to targeted demographics
- negotiate contracts with program suppliers, freelance talent, music licensing organizations, and others

Personal Qualities Audiences and station staff have strong feelings about the programming of radio and television stations and are not hesitant to express them. Accordingly, the program manager must be

- *patient* in listening to various, often contradictory, viewpoints offered by telephone, letter, or E-mail from listeners or viewers and community groups, and in meetings with colleagues;

- *understanding* of the needs and interests of audience members and of the motivations of fellow employees;

- *flexible* in adapting to changing public tastes and programming and technological trends;

- *creative* in developing and executing program and promotion ideas; and

- *ethical* in dealings with others in and outside the station and in programming practices.

Influences

The program manager's decisions and actions are influenced by many factors. A model developed by The Arbitron Company (Figure 4.1) identifies twenty-one factors that comprise the decision-making environment in a radio station

Figure 4.1 *Music-format decision-making environment. (Source: The Arbitron Company. Reprinted with permission.)*

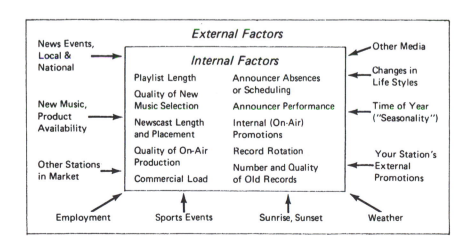

with a music format. Obviously, the station can control all the internal factors listed, such as the performance of announcers, the quality of on-air production, and the music rotation. However, only one of the external factors — external station promotions — is within the station's control. The station has no control over such influences as the availability of new music in its format, the activities of competing stations or other media, and changing lifestyles that may affect audience habits and tastes.

J. David Lewis used responses from 301 stations in the United States to determine influences in television station programming. He developed eight categories, in no particular order of priority:

- *direct feedback* from the audience, including letters, telephone calls, and conversations
- *regulatory*, or rules and standards of practice, such as commitments to the FCC, its rules and regulations, and the station's own policy statement
- *inferential feedback*, or ratings
- *conditional*, a mix of factors including comments of critics and opinions of friends outside the station
- *production staff*, the opinions of station personnel with production responsibilities
- *personal* or *subjective judgment*, including instinct, common sense, and knowledge of the community
- *financial*, or factors related to the station's income and expenditures, such as sales potential, sales manager's opinion, and cost
- *tactical*, that is, methods of program planning, the arrangement of the schedule and viewing trends[8]

RADIO STATION PROGRAMMING

The programming of most radio stations is dominated by one principal content element or sound, known as a *format*. It is designed to appeal to a particular subgroup of the population, usually identified by age, socioeconomic characteristics, or ethnicity.

In reality, few listeners probably know or care what name is used to describe the format of their favorite station. However, the selection of a name is important to management and the sales staff in projecting the station's image and in positioning the station for advertisers.

Formats

There are dozens of formats, but all can be placed in one of the following categories: *music, information,* and *specialty*.

Music   The music format is the most common among commercial radio stations. Describing the format of a particular station in one or two words has become increasingly difficult with the fragmentation of formats and the appeal of some artists in more than one format. In addition, stations use different names to characterize similar sounds.

The major music formats used by radio stations are

Adult Contemporary (AC)   The basic format consists of well-known rock hits and pop standards appealing to persons 25 to 44. However, there has been significant splintering of the format. *Soft adult contemporary*, also called *lite adult contemporary*, targets those aged 32 to 50 and takes two forms. One is oldies-based and relaxing, with songs from the 1960s, 1970s, and 1980s, as well as current hits. The other places more emphasis on the 1980s, but strives for a similarly relaxing atmosphere. *New adult contemporary* is a mix of light jazz and soft rock directed primarily toward persons 25 to 44. *Rock adult contemporary*, also known as *soft rock* and *adult rock and roll*, is a hybrid of adult contemporary and album-oriented rock. It focuses on top hits of the late 1960s and most of the 1970s and has a core audience of 35- to 44-year-olds. *Hot adult contemporary* has many of the features of contemporary hit radio but without the teenage edge.

Album-Oriented Rock (AOR)   Rooted in the protest movements of the 1960s and early 1970s, this heavily male-appeal format still is largely based on album cuts of music that is almost three decades old, combined with current product by some of the original artists. To attract younger listeners, many stations have added heavy metal sounds, but they have not gone over well with the core audience of 25- to 44-year-olds. Some stations try to target both ends of the age spectrum through dayparting, airing classic cuts and new product at times when the respective audiences are most likely to be listening.

Beautiful Music   Also known as *easy listening*, the format has evolved from an unobtrusive background sound with a commitment to a virtually unlimited playlist of instrumentals, to a combination of vocals and instrumentals, a limited playlist, and greater announcer prominence. The aim is to appeal to younger demographics without turning off the core audience, mostly adults over the age of 45. The format performs well only in a few large markets and in resort and vacation areas.

Classic Rock   This format comprises popular rock music of the 1970s and 1980s and has principal appeal to persons aged 25 to 44. Some fragmentation of the format has taken place with the emergence of *mellow adult rock*, which is geared toward males.

Classical   The classical format consists chiefly of recorded classical music and live performances of symphonies, opera, and chamber music. Its audience is among older and better-educated listeners in the higher socioeconomic categories. Many stations program short music selections during the day and concerts in the evening.

Contemporary Hit Radio (CHR)   The name was coined in the 1980s to describe what used to be known as the *top-40* or *top-hits* format. In the 1990s, the format experienced a significant drop in audience as many of its core 18- to 24-year-old listeners found other outlets for their musical tastes, including music videos. Not surprisingly, the number of stations using the format has decreased.

Basically, the format is characterized by a tightly controlled playlist of top-selling rock singles, selected new recordings that are on their way up, and occasional oldies. Strong announcer personality and heavy promotion also are common.

The format continues to witness fragmentation. *Modern rock* targets persons 25 to 34 with 1990s rock. Dance provides a niche for some stations, which bill themselves as *CHR/dance*. *Adult CHR* aims for 25- to 44-year-olds with top-40 hits of 1970 to 1985. Other stations attempt to attract blacks and reclaim young white listeners from urban stations through an emphasis on crossover artists in a format known as *churban*.

Country   The country format is the most popular of all music formats and has broad appeal to men and women aged 25 to 65+ in all socioeconomic categories. Some stations specialize in *traditional country*, others in *contemporary country* or *country-rock*, with heavy use of recordings that appeal both to country and rock audiences. In markets where only one station has adopted the format, the music usually includes both traditional and contemporary.

Jazz   This format has limited appeal, mostly to persons in the higher socioeconomic categories. The music includes both traditional and modern.

Middle-of-the-Road (MOR)   As the name indicates, this format focuses on the mainstream and avoids extremes. Traditional MOR includes a wide variety of music and information content. Typically, the music combines vocal and instrumental versions of contemporary, nonrock popular music and standard hits. There is heavy emphasis on news, sports, weather, and traffic, especially in morning and afternoon drive times. Many stations cover sports events, and some broadcast talk and interviews. The format appeals mostly to adults of age 35+ and makes extensive use of the announcer.

Nostalgia   Drawing most of its audience from persons 50+, this format focuses on popular tunes from the 1930s, 1940s, and 1950s.

Oldies   This format is based on top-40 hits of the 1960s and 1970s, with a core audience of persons aged 35 to 54. Some stations use a variation to appeal to 25- to 44-year-olds with hits of the late 1960s through the early 1980s. They label the format *'70s oldies*.

Urban Contemporary   With strong appeal to persons aged 12 to 34, this format specializes in contemporary rhythm and blues music. A slightly older demographic, persons aged 25 to 44, forms the core audience of the *urban AC* format, also known as *R&B/Adult*.

While music is the dominant program element in music-format stations, a variety of other program content is aired. The kind, amount, and frequency of such content is determined by a number of factors, such as format, the composition of the audience, and the size and location of the community. Examples of nonmusic content include

Community bulletin board: Information on community events

Editorials: The opinions of the station's ownership on local or national issues and events

Features: Stories on a wide range of topics of interest to the station's listeners

Market reports: Both agricultural and business reports

News: Local, regional, national, and international news

Public affairs: Generally interview programs on local or national issues and events

Public service announcements: Announcements for government and non-profit organizations

Religion: Services of various religious denominations or discussions on religion

Sports: Scores, reports, and play-by-play

Traffic reports: Local traffic conditions, especially in large communities and most frequently in drive times

Weather reports: Local and regional conditions and forecasts, but more extensive in times of weather emergencies

Information   There are two basic information formats, *all news* and *all talk*. A third consists of a combination of the two, and is called *news/talk*.

All News   The all-news format consists of news (local, regional, national, and international), information and service features, analysis, commentary, and editorials. It appeals mostly to adults 35+, especially better-educated males.

Stations assume that the audience will tune in only for short periods of time to catch up on the latest developments. Accordingly, they program the format in cycles of 20 or 30 minutes, with frequent repetition of the top stories. This characteristic often is used in promotion, with slogans such as "Give us 20 minutes and we'll give you the world."

The format requires a large staff of anchors, writers, reporters, editors, desk assistants, and stringers, as well as mobile units, cellular telephones, and numerous wire services. As a result, it is expensive and tends to be successful financially only in large markets.

All Talk   Interviews and audience call-ins form the basis of the all-talk format. They are combined with syndicated programs and features, news, weather, sports, and public affairs.

The subject matter of the interviews and call-ins varies greatly. Interview guests may generate discussion of their personal or professional lives. A call-in may focus on a timely or controversial topic selected by the program host. Many stations have hosts with expertise as psychologists, marriage counselors, and sex therapists, and callers use the program to expound on their personal problems.

Adults aged 35 to 65+ are the most consistent listeners. Most often, they are persons in search of companionship or a forum for their views.[9]

Each hour or daypart is programmed to appeal to key available demographics. Success is tied closely to the skills of the host, who must be knowledgeable on a wide range of topics, easy in conversation, and perceptive. Good judgment and the ability to maintain control of the conversation are other desirable attributes.

The format also requires producers who have a keen awareness of local and national issues, and the ability to schedule guests who are informed, eloquent, and provocative. Screeners are used to rank incoming calls for relevance and to screen out crank calls.

News/Talk   This combination of the news and talk formats is the country's most-listened-to format and takes different forms. Typically, it consists of news in morning and afternoon drive times, with talk during the remainder of the broadcast day. Some stations air play-by-play sports on evenings and weekends. The format's chief demographic appeal is to persons aged 35 to 65+.

Specialty   There are many specialty formats. However, the following are the most common:

Ethnic   Ethnic formats are targeted toward ethnic groups or people united by a language other than English. Blacks constitute a major ethnic group in many large markets and in towns of various sizes in the South. The programming of Black stations consists of beat and disco music featuring Black artists, and information of interest to the Black community. Usually, announcers are Black.

Spanish-language stations program music and information for Cuban Americans, Mexican Americans, and Puerto Ricans. In addition, many stations broadcast a variety of content in one or more foreign languages, including French, Polish, Japanese, and Greek.

Religion   This format is characterized by hymns and other religious music, sermons, religious services, talks, interviews, and discussions. The particular program makeup is influenced heavily by the type of licensee. Some stations are licensed to churches and religious organizations that are more interested in spreading their message than in the size or composition of the audience. However, ratings and demographics are of major concern to a second type of licensee, the conventional private entrepreneur who sells blocks of time to churches and religious organizations and spots to advertisers.

Variety   The variety format exists chiefly in one-station markets or where other formats do not meet the music or information needs of several desirable demographics. In a one-station market, for example, the format may include music for all age groups 12 to 54, news, weather, sports, and public affairs. Features would be selected for their appeal to the makeup of the community.

The variety format is programmed to satisfy the available audience. During the morning hours, music may be suited to adults at home. In the afternoon and evening, the sound may become more contemporary for teenagers and young adults.

Program Sources

Radio stations use three major sources of programs: *local*, *syndicated*, and *network*.

Local   Local programming is the principal source for most stations. For stations with a music format, it includes both music and information content.

Recording companies are anxious to have their product played on radio stations, since airplay is an important determinant of sales. Accordingly, they provide most stations with free, promotional copies. To ensure good service, the station must nurture close relationships with the companies. That can be done by maintaining regular contact, sending them copies of the playlist, and keeping them informed of success in reaching those demographics to which the recordings appeal.

Some stations obtain recordings from local stores under a trade-out arrangement. Stations in many small markets do not receive promotional copies and subscribe to a recording service for current releases.

Examples of locally produced information content on a music-format station include news, sports, and public affairs. Stations with an information format rely heavily on local production for news, talk, features, sports, and public affairs.

Radio stations also engage in remote broadcasts from retail stores and malls. They can be a useful promotional tool. Indeed, many stations have bought fiberglass or inflatable studios in the shape of giant radio receivers to increase their visibility on such occasions. However, remotes must be selected with care, since they may interrupt the regular flow of programming. They must also be planned in close cooperation with the sales department.

Syndicated   Syndicators provide stations with *programs* and with complete music *formats*.

Programs   Syndicated offerings range from 60- or 90-second features on health, finance, politics, and assorted other subjects, to programs of several hours' duration.

Long-form programming featuring nationally known talk personalities like Rush Limbaugh and Dr. Laura Schlessinger offers stations quality and cost-efficient content. Such is the appeal of syndicated product that it has even taken over the traditionally locally produced morning drive period on many stations and replaced station hosts with the likes of Don Imus and Howard Stern. Regional morning team programs are also available, especially in the South.

Barter is the primary method of syndicated program acquisition. Other programs are offered on a cash basis, the price determined by factors such as market size, the appeal of the program, and competition for it. Still other programs are available to the station without charge.

Formats   The entire music programming of some stations is provided by format syndicators.

Stations receive from the syndicator, typically via satellite, music in the desired format and then insert commercials, promotional, public service, and ID announcements, and other nonmusic content.

Syndicated formats are found mostly in fully automated stations. However, many formats may be used in semi-automated and live-operated stations.

Some formats are sold to stations and others are leased. Cost is determined mostly by the type of format and size of the market.

In addition to providing music, many format syndicators offer their services to stations as consultants on programming, promotion, and research.

Network The programming of most national networks is designed for specific demographics or formats. The staples are music, news, and talk. Other programs vary according to the interests of the targeted audiences.

Many stations also receive news and other informational programming from regional or state networks. Ad-hoc networks are organized in many parts of the country for the coverage of special events and sports.

Strategies

Selection of a format is the first and most important step in the development of a station's programming strategy. It is also the most difficult. In most markets, music formats with the greatest appeal to the most-sought demographics (persons aged 25 to 54) already have been taken. AM stations experience particular problems, as evidenced by their movement away from music formats and toward news, talk, or a combination. With the increasing fragmentation of formats, FM stations also face difficulties in trying to position themselves in a way that sets them apart from stations with similar formats. "Niche programming" has become the key in an era in which the programmer has to add to existing skills those of promotion, marketing, sales, and finance.

Among the factors that influence the format selection are

Market Size
Generally, the larger the market, the more specialized the format must be to attract an audience.

Community Composition and Location
Demographic characteristics and trends are important in predicting the appeal of particular formats since, as we have seen, music and other program preferences are linked closely to age, gender, income levels, and ethnicity. The makeup of the work force and the proportion of professional, industrial, and agricultural employees also provide useful pointers. The region of the country in which the station is located and the extent to which it serves chiefly urban, suburban, or rural residents, or some combination, give additional clues to content appeal.

Competition
Consideration of the degree to which competing stations have targeted all desirable demographics will indicate if there is a void in the marketplace. Persons deemed most desirable by advertisers are, in order, adults aged 25 to 54, 18 to 49, and 25 to 49. If there is a void, the station may select a format that meets the needs of the unserved or underserved audience. On the

other hand, it may be determined that one or more stations are vulnerable to direct format competition, and that audience may be taken from them by better format execution and promotion.

Potential Audience and Revenues

The size and demographic composition of the audience are key factors in generating advertising dollars. For that reason, projections of the potential audience and of advertising revenues are major criteria in the format-decision process.

Technical Considerations

The size of the potential audience is determined by the number of people who can receive the station's programs. Accordingly, the power at which a station is authorized to broadcast is important. The greater the power, the greater the coverage. Coverage also is influenced by the frequency of an AM station and the antenna height of an FM station. The lower the frequency and the higher the antenna, the greater the range of the station's signal.

Format selection may take into account another technical consideration. The superiority of FM over AM sound fidelity has attracted a majority of music listeners to FM stations and posed programming dilemmas for AM stations in many markets.

Finances

The financial cost of the format and of promoting the station to capture enough listeners to appeal to advertisers must be considered.

Stations that opt for a music format also must decide on other content elements to include in their programming.

Next, the station decides how to execute the programming to attract and retain the target audience. The decision must take into account the needs and expectations of the listeners.

People turn to a music-format station chiefly for entertainment or relaxation, to an all-news station for information, and to an all-talk station for a variety of reasons, including information, opinion, and companionship. They expect to hear a familiar sound, one with which they feel comfortable. The format, therefore, must be executed with consistency.

The most common tool to obtain consistency is the *format wheel* or *format clock*, which identifies the mix and sequence of program elements in a one-hour period. Figure 4.2 shows a format wheel for a contemporary hit station in morning drive time.

The particular composition of an audience, its needs, moods, and the activities in which it engages change during the day. Stations attempt to respond to those changes through *dayparting*. On weekdays, the dayparts are

Morning drive time (6:00 A.M. to 10:00 A.M.): Most listeners want to be brought up-to-date with news and with weather and traffic conditions.

Midday (10:00 A.M. to 3:00 P.M.): The majority of listeners are homemakers, and both music and information programming are tailored to their needs.

Figure 4.2 *Morning drive format wheel: contemporary hit radio station. Hot: chart position 1–10; A Current: 11–20; B Current: 21–30; C Current: 31–40.*

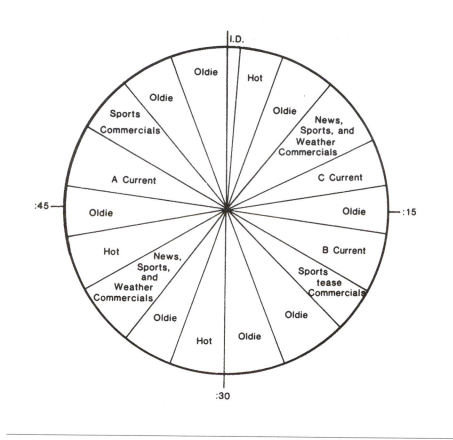

Afternoon drive time (3:00 P.M. to 7:00 P.M.): Teenagers return from school and adults drive home from work. For the most part, the former seek entertainment and the latter a mix of entertainment and information.

Evening (7:00 P.M. to midnight): The audience of most stations is composed chiefly of people desiring entertainment or relaxation.

Overnight (midnight to 6:00 A.M.): Shift workers, college students seeking entertainment, and persons seeking companionship constitute the bulk of the audience.

All-news stations broadcast their content in cycles, with a certain time elapsing before each element is repeated. Figure 4.3 shows a format wheel for such a station.

Audience size is computed by quarter hour, and so stations strive to attract the maximum possible audience in each quarter-hour period. However, audience members do not have to listen continuously for fifteen minutes to be counted. Audience measurement companies credit a station

Figure 4.3 *Format wheel: All-news station.*

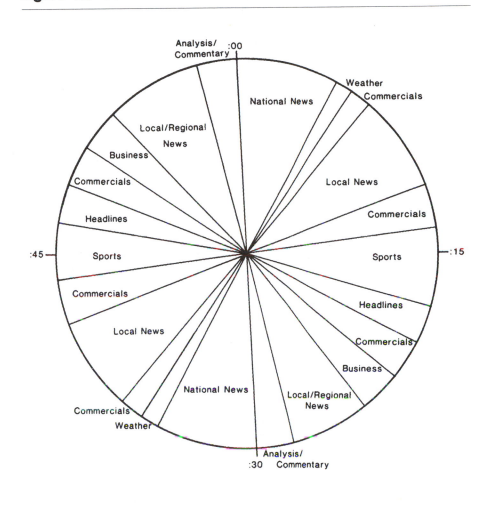

with a listener if a person is tuned in for five or more minutes in any quarter hour. One technique to retain listeners from one quarter hour to the next is to schedule a *music sweep* (i.e., uninterrupted music) over each quarter-hour mark. Nonmusic content, which often prompts dial-switching, is placed within the quarter hour.

A station's success in maintaining audience may be judged by the amount of time a person listens during a specific daypart. This is known as *time spent listening,* or *TSL.* It is calculated by multiplying the number of quarter hours in a daypart by the average quarter-hour audience and dividing the result by the cumulative audience. For example, a station has an average audience of 5,700 and a cumulative audience of 25,500 among persons aged 25 to 49 during morning drive Monday through Friday. The TSL is 80 (number of quarter hours) times 5,700 (average audience) divided by 25,500 (cumulative audience), or 17.9 quarter hours. To determine audience turnover, or the number of times an audience changes during a time period, the cumulative audience is divided by the average audience. In this example, it is 4.5.

Essentially the same music is available to all stations in a market with a particular format. An important strategic consideration, therefore, is the selection of recordings for the *playlist* and their *rotation*. The playlist is the listing of recordings played over the course of a period of time, usually a week. Rotation refers to the frequency with which each is played.

Stations rely on a variety of sources in deciding what to keep on the playlist and what to add and delete. The following are among those used most often:

Trade magazines, such as *Billboard* and *Radio & Records*. They publish lists of top recordings in different formats and draw attention to those that are increasing and decreasing in popularity.

Tip sheets or *newsletters*, including *The Monitor*, *Network 40*, *The Gavin Report*, and *Hitmaker*.

Sales of compact discs and tapes. Trade magazines and tip sheets reflect the popularity of recordings across the nation. To determine local appeal, stations check on sales with area music stores.

To increase their information base, many stations engage in continuing efforts to obtain listener feedback to the music being played or contemplated for addition to the playlist. The most common method is *call-out research*. The station plays over the telephone short excerpts (called "hooks") of music selections and asks respondents for their reactions. The results are tabulated and assist in tracking the popularity of recordings and making decisions on playlist content. Such research is relatively inexpensive, but only a limited number of hooks can be played before participants grow tired.

Another method is *auditorium testing*. About 100 or more people are invited to a large room or auditorium and asked to rate up to 300 or 400 hooks in the space of one or two hours. They are paid and, generally, are chosen from the age group targeted by the station. They may be regular listeners, those who favor a competing station, or a combination. Auditorium testing is more expensive than call-out research and usually is attempted only periodically. That prevents close monitoring of changing music preferences and regular fine tuning of the playlist.

These information sources provide useful insights into the relative appeal of recordings. However, they should not be used to determine the frequency or order of play, which reflect the particular mix the station wants. More and more stations are employing computers to help establish and maintain an appropriate rotation.

In an attempt to ensure that programming is tuned to the needs of the target audience, stations are paying increased attention to nonmusic research. Many are building *databases* to develop listener profiles. Income, lifestyle, product usage, and leisure activity are examples of information that is collected and stored. Images of the station, its programming, personalities, and other elements are obtained through *focus groups*, which bring together ten to twelve people for a controlled discussion led by a moderator. Often, the results provide ideas for more extensive research. *Market perceptual studies* are conducted by telephone interview or mail survey among targeted listeners to identify perceptions of a station's position in the market and its various characteristics. Telephone interviews also are used in *format searches*, attempts to ascertain if there is a need or place for various formats or elements within a format.

In some formats and on some stations, primary emphasis is given to the music or information content. The personality of the announcer is secondary. However, since the announcer is the link between the station and the audience, many stations encourage announcers to project their personality with the expectation that it will provide another competitive weapon. In either situation, announcers are important in the creation of a station's image and are chosen to reflect that image. If personality is emphasized, announcers are scheduled during those dayparts when their personality suits the mood of the audience.

Strategy considerations also may involve the possible use of automation. The station must decide whether its benefits outweigh its shortcomings and whether it may be used advantageously over the entire broadcast day or in certain dayparts. Automation offers the advantages of a consistent, professional sound, eliminates personnel problems, and may result in cost savings. However, it removes the element of personality and deprives the station of spontaneity and flexibility.

Programming must be promoted constantly to retain the existing audience and to attract new listeners. The role of promotion is discussed in Chapter 6, "Broadcast Promotion and Marketing." It should be noted here that stations seek to gain competitive advantage through on-air and off-air promotion of image, programming, and personalities. They hope that the result will be a clear public perception of what the station does and how it can satisfy their needs.

A final and most important strategic consideration is the station's commercial policy. Most listeners to music-format stations have limited tolerance for interruptions in music and may seek out another station when commercials air. Commercial policy usually sets forth the commercial load (i.e., the number of commercials allowed per hour) and the frequency of breaks for commercials and other nonmusic content. Commercial policy is discussed further in Chapter 5, "Broadcast Sales."

TELEVISION STATION PROGRAMMING

Programming a commercial television station differs markedly from programming a radio station. While the radio programmer identifies a specific audience and broadcasts to it throughout the day, the television programmer targets a general audience and attempts to respond to the preferences of those persons who are available to view.

A radio station competes directly for audience against the other radio stations in the market that seek to attract similar demographics. A television station is in competition against all other television stations in the market and, increasingly, against cable and direct broadcast satellite. Additional competition for the viewers' time comes from videocassette recorders.

Network programming occupies only a minor place in the schedule of most radio stations. It is a dominant force in television, providing a major part of the schedule for stations affiliated with ABC, CBS, NBC, and Pax TV. It plays a lesser, though still very important, role in the offerings of affiliates of Fox and of the two emerging networks, The WB and UPN.

Programming success in television rests heavily on the ability to produce or buy programs with audience appeal, air them at times when they can be seen by the audience to which they appeal, and build individual programs into a schedule that encourages viewers to tune to the station and remain with it from one program to another.

Program Sources

Television stations affiliated with a network rely on three principal sources of programs: the *network*, *program syndicators*, and *local production*. Independent stations (i.e., those not affiliated with a permanent network) use syndicated and local production and receive sports and specials from ad-hoc networks.

Network ABC, CBS, and NBC provide affiliates with the bulk of their programming. Weekday daytime hours consist of news magazines, soap operas, a game show, and network news. In prime time, entertainment, news magazines, and some sports are broadcast. Talk-variety, news interviews, and news fill the late night and overnight periods.

On weekends, the major networks schedule programs for children and teenagers on Saturday mornings, sports in the afternoon, and entertainment in prime time. Daytime on Sundays includes news-magazine and news-interview programs and sports, followed by prime-time entertainment.

The networks produce their news and sports broadcasts and a growing number of their prime-time entertainment programs. However, they continue to purchase a significant amount of entertainment from independent production companies based in California.

Pax TV, launched late in 1998, programs all but four hours between 6:00 A.M. and 1:00 A.M. weekdays. Daytime includes talk/variety, a game show, and off-network situation comedy and drama. Off-network drama characterizes prime time and late night. Saturdays and Sundays begin with a children's block, followed later in the day by more dramatic programs and movies.

Fox, The WB, and UPN supply fewer hours for their affiliates than the "Big Three" (ABC, CBS, and NBC) and Pax TV. Fox's programs comprise children's shows in daytime on weekdays and entertainment in prime time. On Saturdays, children's programs are aired in the morning and entertainment in prime time, followed by more entertainment. A morning news-interview program and prime-time entertainment make up the Sunday schedule, joined by afternoon NFL football during the season.

The WB airs two hours of children's programs every weekday afternoon and two hours of entertainment in prime time Monday through Thursday. Saturdays consist of four hours of morning programming for children.

Three hours of prime-time entertainment constitute the network's Sunday offerings.

UPN programs two hours of entertainment on weekdays in prime time. Children are the target on Saturday mornings with one half-hour program and on Sunday mornings with two hours. A noon movie completes the network's Sunday schedule.

Program Syndicators   Syndicated programs are used by network-affiliated stations to fill many of the periods during which the network does not provide programming. Independent stations rely heavily on such programs during all dayparts.

There are two major categories of syndicated programs:[10]

Off-network, which denotes that the programs have been broadcast on a network and now are available for purchase by stations and other outlets. They include a large number of situation comedy and dramatic programs that attracted large and loyal audiences during their network runs.

First-run, which describes programs produced for sale directly to stations. The kind of content available varies from year to year. In the late 1990s, among the most plentiful and popular offerings were talk, news-magazine, and reality-based court programs, and game shows.

Feature films and cartoons also are distributed by syndicators. Decisions on syndicated program acquisitions are based on program availability, cost, and audience appeal.

As noted later in the chapter, the station rep company is an important source of information on available programs. Many stations use additional sources, such as the annual *Television Programming Source Books*, published by BiB Channels. This three-volume series contains information on films and film packages, and lists short- and long-form TV film and tape series, with details of program length, number of episodes, story line, distributor, and distribution terms. Product is available to a station only if it has not already been obtained by another station in the market.

Even though stations often announce that they have bought a syndicated program, what they have bought, in fact, are the exclusive rights to broadcast a program over a specific period of time. Rights for off-network programs generally are granted for five or six years and permit six to eight broadcasts of each episode. For an established or peaking first-run product, they run from two to four years, while the term is one year for new programs and those in the upward part of the growth curve.

The rights are contained in a license agreement between the syndicator and the station. It details, among other items, the series title, license term, number of programs, license fee, method of delivery, and payment terms. The fee is based on a number of factors, including the size of the market, competition for the program from stations in the market, the age of the program, and the time period during which it will be broadcast. The negotiating skills of the person representing the station also may be influential. In the case of feature films, market size, competition, and the age of the films are taken into account, as well as the success they achieved during their showing in movie theaters or on a network.

The dramatic increase in the cost of syndicated product, combined with the emergence and growth of barter programming (discussed below), have led to an important change in the program manager's traditional role in syndicated program purchasing. Today, because of the increased emphasis on the bottom line, the programmer is likely to be only one of several key station personnel involved in purchasing decisions. Others include the general manager, sales manager, and business manager. In many stations, the general manager has primary responsibility, while the program manager merely administers decisions.

In determining what to buy and how much to pay, the station should give particular attention to the ratings potential and projected revenues of syndicated programs. Their appeal may be ascertained by studying their performance in other markets, particularly those with a similar population makeup. Nielsen's *Report on Syndicated Programs* provides detailed information on the size and demographic composition of the audiences for syndicated programs in all markets, in different dayparts, and against different program competition. Clues to the appeal of off-network programs may be gleaned from their performance in the market when they aired on a network.

Calculating revenue potential requires consideration of (1) spot inventory, or the number of 30-second spots available in each program; (2) the average selling price in the daypart in which the program will be broadcast; and (3) the selling level, that is, the percentage of spots likely to be sold. Multiplying the selling price by the number of spots available produces the *gross revenue*. The gross is reduced by 15 percent to allow for commissions paid by the station to account executives, reps, and advertising agencies, producing the *net*. That figure is reduced further by the projected selling level (most stations use 80 percent) to give what is known as the *net net*.

Assume that a network-affiliated station is contemplating the purchase of a half-hour, off-network series. Six commercial minutes are available and the average selling price in the daypart for a 30-second spot is $400. The calculation would be as follows:

Selling price	$400
30-second commercials	× 12
Gross	$4,800
Net revenue level (after commission)	× .85
Net	$4,080
Selling level	× .80
Net net	$3,264

The projected revenue of $3,264 for each episode applies only to the first year. Projections for subsequent years will take into account possible changes in the spot rate. For example, rates in the daypart may increase to keep pace with inflation. A decrease might result if the program were moved to a less costly daypart.

Having calculated the net net revenue potential of each episode over the life of the contract, the station must then consider how much it can afford to pay per episode. It was observed in Chapter 2, "Financial Management," that programming costs for a typical network-affiliated station account for 27.1 percent of revenues. Accordingly, a realistic price per episode would be about 27 percent of its revenue potential.

The actual price will be determined through negotiations between the syndicator and the station.[11] When the contract is signed, the station usually makes a down payment and pays the balance in installments. As noted in Chapter 2, costs are assigned according to an amortization schedule for accounting purposes. The station may select the *straight line* method, which means that an equal value is placed on each broadcast of each episode. Alternatively, it may opt for *accelerated amortization* or the *declining value* method, which assumes that the value of each episode decreases with each broadcast. Accordingly, the station assigns to each broadcast a declining percentage of total cost. A program with six runs may be expensed as follows: run 1 — 40 percent; 2 — 30 percent; 3 — 15 percent; 4 — 10 percent; 5 — 5 percent; 6 — 0 percent.

It is becoming increasingly difficult for stations to buy attractive syndicated programs for cash. Most first-run and some off-network programs in their first year of syndication are available only through *barter*.

In a barter transaction, the syndicator provides the program at no cost but, in return, retains for sale some of the commercial inventory. In a 30-minute program, for example, two minutes may be retained, leaving four minutes for sale by the station. A variation is the *barter-plus-cash* arrangement, whereby the station not only surrenders time to the syndicator but also pays a fee for the program.

At its inception, barter was viewed as a means whereby stations could control soaring program costs. Syndicators emphasized that the value of the commercial time surrendered would represent a much lower cost to the station than if the program were bought on a straight cash basis. Furthermore, the small amount of inventory retained by the syndicator probably would not hurt profits, since 10 to 15 percent of commercial time generally remains unsold.

Barter does permit stations to obtain competitive product without putting out large amounts of cash, and to exchange time that might not be used for lower overall program costs. However, it has become such a dominant force that stations that would be willing to pay cash do not have that option. In addition, program costs have continued to escalate and stations have been left with less inventory to recoup their programming investment. Furthermore, barter now places stations in direct competition with syndicators for the sale of time to national advertisers in the same program.

Local Production   The focus of local production is on local newscasts and public affairs programs, chiefly face-to-face interviews. Other local productions may include magazine, music video, exercise, sports, and children's programs, and occasional documentaries.

Programming Factors

The TV program manager weighs many factors in making program acquisition and scheduling decisions. Among the more important are these:

Strength or Weakness of Competing Stations

Since the size of the television audience is predictable in each daypart, a station attracts viewers at the expense of its competitors. Noting the strength or weakness of the competition, both among total viewers and particular demographics, the station can schedule appropriate programs. In a single time period, there are two basic options. One is to try to draw viewers from competing stations with a program of similar audience appeal. The second is to schedule a program with a different appeal to attract those whose interests are not being addressed.

Building Audience Flow

It is advantageous to a station to air programs that attract large audiences. It is much more advantageous if audiences can be inherited from preceding programs and retained for those that follow. In scheduling, consideration is given to both possibilities.

A challenge in scheduling programs to capitalize on this so-called *audience flow* has grown out of the spread in ownership of remote-control pads to 93 percent of TV households. Viewers use them to switch from channel to channel within and between programs to explore their options. This practice is known as *flipping.*[12]

Building Audience Habit

Series programs scheduled in the same time period each weekday can become part of the audience's daily television viewing routine. Encouraging such habit formation usually is an important goal.

Available Audience

The audience of a market, and the availability of different parts of the audience in various dayparts, are major determinants of program selection and scheduling. Figure 4.4 shows the dayparts on weekdays and the audience available in each.

Weekends present a different picture. In theory, all children and many adults are potential viewers. However, shopping, social, and sporting activities influence the number and kind of people who are free to watch television on Saturdays. The nature of the local economy is important, too. More adults usually are available in white-collar than in blue-collar communities, where Saturday work is not uncommon. On Sundays, religious pursuits may be added to shopping, social, and sporting activities as alternatives to television viewing.

Audience Interest

Audiences are attracted in large numbers to many entertainment programs. If audience interest in other kinds of content is high in a particular market, or if the station believes that interest can be stimulated, it may wish to produce or buy programs that respond to such interest.

Figure 4.4 *Television dayparts and available audience (all times are Eastern).*

Daypart	Available Audience
Early morning (6:00 A.M. to 9:00 A.M.)	Children, homemakers, adult men and women who work outside the home, retired persons. Schoolchildren and working adults are preparing to leave, and most have left by the end of the daypart.
Morning (9:00 A.M. to noon)	Mostly preschoolers, homemakers, the retired, and shift workers.
Afternoon (Noon to 4:00 P.M.)	Early in the daypart, working adults who eat lunch at home are added to the morning audience. They leave, and are replaced from about 2:00 P.M. by children returning from school.
Early Fringe (4:00 P.M. to 6:00 P.M.)	The return of most working adults begins and, in many small and medium markets, is completed.
Early Evening (6:00 P.M. to 7:00 P.M.)	In all but the largest markets, all segments of the audience are home.
Prime Access (7:00 P.M. to 8:00 P.M.)	All audience segments are available to view.
Network Prime Time (8:00 P.M. to 11:00 P.M.)	During the first hour or so, the same as that for prime access. A decrease begins at about 9:30 P.M., chiefly among children, those who have to get up early, and the retired.
Late Fringe (11:00 P.M. to 11:35 P.M.)	Mostly adults.
Late Night (11:35 P.M. to 2:05 A.M.)	Again, mostly adults, including shift workers.
Overnight (2:05 A.M. to 6:00 A.M.)	Shift workers comprise the largest part of the comparatively small available audience.

Advertiser Interest

To be successful, programs must attract advertisers as well as audiences. The principal targets of most local TV advertisers are adults aged 25 to 54. Selecting programs with low audience appeal, or with appeal chiefly to demographics in which advertisers are not interested, leads to financial problems.

Budget

The amount of money available for program production and purchases is an important determinant of what can be programmed. Costs of many popular off-network programs have been driven up significantly in recent years, making it difficult for a station to use large numbers of such programs as a stepping-stone to success.

Program Inventory

Many syndicated program and feature film contracts permit multiple broadcasts over a period of years. In addition to recently purchased product, such content still may be available for airing.

Local Production Capabilities

It has been noted that most stations produce few programs, except news and public affairs. However, a station with an adequate budget, equipment, and technical facilities, competent production personnel, and sources of appropriate talent may contemplate producing other kinds of programs, especially if audience and advertiser interest are strong.

Scheduling Strategies

Consideration of the above factors will suggest program scheduling strategies suited to the competitive situation in which the station finds itself. The following strategies are among those used most commonly:

Head-to-head: A program that appeals to an audience similar to that being sought by a competing station or stations. Early- and late-night newscasts usually are scheduled against each other on network-affiliated stations and provide an example of this strategy.

Counter: A program that appeals to a different audience from that targeted by the competition. A program with principal appeal to adults at the same time as a children's program on another station is an example of counter-programming.

Strip: Scheduling a program series at the same time each day, usually Monday through Friday. This practice, also known as *horizontal programming,* encourages habit formation by the audience. However, if the program does not attract a sizable audience, the strategy may backfire, since failure will be experienced every day. With syndicated series, the strategy is desirable only if there are enough episodes to schedule over several months, at least.

Checkerboard: Airing a different program series in the same time period daily. This strategy has several drawbacks. It is expensive, since the station may have to buy as many as five different series. It is difficult to promote. Finally, it does not permit the station to capitalize on the element of audience habit.

Block: Scheduling several programs with similar audience appeal back-to-back, usually for two hours or more. This strategy also is called *vertical programming* and seeks to encourage audience flow.

Feature films pose a special scheduling challenge. Film packages contain both good and not-so-good movies, and not all have similar audience appeal. Many stations try to surmount the problem by airing films under an umbrella series title and identifying an element for promotional emphasis. If the movie has won awards, for example, the award-winning elements lend themselves to such an approach.

Three decades ago, Philip F. von Ladau, vice president and general manager of Marketron, Inc., set forth ten basic programming principles. Despite changes in audience habits resulting from the massive growth in the number of viewing options and the impact of the remote-control pad, judicious application of the principles can still lead to successful scheduling. They are

1. *Attack where shares of audience are equally divided.* It's a lot easier to take a little audience from each of several stations than a lot of audience from a dominant program.

2. *Build both ways from a strong program.* Take advantage of early tune-in to a strong program creating "free" sampling of a good preceding show; late tune-outs to accomplish the same for the following. This falls under the principle that it's easier to sustain an audience than to build one.

3. *Sequence programs demographically.* Don't force unnecessary audience turnover.

4. *When a change in appeal is called for, accomplish it in easy stages.* When the available audience dictates a change, do so with a program type that will hold as large a share of the preceding audience as possible, rather than attempting to completely change the demographic appeal.

5. *Place "new" programs at time periods of greatest tune-in.* This amounts to free advertising through happenstance sampling. People turning on their sets generally leave them at the station last used; thus, at times of building (increasing) set usage, a significant number of people may inadvertently be exposed to your new show.

6. *Keep a "winning" program in its current position.* Changing competition must, of course, be taken into consideration. But when people are in the habit of finding a popular program in a particular time period, moving it risks an audience loss.

7. *Counter-program to present viewers with a reasonable alternative to the other fare.* It's generally better to offer something different than just another version of the types of programs already being aired by the competition.

8. *Program to those people who are available.* A lot of errors are made here by considering the age/sex makeup of all the audiences using TV. What is really available to most programs, particularly independent and/or individual-station-placed programs, is just the audience that remains after the dominant show has commanded its share.

9. *In buying, always consider how it would be to have the offered program opposite you.* It may be worth a small going-in monetary loss as opposed to the big one that might be created with the subject program opposite your existing properties.

10. *Don't place an expensive program in a time period where there is insufficient audience or revenue potential,* enough at least to break even in combination with its preceding and following properties.[13]

PROGRAMMING THE NETWORK AFFILIATE

Even though stations affiliated with the Fox, The WB, and UPN networks are "network affiliates," their networks' schedules are much more limited than those of the three major networks, ABC, CBS, and NBC. As a result, they operate like independent stations much of the time. For that reason, they will be considered with the independents later in the chapter. In contrast, Pax TV affiliates receive most of their programming from the network. The few hours that are left for the station to program are filled mostly with infomercials. Accordingly, their programming responsibilities are virtually nonexistent and will not be discussed here.

Affiliation with a major network offers many advantages. It has been noted that the network fills a significant part of an affiliate's program schedule, at no direct cost. Indeed, since the network compensates the station for carrying sponsored network programs, affiliation is an important source of station revenue.

Many network programs attract large audiences, thus increasing the value of the time the station sells in and around them. Skillful scheduling and promotion also permit the station to attract audiences to locally scheduled programs before, between, and after network offerings. Similar assistance in boosting audiences is afforded through the network's publicity and promotion, which are most extensive at the start of the fall season.

However, the affiliate programmer's job is not without challenge. By the late 1990s, the average household could select from close to fifty channels, almost double the number available a decade earlier. Cable, Fox and the emerging networks, independent stations, DBS, and VCRs offered stiff competition and had cut deeply into the affiliates' audiences.

Network-Affiliate Relations

The relationship between a network and an affiliated station is governed by an affiliation contract. Specific contracts differ from network to network and are undergoing some changes. Generally, however, they contain the following clauses:

1. The network agrees to provide, and deliver to the station, a variety of programs.

2. The station has the right of first refusal. In other words, the network must offer programs first to its affiliated station in the market.

3. The station may reject any network program it believes to be unsatisfactory, unsuitable, or contrary to the public interest. In such cases, the network may offer the program to another station or program transmission service in the market. In practice, affiliated stations clear (i.e., carry) most of their network's programs. When they refuse, it is generally because they consider the program too controversial or because they wish to broadcast a program of special local interest. Another reason for rejecting a network program is the station's belief that it can attract a larger audience with a different program.

4. The station may broadcast a network program on a delayed basis, but only with network approval. When the delayed broadcast occurs, the station must announce that the program was presented earlier on the network.

5. The station may not add or delete material from a network program without prior written authorization from the network.

6. Within a network program period, the station may not delete any network identification, program promotion, or production credit announcement,

except promotional announcements for a program the station will not carry. In such cases, only a network or station promotional announcement or public service announcement may be substituted.

7. The network may cancel a previously announced program and substitute another program.

8. The station may broadcast locally originated announcements in station break periods between and during network programs. However, the placement and duration of such periods is determined by the network.

9. For each sponsored network program broadcast, the station receives revenue from the network in the form of *station compensation.* It is based on what is known as the *network station rate,* which differs according to market size, the station's audience reach, and other factors that reflect the importance of the station to the network. Special compensation terms are agreed for sports and special events programs. The network deducts from the compensation a sum for its overhead expenses and for music licensing payments. The network may increase or decrease its station rate. In the event of a decrease, the station may terminate the contract.

10. When an affiliated station is sold, the network has the right to determine whether to accept the change.

Network Programming

The three major networks provide their affiliates with programs in most dayparts.

Weekday early-morning network programming consists of news magazines. A women's magazine program (ABC), game show (CBS), and soap opera (NBC) fill part of the morning, followed by an afternoon block of soap operas and news in early evening. Network prime time comprises a variety of programs: situation comedies, dramas, feature films and made-for-TV movies, news magazines, specials, and sports. Late night is made up of news-interview and talk-variety programs, followed by news in the overnight daypart.

The networks' weekend lineup varies, chiefly as a result of sports coverage on Saturday and Sunday afternoons. News magazines, cartoons, and other child- and teen-appeal programs are aired on Saturday mornings. Sports characterize Saturday afternoons, usually followed by the network news. Network prime time consists of entertainment. NBC is the only network that has programs in the late night and overnight slots, with "Saturday Night Live" and the news broadcast "Nightside."

News magazines and news interviews are aired on Sunday mornings, and sports during the afternoons. Network news precedes prime-time programming at 7:00 P.M. and fills the overnight period.

Scheduling

Since a network fills the major part of an affiliated station's broadcast day, the program manager's chief scheduling responsibility is for those periods during which the network is not feeding programs. Of course, if the station determines that it will not clear or will delay broadcast of a network program, additional scheduling decisions must be made. Programming possibilities on weekdays include the following:

Early Morning (6:00 A.M. to 9:00 A.M.)   Many affiliates start the day-part with local news and/or news-magazine programs, and most join the networks at 7:00 A.M. for their respective news magazines. In large markets, stations have found success with their own two-hour news magazines. Children and teenagers are not being served. Locally produced children's programs, syndicated cartoons, and off-network sitcoms or drama-adventure series offer alternatives for part or all of the period.

Morning (9:00 A.M. to Noon)   Homemakers are a principal target in this daypart. During the first two hours, the networks are not providing programs. Options include syndicated talk, discussion, or magazine programs oriented toward women. Off-network situation comedies starring children or with slapstick elements may bring children as well as adults to the set. ABC and CBS return at 11:00 A.M., and most affiliates clear network programming through the end of the period. Some NBC affiliates carry a network soap opera fed earlier in the day, while syndicated talk is the choice of many others.

Afternoon (Noon to 4:00 P.M.)   Between noon and 12:30 P.M., many affiliates opt for local news or a news magazine, both of which provide an opportunity to promote later newscasts. Syndicated entertainment, such as quiz or game shows and situation comedies, is an alternative. From 12:30 to 4:00 P.M., ABC and CBS affiliates generally carry the network soap operas. NBC affiliates usually air their network's two-hour soap opera block and have an opportunity to counter-program starting at 3:00 P.M. The alternatives include syndicated talk with strong appeal to women, or cartoons and situation comedies with teenage and child appeal to target returning schoolchildren and teenagers.

Early Fringe (4:00 P.M. to 6:00 P.M.)   This is the start of the longest period for which an affiliate has programming responsibility. At the same time, it offers a station the opportunity to generate significant advertising revenues and build the adult audience for its local news.

The growth in audience size and diversity allows stations to engage successfully in counter-programming. Thirty-minute and one-hour off-network and first-run syndicated content fit easily into the period, and many stations have discovered that audiences respond well to blocks of programs of the same genre.

Placement of local news is a major strategic factor. Airing it at 5:30 rules out the possibility of back-to-back hour-long programs. However, a succession of three off-network situation comedies with increasingly older appeal can bring youngsters to the set first, followed by teenagers and adults. A block of 30-minute reality programs attracts the adult demographics desired for news. An alternative strategy for building a news audience involves the scheduling of two hour-long syndicated talk programs across the period. Movies may be considered, but their appeal varies. They also pose some scheduling problems because of their varying lengths. Made-for-television movies are consistent in length, but have proven less appealing than feature films.

Early Evening (6:00 P.M. to 7:00 P.M.)   The length of the local newscast and the periods selected both for local and network news influence the schedule in this daypart. The 30-minute network newscast may be preceded or followed by a 30-minute local newscast. An hour-long local news program may be followed by network news in the first half hour of prime access, or a 90-minute news block may start with 30 minutes of local news, followed by network news, and a final 30 minutes of local news. In most major markets, longer news blocks are common. However, many affiliates air one hour of news from 6:00 to 7:00 P.M., comprising 30 minutes of local and 30 minutes of network.

Prime Access (7:00 P.M. to 8:00 P.M.)   The prime-time access rule restricting what could be shown by some network affiliates formerly influenced program choices in this daypart. With the rule's termination in 1996, stations in all markets are free to air whatever they please. Most stations have filled the time slot with syndicated programs. Quiz and game shows as well as off-network situation comedies have proved very strong in this period. News magazine programs enable stations to inherit adults from the preceding newscasts.

Network Prime Time (8:00 P.M. to 11:00 P.M.)   Most affiliates carry network programming during this entire daypart. If a network program is not competitive, or if most of the network's schedule on a given night is faring poorly, the station may consider preempting and substituting its own programming. Syndicated entertainment programs can fill a 30- or 60-minute period, while movies may produce the desired audience for periods of 90 minutes or 2 hours.

Late Fringe (11:00 P.M. to 11:35 P.M.)   Affiliated stations usually air their late local news in this time slot.

Late Night (11:35 P.M. to 2:05 A.M.)   NBC provides affiliates with programming for the entire period, and CBS programs all but 30 minutes. ABC fills only the 11:35 to 12:35 A.M. slot. Options for CBS and ABC affiliates include off-network situation comedies and, for ABC affiliates, syndicated talk or entertainment-based programs, and off-network dramatic series.

Overnight (2:05 A.M. to 6:00 A.M.)   Affiliates that remain on the air during this daypart usually carry news fed by the network.

Weekend scheduling is influenced by network sports programming, which varies from season to season. On Saturday afternoons, the station may have to program a period of two or more hours. Syndicated entertainment and feature films are among the most popular options. Many stations air a 30-minute local newscast at 6:00 P.M. and follow network news with a one-hour or two 30-minute syndicated entertainment programs from 7:00 to 8:00. Local late news follows network prime time on many affiliated stations. ABC and CBS affiliates do not receive network programming during late night and overnight and often run movies, syndicated talk, off-network drama series, or situation comedies in the time periods.

Many affiliates carry religion, public affairs, or children's programs on Sunday morning before joining the network for news-magazine and news-interview broadcasts. Depending on the season, the station may have to schedule afternoon programs before or after network sports. Again, syndicated entertainment and feature films are common choices, with local and network news between 6:00 and 7:00 P.M. After network prime time, most affiliates air a 30-minute local newscast. Movies, syndicated entertainment, and religion are among the alternatives for the late-night period, followed by overnight network news broadcasts.

PROGRAMMING THE INDEPENDENT STATION

Programming an independent television station is a most challenging job. The challenge is less difficult for stations affiliated with Fox, The WB, and UPN, which receive varying amounts of programming from their networks. However, programmers still are left with many hours to fill each day. And they cannot rely to the same degree as competing major network affiliates on network programs to encourage the flow of viewers into locally scheduled time periods, thus enhancing not only audience size but also the value of time the station sells to advertisers.

By definition, the true independent does not have access to programs on any permanent network, many of which attract large audiences to the affiliates with which it competes. It does not benefit from the audience flow that many network programs provide or from network promotion and publicity, which draw viewers to the affiliates. Unlike the affiliate, the true independent must provide all the programs it airs, a task that has been aggravated by the increased competition for attractive off-network syndicated programs and by their growing cost.

The independent has to meet program and other costs without the station compensation that networks pay their affiliates, and it does not enjoy the comparatively high rates that affiliates can charge advertisers for time in and around network programs. Further, the independent often has to contend with a negative attitude on the part of time buyers.

The challenge is difficult but not impossible, as evidenced by the number of independent stations showing a profit. In large measure, their achievement has been based on the wisdom of their program selection, the imagination of their promotion efforts and above all, on the effectiveness of their program scheduling.

For the most part, the programming weapons of independents have been movies, syndicated talk, off-network entertainment programs — especially situation comedies and action-drama series — syndicated or local children's programs, and live sports. Many independents also carry specials and, occasionally, programs rejected by affiliates of the major networks.

Network promotion has aided Fox affiliates in positioning themselves, while station promotion has enabled true independents to benefit from their image as a source of alternative programming or as the station to watch for movies or sports. However, positioning the independent is becoming more difficult with the increase in both alternative and specialized program offerings on cable.

At the heart of the strategy of many independents is the realization that it is unrealistic to try to beat major network affiliates in all time periods. Rather, they have identified dayparts in which they can compete and have programmed accordingly. Generally, the dayparts have been those in which all affiliates seek similar audiences or in which parts of the available audience have been unserved or underserved. Their strategy has been based chiefly on counter-programming.

The success of their counter-programming points to one of the few programming advantages enjoyed by true independent stations: flexibility in scheduling. Affiliates are expected to carry most of the programming of their networks. The network schedule also determines the amount and times of locally programmed periods. The independent, on the other hand, is free to develop its own schedule and to take advantage of the opportunities to attract audiences whose interests are not being satisfied. Among the best opportunities for counter-programming on weekdays are the following:

Early Morning

While most affiliates are carrying adult-appeal network or local news-magazine shows or local news programs, the independent can capture children with syndicated cartoons or locally produced children's programs. Fox affiliates enjoy compatible programming from the network with one hour of cartoons from 7:00 to 8:00 A.M.

Afternoon

With affiliates of the three majors airing network soap operas, the independent has taken advantage of the abundance of syndicated talk programs to offer an alternative. Off-network situation comedies and male-oriented action dramas also have proved effective options. As the daypart progresses, cartoons and other child- and teenage-appeal content is favored by many stations.

Early Fringe

Fox and The WB fill the first hour of the daypart for their affiliates with children's programs. Many stations move to a block of off-network situation comedies with appeal to both children and adults. The strategy also serves as a counter to local news, which often starts before the end of the period, and as a bridge to the adult-appeal programming that follows. True independents also look to situation comedies or counter both Fox and other affiliates with off-network reality shows and hour-long dramas.

Early Evening

An excellent opportunity to counter-program with off-network entertainment is offered during this traditional news block on affiliated stations.

Prime Access

The independent can benefit from audience flow in the 7:00 to 8:00 P.M. period by airing additional entertainment. An alternative for true independents would be to start a two-hour movie at 7:00 in an attempt to attract adults and hold them during the first hour of network prime time.

Late Fringe

During this period, most affiliates of the majors broadcast local news. Independents are able to counter with adult-appeal entertainment programs, such as situation comedies, action dramas, or movies.

Overnight

Entertainment of any kind geared toward adults provides an alternative to news broadcasts on affiliates of the three major networks.

Most other periods do not offer significant advantages to independent stations, though effective counter-programming still is possible.

During the morning hours when affiliates are not receiving network programs, the independent is on an equal footing. Homemakers constitute a significant part of the available audience and are the principal target of advertisers. With their appeal to women in the 25 to 54 age group, movies could offer strong competition to the affiliates' offerings. Alternatives include syndicated talk and off-network situation comedies and dramatic series with strong female appeal. Similar programs may be the most effective way of competing against the network soap operas before the return of children in midafternoon.

Prime time poses a difficult problem for the true independent. The networks' lineup of entertainment programs attracts large audiences during this period. Movies, off-network dramatic series, and specials offer the best opportunities to attract audiences. From 10:00 to 10:30 P.M., the independent can counter entertainment on the affiliates with local news.

In the late night daypart, syndicated talk-variety, off-network situation comedies and adventure dramas, or movies are effective competition against network programming.

Weekends provide true independent stations with several opportunities to counter-program. While affiliates are carrying network cartoons or other child- or teen-appeal programs on Saturday mornings, the independent may target adults and older teenagers with movies or sports, such as wrestling. Syndicated popular music, adventure drama, and movies offer alternatives to network sports during the afternoons.

As noted earlier, affiliate programming on Sunday mornings consists primarily of religion, public affairs, and network news magazines and news interviews. The independent station can attract children with cartoons, and young viewers and adults with situation comedies and adventure dramas. Movies are another vehicle to bring adults to the set. Popular-music programs and movies are among the most attractive alternatives to network sports on Sunday afternoons, though some independents go head-to-head against affiliates with regional or minor sports.

PROGRAMMING AND THE STATION REPRESENTATIVE

The traditional role of the station representative firm, or station rep, has been to sell time on client stations to national and regional spot advertisers. However, in the increasingly competitive environment in which television stations operate, reps have assumed an important role in local station programming. Today, all rep firms have departments that are experienced in advising stations on the purchasing, scheduling, and promotion of programs.

The move is not surprising. After all, the more competitive the station's programming, the easier it is to sell time. Competitive programming requires sound information and advice on which to base program purchase and scheduling decisions. The rep can provide such services.

The rep has access to a wealth of information that can be used to strengthen the station's competitive position. Details of the current performance of network offerings and network program plans, including specials, can provide the station with useful insights for its own planning.

The rep knows which syndicated programs are available or are about to become available. Additionally, the rep is privy to a wide range of information on such programs, including the track records of those that have been broadcast; how they fared in other markets or geographic areas similar to that of the client station; their strength against different kinds of competing programs and among different demographics; and, with off-network programs, how they performed when they were broadcast originally in the market. Using this and other information, the rep can recommend desirable program purchases and realistic purchase prices.

With a proposed new program, the challenge is more difficult. An important consideration is whether it will actually make it to the air. The rep firm programming department can evaluate the program's prospects before the station commits to it. If a commitment is made, the rep can suggest likely demographic appeal and possible time periods.

The rep programmer also has information on the availability of feature film packages and the performance of individual films in movie theater and network showings.

It has been emphasized that a station's programming success derives not only from individual programs, but the way in which they are assembled in a schedule. Here, again, the rep's expertise can be valuable.

Through a close study of the market and competing stations, the rep can identify strengths and weaknesses in the station's current schedule and propose appropriate changes. It is unlikely that the rep will recommend program purchases in isolation. Generally, such purchases are proposed with an eye to strengthening a daypart, not just a time period.

The rep firm can help the station decide on expanding or contracting the amount of local news programming. For example, the station may be considering adding a half-hour to its early news, starting a Saturday morning newscast, or supplying a newscast to the local independent station. The rep can analyze what has happened in other markets under similar circumstances and can assist the station in making intelligent forecasts in its own market. To achieve the strongest possible lead-in for early news, the rep routinely aids the station in programming the early-fringe time period.

PROGRAMMING FOR CHILDREN

Television stations have wide discretion in selecting the programs they broadcast. Children's programming is a notable exception.

In accordance with the Children's Television Act of 1990 and the FCC rules adopted under the act, commercial stations are required to (1) broadcast programming that is responsive to the educational and informational needs of children 16 years of age and younger; and (2) complete FCC Form 398, which requests information about such programming. Noncommercial stations must air responsive programming, but are exempt from the obligation to complete Form 398.

Children's programming constitutes an important part of the licensing process. To receive FCC staff-level approval of an application for license renewal, a station must demonstrate that it has aired at least three hours of *core programming*, on average, each week over each six-month period. The FCC characterizes such programming as programming

- that has as a significant purpose meeting the educational and informational needs of children 16 years old or younger

- whose educational purpose is specified in writing

- that is at least 30 minutes in length

- that is aired weekly on a regular basis between 7:00 A.M. and 10:00 P.M.

- that is identified at the time of airing and to program guide publishers as being "core programming" designed for a specific age range of children[14]

A station that airs "somewhat less" than an average of three hours per week of such programming may still receive staff approval of its license renewal. However, it must show that it has broadcast a package of programming that demonstrates a commitment at least equivalent to airing three hours a week of core programming.

If a station fails to meet either the core or equivalent guideline, its license renewal application is reviewed by the FCC's members.

Form 398 (Figure 4.5) provides the means by which a station may document its efforts to comply with the children's programming requirements. It asks for details of both core and non-core educational and informational programming aired in the preceding calendar quarter, core programming planned for airing in the next quarter, and core programming sponsored by the licensee and aired on any other station in the market. The form must be completed quarterly and a copy placed in the station's public inspection file. For an experimental three-year period (1997 through 1999), all four quarterly reports must be filed annually with the FCC.

Television broadcasters also are required to alert parents and others to the content of programs through use of a ratings system for all programs except news and sports. That obligation is in response to a mandate in the Telecommunications Act of 1996 and follows an FCC-approved agreement adopted jointly by the National Association of Broadcasters, the National Cable Television Association (NCTA), and the Motion Picture Association of America (MPAA), and titled *TV Parental Guidelines*.

The guidelines apply to programs designed solely for children and to those designed for the entire audience, including children. They consist of six general categories of programs, with additional content indicators for fantasy violence,

Figure 4.5 *FCC 398 Children's Television Programming Report.*

Federal Communications Commission
Washington, D. C. 20554

Approved by OMB
3060-0754

FCC 398
Children's Television Programming Report

Report reflects information for quarter ending (mm/dd/yy) _____

1. Call Sign	Channel Number	Community of License				
		City	State	County		ZIP Code
Licensee						Previous call sign (if applicable)
☐ Network Affiliation: _____		☐ Independent	Nielsen DMA	World Wide Web Home Page Address (if applicable)		

Core Programming

2. State the average number of hours of Core Programming per week broadcast by the station. See 47 C.F.R. Section 73.671(c).

3. Does the licensee identify each Core Program at the beginning of the airing of each program as required by 47 C.F.R. Section 73.673?   ☐ Yes   ☐ No

4. Does the licensee provide information identifying each Core Program aired on its station, including an indication of the target child audience, to publishers of program guides as required by 47 C.F.R. Section 73.673?   ☐ Yes   ☐ No

5. Complete the following for each program that you aired during the past three months that meets the definition of Core Programming. Complete chart below for each Core Program. (Use supplemental page for additional programs.)

Title of Program:				Origination		
				Local	Network	Syndicated
Days/Times Program Regularly Scheduled:	Total times aired	Number of Preemptions	If preempted and rescheduled, list date and time aired.			
			Dates		Times	
Length of Program: (minutes)						
Age of Target Child Audience: from _____ years to _____ years.						
Describe the educational and informational objective of the program and how it meets the definition of Core Programming.						

FCC 398 (Page 1)
January 1997

Figure 4.5 *Continued*

6. Complete the following for each program that you aired during the past three months that is specifically designed to meet the educational and informational needs of children ages 16 and under, but does not meet one or more elements of the definition of Core Programming.   See 47 C.F.R. Section 73.671.   Complete chart below for each additional such educational and informational program. (Use supplemental page for additional programs.)

Title of Program:		Origination		
		Local	Network	Syndicated
Dates/Times Program Aired:	Total times aired	Number of Preemptions	If preempted and rescheduled, list date and time aired.	
			Dates	Times
Length of Program: (minutes)				
Age of Target Child Audience (if applicable): from __ years to __ years.				
Describe the program.				
Does the program have educating and informing children ages 16 and under as a significant purpose?			☐ Yes ☐ No	
If Yes, does the licensee identify each program at the beginning of its airing consistent with 47 C.F.R. Section 73.673?			☐ Yes ☐ No	
If Yes, does the licensee provide information regarding the program, including an indication of the target child audience, to publishers of program guides consistent with 47 C.F.R. Section 73.673?			☐ Yes ☐ No	

Other Matters

7. Complete the following for each program that you plan to air for the next quarter that meets the definition of Core Programming. Complete chart below for each Core Program. (Use supplemental page for additional programs.)

Title of Program:		Origination		
		Local	Network	Syndicated
Days/Times Program Regularly Scheduled:	Total times to be aired	Length of Program: (minutes)	Age of Target Child Audience: from ___ years to___ years.	
Describe the educational and informational objective of the program and how it meets the definition of Core Programming.				

8. Does the licensee publicize the existence and location of the station's Children's Television   ☐ Yes   ☐ No
    Programming Reports (FCC 398) as required by 47 C.F.R. Section 73.3526(a)(8)(iii)?

Figure 4.5 *Continued*

9. List Core Programs, if any, aired by other stations that are sponsored by the licensee and that meet the criteria set forth in 47 C.F.R. Section 73.671. Also indicate whether the amount of total Core Programming broadcast by another station increased.

Name of Program	Call Letters of Station Airing Sponsored Program	Channel Number of Station Airing Sponsored Program	Did total programming increase?
			☐ Yes ☐ No
			☐ Yes ☐ No
			☐ Yes ☐ No

For each Core Program sponsored by the licensee, complete the chart below.

Title of Program:				Origination		
				Local	Network	Syndicated

Days/Times Program Regularly Scheduled:	Total times aired	Number of Preemptions	If preempted and rescheduled, list date and time aired.	
			Dates	Times

Length of Program: _____ (minutes)

Target Child Audience: from ____ years to ____ years.

Describe the educational and informational objective of the program and how it meets the definition of Core Programming.

10. Name of children's programming liaison:		
Name		Telephone Number (include area code)
Address		Internet Mail Address (if applicable)
City	State	

11. Include any other comments or information you want the Commission to consider in evaluating your compliance with the Children's Television Act (or use this space for supplemental explanations). This may include information on any other non-core educational and informational programming that you aired this quarter or plan to air during the next quarter, or any existing or proposed non-broadcast efforts that will enhance the educational and informational value of such programming to children. See 47 C.F.R. Section 73.671, NOTE 2.

WILLFUL FALSE STATEMENTS MADE ON THIS FORM ARE PUNISHABLE BY FINE AND/OR IMPRISONMENT (U.S. CODE, TITLE 18, SECTION 1001), AND/OR REVOCATION OF ANY STATION LICENSE OR CONSTRUCTION PERMIT (U.S. CODE, TITLE 47, SECTION 312(a)(1)), AND/OR FORFEITURE (U.S. CODE, TITLE 47, SECTION 503).

I certify that the statements in this application are true, complete, and correct to the best of my knowledge and belief, and are made in good faith.

Name of Licensee	Signature
Date	

FCC 398 (Page 3)
January 1997

sexual situations, violence, language, and dialogue (see Appendix A). Rating icons and content symbols must be displayed on-screen for the first 15 seconds of each rated program.

PROGRAMMING AND THE COMMUNITY

The Communications Act imposes on broadcasters the obligation to serve the public interest, convenience, and necessity. Programming is the principal tool used to satisfy that requirement.

Entertainment dominates the programming of most commercial television stations and music-format radio stations. Information is included in the schedule of most stations and is the sole element for many radio stations.

Problems confronting the community of license must not be overlooked in programming. Every three months, stations must place in their public file a quarterly list reflecting the "licensee's most significant programming treatment of community issues."

To help determine the issues of concern, the program manager and others in managerial capacities must develop a personal involvement with the community. Riding the bus to work and speaking with other passengers, and talking with garage attendants, laborers on construction projects, and others outside the broadcast workplace may result in some valuable insights. Membership in service clubs and nonprofit organizations can be useful, too.

The public interest is served best, however, when the station demonstrates a sincere commitment to community service. Many stations render off-air service through participation in, and sponsorship of, selected events. Opportunities through use of the station's air time are numerous. They include the following:

Local Newscasts
Radio and television newscasts are important sources of information on day-to-day events and activities in the community. Investigative reports and series enable the station to bring to public attention questionable or illegal practices by individuals or institutions, often with results that are beneficial to the community.

A major police crackdown on drug dealers occurred after a Nashville radio station broadcast a series of reports on the surge in violent crime in that city. Television stations that produce and air the "Crime Stoppers" series frequently are successful in solving crimes in the community.

Public Affairs Programs
Interview programs are the most common method of exploring community issues in depth. On television, such programs often are criticized for their reliance on "talking heads." Radio stations find it difficult to engage the sustained interest of listeners accustomed to almost continuous music. Nevertheless, public affairs programs of this kind can be instructive and allow the station to compensate for the brevity with which complex issues usually are covered in newscasts.

Stations with adequate staff and production resources periodically air 30- or 60-minute specials or documentaries on community problems. In one half-hour special, a Cincinnati television station revealed that an orderly at a local hospital was a serial killer. A station in Washington, D.C., examined ways in which medical laboratory errors led women with cancer to believe that they were healthy.

Station Editorials

Editorials offer the station the opportunity to focus listener or viewer attention on community issues and problems and to play a leadership role in effecting change.

Recognizing the needs of the community, a Chicago radio station aired a series of editorials calling for flexible hours in the city's health clinics. A series on a TV station in New Orleans led to the forced retirement of the warden and the replacement of all other administrators at a prison for young, first-time offenders. The editorials attacked the administration for failing to put a stop to gang rapes and for allowing hardened criminals who did not belong in the institution to "sell" some young inmates to other convicts.

Public Service Announcements

The National Association of Broadcasters calculates that the broadcast industry provides almost $7 billion a year in public service.[15] Public service announcements (PSAs) aired by stations and national networks constitute about two-thirds of that amount, a total of $4.6 billion.[16]

Most PSAs contain information about the activities of nonprofit groups. However, many stations have discovered that they can be very effective in soliciting volunteers. A Chicago radio station used them as the basis of a successful ten-week campaign to recruit and match volunteers with community organizations. Member radio and television stations of the West Virginia Broadcasters' Association aired them to encourage clubs and organizations to adopt and clean up stretches of roads in their communities as part of an "Adopt-a-Highway" program. Over 800 groups responded and more than 14,000 volunteers set to work on about 2,400 miles of roads.

Radiothons and Telethons

Raising funds to support their activities is a constant challenge for most nonprofit organizations. Many broadcast stations have become partners in that endeavor by donating air time for radiothons or telethons or by making time available at a modest cost.

A radio station in Atlanta raised more than $800,000 during a 40-hour radiothon to benefit St. Jude Children's Research Hospital in Memphis. Almost 200 television stations join together annually in the so-called "love network" for Jerry Lewis' Labor Day telethon for the Muscular Dystrophy Association. Since 1966, the telethon has generated more than $500 million in viewer pledges.

Some stations respond immediately to the need for funds, whether that need is domestic or foreign. A radio station in Atlantic City devoted ten hours of air time and collected more than $70,000 to help children orphaned by an earthquake in Armenia.

Fund-raising activities need not be restricted to radiothons or telethons. Staff often volunteer their time off the air to assist community groups in their efforts. A morning personality on a radio station in Portland, OR, collected more than $44,000 for underprivileged schoolchildren by swimming 35 miles in a hot tub. Staffers of two radio stations in Exeter, NH, joined 300 people in a 10-mile walk, which raised over $19,000 for the state chapter of the National Head Injury Foundation.

Such methods of serving the public interest can go far toward stilling criticisms that broadcast stations are merely vendors of entertainment. In addition, they can lead to improved ratings and increased business by enhancing the station's image in the community. One observer summarized the importance of public service to the broadcaster in this way:

> If . . . you are seen as somebody working hard to make people's downtown safe, protect their kids from drugs and alcohol and lead their community to invest more in itself and its improvement, they will treat you not as a vendor but as a friend and ally.[17]

Active participation in the community, and service to it, are valuable tools for forestalling threats from citizen groups and fending off challenges to license renewal. They also permit the station to show that it is living up to its responsibility as a public trustee.

The discharge of that responsibility has become even more important in this era of deregulation. Instead of dictating standards, the Federal Communications Commission has entrusted to listeners and viewers the task of deciding the public's interest. However, the commission retains its responsibility to ensure that broadcasters remain responsive to the needs, interests, and tastes of their audiences.

Keeping a close watch on both broadcasters and the FCC are those members of Congress who are not convinced that loosening regulations will benefit the public. One of them, Representative Edward Markey, former chairman of the powerful House Telecommunications and Finance Subcommittee, has warned of what might happen if stations ignore their public interest obligations:

> The broadcasting industry will remain "special" as long as the public-trustee concept remains its fundamental underpinning. Its special niche in the marketplace has been protected because it is viewed as having a special role. If broadcasters eschew that role, Congress will take a Darwinian view of their faith and there will be no need for us to protect them.[18]

WHAT'S AHEAD?

On the occasion of its fiftieth anniversary in 1981, *Broadcasting* magazine speculated on the world of communications in 2001. It quoted the late physicist Niels Bohr: "It is very difficult to make predictions — especially about the future."[19]

Despite Bohr's amusing observation, one assertion can be made with confidence: The United States is growing older. The Census Bureau estimates that the median age will be 36.5 at the start of the twenty-first century, up from 33 in 1990 and 30 in 1980. By 2010, it will reach 39 — its highest ever — and will exceed 40 in more than one-quarter of the states.

A dominant element in this phenomenon is the more than 70 million babies born between 1946 and 1964, the so-called "baby boom" generation.

Today, they account for more than 25 percent of the population and almost 45 percent of all households. And they are no longer babies. By the end of the 1990s, the youngest boomer was 35 and the oldest was 53.

The aging of the United States poses many challenges and opportunities for radio and television station programmers. Typically, older audiences have a need for more news and information, and stations must be able to respond. Many radio stations already have, making the news/talk format the most popular in the country. As younger boomers age, they will rely increasingly on information to aid them in their work and leisure pursuits, and will reward responsive stations with their listenership.

Local news has long been a profit-center for network-affiliated television stations. It will continue to be profitable, but only for stations that rise to the challenge of meeting viewers' changing needs. The major events of the day still will have to be reported. However, news and features on health, travel, finance, retirement, and associated topics will have to be included.

The music that entertained earlier generations of older listeners is giving way to radio formats offering baby boomers the sounds with which they grew up. It is no coincidence that three of the four most-listened-to music formats — adult contemporary, country, and oldies — draw 60 percent or more of their audience from adults 35 and over. As the audience continues to age, programmers must be alert to the opportunities presented and consider appropriate format changes or adjustments.

Out of economic necessity, independent television stations have long been accustomed to broadcasting programs that had their first airing during the baby boomers' earliest acquaintance with the television medium. Today, many of those programs continue to attract their original audience, now much older and seeking an outlet for their nostalgia. Given the networks' infatuation with persons aged 18 to 49, it may be difficult for affiliated stations to satisfy older baby boomers' desire to recapture their youth. Nonetheless, station programmers should strive to respond — through their local production and syndicated purchases — to the entertainment needs of viewers 50 and over, whose discretionary income per capita surpasses that of most other audience segments.

Broadcast programmers will also have to continue to respond to changes in the country's ethnic composition. Despite a slowdown in overall population growth, the proportion of minorities is increasing and will reach 29 percent at the start of the new century. That compares to 25 percent in 1990. One in four Americans is of African, Asian, Latino, or Native American ancestry. Latino Americans will register the greatest growth and will pass African Americans as the nation's largest minority group by 2010.[20]

Stations will have to take into account the content needs of these increasingly important audiences. Both Latino Americans and African Americans are heavy users of radio and television. Their program choices are easy to understand. Forty-eight percent of Latino Americans aged 12 and over prefer to listen to Spanish formats and more than 60 percent of African Americans favor urban and urban adult contemporary formats.[21] Spanish-language television programming ranks highest among persons in Latino American households.[22] African American viewers show a clear preference for programs with predominantly African American casts.[23]

Many radio stations already are positioned to attract listeners characterized by ethnicity or a language other than English. Others are likely to follow. Television stations in communities with significant ethnic or foreign-language populations may find it profitable to program to them or to speak to them in their own language. Almost half of all Latino Americans, for example, do not speak English, and another 40 percent prefer to communicate in Spanish.[24]

Attracting audiences — and retaining them — will not be easy for radio and television stations confronting fierce competition. The nature of that competition, both existing and projected, was described in Chapter 1, "Broadcast Station Management." However, it bears repeating here that the array of communication choices available will render audiences much more selective in their allocation of time. Finding the content that best meets their needs, and marketing it in a way that captures their attention, will be a difficult challenge.

Broadcast stations have a powerful weapon, one that will set them apart from much of the competition: Their local connection. Indications are that they can use that uniqueness to their advantage. More than 50 percent of Web users — with access to the world, literally — say they search the Internet for local news.[25]

For some radio stations, a return to localism will mean turning away from nationally distributed content, to which some attribute the continuing decline in audience. For others, it will require a return to local air talent. For all, it may mean turning to the Internet to distribute niche formats that could develop a loyal local following, even though they may not be economically attractive for broadcast.

Affiliated television station programmers should not stand by idly while their audiences continue to diminish. They should move aggressively to identify themselves even more closely with their market. That means doing what most competitors cannot — responding to the interests and needs of the community through diverse local programming of high quality. Such a move will require courage. The future, however, does not belong to the faint-hearted. It will also require money. But the investment offers at least the opportunity to compete.

Localism may not be enough for single-station radio operators facing stiff competition in the market from duopolies and superduopolies. Their best hope lies in a battle among their larger, well-financed competitors for the audiences of mainstream formats, thus opening a window for some niche or specialty formats. Such an outcome appears unlikely, however. What is more likely is that multistation owners will strive for market domination, either through *horizontal* or *vertical positioning*. Horizontal positioning would enable them to program their different stations to attract different demographics covering the entire age span of listeners. Through vertical positioning, they would seek to control all audience elements in a single age demographic.

Audience retention is one of the issues behind proposed changes in the relationship between the major television networks and their affiliated stations. Faced with continuing audience erosion, advertiser resistance to increased spot rates, and higher programming costs, the networks argue that they can no longer afford to bear all the economic risks and compensate stations at present levels. They want affiliates to lend a financial hand. Many stations reply that the networks should manage their costs more efficiently. They, too, are having to contend with program cost increases and they are facing huge outlays as they make the transition to digital transmission.

To ease their financial plight, the networks want to *re-purpose* their programming, or repackage it for sale to other outlets. Affiliates counter that such a move would draw viewers away from program airings on the networks and lead to further audience loss. Accordingly, they are seeking to protect themselves by demanding network exclusivity.

Changes are already in the works and more are likely to follow. CBS affiliates agreed to swap commercial inventory and pay some cash to help their network meet the costs of NFL coverage. And CBS was the first to commit formally to exclusivity. If NBC has its way, a network-affiliate economic partnership will replace the current business relationship. It has suggested a joint venture with affiliates for an initial ten-year period, during which compensation payments would be phased out. Whatever the results, it is obvious that the first major overhaul of station-network relations is underway, with significant implications for affiliate programmers and audiences.

Another change is in progress — one with a much less certain outcome for program managers and directors. It grows out of the explosion in the use of the Internet. Depending on one's perception, this new medium may be considered a competitor or an ally.

Those who count it among the competition point to its immediate threat to radio stations, as listeners tune to stations Webcasting from other markets and even other countries. Already, Web-listening is showing up in audience measurement studies conducted by Arbitron. As video-streaming technology improves, television stations may face similar inroads on their audiences. Nor is the competition restricted to other existing broadcasters. No one can predict how many companies, organizations, and individuals will seek to become audio and video content distributors. Some have entered the arena as Internet-only "broadcasters," and their number is increasing. Many others are eyeing the opportunities offered by a medium whose use does not carry with it the cost of station purchase or construction or acquisition of an FCC license to operate.

Broadcasters who have already established a presence on the Internet take a different view. They see it as a means of adding to their competitive strength. Hundreds of radio stations number among their audience listeners in distant communities and countries. Television stations will follow, albeit at a much slower pace. Both radio and television stations are putting on their Websites current and archived newscasts, complete with audio and video clips. In time, other content will be available there for on-demand use. Stations also can use the medium for content experimentation, at a modest cost and without risk to their current programming.

The challenge to programmers is to seek ways of capitalizing on the new medium to expand and build station audiences.

SUMMARY

Radio and television station programming reaches virtually every household in the United States, and it is influenced by the interests of the audience, the broadcaster, the advertiser, and the regulator.

Entertainment is the dominant program element both in radio and television, with the exception of information-format radio stations. However, most stations broadcast a variety of other programs.

Responsibility for a station's programming rests with the program department, headed by a program manager or program director. In a music-format radio station, department staff generally includes a music director, production director, and announcers. In a station with an information format, editors, producers, hosts, anchors, reporters, writers, and desk assistants constitute the majority of the staff. In television, the program department comprises a production manager, production staff, a film or film and videotape director, and an art director. In some radio and television stations, news is a function of the department.

The principal duties of the program manager are to plan, acquire, execute, and control the station's programming. To carry out those duties effectively requires knowledge, administrative and professional skills, and certain personal qualities.

The programming of most radio stations revolves around one principal content element, called a format. Usually it is designed to appeal to a particular subgroup of the population, identified by age, ethnicity, or socioeconomic status. Music is the most common format. Other format categories are information and specialty.

The major sources of radio station programs are the station itself, syndicators who distribute both programs and entire music formats, and networks.

In developing a programming strategy, a radio station selects a format and decides how to execute it. Consistency of sound is a major consideration, and stations seek to attain it through use of a format wheel or clock. The wheel identifies the combination of content elements in a one-hour period and the sequence in which each element is aired. All-news stations broadcast their content in cycles, with a period of time elapsing before each element is repeated. Other important strategic considerations include dayparting, playlist selection, music rotation, and the frequency and length of commercial interruptions.

Television station programming is quite different from radio station programming. In radio, a major goal is to identify a segment of the population and broadcast to it throughout the day. In television, the programmer seeks to attract and retain those persons who are available to view.

Network affiliates use three major program sources: the network, program and feature film syndicators, and the station itself. Independent stations rely on syndicators, station productions, and on ad-hoc networks.

In acquiring and scheduling programs, the television station program manager considers many factors. Chief among them are the programming of competing stations, the kinds of people available to view, and the station's program budget. Attention is also paid to the possibility of building audience flow and habit. The basic scheduling strategies are head-to-head, counter, strip, checkerboard, and block.

The three major networks and Pax TV fill a large part of their affiliates' schedules. Fox, The WB, and UPN provide considerably less programming to their affiliates. Independent stations, must program all time periods themselves.

Despite the challenge, many independents have achieved profitability by concentrating on dayparts in which they can compete effectively. Counter-programming has played an important part in their success.

Many television stations seek program information from their rep company, which is aware of the availability and performance of all syndicated programming. Additionally, the rep can offer advice on scheduling and promoting programs.

Television stations are required to air programming that meets the educational and informational needs of children and to use a ratings system for all content, except news and sports.

Programming is the chief method whereby stations carry out their obligation to serve the public interest. They are required to treat community issues and can use their air time in a variety of ways to demonstrate a commitment to public service. Service also can be rendered by station involvement in community activities.

Increasingly, radio and television station program directors and managers will have to respond to the needs of audiences that are older and ethnically more diverse. They will also have to use their local connection to stave off competition. Programmers of stations affiliated with the major television networks will have to contend with changes in the station-network relationship. And all broadcast programmers will have to adjust to the challenges and opportunities resulting from the growing influence of the Internet.

CASE STUDY: RADIO

A market in the South has an estimated metro survey area population (persons 12+) of 380,600. Blacks constitute 48,500 (12.7 percent) of that number. Teens (12 to 17) account for 40,000 (10.5 percent). The following table describes the rest of the population:

Age	Men	%	Women	%
18–24	19,300	5.1	19,800	5.2
25–34	31,500	8.3	32,900	8.6
35–44	36,500	9.6	38,600	10.1
45–49	17,000	4.5	17,700	4.7
50–54	12,700	3.3	14,100	3.7
55–64	19,200	5.0	22,100	5.8
65+	22,800	6.0	36,400	9.6

Fifty-four percent live in owner-occupied homes with a median value of $57,000. Household median income is $37,511. The occupation of persons 16 and older is as follows:

Managerial	22.8%
Technical	31.2%
Service worker	12.2%
Farm worker	1.3%
Precision production	12.0%
Operator	20.5%

Sixteen percent of persons 25 and older have completed four or more years of college, and 23 percent one to three years. Of the remainder, 29 percent are high school graduates. Twenty-one stations serve the market:

	Power (Watts)		
Station	**Day**	**Night**	**Format**
WAAA-FM	500	500	Adult contemporary
WBBB	5,000	5,000	News/talk
WBBB-FM	100,000	100,000	Soft adult contemporary
WCCC	5,000	5,000	Nostalgia
WCCC-FM	100,000	100,000	Country
WDDD	5,000	5,000	Country
WEEE	50,000	2,500	Religious
WFFF-FM	6,000	6,000	News/talk
WGGG	5,000	1,000	News/talk
WHHH-FM	3,000	3,000	Urban contemporary
WIII-FM	16,000	16,000	Contemporary hit radio
WJJJ-FM	1,550	1,550	Adult contemporary
WKKK-FM	3,000	3,000	Urban adult contemporary
WLLL	5,000	—	Urban adult contemporary
WMMM-FM	2,850	2,850	Oldies
WNNN	5,000	—	Country
WOOO-FM	1,300	1,300	Classic country
WPPP-FM	100,000	100,000	Adult contemporary
WQQQ-FM	100,000	100,000	Country
WRRR	1,000	—	Religious
WSSS-FM	1,000	1,000	Contemporary hit radio

The Spring ratings book reflects the trends in metro share over the past year for each station among persons 25 to 54, Monday to Sunday, 6:00 A.M. to midnight:

	Summer	Fall	Winter	Spring
WAAA-FM	1.2	2.9	1.7	3.4
WBBB	.3	.3	.3	.6
WBBB-FM	10.7	9.4	7.8	6.0
WCCC	.3	.9	.6	.9
WCCC-FM	2.7	2.9	3.5	5.7
WDDD	.3	.3	.3	.9
WEEE	.3	.6	.6	.3
WFFF-FM	3.3	5.0	4.3	2.8
WGGG	3.6	2.9	3.5	4.3
WHHH-FM	5.9	7.4	7.2	5.7
WIII-FM	2.7	1.8	2.3	1.4
WJJJ-FM	4.4	5.3	5.2	4.0
WKKK-FM	2.1	2.1	2.0	2.3
WLLL	2.7	2.4	2.3	3.4
WMMM-FM	5.0	4.4	4.9	6.3
WNNN	.3	.3	.3	.3
WOOO-FM	1.8	1.9	2.3	3.4
WPPP-FM	13.3	11.2	10.4	12.5
WQQQ-FM	18.6	23.8	21.0	18.8
WRRR	.3	.3	.3	1.1
WSSS-FM	2.1	2.6	2.3	2.3

You are the program director of WQQQ-FM. The general manager tells you that your company is contemplating the purchase of WJJJ-FM and WSSS-FM. The company president wants you to analyze the stations' performance and make a recommendation on formats, should the purchase be completed.

Exercises

1. What is your assessment of the performance trends of the two stations?

2. What does your assessment suggest about the desirability of format changes?

3. If you conclude that changes are appropriate, what formats would you recommend? Why?

CASE STUDY: TELEVISION

You are program manager of WCCC, a Fox affiliate in a top-100 market in the Southeast. The other stations in the market are WBBB (CBS), WDDD (UPN), WEEE (NBC), WFFF (PBS), and WGGG (ABC). WAAA is a PBS affiliate in a community about 30 miles away and is carried on your market's cable television system.

Margaret Smith is your GM. She has just received the May ratings book and stops by your office on the way to a meeting of the United Way board. She hands the book to you and says: "I'm not at all happy with our Saturday morning performance. I've scanned the numbers and our share trends are not looking good. We may have to make some changes. Take a closer look and let me know what you think. I'll be back in a couple of hours."

You set to work and compile the DMA rating and share data, the share trends over the past year, and the ratings for teens (12–17) and children (2–11).

		DMA Household		Share Trend			DMA Rating	
		Rating	Share	Feb	Nov	May	12–17	2–11
8:00 A.M.								
WAAA	Arthur	1	4	3	3	3		2
WBBB	New Ghostwriter	1	4	3	4	4	1	2
WCCC	Mr. Potato Head	1	4	4	4	4	2	3
WDDD	Monkey Magic	<<						1
WEEE	Saturday Today	6	31	23	29	25	1	1
WFFF	Sesame Street	1	3	3	3	3		1
WGGG	Disney's Hercules	1	5	7	8	14		4
8:30								
WAAA	Arthur	<<						
WBBB	Wheel of Fortune 2000	1	5	6	4	7		3
WCCC	Power Rangers in Space	1	4	4	5	5	2	3
WDDD	War Planet	<<						
WEEE	Saturday Today	7	29	22	25	23	1	
WFFF	Sesame Street	1	6	4	3	4		3
WGGG	Disney's One Saturday Morning	1	6	6	5	11	1	4
9:00								
WAAA	Woof! It's a Dog's Life	1	3	4	4	4		2
WBBB	Saturday Morning	2	9	4	6	10	1	
WCCC	Godzilla	1	6	6	6	5	1	4

		DMA Household		Share Trend			DMA Rating	
		Rating	Share	Feb	Nov	May	12–17	2–11
WDDD	Infomercial	<<						
WEEE	Infomercial	1	6	6	6	3		
WFFF	Mister Rogers' Neighborhood	1	4	4	3	3		1
WGGG	Disney's One Saturday Morning	2	8	5	8	11	3	5
9:30								
WAAA	Debbie Travis' Painted House	<<						
WBBB	Saturday Morning	1	4	3	4	5	1	
WCCC	Young Hercules	1	7	7	7	3	1	4
WDDD	Infomercial	<<						
WEEE	Our Town	1	5	4	9	7	1	
WFFF	Mister Rogers' Neighborhood	1	3	3	4	4		1
WGGG	Disney's One Saturday Morning	2	10	6	11	10	2	7
10:00								
WAAA	Today's Classic Homes	<<						
WBBB	Saturday Morning	1	7	5	4	4	1	
WCCC	Spider-Man	1	6	9	7	5	2	5
WDDD	Saturday Morning Movie	<<						
WEEE	Saved by the Bell: New Class	2	9	9	10	14	5	2
WFFF	Charlie Horse Music Pizza	1	2	1	1	1		1
WGGG	Disney's One Saturday Morning	3	13	11	14	8	1	8
10:30								
WAAA	New Tastes from Texas	<<						
WBBB	Saturday Morning	1	4	3	3	5	1	

		DMA Household		Share Trend			DMA Rating	
		Rating	Share	Feb	Nov	May	12–17	2–11
WCCC	Secret Files of Spy Dogs	1	6	9	7	8	3	5
WDDD	Saturday Morning Movie	<<						
WEEE	One World	2	10	7	8	13	6	3
WFFF	Wishbone	1	3	3	4	3		2
WGGG	Bugs Bunny	3	13	9	14	6	2	7
11:00								
WAAA	Nathalie Dupree Cooks	<<						
WBBB	Sports Illustrated for Kids	2	8	3	3	5	2	4
WCCC	Mad Jack	1	5	10	10	9	2	1
WDDD	Saturday Morning Movie	<<						
WEEE	Hang Time	2	11	10	14	13	4	4
WFFF	Best of Joy of Painting	1	5	4	4	6		
WGGG	Bugs Bunny	2	10	4	7	8	1	4
11:30								
WAAA	Great Food	<<						
WBBB	Weird Al	1	6	2	3	3		3
WCCC	Oggy & the Cockroaches	1	3	9	9	7	1	
WDDD	Saturday Morning Movie	<<						
WEEE	City Guys	2	9	10	11	15	3	2
WFFF	Sewing With Nancy	1	4	2	3	4		
WGGG	Disney's 101 Dalmatians	2	13	6	5	10	3	6

<< Below minimum audience standards

Exercises

1. How accurate is Margaret's assessment of the trends?

2. In her haste, has she overlooked other relevant data? If so, what?

3. Do you agree with her that changes may be necessary? If so, give details. If not, why?

4. What will you tell her on her return?

NOTES

1. *Radio Marketing Guide and Factbook for Advertisers* and *Radio Today: How America Listens to Radio.*

2. *1998 Report on Television* and "Who Watches TV?" <http://www.nab.org/Television/tvindus.asp>.

3. *Radio Today: How America Listens to Radio,* p. 5.

4. *Ibid.,* p. 4.

5. *1998 Report on Television,* p. 17.

6. *Ibid.*

7. *Ibid.,* p. 18.

8. J. David Lewis, "Programmer's Choice: Eight Factors in Program Decision-Making," *Journal of Broadcasting,* 14:1 (Winter, 1969–70), pp. 74–75.

9. Harriett Tramer and Leo W. Jeffres, "Talk Radio — Forum and Companion," *Journal of Broadcasting,* 27:3 (Summer, 1983), p. 300.

10. Other categories are *off-first run, off-Fox,* and *off-cable.* The first refers to series produced for syndication with only a limited number of episodes but now with enough to permit daily broadcast, or stripping. The second indicates that the series was carried originally on the Fox network, and the third on a cable network.

11. Syndicators of some highly successful network programs have sold off-network syndicated rights by confidential bid rather than negotiation. "The Cosby Show" and "Who's the Boss?" are examples.

12. Remote-control pads have given rise to another habit that causes headaches for the program manager. Many viewers employ them to scan the dial continuously, a practice known as *grazing.* The virtual saturation of the remote control also has implications for the sales department as viewers practice *zapping,* the term given to changing channels to avoid commercials. The device also permits *zipping,* the fast-forwarding of videocassette recorders through commercials in recorded programs.

13. *Broadcast Financial Journal,* March, 1976, p. 23. Used with permission of Broadcast Cable Financial Management Association.

14. 47 *CFR* 73.671(c).

15. Chris McConnell and Paige Albiniak, "Putting a Price on Public Service," *Broadcasting & Cable,* April 6, 1998, p. 70.

16. *Ibid.*

17. Jerry Wishnow, "Stand Up and Stand Out with Public Service," *Broadcasting,* May 9, 1988, p. 21.

18. *Channels: The Business of Communications,* January, 1989, p. 64.

19. "2001 Overview," *Broadcasting,* October 12, 1981, p. 214.

20. "Hispanics Set to Become Largest Minority in U.S.," *Chattanooga Times,* September 29, 1993, p. A6.

21. *Hispanic Radio Today: How Hispanics Use Radio in 1997* (New York: The Arbitron Company, 1997).

22. *1998 Report on Television*, p. 34.

23. *Ibid.*, p. 31.

24. "Advertisers Rush into Growing Market," *Broadcasting & Cable*, November 15, 1993, p. 46.

25. "Go Figure," *New Media*, November 3, 1997, p. 11.

ADDITIONAL READINGS

Broadcasting & Cable Yearbook. New Providence, NJ: R.R. Bowker, published annually.

Cantor, Muriel G., and Joel M. Cantor. *Prime-Time Television: Content and Control*, 2nd ed. Newbury Park, CA: Sage, 1991.

Carroll, Raymond L., and Donald M. Davis. *Electronic Media Programming: Strategies and Decision Making*. New York: McGraw-Hill, 1993.

Eastman, Susan Tyler, and Douglas A. Ferguson. *Broadcast/Cable Programming: Strategies and Practices*, 5th ed. Belmont, CA: Wadsworth, 1997.

Halper, Donna L. *Radio Music Directing*. Boston: Focal Press, 1991.

Howard, Herbert H., Michael S. Kievman, and Barbara A. Moore. *Radio, TV, and Cable Programming*, 2nd ed. Ames, IA: Iowa State University Press, 1994.

Langevin, Michael J. *Basic Radio Programming Manual*. Washington, DC: National Association of Broadcasters, 1996.

MacFarland, David T. *Future Radio Programming Strategies: Cultivating Listenership in the Digital Age*, 2nd ed. Mahwah, NJ: Lawrence Erlbaum, 1997.

Matelski, Marilyn J. *Daytime Television Programming*. Boston: Focal Press, 1991.

Miles, Peggy. *Internet World Guide to Webcasting: The Complete Guide to Broadcasting on the Web*. New York: John Wiley, 1998.

Norberg, Eric G. *Radio Programming: Tactics and Strategy*. Boston: Focal Press, 1996.

Vane, Edwin T., and Lynne S. Gross. *Programming for TV, Radio, and Cable*. Boston: Focal Press, 1994.

5 BROADCAST SALES

This chapter considers

- [ ] the functions of the sales department and the responsibilities and attributes of its personnel

- [ ] the sale of time to local, regional, and national advertisers

- [ ] research methods and the uses of research in sales

A broadcast station serves two kinds of customers:

Audiences, which tune to a station to hear or view its programs and which make no direct payment for the product (i.e., programs) they receive. As we have seen, obtaining audiences is the responsibility of the program department.

Advertisers, who gain access to those audiences with information on their products and services by purchasing advertising time. Obtaining advertisers is the responsibility of the sales department.

Broadcast advertisers fall into three categories:

Local: Those in the immediate geographical area of the station.

Regional: Those whose products or services are available in the area covered by the station.

National: Those whose products or services are available nationwide, including the area covered by the station.

Time is sold to local advertisers by members of the station's sales staff called *account executives.* Sales to national and regional advertisers are carried out by the station's national sales representative, or *station representative* (*station rep*) *company.*

The sales department is the principal generator of revenues for the station. However, its ability to sell time is determined to a large degree by the program department's success in drawing audiences, especially those that advertisers want to reach. Good programming attracts audiences, which in turn attract advertisers and dollars. The greater the sales revenues, the better the programming the station can provide. Together, therefore, the program department and the sales department are important parts of a cycle that has a major impact on the station's financial strength.

THE SALES DEPARTMENT

The number of sales department employees of a particular station is influenced largely by market size. Local competitive conditions also may be influential. However, departments in markets of all sizes have similar responsibilities.

Functions

The major functions of the sales department are to

- sell time to advertisers
- provide vehicles whereby advertisers can reach targeted audiences with their commercial messages at a competitive cost
- develop promotions for advertisers
- generate sufficient revenues to permit the station to operate competitively
- produce a profit for the station's owners
- contribute to the worth of the station by developing and maintaining a strong base of advertiser support

Organization

The staff and activities of the department are directed by a general sales manager (GSM), who answers to the general manager and whose specific responsibilities are described later. The following are the principal department staff:

National Sales Manager

Coordinating the sale of time to national and regional advertisers through the station rep company and maintaining contacts with local offices of national and regional accounts are the chief responsibilities of the national sales manager, who reports to the general sales manager. In many stations, the duties are carried out by the general sales manager.

Local Sales Manager

The local sales manager reports to the general sales manager and is responsible for

- planning and administering local sales
- directing and supervising account executives
- assigning actual or prospective clients to account executives
- establishing account executive sales quotas
- in some stations, carrying a list of clients

Account Executives

Account executives report to the local sales manager and

- seek out and develop new accounts
- service existing accounts
- prepare and make sales presentations
- in radio, often write and produce commercials

Co-op Coordinator

Many manufacturers reimburse retailers for part of the cost of advertising that promotes the manufacturer's product. This arrangement is known as *cooperative*, or *co-op*, *advertising*, and stations often employ a coordinator to provide co-op data to account executives. However, the responsibilities may be more extensive and may consist of

- identifying co-op opportunities
- working with retailers in the development of co-op campaigns using advertising allowance credits, called *accruals*
- handling the various elements of the campaign, such as copy and production, and overseeing the campaign's execution
- assisting retailers in filing for reimbursement of co-op expenditures

In many stations, the co-op coordinator's job has evolved to include vendor support programs. They will be discussed later in the chapter.

Once sales orders have been received and checked by the sales manager, they are confirmed and processed. Those are among the responsibilities of the *traffic department*, which often is a unit of the sales department. It is headed by a traffic manager, who reports to the general sales manager. The traffic department also

- prepares the daily program log detailing all content to be aired, including commercials
- maintains and keeps current a list of availabilities, called *avails*—in other words, time available for purchase by advertisers
- advises the sales department and the station rep company of avails
- schedules commercials and enters appropriate details on the program log
- checks that commercials are aired as ordered and scheduled
- advises the general sales manager if commercials are not broadcast or are not broadcast as scheduled, and coordinates the scheduling of *make-goods*

Clients who do not use the services of an advertising agency often require the station's assistance in writing and producing commercials. The writing usually is assigned to copywriters in the *continuity* or *creative services department*, which may be a unit of the sales or program department and which is headed by a director. Commercial production is carried out by the production staff.

THE GENERAL SALES MANAGER

Responsibilities

Like all managers, the general sales manager plans, organizes, influences, and controls. The proportion of time spent on those and other functions varies. In a large station, for example, the position may be chiefly administrative. In a smaller station, the general sales manager may be a combination national/regional and local sales manager and account executive. However, included in the major responsibilities of most general sales managers are the following:

- Developing overall sales objectives and strategies. They are drawn up in agreement with the station rep and national sales manager for national and regional sales, and with the local sales manager for local sales.
- Selecting the station representative company, in consultation with the general manager and the national sales manager.
- Preparing and controlling the department's budget, and coordinating with the business department collections, the processing of delinquent accounts, and credit checks on prospective clients.
- Developing the rate card and controlling the advertising inventory.
- Selecting, or approving the selection of, all departmental personnel and arranging for their training, if necessary.
- Setting and enforcing sales policies, and reviewing all commercial copy, recorded commercials, and sales contracts.

General sales managers engage in a variety of other duties, including the conduct of sales meetings, approval of account executive client lists, and the handling of *house accounts*, or accounts that require no selling or servicing and on which no commissions are paid. However, one of their most significant activities is the establishment of sales quotas.

The importance of revenue and expense projections in the preparation of the station's annual budget was noted in Chapter 2, "Financial Management." As the major generator of revenues, the sales department plays a key role in the station's success. If its projections are unrealistic and fall short of expectations, cost-cutting measures will have to be introduced to keep the budget in balance. Those measures might include the termination of personnel and the modification or elimination of plans for equipment purchases, programming, promotion, and other areas of station operation.

To try to avoid such an upheaval, most sales departments establish attainable annual dollar targets. In many stations, account executives are asked to submit their local sales goals for each month of the next fiscal or calendar year, reflecting adjustments for the number of weeks per month compared to the current year and the proposed percentage increase. The general sales manager and the local sales manager review them, determine their appropriateness, and make changes they deem necessary. Finally, the sales managers meet with each account executive and, together, the three agree on a final quota. In the meantime, the GSM consults with the station rep to settle on targets for national and regional sales.

When these steps have been completed, the GSM sends to the general manager the department's budget proposal listing projected revenues from local, regional, and national sales and estimated expenses. It is analyzed with the submissions from other departments, and adjustments are made to develop a balanced budget. They may consist of a reduction in requested expenditures, an increase in revenues, or both. If more revenues are called for, the GSM considers the options with the local sales manager, account executives, and the station rep, and higher goals are established by mutual agreement.

Monthly goals provide continuing, short-term targets. They may not always be met. A delay in receipt of an order, a change in a client's advertising schedule, or a temporary lull in the economy can play havoc with an account executive's expectations in a single month. Accordingly, much more serious attention is paid to the attainment of quarterly goals.

If business remains sluggish over an extended period, the general sales manager will contemplate steps to revive it. Rates may be lowered temporarily, for example. Additional sales incentives may be introduced. One station offered a ski trip to account executives who made calls on ten potential new clients in two weeks and completed at least one sale. All met the challenge and won a trip, and the station wrote $10,000 in brand new business. Of course, if these and other actions fail to produce the projected revenues, the only alternative will be a reduction in expenditures.

Qualities

To be effective, a GSM must possess many attributes. Chief among them are *knowledge*, administrative and professional *skills*, and certain *personal qualities*.

Knowledge   The general sales manager should have knowledge of

Station ownership and management: The objectives and plans of the station's owners and the general manager, and the role of the sales department in accomplishing them.

The station and staff: The station's strengths and weaknesses as an advertising medium, and the ways in which the sales function relates to the activities and functions of other departments; awareness of the motivations, potential, and limitations of sales department employees, and of their working relationship with staff in other departments.

The market and the competition: Population makeup, employment patterns, cultural and recreational activities, and business climate and trends; the sales activities and plans of competing stations and media, their successes and failures.

Sales management: The responsibilities of sales management and ways of discharging them. This includes familiarity with techniques, practices, and trends in broadcast sales and advertising; methods of estimating revenues and expenses, and of increasing revenues and controlling costs; methods, sources, and uses of marketing, sales, and audience research; marketing and sales techniques and practices, especially those used by retail stores and service companies; and the business, sales, and advertising objectives of clients and their past and present advertising practices.

Content and audiences: Types of formats, programs, and other content, their demographic appeal, and audience listening or viewing habits.

Skills   Knowledge will be translated into success only if the general sales manager is able to combine it with both managerial and professional competence in

- planning the department's objectives and strategies, explaining and justifying them to the general manager, and coordinating their accomplishment with staff and other departments

- organizing personnel and activities to attain stated objectives, and stimulating and directing employees toward their attainment

- managing the advertising inventory — that is, balancing the number of commercial units, availabilities, and cost-per-spot to maximize revenue

- controlling the department's activities by careful attention to budget, personnel strengths and shortcomings, the achievements of competing stations and media, and research findings, and by taking appropriate actions

Personal Qualities   Selling often is referred to as a "people" business. For that reason, the GSM must be able to get along with people, both inside and outside the station. An outgoing personality, combined with a cooperative attitude and high ethical standards, are absolute necessities. But a friendly exterior will not spell success in the absence of other qualities.

General sales managers are charged with generating the bulk of the station's revenues. Accordingly, they have to be

- *ambitious* in striving for the accomplishment of objectives;
- *competitive* in approaching their responsibilities and meeting the challenges posed by other stations and media; and
- *persuasive* in their dealings with clients, advertising agencies, and the station rep.

Finally, they must be *adaptable* to changing business conditions, and *creative* in developing sales techniques and promotions and in motivating their staff.

TIME SALES

Time is sold to advertisers by the second. The majority of sales in radio are 30- or 60-second spot announcements, called *spots*. In television, the 30-second spot is standard, and a limited number of 15- and 10-second spots are also available. Many broadcast stations also sell blocks of time for the airing of programs.

The Rate Card

Traditionally, radio stations listed the cost of time on a published rate card. The major factors in determining cost were the time of day at which the spots were to run and the number of spots purchased, hence the name *frequency card*.

In time, most stations moved to a *grid card* in which the principal determinants are the supply of, and demand for, time. Grid cards are still used by many radio stations. Increasingly, however, computerization has permitted stations to introduce an *electronic rate card*. Using revenue goals and a variety of other variables, such as supply and demand, daypart, traditional sellout periods, and the flow of demand during the week, the station may select from a number of software programs to develop its rate structure.

The electronic rate card in Figure 5.1 shows that the station sells time in four dayparts and that the cost of a 60-second spot varies by daypart and day of the week. Morning drive Monday through Friday carries a high price tag because the station airs a syndicated program with a limited number of local avails. Although not included in the rate card, 30-second spots also may be purchased. In addition, the station offers a *Total Audience Plan* (*TAP*), whereby advertisers may obtain equal distribution of spots in the first three dayparts or in all four.

Figure 5.1 *Radio station electronic rate card.*

	Mon	Tue	Wed	Thu	Fri	Sat	Sun
6:00 A.M.–10:00 A.M.	100	100	100	100	100	25	15
10:00 A.M.–3:00 P.M.	60	60	60	65	65	65	25
3:00 P.M.–7:00 P.M.	60	60	70	75	75	50	25
7:00 P.M.–12:00 A.M.	15	15	20	20	20	15	15

The electronic rate card offers several advantages. It compels the sales manager to pay continuing attention to inventory. As a result, inventory should be easier to manage and the station should be able to generate maximum revenues by pricing available time to reflect current supply and demand. At the same time, however, it reduces the account executive's flexibility because special rates cannot be offered. Clients also may conclude that rates are negotiable because of their wide variation.

In addition to selling by daypart, most radio stations sell sponsorships in certain programs (e.g., news, sports) and in daily features (e.g., business report), with specific rates for each.

For the most-part, television stations sell time in, and adjacent to, programs and not by daypart. They have used grid cards for many years to adjust rates in response to demand.

Figure 5.2 shows part of a grid rate card used by a television station that sells at five levels. As an example of how the selling level is determined, assume that demand for time in "Entertainment Tonight" is low. An advertiser may be able to buy 30-second spots at level 5, or $150 each. However, if demand is high, the advertiser may have to pay $350 at level 1.

Note the following:

- Local news is in high demand and is priced accordingly.

- Prices of other programs rise and fall as audience size increases and decreases.

- The same rates are set for all time periods in the three-hour news and news magazine block from 6:00 A.M. to 9:00 A.M. and in the two-hour afternoon soap opera block, without regard to the program in which the spot appears. A similar practice is followed in other blocks, also.

- Only the cost of 30-second spots is included on the card. However, other lengths are sold: 60-second spots at double the 30-second rate, and 15- and 10-second spots at 75 percent and 50 percent of the 30-second rate, respectively.

The rate card in Figure 5.2 reflects costs in regularly scheduled, Monday-through-Friday programs on a network-affiliated station. Costs vary according to audience size for network prime-time programs. They vary, too, for weekend network sports programs, specials, and movies, and are influenced by the anticipated appeal of each to the station's audience. Special rates are used for news updates, which usually include a 10-second spot and an open billboard announcing sponsorship.

Even though a rate card lists the costs of time, cash does not always change hands every time an advertiser obtains time on a broadcast station. Many stations exchange time for merchandise or services in a transaction known variously as a *trade, tradeout,* or *barter.* For example, advertisers may provide the station with travel, food, or furniture for its own use or as contest prizes, in return for advertising time with an equivalent cost. Some stations use trades to persuade hesitant businesses to advertise, and hope that they will be able to convert to a cash sale later. Merchandise or services instead of cash are accepted by many stations to settle delinquent accounts.

Figure 5.2   *Excerpt from television station grid rate card.*

Monday to Friday

			30 Second			
		1	2	3	4	5
A.M.						
6:00–7:00	Action News Today	200	175	150	125	100
7:00–9:00	Today Show	200	175	150	125	100
9:00–10:00	Sally Jessy Raphael	80	70	60	50	40
10:00–11:00	Howie Mandel	70	60	50	40	30
11:00–11:30	Martha Stewart Living	60	50	40	30	20
11:30–12:00	Gayle King	60	50	40	30	20
P.M.						
12:00–1:00	Sunset Beach	60	50	40	30	20
1:00–2:00	Leeza	60	50	40	30	20
2:00–3:00	Another World	150	125	100	90	80
3:00–4:00	Days of Our Lives	150	125	100	90	80
4:00–5:00	Montel Williams	125	100	80	70	60
5:00–5:30	Action News at 5:00	350	300	250	200	175
5:30–6:00	Action News at 5:30	350	300	250	200	175
6:00–6:30	Action News at 6:00	500	450	400	350	300
7:00–7:30	Entertainment Tonight	350	300	250	200	150
7:30–8:00	Hard Copy	350	300	250	200	150
11:00–11:35	Action News Tonight	600	500	400	350	300

Barter programming also is used to acquire time. As noted in Chapter 4, "Broadcast Programming," it permits a syndicator to obtain time, at no cost, for sale to national advertisers in return for supplying programs to the station without charge.

Cooperative, or *co-op, advertising* was mentioned earlier in the chapter. It allows a retailer to enjoy the benefits of advertising at less than rate card prices. In a co-op deal, the retailer receives from the manufacturer reimbursement for part or all of the cost of advertising that features the manufacturer's product. The percentage of reimbursement usually is tied to the value of the retailer's product purchase and carries a dollar limit. For instance, a hardware store may buy $20,000 worth of lawnmowers and qualify for 50 percent reimbursement to a maximum of $2,000.

Vendor support programs enable a retailer to obtain manufacturer (vendor) dollars to cover the advertising costs. In a *direct vendor program,* the retailer develops a proposal (often in cooperation with a station account executive) to promote the sale of a product, and presents it to the vendor or product distributor for financial support. For example, a grocery store may plan to highlight a product in an in-store promotion. It may propose a schedule of radio commercials that would advertise both the product and the store. In a *reverse vendor program*, the vendor approaches the retailer with funding to support a promotion. Monies provided under a vendor program are not subject to the kinds of product purchase requirements that apply to co-op, and represent another method whereby a retailer may acquire time without paying rate card prices.

Another method is through *per-inquiry advertising*, whereby an advertiser pays on the basis of the number of responses generated by the advertising. The practice is not widespread, but it is used by some stations, especially with mail order companies that pay the station a percentage of money received on sales of the advertised product.

Per-inquiry advertising is frowned on by most stations. So, too, is rate cutting, often called "selling below the card" or "selling off the card." Most stations express verbal opposition to cutting rates but many engage in it, especially when business is bad or when an advertiser threatens to make the buy on a competing station unless the rate is reduced.

Some stations disguise rate cutting by awarding advertisers *bonus spots*, also called *spins*. No charge is made for them since they are given as a consideration for buying other spots. The effect is that the advertiser receives time for less than the price quoted on the rate card.

Even though rate cutting may lead to a short-term spurt in sales for the station, it can result in a price war and create instability in the market. It conditions advertisers to believe that prices are negotiable and brings into question the value of commercial time on all stations. Ultimately, of course, it may be self-defeating, since stations have a limited amount of time to sell, and an increase in sales at less than the rate card price may not produce an increase in revenues.

Sales Policies

Time is a perishable commodity. Once it has passed, it cannot be sold to an advertiser. This fact imposes on the sales department an obligation to manage its commercial inventory in such a way that it produces the maximum possible financial return.

As a first step, the department must ensure that the rate card is realistic, based on considerations such as the size or characteristics of the audience, market size, and competitive conditions. But inventory management also requires the development of sales policies that will make time available and attractive to advertisers, and that will not result in audience tune-out.

Most stations have policies on the following:

Amounts of Time that May Be Purchased
As noted earlier, radio stations sell mostly commercial units of 30 and 60 seconds. Thirty-second units are the norm in television. Longer periods of time usually may be bought in both media for the broadcast of entire programs.

Number of Commercial Breaks per Hour

Most stations limit the number of breaks for commercials and other non-program material to reduce the possibility of alienating the audience with frequent interruptions in programming.

Number of Commercials per Break

Stations that have only a few breaks per hour may have to air several minutes of commercials in each to meet revenue needs. Infrequent breaks may please the audience but upset the advertiser, whose commercial may become lost in a succession of announcements, a situation known as *clutter*.

Number of Commercial Minutes per Hour

Again, the goal is to schedule enough commercials to satisfy revenue demands, but not so many as to drive away audiences, especially to competing stations. Many stations continue to adhere to the standards of the now-discontinued radio and television codes of the National Association of Broadcasters. Under the Radio Code, stations agreed not to broadcast more than 18 minutes of commercials per hour. The Television Code limited network-affiliated stations to not more than 9 minutes and 30 seconds of commercials and other nonprogram material (e.g., promotional announcements) in prime time, and 16 minutes at other times. For independent stations, the limits were 14 and 16 minutes, respectively.

Rate Protection

Most stations guarantee advertisers that the price in effect at the time a sales contract is signed will not change for a specific length of time, even if rates are increased in the meantime.

Product Protection

Advertisers prefer that commercials for competing products or services not be aired adjacent to, or in the same breaks, as theirs. A product protection policy guarantees that a certain time will elapse before such spots are broadcast. If spots for competing products do run back to back for some reason, most stations allow advertisers a choice of a rebate, credit, or make-good.

Product Acceptance

A policy that states the categories of products or services for which the station will not accept advertising.

Continuity Acceptance

The wording and/or visuals of commercials must meet standards determined by the station.

Make-Goods

When a spot does not run or is aired improperly, the station offers the advertiser a *make-good*, or another time for the commercial.

Additional Costs

A policy on costs the advertiser will incur beyond the purchase of time. Many radio stations include production and talent costs in the rate card price. However, such costs may be added to the purchase price if the commercials are sent for broadcast on other stations.

With two exceptions, a station creates sales policies that are consistent with its revenue objectives and its perception of responsible operation. The first exception grows out of the Children's Television Act of 1990, which directed the FCC to adopt rules limiting the amount of commercial matter that television stations may air during children's programming. As a result, the commission approved a restriction on commercial time in programs directed toward viewers 12 and under to 10.5 minutes per hour on weekends and 12 minutes per hour on weekdays. At the same time, it reaffirmed its long-standing prohibition on "program-length commercials" (i.e., programs associated with a product and within which a commercial for the product is broadcast), and on "host selling," or the use of program talent to advertise products.

The second exception applies to both radio and television stations and deals with the sale of time to candidates for public office. The following policies apply:

Access Section 312 of the Communications Act of 1934, as amended, gives the Federal Communications Commission the right to revoke a broadcast station's license "for willful or repeated failure to allow reasonable access to or to permit purchase of reasonable amounts of time for the use of a broadcasting station by a legally qualified candidate for Federal elective office on behalf of his candidacy."

Federal candidates are the only ones to whom a station must grant access or sell time. However, if time is sold to a candidate for any elective office, Section 315(a) of the Communications Act applies:

> If any licensee shall permit any person who is a legally qualified candidate for any public office to use a broadcasting station, he shall afford equal opportunities to all other such candidates for that office in the use of such broadcasting station: *Provided*, That such licensee shall have no power of censorship over the material broadcast under the provisions of this section.

Charges Section 73.1942 of the FCC's Rules and Regulations stipulates the prices that the station may charge political candidates:

> The charges, if any, made for the use of any broadcasting station by any person who is a legally qualified candidate for any public office in connection with his or her campaign for nomination for election, or election, to such office shall not exceed: (1) During the 45 days preceding the date of a primary or primary runoff election and during the 60 days preceding the date of a general or special election in which such person is a candidate, the lowest unit charge of the station for the same class and amount of time for the same period. (i) A candidate shall be charged no more per unit than the station charges its most favored commercial advertisers for the same classes and amounts of time for the same periods. Any station practices offered to commercial advertisers that enhance the value of advertising spots must be disclosed and made available to candidates on equal terms. Such practices include but are not limited to any discount privileges that affect the value of advertising, such as bonus spots, time-sensitive make goods, preemption priorities, or any other factors that enhance the value of the announcement. (2) At any time other than the respective periods set forth in paragraph (a) (1) of

this section, stations may charge legally qualified candidates for public office no more than the charges made for comparable use of the station by commercial advertisers. The rates, if any, charged all such candidates for the same office shall be uniform and shall not be rebated by any means, direct or indirect. A candidate shall be charged no more than the rate the station would charge for comparable commercial advertising. All discount privileges otherwise offered by a station to commercial advertisers must be disclosed and made available upon equal terms to all candidates for public office.[1]

Discrimination Section 73.1941 provides that

In making time available to candidates for public office, no licensee shall make any discrimination between candidates in practices, regulations, facilities, or services for or in connection with the service rendered pursuant to this part, or make or give any preference to any candidate for public office or subject any such candidate to any prejudice or disadvantage; nor shall any licensee make any contract or other agreement which shall have the effect of permitting any legally qualified candidate for any public office to broadcast to the exclusion of other legally qualified candidates for the same public office.[2]

Records Section 73.1943 requires stations to maintain and make available for public inspection certain political records:

Every licensee shall keep and permit public inspection of a complete and orderly record (political file) of all requests for broadcast time made by or on behalf of a candidate for public office, together with an appropriate notation showing the disposition made' by the licensee of such requests, and the charges made, if any, if the request is granted. The "disposition" includes the schedule of time purchased, when spots actually aired, the rates charged, and the classes of time purchased. When free time is provided for use by or on behalf of candidates, a record of the free time provided shall be placed in the political file. All records required by this paragraph shall be placed in the political file as soon as possible and shall be retained for a period of two years. As soon as possible means immediately absent unusual circumstances.

Time Requests The candidate is responsible for requesting equal opportunities:

A request for equal opportunities must be submitted to the licensee within 1 week of the day on which the first prior use giving rise to the right of equal opportunities occurred: Provided, however, That where the person was not a candidate at the time of such first prior use, he or she shall submit his or her request within 1 week of the first subsequent use after he or she has become a legally qualified candidate for the office in question.[3]

Proof Additionally, proving that the equal opportunities provision applies rests with the candidate:

A candidate requesting equal opportunities of the licensee or complaining of noncompliance to the Commission shall have the burden of proving that he or she and his or her opponent are legally qualified candidates for the same public office.[4]

Local Sales: The Account Executive

As indicated earlier, local sales are the responsibility of staff members known as account executives.

Hiring Success in attaining local sales objectives is tied closely to the station's ability to attract and select persons with the appropriate background and personal attributes. If they are selected wisely, the station will reap significant financial returns; if not, the station will face constant turnover, resulting in lost sales, disruptions in relationships with clients, and the time, effort, and expense of finding and training replacements.

Sources Many people are attracted to careers in broadcasting because of the glamour that accompanies work as a disc jockey or television news anchor, or the opportunity for creative expression through writing or production. Relatively few show an initial interest in sales, despite the fact that it offers better financial prospects and an avenue for advancement to top management.

In their search for account executives, stations turn to various sources:

Other stations: Persons working as account executives in other stations in the market bring with them familiarity with broadcast sales, local clients, and the community. Those hired from outside the market are familiar with the first, but have to develop relationships with local clients and an awareness of the community.

Other media: Newspapers, outdoor, transit, and other advertising media provide a source of employees with knowledge of sales and advertising and an understanding of the methods, strengths, and shortcomings of the medium in which they have been employed.

Advertising agencies: Awareness of agency practices, clients, and the relative advantages and disadvantages of different media are among the qualities offered by advertising agency account executives and media buyers.

College or university graduates: Broadcasting or communication graduates bring to the position some knowledge of media theory and practices. Business graduates may be equipped similarly in sales and marketing. The best prospects are those who have included in their academic program an internship, or who have gained practical experience through part-time work.

Other: Other sources include persons currently working in the station, especially in sales, traffic, continuity or creative services, or production. They are familiar with the station and its personnel, and should understand the role and responsibilities of the account executive. Persons with a successful background in selling, especially in the sale of intangibles, also may have the experience and potential to succeed.

Qualifications Probably the best predictor of success as an account executive is a record of accomplishment in broadcast sales. However, in selecting among all candidates, the station should consider *knowledge, skills,* and *personal qualities.*

Knowledge   Applicants for account executive positions should have, or show the ability to develop, knowledge of

Broadcast and other media: their operations, personnel, and relative strengths and weaknesses as advertising vehicles

The station and its competitors: programming, personalities, coverage, and the characteristics of audiences for different formats or programs

The market: employment, work hours, households, retail sales, consumer spendable income, buying habits, and the listening or viewing population

Sales and marketing: techniques and practices, and the categories, sales cycles, and special sales periods of retailers

Research: terminology, and the uses of research in sales

Skills   The account executive should have the ability or potential to set and attain objectives, plan and manage time, communicate effectively, keep accurate records, and relate to people and their problems. On a daily basis, skills in preparing and delivering sales presentations, selling and servicing accounts, and interpreting and using research are required.

Personal Qualities   Ambition, initiative, and energy are prerequisites for anyone seeking success in sales. Persistence, persuasiveness, imagination, integrity, and professionalism in behavior and dress are equally necessary for the broadcast account executive.

Training   Stations recognize that new employees with little or no experience will be productive only if they understand what is expected of them and are equipped with the knowledge and skills to function effectively. Many stations organize formal training programs to introduce new account executives to their responsibilities and to the information and techniques they will be required to master to achieve success.

Typically, a training program includes details of the station's expectations on the number of contacts and sales presentations, and the amount of business that should be accomplished within a certain period of time. It introduces the employee to the medium, and to the station and its personnel, particularly those departments and people whose work affects, or is affected by, the sales department.

For example, the new account executive should become familiar as soon as possible with the station's format or programming, and with traffic, continuity or creative services, and production personnel and practices. Methods of prospecting or finding new business, preparing and presenting sales proposals, processing orders, maintaining records, and compiling activity reports should also be covered.

Figure 5.3 contains an example of a two-week training program for radio station account executives. In addition to the activities listed, trainees are required to complete daily readings, listen to audiotapes, view videotapes and slide-tape presentations, and spend part of each day observing the work of the sales department.

Figure 5.3 *Training program for radio station account executives.*

Day	Activities
1.	Tour of station and introduction to staff Role of the salesperson The radio medium Advertising on radio Presentations by the news director, program director, and a disc jockey Rate cards
2.	Attend sales meeting Audience research: how to read, understand, and use as a sales tool Exercise in the use of research Conducting research on clients and prospects
3.	Interpersonal relations: dealing with clients and prospects Role-playing exercises on interpersonal relations Prospecting Making the appointment
4.	Selling techniques Written sales proposals Sales presentations Time management Co-op advertising: opportunities and pitfalls Processing orders Availabilities Make-goods
5.	Competitive media: strengths and weaknesses Radio positioning proposals Attempt to schedule three appointments for days 7–9
6.	Follow-up on appointments Collections Presentations by traffic manager, continuity director, sales secretary Sales promotions
7.	Appointments or introductions to clients Review of appointments or introductions
8.	Appointments Introductions to clients Ride with another account executive
9.	Prospecting/appointments for following week Appointments Introductions to clients Ride with another account executive
10.	Deliver sample sales presentation to general and local sales managers Presentation review Review of training program Appointments for following week Introductions to clients

New employees with previous broadcast sales experience may not be required to participate in all training activities. However, they should attend those that permit them to become familiar with the station and its personnel and with the department's sales policies and practices.

Training does not end with an initial program of the kind outlined in Figure 5.3. It should be a continuing requirement for new and existing account executives so that they may enhance their knowledge, stay abreast of new sales techniques and strategies, and improve their performance.

Sales Tools   The most important tool of the account executive is knowledge that will permit the creation of a sales proposal geared to the interests and needs of each client or prospect. Knowledge of the *market*, the *station*, and the *client* are of particular importance.

Market Data   The account executive should be familiar with the people and business activity of the market, including the size and composition of the population, median income and purchasing power, and retail sales and buying patterns. Knowledge of the work force and working hours, and of cultural and recreational pursuits, also should be part of the account executive's database.

Station Data   To show how the station can assist the client or prospect in attaining objectives, the account executive should have knowledge of the station's

- audience, especially those characteristics that are important to the advertiser and how they compare to the characteristics of audiences for competing stations or programs
- format or programs, and their appeal to the advertiser's actual or potential customers
- commercial policies, particularly those that will afford the advertiser distinctive, uncluttered access to the audience
- availabilities, to show how the prospect can gain access to targeted customers
- rate card, to present a package that meets the advertiser's objectives at an acceptable cost

Other data that may be helpful in making a sale include the success achieved by advertisers currently using the station, awards won by the station and its employees, and the quality of staff and the facilities available to produce commercial messages.

Client Data   One of the most frequent objections by advertisers is that account executives do not know the advertiser's business. Some stations try to alleviate that problem by inviting current advertisers to station sales meetings to educate the sales staff. However, in compiling a tailor-made proposal, the account executive must understand the particular needs of each client or prospect.

To do that effectively calls for detailed knowledge of the product or service category, business location or locations, customer characteristics, and major competitors. Familiarity with the client's or prospect's objectives, successes, and problems, their past and present advertising, sales, and marketing activities, and their advertising budget and its current disposition also is required.

To obtain such information, the Radio Advertising Bureau (RAB) recommends an interview with prospects using the form in Figure 5.4. The form can easily be adapted for use by television stations. Answers to the questions should permit the account executive to develop a profile of the business and to prepare a sales proposal that will be responsive to the prospect's needs.

Knowledge of the market, station, and prospective client may not be sufficient for prospects who have not engaged in paid advertising in the past. They may have to be convinced of the value of advertising and, for that reason, the account executive should be familiar with the benefits that advertising brings. The RAB's list of ten reasons to advertise (Figure 5.5) provides useful information to meet such a challenge.

Prospects who have not used radio or television previously may have to be persuaded of the medium's advantages as an advertising vehicle. The radio account executive may cite some of that medium's strengths:

- Radio reaches virtually every U.S. consumer.

   Radio is heard by virtually every American, every week of the year. They listen more than three hours each and every day.

- Radio is everywhere.

   Whatever they're doing (working, relaxing, exercising, traveling, shopping), wherever they are (at home, at play, behind the wheel, and even at work), only radio accompanies your customers and prospects wherever they go, whatever they do.

- Radio offers the ultimate in targetability via a host of programming and format options.

- Radio reaches the big spenders.

   Upscale individuals with above-average incomes and affluent lifestyles spend more of their disposable income on big-ticket items — and spend more of their time with radio.

- Radio allows you to achieve the message frequency necessary to stand out from the competition.

   The average American is bombarded by 3,000 to 5,000 marketing impressions each day. To break through this clutter successfully, you need a medium that not only targets your best prospects, but also delivers the message *enough times* to make a lasting impression. Radio advertising uniquely is intrusive. Consumers listen only to their favorite stations — and they listen for long periods of time, giving you the best possible opportunity to achieve the *message repetition* so necessary to a successful advertising campaign.

- Radio is the only truly portable, mobile medium.

   Most Americans spend their lives on the run. Only radio takes your selling message to today's active, acquisitive consumers wherever they are and however they got there.

Figure 5.4 *Radio Advertising Bureau Sales Consultancy Interview form.*
(© Radio Advertising Bureau. Used with permission.)

THE RAB SALES CONSULTANCY INTERVIEW

TO BE FILLED IN IN ADVANCE OF INTERVIEW IF POSSIBLE

Name of firm _____   Business Type _____

Address _____   Phone Number _____

Slogan _____   Landmarks (near any well-known locations, in

shopping center, downtown?) _____

Name of person being interviewed. Should be primary decision maker.

Name_____   Title _____

Name of others involved in advertising decisions. (At business or agency) _____

Name _____   Title _____

Name _____   Title _____

Co-op Sources (Brands carried by advertiser that give co-op)_____

_____

1. Thanks for giving me this time. To arrive at an effective media strategy, it's necessary to learn about your business. First, how long have you been in business? _____Date opened?_____

2. How many stores (branches) do you have?_____ 3. Where are they?_____

_____

4. What do you consider your biggest advantages? Why do people come to you rather than a competitor?

_____

5. What exclusive advantages do you have?_____

_____

6. Who are your major competitors? _____

_____

7. You run such an excellent operation here, why do people go to your competitors?_____

_____

8. As you know, more and more advertisers use Radio co-op with manufacturer support. To save your time I've written down some of the brands you carry which give Radio co-op (mention those listed above), like_____

_____

Are there others you'd like to include?_____

_____

Figure 5.4   *Continued*

9. It's important to our planning to learn about your customers. **What percentage would you say are**
   Adult Males? _____ Adult Women? _____ Male Teens? _____ Female Teens? _____

10. Generally what is the age range of most of your customers? _____

11. What would you judge their income to be? Lower, middle, upper? _____

12. Where do most of your customers live? _____

13. What are your best months? _____ 14.   Your best days? _____

15. Are you open Sunday? _____ 16.   What nights are you open late? _____

17. Now, in the order of importance, please give me your most important sales events. Give me them all
   for the last year, with dates, please.

   _____   _____

   _____   _____

   _____   _____

18. Now, let's think about what we're trying to accomplish. What image of your business would you
   most like to put into the heads of shoppers? _____

   _____

19. Thinking about advertising, what do you like most about Newspapers? _____

   _____ TV _____

   Radio_____

   Others?_____

20. What do you like least about Newspaper? _____

   _____ TV? _____

   Radio? _____

   Others? _____

21. What's your basic advertising medium? _____ What percentage of the budget does it get? _____

22. What is your total advertising budget in dollars? _____

23. Finally, how would you like your message on Radio to sound? Are there Radio commercials you particularly like? _____

   _____

Thanks for your time and confidence. Let's set a date now for our next meeting, when I'll be back with a
specific proposal...after I've analysed the interview, talked to my management and called on outside advertising resources.

- Radio reaches your customers and prospects right up to the time of
  purchase.

  The closer a selling message can get to the cash register, the better its
  chance of actually influencing the purchase. A new major study shows that

more consumers are reached by radio than any other major medium within an hour of making their largest purchase of the day.

- Radio listeners are almost fanatically loyal to their favorite stations and personalities and, as a result, they spend more time with radio than with any other medium.

- Radio not only mixes well with other media, but it also takes up where other media fall short.

  Using radio with newspaper increases your reach and helps ensure coverage among light readers and younger consumers.

  Light TV viewers (38 percent of adults) spend more than three hours per day with radio. By adding radio to your media plan, you reach this upscale segment of the market that you might otherwise miss.

  Outdoor exposure decreases during bad weather and adverse traffic conditions, but radio listening actually increases during these times.

  Since almost half of all direct mail is never opened, you need the intrusive power of radio to call attention to your mailings and precondition recipients to the benefits of reading and responding to your direct mail offers.

- Radio is the most flexible of all your advertising options.

  Copy changes can be made at a moment's notice. New commercials can be produced quickly and efficiently. If your supplier surprises you with a double order this morning, you can advertise a fire sale tonight. Whatever the changes, whenever they occur, you can react instantly with radio.

- Radio is the most cost-effective of all advertising media.

  Radio targets and motivates the specific customers you select and does it more cost-efficiently than any other medium. Minimum production time and expense make it the most cost-efficient advertising medium in America today.

- Radio uniquely offers proactive, promotional opportunities simply not available from any other medium.

  Radio stations know how to build and maintain an audience — through great programming often supported by promotional activities that keep listeners coming back for more. And no other medium knows more about how to plan and execute a successful promotion than radio. [5]

The television account executive may point to that medium's

- persuasiveness, growing out of its combination of sight, sound, motion, and color

- reputation as the most memorable, credible, exciting, and influential advertising medium

- capacity to involve viewers emotionally

- ability to demonstrate products and plant in viewers' minds images of product packaging, uses, and benefits

- broad demographic appeal and ability to reach *all* demographics

- large daily audiences

- wide geographic coverage

- record of bestowing prestige on advertisers and products

Figure 5.5 *RAB's Ten Reasons to Advertise. (Used with permission.)*

---

1. Advertising Creates Store Traffic
Continuous store traffic is the first step toward increasing sales and expanding your base of shoppers. The more people who come into the store, the more opportunities you have to make sales. A National Retail Federation survey found that for every 100 items shoppers plan to buy, they make 30 unanticipated purchases.

2. Advertising Attracts New Customers
Your market changes constantly. Newcomers to your area mean new customers to reach. People earn more money, which means changes in lifestyles and buying habits. The shopper who wouldn't consider your business a few years ago may be a prime customer now.

3. Advertising Encourages Repeat Business
Shoppers don't have the store loyalty they once did. Shoppers have mobility and freedom of choice. You must advertise to keep pace with your competition. The National Retail Federation states: "Mobility and non-loyalty are rampant. Stores must promote to get former customers to return, and to seek new ones."

4. Advertising Generates Continuous Business
Your doors are open. Employees are on the payroll. Even the slowest days produce sales. As long as you're in business, you've got overhead to meet and new people to reach. Advertising can generate traffic now . . . and in the future.

5. Advertising Is an Investment in Success
Advertising gives you a long-term advantage over competitors who cut back or cancel advertising. A survey of more than 3,000 companies found . . .
* Advertisers who maintained or expanded advertising over a five-year period saw their sales increase on average of 100%.
* Companies which cut advertising grew at less than half the rate of those that advertised steadily.

6. Advertising Keeps You in the Competitive Race
There are only so many consumers in the market ready to buy at any one time. You have to advertise to keep regular customers, and to counterbalance the advertising of your competition. You must advertise to keep or expand your market share or you will lose to more aggressive competitors.

7. Advertising Keeps Your Business Top-of-Mind with Shoppers
Many people postpone buying decisions. They often go from store to store comparing prices, quality and service. Advertising must reach them steadily throughout the entire decision-making process. Your name must be fresh in their minds when they decide to buy.

8. Advertising Gives Your Business a Successful Image
In a competitive market, rumors and bad news travel fast. Nothing sets the record straight faster than advertising; it tells your customers and competitors that your doors are open and you're ready for business. Advertising that is vigorous and positive can bring shoppers into the marketplace, regardless of the economy.

9. Advertising Maintains Morale
Positive advertising boosts morale. It gives your staff strong, additional support. When advertising or promotion is suddenly cut or canceled, salespeople and employees may become alarmed or demoralized. They may start false rumors in the honest belief that your business is in trouble.

10. Advertising Brings in Big Bucks for Your Business
Advertising works. Businesses that succeed are usually strong, steady advertisers. Look around. You'll find the most aggressive and consistent advertisers are almost invariably the most successful. Join their ranks by advertising, and watch your business grow!

Many stations include relevant market and station data in a sales kit, a variety of materials usually contained in an attractive folder and designed to demonstrate the station's ability to generate traffic for the prospect. The kit might consist of details of the market's population, the size and characteristics of the audience, personality profiles, a coverage map, cost and effectiveness comparisons with other media, and reprints of newspaper or magazine articles about the station and of the station's trade and consumer advertising.

The Sales Proposal   In the past, account executives relied heavily on the sales kit to obtain an order. They expected that an impressive array of information about the station would be sufficiently persuasive. What they failed to realize is that advertisers are interested in the station only when they understand how it can help further their business.

Today, many sales managers are demanding written, custom sales proposals. Instead of an all-purpose collection of materials, account executives are being required to develop a personalized proposal that addresses the special needs of each potential client. The proposal includes frequent references to the prospect, and the material is organized to make reading easy. It is brief and to the point.

For example, a radio station's proposal to an above-ground pool retailer that does not advertise on radio might begin with a list of campaign objectives: for example, position the store as the best in the market and pool ownership as simple, economical, and fun; and identify the targets as families with children, living in outlying areas. That might be followed by a description of campaign strategy: such as a heavy schedule of commercials to make the message inescapable; a repetition of the themes of speed and ease of installation, simplicity of maintenance, and low monthly payments. A statement about radio's ability to reach families throughout the day and to do so at a lower cost than competing media might be followed by details of the target audience (adults 25 to 54) that listen to the station in outlying and rural areas where above-ground pools are very popular. Finally, the campaign objectives are repeated and a specific advertising schedule is presented, showing the number of spots proposed, when they would air, and the weekly cost.

Note that the proposal includes a recommended advertising schedule. Merely to sell time would bring the account executive a commission, but might not produce increased business for the advertiser and could make it difficult or impossible to obtain a subsequent order.

The most widely accepted measures of a schedule's effectiveness are *reach* and *frequency*. Reach refers to the number of different homes or persons targeted by the advertiser who see or hear the commercial. Frequency is the number of times the targeted homes or persons are exposed to it.

Both goals may be accomplished through a *saturation schedule*, a heavy load of commercials aired in time periods when the targeted homes or persons are tuned in. In contrast, a *spectrum plan* exposes different people to the commercial, but only occasionally. It involves the purchase of a moderate number of spots distributed throughout the day.

A *spot schedule* is a series of commercials aired in only one or two periods of the day, and is aimed at reaching the target audience that is most available during those periods. It is used to reach a large number of people in a particular demographic category.

A *rotation plan* gives an advertiser exposure to a similar or different audience over a period of time. With *horizontal rotation*, the commercials are broadcast at or about the same time daily. *Vertical rotation* places the commercials throughout the day.

Advertisers who want to stretch their campaign may buy time on an "on-and-off" basis. In other words, they may run a succession of two-week schedules with a one-week interruption between them. Some account executives refer to this practice as a *blinking schedule*.

The Sales Call Account executives handle two kinds of accounts:

Direct: The account executive deals directly with the advertiser, obtaining the order and receiving the copy and/or tape or arranging for the commercial to be written and/or produced by the station. The station bills the advertiser.

Agency: An advertising agency writes and/or produces (or arranges for the production of) the client's commercial and buys time from the account executive on the client's behalf. The station bills the agency, which receives a commission of 15 percent on the dollar amount of time purchased.

Each account executive is given an exclusive list of accounts on which to call. The most equitable method of compiling the list is to assign a variety of product or service categories to each salesperson. Assigning on a geographical basis so that all areas of the market are covered can lead to imbalances in sales opportunities and create morale problems. Assigning by category (e.g., furniture stores, automobile dealerships) enables the account executive to develop a good knowledge of the product and of category sales and marketing practices, but many advertisers object to dealing with someone who does business with competing companies.

In addition to equity, a major consideration in assigning accounts is compatibility. Usually, attempts are made to match an account executive with a prospect or client on the basis of their respective personalities and temperaments.

The purpose of sales calls is to obtain an order. However, few sales are made the first time an account executive calls on a prospect. Often, the first meeting is used to learn as much as possible about the prospect's business and needs so that a proposal may be prepared for presentation during a second visit.

To successfully generate initial and repeat sales to a direct account, the account executive should take certain actions *before, during,* and *after the call:*

Before Identify the person who handles the prospect's advertising and is authorized to buy time and sign a sales contract.

Make an appointment to meet with individuals at their convenience. Develop knowledge of the prospect's

- business or service
- customer characteristics
- past and present advertising activity

- advertising budget (or an approximation) and how and when it is allocated
- objectives and problems
- previous dealings with the station, if any

Be aware of the interests and personalities of the persons to whom the proposal will be presented, and of their buying habits (e.g., whether they buy in small or large quantities).

Prepare a written proposal that addresses the prospect's needs and includes an advertising schedule and its costs.

Ensure that printed or other materials (e.g., a spec tape or sample commercial) to be used in the presentation are ready and taken on the call.

During   Describe and explain the proposal, with frequent reference to the prospect's needs and the ways in which the proposal will help meet them. Remember to

- Keep the presentation brief.
- Invite questions, and design the answers so that they reinforce major points contained in the proposal.
- Ask for the order.
- Have the client sign and date the sales contract.
- Obtain a production order if the client wants the station to write and/or produce the commercial.

After   Process the order. The routing of the order varies, but generally it is checked by the local sales manager and then cleared against availabilities. If requested times are available, details are sent to traffic for entry on the program log. If copy and/or production are required, relevant information is provided to the persons responsible. In some stations, bookkeeping receives a copy of the order for billing purposes; in others, clients are billed from the log.

Prepare a report on the call, noting the name of the client and the person seen, the date, the content of the presentation, its results, and comments.

Service the account. Diligent servicing paves the way for subsequent sales. It begins with monitoring the progress of the order from its delivery at the station to the time the commercial begins to air.

Problems can occur, and it is the responsibility of the account executive to ensure that they are resolved. Additionally, the account executive should check with the client regularly during the advertising's schedule to assess its results. Adjustments may be necessary if the commercial appears to be having limited or no effect. Maintaining contact with the client is a continuing responsibility, and should be accompanied by acts of appreciation, such as invitations to lunch or dinner, offers of tickets to cultural, sports, and other events, or similar gestures.

If a sale did not result from the call, the account executive should analyze the reasons why and develop another proposal that addresses the prospect's reservations or concerns. Often, the reason may lie in the account executive's inability to deal with objections raised by the prospect. Most are predictable, and the account executive should anticipate them and be ready to respond.

The following are among the objections mentioned most frequently, and the actions that may be taken to counter them:

"You're too expensive."

Probe to discover what the prospect is using for comparison. Another station? Another medium? Point to the prospect's selection of a superior (and more expensive) location for doing business or to something about the business (e.g., a large and impressive sign) that is expensive but, presumably, successful. Stress that the prospect will be buying much more than a schedule of commercials, such as the number of people who will be reached, their characteristics (underlining the fact that they are potential customers), the station's expertise in commercial production, and so on. Rather than speaking of the cost of the schedule, emphasize the cost of reaching individuals and how it compares to other stations or media. Use the experience of other advertisers on your station to show that you can help the prospect increase business and profits.

"I don't have enough budget."

If you don't know the prospect's current advertising budget and its disposition, try to find out. Use that information, or your estimate, to demonstrate the affordability of your station and its ability to reach more potential customers. If appropriate, raise the possibility of co-op or vendor support programs to exemplify how the prospect can enjoy the benefits of additional advertising at little or no added cost, and detail the assistance the station will give in carrying out such programs.

"Radio (or television) doesn't work."

Ask for more information. You will probably learn that the prospect bought a short and inexpensive schedule on a radio station or in a TV daypart with the wrong demographics, or that the commercial was poorly written or produced. Point out those likely causes of disappointment and explain how you will do things differently. Again, use facts and examples to illustrate the effectiveness of radio or television advertising and the ability of your station to reach the prospect's customers.

"My customers don't listen to (or watch) your station."

Refer to data on who buys what and show how many of them are reached by your station. This response also can be used to meet a price objection if the prospect is advertising on a radio station that does not attract large numbers of the prospect's potential customers, or in TV dayparts or programs that skew to less-than-desirable demographics.

"I tried your station once and I had a bad experience with your rep, John Smith. He screwed up everything."

Tell the prospect what happened to John Smith. If he has been fired, so much the better. You can use that information to emphasize your station's commitment to giving clients the best service. If he is still employed by the station, make the point that the station considers the prospect important enough to assign another account executive. Give an assurance that similar bad experiences will not occur in the future.

"I've been advertising with WAAA for years and I don't want to change."
This objection reflects a fear of change. Find out when the prospect first advertised with WAAA. Speculate aloud about the concerns that accompanied that decision and reinforce the success that resulted from it. How will the prospect's business grow from this point? Your station provides that opportunity by offering the means of reaching new or larger audiences of potential customers or by adding to the mix of customers. Again, it may be advantageous to compare your station's cost and production quality with those of WAAA.

The account executive should listen closely to every objection and seek clarification or additional details. For example, a blanket statement like, "I tried radio and it doesn't work" is not specific enough to understand what gave rise to it or to frame a satisfactory response. Further questioning may reveal that the prospect spent $250 on a schedule with a station whose listeners were not potential customers. Now, the objection has moved from radio in general to a specific radio station, and that is easier to handle. The account executive can use the new information to speak about radio's ability to target particular demographics and to describe the represented station's proven record of attracting listeners in the demographic group that buys the prospect's products.

The account executive's principal contact in agency accounts is with *media buyers*. Generally, they are much more knowledgeable than retailers about broadcast advertising, and their concerns are different. While a retailer is interested in results (i.e., generating more customers), a media buyer focuses on rating points and costs.

Assume that a decision has been made to buy a schedule on a television station. A request is made for a list of avails for the quarter. The buyer will identify the required demographic (e.g., men and women aged 25 to 54), restrictions (e.g., no time before 4:00 P.M. or after midnight), the amount budgeted (e.g., $25,000), and the cost-per-point sought (e.g., $20). The account executive enters this information in the computer and comes up with the most efficient schedule based on the buyer's stipulations. Negotiations continue until agreement is reached on schedule and cost. If the schedule fails to deliver the promised ratings, the media buyer usually requests additional spots at no cost to make up for the difference.

Sales presentations to agencies are prepared in much the same way as those for retailers and must be scheduled to meet the buyer's quarterly purchasing cycles. They pay special attention to client needs, but they also recognize the buyer's interest in rating points and costs, and are designed to address it.

Compensation   As noted in Chapter 3, "Human Resource Management," financial compensation for sales personnel differs from that of other staff. The seven principal methods are

Salary only: Sales managers who do not service clients, co-op coordinators, and trainees are most likely to be compensated on a straight salary basis.

Salary and bonus: Salary combined with a bonus based on net sales revenues; used mostly for sales managers.

Straight commission: The most common method for account executives. It permits the more successful to earn comparatively large salaries.

Draw against commission: Account executives establish their own minimum compensation, or *draw,* and receive that amount as long as their sales commissions meet the goal during the specified period, usually a week or month. Commission is paid on all sales that exceed it. Some stations provide a guaranteed draw. In other words, the compensation is paid even if the sales goal is not met. However, the guarantee generally remains in force for a limited period.

Salary and commission: Used for managers with a client list, account executives, and coop coordinators.

Salary, bonus, and commission: Managers who continue to service clients are most likely to fall into this category.

Straight commission with bonus: Account executives and managers servicing clients may be compensated in this way.

The account executive must receive enough money to enjoy a reasonable standard of living and a sense of security during the initial period of employment. Some stations attempt to provide both by using straight salary for several months, moving to commission and a smaller salary and, ultimately, to straight commission.

Commissions may be paid on billings or on billings collected. If billings are used, commissions are adjusted later if payment is not received from the advertiser. The billings collected method usually leads the account executive to check the credit rating of prospective clients before attempting a sale, and to take extra effort to ensure that bills are paid and delinquent accounts settled.

With the exception of salary only, all compensation methods use commissions and quotas to stimulate effort and productivity. Most stations employ additional incentives, with monetary or other prizes as inducements.

Individual or team sales contests are common in many stations, with points determined on the level of accomplishment. For example, new accounts may be worth 25 points, new business from clients who have used competing stations, 20, and increasing sales to current accounts, 15. Other accomplishments meriting points might include generation of the greatest dollar amount of new business or the greatest percentage increase in business.

Other incentives include extra commissions, such as paying a higher percentage commission on new than on repeat business or on production beyond quota, and bonuses, as when all account executives meet their quota.

Prizes should take into account the motivations of employees. A small monetary reward may not be very appealing to an account executive earning more than $100,000 a year. Similarly, a trip to a nearby resort may not be viewed as valuable by someone who does a lot of traveling.

Contests that are won regularly by the same few people may injure rather than assist the sales effort. For that reason, many stations prefer group incentives. Everybody has a reason to lend their best efforts to the endeavor since all benefit if the goal is achieved.

One way of reaching for any sales goal is through additional sales to existing clients. Another is through the attraction of new clients, a responsibility of all account executives. It is particularly important for the new employee, who may have only a short client list, or no list at all.

Monitoring other media can provide useful leads in identifying new accounts. Thumbing through the local newspaper and tuning to other stations will reveal who is advertising, what they are advertising, and the targets and appeals being used. Analyzing the ads permits the account executive to develop a sales proposal for the advertiser, using the products, audiences, and appeals of the current campaign.

Many newspapers carry stories announcing the opening of new businesses. Government offices maintain records of business licenses granted and building permits issued. These and other sources provide valuable clues for the account executive in search of clients.

National and Regional Sales: The Station Rep

Most national and regional advertising is bought by advertising agencies with offices in large cities such as New York, Chicago, Los Angeles, Atlanta, and Dallas. Since it would be impossible for the majority of broadcast stations to maintain a sales staff in those cities where major agencies buy time, they engage a station representative company, or rep, to sell time on their behalf.

The rep is, in effect, an extension of the local sales force. Rep sales are billed by the station to the agency, which deducts its 15 percent commission. From the balance, the station pays the rep a commission, as set forth in the contract between the two. It may range from 5 to 15 percent of the gross business ordered (i.e., the amount billed to the agency).

Selecting the Rep   National and regional sales account for as much as 20 percent of a radio station's sales revenues and up to 45 percent of the revenues of a television station. Selection of a rep, therefore, is an important decision. Among the considerations to be weighed before contracting for the services of a rep firm are these:

Ownership and management: Who owns and who manages? Who provides direction and leadership, and how are they provided?

Services: In addition to national and regional sales, what services will the company provide? Will advice be available on programming, promotion, research, and local sales? What about assistance in collecting past-due national and regional accounts?

Offices: Does the firm have enough offices, and are they located in appropriate cities to give effective national sales coverage?

Staff: How many employees are assigned to sales and to other services in the company's offices? What kind of educational and professional background do they have? How are they trained and compensated? Is the staff stable?

Stations represented: Does the company specialize in representing particular kinds of stations or stations in particular kinds of markets? How many stations does the company represent, and how long has it represented them? Which stations? Do they include similar properties?

Sales teams: How many sales teams does the rep have? How many stations are on each team? Are TV affiliates and independents mixed?

Reputation: What is the company's reputation with national advertising agencies and with stations already represented? How is it perceived by other station rep companies?

Sales philosophy and practices: Are they compatible with those of the station?

Cost: Is the commission realistic? How does it compare to that paid by similar stations in similar markets for the same services?

Rep Services   The basic service offered by a rep company is the sale of national and regional spot advertising on stations it represents. Some of the larger companies also put together groups of stations to sell as a package in what are known as *unwired networks.* Sales are accomplished through rep account executives, who make regular calls on media buyers in advertising agencies.

Much of the information used by the account executives is developed by rep employees engaged in research on, among other things, programming, products, advertisers, and broadcast markets and audiences. Their work enables the rep company to offer a second service: consulting on a range of station activities, all of which have an impact on the sales effort.

Most rep firms offer advice to stations on the following:

Sales and sales strategy: Sales includes rate-card development, sales training, and presentation materials; sales strategy includes the basic posture of the station as it enters a given quarter and changes in that posture as time passes.

Budget development: The rep's projections of market and station billings for a future year.

Programming: Local programming and the purchase of syndicated programs and features.

Research: Research methods, interpretation of research, application of findings; information and analysis on business considerations (e.g., switching network affiliation, expanding local news, financial impact of airing a syndicated program instead of clearing the network lineup).

Promotion: Audience and sales promotion methods, preparation of trade and consumer advertisements, public relations.

To represent the station effectively and to maximize the advertising dollars flowing to the station, the rep must be supplied with data on the *station*, the *competition*, and the *market.* Information on the station would include

- availabilities and rate card
- audience coverage, ratings, and other research reports (e.g., local marketing research)
- format or program schedule, features, specials, and sporting events
- news releases on the station, its personnel, and achievements and awards
- promotions, and examples of trade and consumer advertising
- local, regional, and national clients, and advertising effectiveness as documented in letters from advertisers and agencies

The rep also would find it helpful to receive details of station facilities, especially those that distinguish it from the competition, the station's role and image in the community and, for radio, an air check and personality profiles.

To the degree possible, the station should provide the rep with similar information on competing stations in the market, drawing particular attention to those characteristics that suggest, or demonstrate, the represented station's superiority.

The rep may have to sell agencies on the worth of the market as well as the station. Accordingly, the station should supply details of the community's media and their circulation, population makeup and trends, employment categories, major employers, and pay days. Details of the market's educational institutions and cultural and recreational activities also would give the rep a profile of the market.

Station-Rep Relations   The principal contact between the station and the rep company is the person responsible for national and regional sales, usually the general sales manager or the national sales manager. If the relationship is to be productive, it must be characterized by trust and confidence.

To establish and maintain such an atmosphere requires open and constant communication. The station must satisfy the rep's information needs promptly and accurately. In particular, the rep must be aware of all availabilities and of modifications in the rate card, and must be provided with details and explanations if spots are not aired as ordered. The rep must also be advised of changes in the programming of the station and of competing stations. The station should be informed of the status of ongoing negotiations with agency buyers, and has a right to an explanation if potential sales are not closed by the rep.

Communication can be enhanced through regular visits to the rep's offices by the station's general manager as well as the general and national sales managers. Such visits provide opportunities to sell the market and the station and to exchange ideas and information. Similarly, appropriate members of the rep's management team should visit the station periodically.

The station should reply promptly to rep requests for availabilities, and clear and confirm sales orders as quickly as possible. Timely payment of commissions also contributes to good relations.

Since the rep company is a partner in the sales effort, it should be involved in the development of sales objectives and plans, and in the review of their progress. And the rep should be recognized for significant accomplishments through congratulatory letters and awards.

RESEARCH AND SALES

The sales department relies heavily on market and audience measurement research. For the most part, market research is qualitative. It includes, for example, information on new businesses and on demographic and employment changes, much of which the department may obtain from the chamber of commerce, business news announcements and stories in local newspapers, and census reports. More comprehensive data on factors such as the occupation, education, income, and buying habits of station audiences and the population in general may be purchased from market research companies.

Typically, audience research is quantitative and consists of a count of listeners or viewers categorized by age and gender. It is usually bought from independent companies. Account executives use it to provide clients with details of audiences that will be reached through a commercial schedule and to demonstrate the schedule's efficiency. It is also a useful tool for reviewing the rate card.

Three principal methods are used to estimate audiences for radio and television stations. A fourth is used only for television. Each employs a process known as random sampling, which means that each household or person in the population being surveyed has an equal chance of being selected. Accordingly, the viewing or listening behavior of persons or households in the sample group can be projected to that population. The measurements are estimates, and are subject to a sampling error. In other words, the actual audience may be a little larger or smaller than reported. The survey methods are as follows:

Diary: Daily viewing or listening activity is recorded in a small booklet or log for one week.

Telephone: Interviewers ask what station or program is being listened to or watched at the time of the call. This is known as the *telephone-coincidental* method. In the *telephone-recall* method, participants are asked which stations or programs were listened to or viewed during an earlier period of time (e.g., the previous day or evening).

Personal interview: Interviewers visit people in their homes and question them about their listening or viewing.

Meter: A monitoring device is connected by telephone to a central computer and records the channel to which the television set is tuned.

Each method has advantages and disadvantages, and some of them are listed in Figure 5.6.

The sales department, station rep, and advertising agencies use audience estimates compiled chiefly by Nielsen Media Research (television) and The Arbitron Company (radio).

Nielsen surveys the more than 200 television markets for four-week periods in November, February, May, and July. Some of the larger markets are surveyed seven times a year, through the addition of October, January, and March. These simultaneous surveys are known as "sweeps."

Arbitron conducts continuous measurements in most of the top-100 radio markets for forty-eight weeks a year, in four twelve-week cycles. Other markets are measured for twelve weeks twice a year (spring and fall).

In more than forty large markets, Nielsen uses a household meter to collect TV set usage data (i.e., set on/off, channel tuned) in the preparation of overnight reports.[6] However, the basic measurement method for television stations in all markets is a diary, which sample households complete for each television set for one week. Each day is broken down into 15-minute periods. Respondents are asked to note the station or channel name, the channel number, and the program to which the set was tuned in each period, together with the age and gender of all family members, as well as visitors viewing and the number of hours each person works per week. VCR record and playback activity also must be included.

For radio, Arbitron supplies a one-week diary to each member of selected households 12 years of age and older. Respondents enter in the diary (1) the times during which they heard a radio, and whether they chose the station or not; (2) the call letters or station name (if they do not know either, they are asked to write the program name or dial setting); (3) whether the station was AM or FM; and (4) whether they heard it at home, in a car, at work, or in some other place.

At the end of the week, the completed television or radio diaries are mailed to the respective companies. The information they contain is processed and some of the results published in a local market report, more commonly called a ratings book or, simply, the book. In metered television markets, the report comprises demographic information from the diaries integrated with household tuning data from the meters.

The television report estimates, by age and gender and for different time periods and programs, the audience for stations in the market. The radio report lists audience estimates by age and gender for different time periods. It also contains details of away-from-home listening, time spent listening, and the ethnic composition of station audiences.

Market report information prepared by Nielsen and Arbitron is organized according to the geographic area in which viewing or listening took place. The following areas are used in the Nielsen Station Index (NSI) report:

Metro area, which generally corresponds to the metropolitan statistical area (MSA), as defined by the U.S. Office of Management and Budget

Designated market area (*DMA*), those counties in which commercial stations in the market being surveyed achieve the largest share of the 7:00 A.M. to 1:00 A.M. average quarter-hour audience

NSI area, a market's metro and DMA counties, plus other counties necessary to account for approximately 95 percent of the average quarter-hour audience of stations in the market

Audience Measurement Terminology

To use the market report effectively, the account executive and other members of the sales department staff must understand the information it

Figure 5.6 *Advantages and disadvantages of broadcast audience measurement methods.*

Advantages	Disadvantages
Diary	
Provides detailed information	Diary-keeper may
Reports individual viewing or listening behavior	—lie
	—fail to complete it
Relatively inexpensive	—fail to return it
	—enter inaccurate information (e.g., call letters, dial position)
	—write illegibly
	—forget what was listened to or viewed before completing
	Diary has to be carried for away-from-home listening
	Slow results
	Infrequent surveys in many markets
Telephone-coincidental	
Eliminates possibility of respondent forgetfulness	Non-telephone or unlisted homes excluded (unless random digit dialing used)
Fast results	Non-cooperation by respondents
Relatively inexpensive	Questions must be brief
	Difficult to obtain detailed responses
	Possibility of interviewer bias (e.g., in wording of questions, recording of responses)
Telephone-Recall	
As for telephone-coincidental, except respondent forgetfulness	As for telephone-coincidental. Add possibility of respondent forgetfulness, unless aided-recall used.
Personal interview	
More personal than other methods	Respondents may lie
Provides detailed information	Possibility of interviewer bias
With aided-recall, reduces possibility of of audience forgetfulness	Time-consuming
	Relatively expensive
Meter	
Records actual set operation and channel	Does not indicate if anyone is watching
Eliminates possibility of human error	Does not provide demographic information (e.g., viewer sex, age)
Avoids interviewer bias	Subject to mechanical failure
Fast results	Relatively expensive

contains. Understanding begins with knowledge of basic audience measurement terminology.

The following are among the terms used most frequently:

Rating In television, the percentage of all TV households or persons tuned to a specific station:

$$\text{Rating} = \frac{\text{Number of households viewing station}}{\text{Number of TV households in survey area}}$$

Or

$$\frac{\text{Number of viewers to station}}{\text{Total viewer population}}$$

To say that a television program has a household rating of 10 means, therefore, that 10 percent of all TV households in the survey area were watching it.

In radio, rating denotes the percentage of all people in the survey area listening to a specific station:

$$\text{Rating} = \frac{\text{Number of listeners to station}}{\text{Population of survey area}}$$

Households Using Television (HUT) The percentage of all television households with TV sets in operation at a particular time:

$$\text{HUT} = \frac{\text{Number of TV households with sets on}}{\text{Number of TV households in survey area}}$$

Share The percentage of households using television (HUT) or persons using television (PUT) tuned to a specific station:

$$\text{Share} = \frac{\text{Number of TV households viewing station}}{\text{Number of TV households with sets on}}$$

Or

$$\frac{\text{Number of viewers to TV station}}{\text{Number of people viewing TV}}$$

In radio, share represents the percentage of listeners to a station:

$$\text{Share} = \frac{\text{Number of listeners to station}}{\text{Number of listeners to all stations}}$$

Rating, share, and households using television are interrelated, as indicated by the formula used to calculate each:

$$\text{Rating} = \text{Share} \times \text{HUT}$$

$$\text{HUT} = \frac{\text{Rating}}{\text{Share}}$$

$$\text{Share} = \frac{\text{Rating}}{\text{HUT}}$$

Assume that a TV market report gave the following information for the period 6:00 P.M. to 6:30 P.M.:

STATION	DMA HOUSEHOLD RATING
WAAA	15
WBBB	5
WCCC	10
WDDD	8
HUT	60

If you wanted to calculate the share for WCCC, you would merely divide 10 (rating) by 60 (HUT) to give a share of 17 percent. Note that the HUT level is greater than the sum of ratings for stations in the market. That is explained by the fact that some households (22 percent) were viewing cable services or stations from outside the market.

Similarly, if you knew that 60 percent of households were watching television, and that WCCC had a 17 share, you could figure the station's rating. Simply multiply 17 (share) by .60 (HUT). To determine HUT, divide 10 (rating) by 17 (share).

Other commonly used audience measurement terms include these:

Average quarter-hour (AQH) audience: An estimate of households or persons viewing or listening for at least five minutes during a quarter-hour period

Cume: Short for *cumulative audience,* an estimate of the number of *different* households or persons viewing or listening for at least five minutes in a specified period

Gross rating points (GRPs): The total of all rating points achieved for a schedule of commercials

Gross impressions (GIs): The total number of exposures to a schedule of commercials

Advertisers want to broadcast their messages to people who use, or might use, their products or services, and at a reasonable cost. With an understanding of the terminology in the market report, the account executive can interpret the information it contains and incorporate relevant parts of it in a sales presentation.

The advertiser who is interested only in total numbers of people, or people with certain age or gender characteristics, may be impressed by ratings converted to numbers of households or persons. The account executive can go further and use share information to show that the station reaches more of the advertiser's clientele than the competition, or cumes to indicate how many different people would be exposed to the commercial.

Advertisers also are concerned with the efficiency of their advertising buys, or what it costs them to reach target audiences. Often, this is calculated on the basis of *cost-per-thousand* (*CPM*) households or persons:

$$CPM = \frac{\text{Cost of spot or advertising schedule}}{\text{Number of households or persons reached}} \times 1000.$$

For example, if a spot costs $300 and is aired in a program seen in 20,000 households, the household CPM is $15 (300 divided by 20,000 and multiplied by 1000).

Another measure of efficiency is *cost-per-rating point* (*CPP*), which is calculated by dividing the cost of a spot by the rating for the period or program in which it was broadcast. If a spot costs $300 and the rating is 5, the CPP is $60. For an advertising schedule, the cost is determined by dividing the cost of the schedule by the gross rating points (GRPs), or the sum of ratings, obtained.

Audience measurement estimates are important tools for advertising agencies and station rep companies as well. Agency time buyers use them to select markets and stations on which to place their clients' advertising.

The station rep uses the market report in much the same way as the station's account executives: to persuade advertisers and agencies that they can achieve their objectives effectively and efficiently by purchasing schedules on the represented station. Acting in an advisory capacity, the rep can use the report to support recommendations for changes in the station's price structure.

The market report provides essential information for station and rep account executives and advertising agencies. However, much of the data collected is not contained in it, including such key details as reach and frequency. To obtain that and other information, stations often purchase additional services from the audience measurement companies.

Traditionally, audience research has focused on quantitative data of the kinds described. As competition for advertising dollars has intensified, many stations have sought information that goes beyond the age and gender of audience members. Income, home ownership, occupation, educational level, and other characteristics provide important pointers to consumer motivations. They help the station to develop a more complete profile of listeners or viewers. They also permit the sales department to incorporate qualitative data in presentations and to give the client or advertising agency more precise details on which to base media buying decisions.

Such information is available from many sources, including Arbitron and Nielsen. Arbitron delivers measures of consumer behavior for retail shopping and media usage in most of the markets it surveys. Nielsen provides details of diary keepers' shopping and product purchases, dining out, leisure activities, and use of media other than television. GRR, Inc. uses local market surveys to produce the *Griffin Radio Reports*. They consist of three profiles of each station's listenership: demographic (age, sex, race, income, education, marital status, employment, and residence information); lifestyle (eating-out habits, use of credit cards and health-care facilities, vehicle ownership, and shopping and buying practices); and media (radio listening, television viewing, and newspaper reading). In some markets, Leigh Stowell, Marshall Marketing, and Scarborough Research Company provide details of TV viewing and product usage. Mediamark Research Inc. (MRI) publishes the results of a nationwide survey of media and product purchase behavior twice a year. Claritas Corporation breaks down the country into areas smaller than zip codes to develop age, education, income, political, and other characteristics of people who live there.

WHAT'S AHEAD?

The large-scale trading of commercial radio stations that followed passage of the Telecommunications Act of 1996 offers both challenges and opportunities for many radio sales managers.

Almost two-thirds of Arbitron-rated stations now are part of a duopoly or superduopoly.[7] One of the results is that managers are responsible for handling not only a larger sales force but one that consists, in part, of former competitors. Added to that is the continuing pressure from owners for ever-increasing revenues.

At the same time, the multistation environment provides unprecedented opportunities for revenue enhancement. For the first time, radio can compete as a reach medium with newspapers and television and, thus, access advertising dollars never before available. That is true, in particular, where owned stations complement each other in audience appeal. Success will hinge on management's ability to adapt its operating methods to the new reality and train account executives accordingly.

However, ownership of multiple stations in a market does not necessarily mean an increase in the total amount of advertising time per station. Increasingly, therefore, sales managers will be required to explore nontraditional revenue sources if they are to satisfy owner expectations.

One that has proved popular with merchants and profitable for stations is the Automatic Prize Machine (APM). Leased to businesses for a week or more, the machine permits holders of station-distributed cards similar to credit cards to "swipe and win" cash and other prizes. During the visit to the business location, they respond to questions on the machine's screen, enabling the business to develop information about them and compile a mailing list for follow-up direct mail contacts. This is just one method being employed by stations seeking to open up additional revenue streams without compromising their customary time sales operation.

Radio's transformation from a targeted medium to both a targeted and reach medium will pose a direct challenge to television sales in many markets. Already, the fragmentation of the television audience has compelled stations to contemplate ways of delivering targeted advertising to smaller audiences. In the future, the pressure will intensify.

TV sales managers will also have to consider the effects of the escalating consolidation of non-media businesses, such as banks, grocery stores, automobile dealerships, and other traditionally heavy buyers of television time. Typically, these changes in ownership remove advertising decisions from local to regional or national offices, reducing the amount of station-client contact and the degree of station influence over time purchases. In many cases, regional or national coverage goals replace strictly market goals, and stations find themselves competing fiercely for advertising dollars that are allocated on a regional or national basis.

As noted in Chapter 1, "Broadcast Station Management," the Internet offers both radio and television stations opportunities for revenue enhancement through advertising sales.

Revenue for all online advertising is projected to increase dramatically, from $1 billion in 1997, to $7.7 billion in 2002.[8] Broadcasters can benefit from that growth in several ways.

Most obviously, they can sell ads on their own Website as part of a combined on-air and Internet package, or sell them separately. The sale of links from the station's site to those of advertisers provides another vehicle for revenue.

A potentially more lucrative method is station involvement in the direct marketing process. In 1997, online purchases totaled $3.3 billion and an additional $4.2 billion in purchases were shopped for online but bought off-line.[9] It is predicted that the percentage of Internet households buying products or services online will increase from 19 percent in 1997 to 49 percent in 2001, and that the average online purchase value will grow from $511 to $1,660 in the same period.[10]

Radio stations can look for assistance from the Association of Internet and Radio, which enables them to partner with Internet retailers and earn commissions by selling retailer products through the station's Website. Radio and television stations can generate revenue directly by developing and maintaining for businesses a Website linked to that of the station.

All such ventures will require sales managers to remain alert to continuing possibilities for diversifying their revenue sources and to ensure that account executives are prepared adequately to discharge their new role. Failure to do so carries with it the risk of being left behind in this new era of advertising and sales.

SUMMARY

Broadcast stations generate the majority of their revenue through the sale of time to local, regional, and national advertisers.

Obtaining advertisers is the responsibility of the sales department. It is headed by a general sales manager and includes a national sales manager, local sales manager, and account executives.

The general sales manager develops sales objectives and strategies, prepares and controls the department's budget, and directs and supervises the work of the departmental staff. Knowledge of the financial objectives of the station's owners, broadcast sales and advertising, and the sales activities of competing stations are among the qualities the general sales manager should possess. They should be combined with administrative and sales skills, and with an energetic and competitive personality.

The national sales manager coordinates the sale of time to national and regional advertisers, and the local sales manager supervises the account executives.

Most of the time sold is for 30- or 60-second commercials, or spots. Many stations also sell longer periods of time for the broadcast of complete programs.

The cost of time in different dayparts on a radio station is listed on a rate card. It is influenced by several factors, including supply and demand, the time of day, and the length of the spot. Television stations sell time in, and adjacent to, programs. Rates are determined by supply and demand and spot length.

Instead of accepting money, stations may exchange some of their time for advertiser-provided merchandise or services in a transaction known as a trade or tradeout. Barter programming, co-op, vendor support, and per-inquiry advertising permit advertisers to obtain time at less than rate card prices. Some stations cut their rates or provide bonus spots to attract clients.

Sales and advertising practices are governed by policies the station implements according to its revenue objectives and its notion of responsible operation. However, the government dictates policies on the amount of time that may be sold in children's TV programs and on the use of radio and television stations by candidates for public office.

The effectiveness of the local sales effort is determined largely by the abilities of the account executives. Knowledge of the market, the station, and prospective clients are among the tools necessary for success.

To obtain orders, account executives present custom sales proposals to prospective advertisers and to advertising agencies, emphasizing ways in which the station can assist in attaining client objectives. They are compensated in various ways, and commissions and other incentives usually are employed to encourage effort and productivity.

Sales to national and regional advertisers are accomplished by station representative companies, or station reps, which obtain orders from advertising agencies located in major cities. In addition to selling, most reps offer advice to the station on sales and sales strategy, budget development, programming, research, and promotion.

Market and audience measurement research are important tools of the sales department. Radio and television audiences are measured mostly by diary. Television audiences are measured by meter as well. The research results in estimates of the size and composition of the audience, and enables the station to advise advertisers of the number and kinds of people who hear or see its programs, and the costs of reaching particular demographic categories.

Sales managers will be faced with continuing pressures to enhance revenues. Radio stations that are part of a duopoly or superduopoly are well poised to meet the challenge. Both radio and television stations will be required to explore and respond to opportunities made available by the Internet.

CASE STUDY: RADIO

You are the local sales manager of classic rock station WZZZ-FM in a medium market in the Midwest. Account executive Sam Wall stops by your office on Monday morning. He does not seem happy — and with good reason. Bob Weeks, the advertising manager of City Ford, has just called to tell him that he is going to cancel his $4,000-a-month contract with the station and switch to television.

"What's the problem?" you ask.

"He says his radio spots just aren't working," Sam replies.

Even though the news is unwelcome, it does not surprise you. For some time, you have been concerned about what you consider the "Hee-Haw"-type humor used in the spots. And you have had reservations about Bob's demand that all spots air between 7:00 and 9:00 A.M., Monday through Friday.

You tell Sam to try to schedule an appointment with Bob to discuss his decision. What you really want is an opportunity to change his mind.

Exercises

1. What responsibility, if any, do you bear for Bob's action?

2. What, if anything, might Sam have done to prevent Bob's conclusion that the spots are not working?

3. How will you attempt to persuade Bob to reconsider his decision and remain with your station?

CASE STUDY: TELEVISION

You are local sales manager of WXYT-TV, an NBC affiliate in a medium market in the South.

At the monthly ad club meeting, you run into Joe Jackson, president of the Jackson Group advertising agency. He asks you to call him. He wants to speak with you about the Markhurst Jewelry account, which averages $60,000 a year for your station. The store is locally owned and is the market leader in jewelry sales, attracting new and repeat customers from ages 18 through 65.

At your meeting, Joe tells you that he has listened to a presentation by the general sales manager and an account executive from the Sunrise Company. The company owns country-formatted WSYU-FM, the number one station among person 12+. Within the past year, it has purchased three additional FM stations in the market: WTJJ, urban contemporary; WJKX, contemporary hits; and WTGO, oldies. All the purchased stations rank among the top 10 in the 20-station market.

Joe assures you that your station has been a major factor in the store's success. However, he has run the numbers and they show that a buy on the four Sunrise stations will reach all the required demographics and do so at a significantly lower cost-per-point than what he's paying you. He adds that radio will offer greater production flexibility and lower production costs. You thank him and agree to get back with him within the week to talk again.

Exercises

1. How will you respond to Joe's cost-per-point argument?

2. Is Joe's assertion about production flexibility and cost valid? Can it be countered?

3. Develop a proposal designed to persuade Joe of the desirability of renewing the Markhurst Jewelry contract.

NOTES

1. 47 *CFR* 73.1942(a).

2. 47 *CFR* 73.1941(e).

3. *Ibid.*, (c).

4. *Ibid.*, (d).

5. Adapted from *Sound Solutions: Why Radio Can Help You Solve Your Toughest Marketing Problems.* Used with permission.

6. For its national reports, Nielsen uses a people meter. The meter is placed on each television receiver or video tuning device in the 5,000 sample households and an accompanying remote-control unit permits those in the room to make electronic entries. Family members are assigned a personal viewing button on the meter, which also includes buttons for visitors.

7. *Radio Today: How America Listens to Radio*, p. 2.

8. "On-line Ads Beginning to Click," *USA Today*, February 24, 1998, p. 6B.

9. *The Industry Standard*, May 18, 1998, p. 37.

10. *Ibid.*

ADDITIONAL READINGS

Brady, Frank R., and J. Angel Vasquez. *Direct Response Television: The Authoritative Guide.* Lincolnwood, IL: NTC Publishing Group, 1995.

Buzzard, Karen. *Electronic Media Ratings.* Boston: Focal Press, 1992.

Buzzard, Karen S. *Chains of Gold: Marketing the Ratings and Rating the Markets.* Metuchen, NJ: Scarecrow Press, 1990.

Eicoff, Alvin, and Anne Knudsen. *Direct Marketing through Broadcast Media: TV, Radio, Cable, Infomercials, Home Shopping and More.* Lincolnwood, IL: NTC Publishing Group, 1995.

Evans, Craig Robert. *Marketing Channels: Infomercials and the Future of Televised Marketing.* Englewood Cliffs, NJ: Prentice Hall, 1994.

Greenwood, Ken. *High Performance Selling.* West Palm Beach, FL: Streamline Press, 1995.

Herweg, Ashley, and Godfrey Herweg. *Recruiting, Interviewing, Hiring and Developing Superior Salespeople*, 4th ed. Washington, DC: National Association of Broadcasters, 1993.

Herweg, Godfrey, and Ashley Herweg. *Making More Money: Selling Radio Advertising Without Numbers*, 2nd ed. Washington, DC: National Association of Broadcasters, 1995.

Keith, Michael C. *Selling Radio Direct.* Boston: Focal Press, 1992.

Marx, Steve, and Pierre Bouvard. *Radio Advertising's Missing Ingredient: The Optimum Effective Scheduling System*, 2nd ed. Washington, DC: National Association of Broadcasters, 1993.

Pricing and Rate Forecasting Using Broadcast Yield Management. Washington, DC: National Association of Broadcasters, 1992.

Schulberg, Pete. *Radio Advertising: The Authoritative Handbook*, 2nd ed. Lincolnwood, IL: NTC Publishing Group, 1996.

Warner, Charles, and Joseph Buchman. *Broadcast and Cable Selling*, 2nd ed. updated. Belmont, CA: Wadsworth, 1993.

6 BROADCAST PROMOTION AND MARKETING

This chapter focuses on the promotion and marketing of radio and television stations to audiences and advertisers. It considers

- [ ] the responsibilities and qualities of the promotion and marketing director

- [ ] the development of a promotion plan

- [ ] the goals and methods of effective audience and sales promotion campaigns

Commercial radio and television stations spend considerable time and energy promoting the interests of others directly through advertising and public service announcements. Indirectly, they promote the interests and careers of recording artists and an array of other personalities.

Broadcast promotion and marketing refers to a station's efforts to promote itself, and is directed toward the two groups whose support is necessary to ensure its continued operation: audiences and advertisers.

Without an audience, even the best programs attract little advertiser interest. Through *audience promotion*, a station seeks to persuade people to continue to tune in or to sample its programming.

In the increasingly competitive media marketplace, a station has to fight for its share of advertising dollars. Through *sales promotion*, a station seeks to persuade advertisers and advertising agencies to buy time.

Promotion is so important to success that many stations entrust it to a department headed by a promotion and marketing director, who reports to the general manager.[1] The size of the department varies.[2] It is determined by many factors, including station and market size, the competition, and the importance assigned to promotion by station management. In some stations, the director may have the assistance of only a secretary. In others, the staff may number a dozen or more, and may be organized to reflect the various functions of the department.

Some stations do not give promotion responsibilities to a separate department. Audience promotion may be carried out by the program department, for example, and sales promotion by the sales department. In small stations, the general manager may play the prominent role in promotion.

Here, emphasis will be on the promotion and marketing director and the promotion functions, no matter who discharges them.

THE PROMOTION AND MARKETING DIRECTOR

Responsibilities

The promotion and marketing director is responsible for marketing the station and its programs to audiences, and its audiences to advertisers. In a small department, the director may have to handle all the details. In a large department, specific responsibilities may be assigned to different staff members, with the director supervising their work and carrying out general administrative tasks.

Whether directly involved or acting chiefly in a supervisory capacity, the promotion and marketing director has responsibility for a wide variety of activities. They include

- assisting in the development of a promotion plan
- creating and planning audience and sales promotion campaigns
- implementing campaigns through the preparation and/or coordination of advertising and promotional materials and their scheduling
- evaluating campaigns
- conducting or contracting for research and employing appropriate data in campaign creation, planning, implementation, and evaluation

- planning and overseeing public service activities, unless those duties are handled by a public service director
- coordinating the station's overall graphic look
- maintaining media relations
- administering the activities of the promotion department and coordinating them with other station departments

Qualities

The qualities required of an effective promotion and marketing director are as numerous and varied as the responsibilities.

Knowledge   The director should have knowledge of the following:

Marketing, its functions and processes, and their application to audience and sales promotion.

Promotion methods used most frequently, especially (1) advertising — characteristics of all advertising media, media selection, buying, and tradeouts; (2) publicity — available avenues and the cultivation of publicity sources; (3) public relations — role in promotion and the fostering of effective public relations; (4) promotions — vehicles for on-air and off-air promotion and their utilization; and (5) public service — ways in which it can assist in the promotional mix.

Research, conducting or contracting for research, and its interpretation and use in promotion.

Professional services, such as those available from printers, advertising and public relations agencies, companies specializing in the production of promotion materials, and from Promax International, a professional association of promotion and marketing executives.

Laws and regulations, especially those that apply to advertising, copyright, and contests.

Skills   The promotion and marketing director should display skills in

- creating, planning, implementing, and evaluating promotion campaigns
- planning and coordinating in-house research
- writing advertising and promotion copy, news and feature releases, program listings, and sales promotion materials, such as station and market data sheets, ratings analyses, and program and personality profiles
- producing art work and layouts for print advertising and promotion, radio and/or television commercials and promos, and audiovisuals for sales presentations
- planning, creating, operating, and maintaining the station's Website
- coordinating promotions with other station departments
- maintaining records of departmental personnel, budget, and promotional activities

Personal Qualities   The promotion and marketing director should be

- *alert* to the changing fortunes of the station and its competitors and *adaptable* in responding to the demands that may be placed on the department as a result;
- *creative* in developing and executing promotion ideas;
- *communicative* and *cooperative* in contacts with departmental and station personnel and with persons, companies, and organizations outside the station;
- *enthusiastic* and *energetic* in approaching and carrying out the varied responsibilities of the position; and
- *ethical* in dealings with others and in promotion practices.

THE PROMOTION PLAN

A promotion plan is the product of discussions among the promotion and marketing director, general manager, and the heads of the program and sales departments and, often, the news department. Carrying out the plan is the function of the promotion and marketing director.

Developing and executing the plan is a six-step process:

1. Determine the percentage of the market that is watching or listening to the station's product and that of competitors, together with the audience's demographic and psychographic characteristics.
2. Identify the reasons why listeners and viewers select a station. Find out, also, why the station's potential audience is not tuning in.
3. Assess the station's strengths and weaknesses and, especially, effectiveness in positioning itself to attract the desired demographics.
4. Having established the strengths, draw up a plan that addresses the weaknesses and how to correct them.
5. Implement the plan.
6. Evaluate the effectiveness of the plan and, if necessary, refine it.

AUDIENCE PROMOTION

The principal goal of audience promotion is to increase audience by maintaining current listeners or viewers and persuading nonlisteners or nonviewers to sample the station's programs. The goal is accomplished through *image promotion* and *program promotion*.

Like the products they advertise, stations must stand out from the competition by winning a place in the public's mind or *positioning* themselves. Image promotion seeks to satisfy that need by establishing, shifting, or solidifying public perceptions of the station.

Traditionally, radio stations have used their format as their image, so that people refer to a station as "the rock station" or "the news station." Stations that air a significant amount of sports programming may project the image of

Figure 6.1 *This bus board reflects the practice of many Fox affiliates that position themselves by combining the name of the network with their channel number. (Courtesy WDSI-TV.)*

"the sports station." If the station has a heavy schedule of community affairs programming and is closely involved in community activities, the image of "the community station" may be selected.

In today's competitive marketplace, such broad positioning statements often are inadequate. For example, how does "rock" position a station if the community has stations with contemporary rock, album rock, classic rock, and country rock formats?

Because of the similarity of program types on the major broadcast television networks, and the frequent changes in programming, network-affiliated television stations usually have looked to their local programming for image promotion. Often, their efforts center on local news, with themes such as "Eyewitness News" or "Action News." Independent television stations, many of which do not attempt to compete with affiliates in news, usually turn for their image to other competitive programming, such as sports or movies. Some position themselves as "the alternative station," by which they mean that they offer program types different from affiliated stations during certain dayparts. Stations that are affiliated with Fox, The WB, or UPN often position themselves simply by identifying with the network (see Figure 6.1).

Again, these general themes do not permit a station to occupy a niche. Remote trucks enable most stations to be "eyewitnesses" to the news. In addition, as noted in Chapter 4, "Broadcast Programming," "alternative" programming is insufficient ammunition for an independent competing against an array of alternatives offered by cable. And "Fox" may conjure up many images, from "The Simpsons" to NFL football.

Today, selection of an image must be based on a clear understanding of perceptions of the station and its competitors, the targeted audience, the audience's needs and how the station fulfills them, and of *specific* ways in which the station differs from the competition.

The required understanding should emerge from the research carried out in completing the first three steps of the promotion plan. Focus groups, interviews, and surveys can provide valuable insights into current perceptions of the station and its competitors and suggest an appropriate image. However, the positioning statement must say *exactly* what the station is. "More music" says something, but "More music, 12 in-a-row" says much more. Research may reveal that a major competitor is perceived as having disc jockeys who talk too much. "Less talk" could be a strong and effective positioner. If technology is determined to be a significant listener benefit, "The all-digital station" may be considered.

Occasionally, research suggests a statement that tells what the station is *not*. One station changed its format to light adult contemporary and wanted to avoid the notion that it was playing elevator music, which, according to focus groups, was the perception held of a competitor. The positioner that resulted was "No hard rock. No elevator music."

The diversity and wide appeal of programming on all television stations make it difficult for a station to develop a positioning statement that sets it apart from the competition. Some stations select an umbrella theme, such as "Making a Difference," and use it as part of all their promotions.

More frequently, stations affiliated with the three major television networks try to position themselves through locally programmed dayparts or local programming. Local news plays such a key role in influencing public perceptions that it usually is chosen for image promotion emphasis (see Figure 6.2). Anchors, reporters, technology, comprehensive coverage — all can enhance the station's image. Successful promotion, however, demands that the station identify viewer and nonviewer perceptions and proceed to tackle those that are important in establishing or reinforcing the image necessary to attract or retain desired demographics.

For instance, a station may view a veteran anchor and the stability of its reporters as major competitive advantages. Research may reveal that viewers

Figure 6.2   *The importance of local news promotion to a station affiliated with one of the three major TV networks is demonstrated in this billboard bearing the station's slogan. (Courtesy WRCB-TV.)*

perceive as a benefit the fact that the anchor and reporters have worked at the station for a long time, in contrast with the frequent turnover in personnel at other stations. The research may also indicate that certain of the station's newspeople are seen as lacking warmth. That kind of information provides a basis for an image campaign stressing stability and market familiarity, presented in a warm and appealing manner.

Program promotion revolves around a station's efforts to promote its content. In radio, the principal emphasis is on the station's format and personalities. Television stations, on the other hand, draw attention to individual programs or dayparts.

Stations have discovered that effective program promotion requires more than a recitation of format or programs. An important key to success lies in stressing the benefits to the audience by identifying the ways in which the programming is meeting, or could meet, its desires.

News and public affairs programs may meet the desire for information, music for relaxation, entertainment programs for amusement, and so on. Promoting the benefits of tuning in reinforces listening and viewing habits among the current audience and can be a strong motivator for others.

Affiliated television stations can rely on the network to promote network programs. Accordingly, much of the station's promotion effort is directed toward local news or syndicated programs. In theory, independent stations must promote all their programming. In practice, however, most direct their efforts to the promotion of entertainment programs or those for which the station has staked a claim in the marketplace.

Before embarking on an audience promotion campaign, a strategy must be developed. It must take into account several considerations, including the following:

Campaign Purpose

Is the purpose to promote image or programming? If the former, is the concern with establishing, reinforcing, or changing image? If the latter, what element of programming? Are results expected in a short time or over a longer period?

Target Audience

To whom is the campaign to be directed? What kinds of people are most likely to respond?

Audience Benefits

Why should the targeted audience respond? What benefits can they expect?

Promotion Methods

How can the targeted audience be reached? Which medium or media will be used? Will the campaign rely chiefly on one method of promotion or on a combination? What about the time schedule?

Content

What kind of content will be most suited to the promotion method or methods selected? Can the content be developed by the station or will outside services be required?

Budget

What kinds of costs will be incurred? Does the purpose justify the costs?

Evaluation

How will the results of the campaign be determined? Will it be necessary for the station to develop an instrument to measure the results? Or will telephone calls, letters, E-mail, ratings, or other feedback indicate the degree of success achieved?

Promotion Methods

The methods by which a station seeks to accomplish its audience promotion goals are limited only by the imagination of those involved in planning the promotion and the available budget. There are four major methods: (1) *advertising*, (2) *publicity* and *public relations*, (3) *on-air* and *off-air promotions*, and (4) *public service*. In most campaigns, a combination of methods is used.

Advertising   Advertising refers to the purchase of time or space. In some cases, stations trade for time or space with other media. Instead of making a payment, they offer to the other media advertising time on their stations that would cost an equivalent amount of money.

Stations may plan, develop, and supervise the advertising themselves or engage the services of an advertising agency.

In audience promotion, the major advantage of advertising is that the station has control over the content as well as when and where it appears. But some stations consider advertising expensive, especially when compared to some of the other available promotion methods.

Among the advertising media that stations use are newspapers, magazines, outdoor, transit, and broadcast.

Newspapers   Daily or weekly newspapers are published in most communities and reach people who are not regular listeners or viewers. It may be assumed that most readers are interested in being informed. For that reason, many stations use newspapers to advertise news programs, special news features, or other informational programming.

Often, advertisements are placed in the newspaper's TV/radio or entertainment sections. If a program with special appeal is being promoted, an ad may be placed in another section. Advertisements for sports programs, for example, probably will reach more of the interested audience in the sports section. Advertisements for business, travel, and several other kinds of programs will reach the most interested through placement in appropriate sections.

The television supplement published by many newspapers on Sundays represents a valuable vehicle for television stations. It is used by viewers and usually remains around the home for at least a week. An advertisement for a program on a given day may be placed on the page containing program information for that day.

Many stations engage in tradeouts with newspapers, and network-affiliated television stations often participate in co-op advertising with the network, especially at the start of the fall season. The network agrees to pay part of the

Figure 6.3 *A news/talk station includes its positioning statement in all its promotions, including billboard advertising. (Courtesy WGOW-AM.)*

cost of advertising its programs. The station benefits, since it lists its call letters or channel number in the advertisements.

Magazines Many radio and television stations operate in markets where no general-interest magazine is published. However, large-market stations often have access to the so-called "city magazine" and use it to promote image and format or programs. Additionally, some stations place advertisements on regional pages of nationally circulated magazines, such as *Time* and *Newsweek*.

A very useful magazine for television stations is *TV Guide*, which offers advantages similar to those of the newspaper television supplement. Even though it has discontinued the use of tradeouts, many stations advertise in the publication because of its ability to target viewers directly.

Outdoor Billboards offer several advantages as an advertising medium. They are available in a variety of sizes, can incorporate special effects, and can be illuminated so that their impact can be felt around the clock. Obviously, they are most useful if they are located in areas with heavy traffic, especially if it is slow-moving.

Many radio stations favor billboard advertisements because they can stimulate drivers to take immediate action by tuning in the station whose call letters and frequency are displayed (see Figure 6.3). Billboards serve also as useful reminders of television programs, which people can view when they reach home. They have proved valuable to both radio and television stations in promoting the station's slogan and its *logo*, a distinctive symbol that identifies the station and incorporates its call letters and frequency or channel number.

Transit In many cities, buses travel great distances daily, and advertisements on the outside are seen by vehicle drivers, pedestrians, and bus riders (see Figure 6.4). The advertisements come in various sizes and often are displayed on all four sides of the bus. Advertisements on the inside are seen only by riders, but usually they are read, since they have little competition for attention. Interior cards are available in trains also, and platform posters are seen by a sizable number of commuters.

Figure 6.4   *A station's logo may be incorporated in advertisements in all visual media, as shown in this bus board. (Courtesy WSKZ-FM.)*

Taxicabs operate in most communities, regardless of size. Like buses, they travel many miles each day, and advertisements in the rear or on the rooftop are seen by vehicle drivers and pedestrians.

Other transit advertising media used by many stations include display cases at airports, the walls of bus shelters, and bus benches.

Broadcast   Broadcast advertising refers to the use of radio advertising by a television station or television advertising by a radio station. It does not include the use of one's own station, an activity known as *promotion* and discussed later in the chapter. Using audience demographic information for particular television programs or dayparts, a radio station can direct its television advertising to the kinds of people who are most likely to listen to the format or program being promoted. The television medium's combination of sight, sound, color, and motion can be very persuasive and influence people to sample the product.

Many stations avoid television because of what they consider the relatively high cost of producing and airing commercials. However, some stations are reducing the production cost problem by using syndicated spots for their format and a tag line or other device to draw attention to their call letters and frequency.

Radio's mobility means that advertisements on radio can reach people virtually everywhere, no matter what they are doing. Radio stations attract specific demographics, and television stations can reach the sought-after audience by placing advertisements on stations whose formats attract those demographics.

Many television stations consider radio stations particularly effective during the evening drive-time period to advertise their early evening news programs. Some use their anchors to give headlines and invite listeners to view.

The advertising media described above are not the only ones available. Additional locations or outlets might include the sides of buildings, malls and shopping centers, shows, displays, conventions, ballparks, time and temperature displays, skywriting, and direct mail.

Publicity and Public Relations   As used here, the term *publicity* refers to space in print publications or air time on other broadcast stations in which information about the radio or television station appears and for which the station makes no payment.

In a sense, publicity, advertising, and anything else a station and its personnel do influence perceptions of the station and may be considered *public relations*. Here, the focus is on personal contacts between the station and its various publics.

Publicity   In seeking to gain publicity through other media, broadcast stations recognize that other stations rarely are interested in publicizing their activities. Why should they aid the competition? However, they may be interested if the information is of wide public interest. Usually, such information deals with events or actions that do not reflect well on the station and represents the kind of publicity it could do without.

As a result, most stations concentrate their publicity efforts on the print media, particularly newspapers. Their activities generally center on the preparation of *publicity materials* and the organization of *publicity events*. Among the more common materials are these:

News and Feature Releases
News and feature stories about the station and its employees. Typical examples would include stories about new personnel, awards won by the station or a staff member, and ratings successes.

Photographs
When appropriate, photographs are included with news and feature releases. Sometimes, however, a photograph and caption may be used alone. A photograph of a new transmitter tower, for instance, may be considered an effective publicity device.

Press Kits
When stations wish to publicize special programs or events or, in television, the start of a new season or new program, often they compile a kit for the press. Releases, photographs, and other materials deemed important are included.

Program Listings
Television stations prepare complete broadcast schedules for use by daily newspapers and in the Sunday television supplement. Radio stations do not use listings as extensively. However, many stations list special programs or features, and the guests or subject matter of interview or call-in programs.

Like publicity materials, publicity events are intended to attract the attention of the media, particularly newspapers. It is hoped that, as a result, stories about the station will appear in print. The following are typical of events staged by many stations:

News Conferences

When a station has news that it considers especially significant, it may schedule a news conference and invite reporters and photographers from all media. Usually, the general manager and other appropriate station personnel are in attendance to make the announcement and answer questions. A press kit usually is distributed.

Celebrity Appearances

Radio and television stations try to obtain maximum publicity when celebrities visit their community, particularly if the station has organized the visit or can claim some connection with it. The purpose of the visit, schedule, interests, and personality of the visitor will determine the kinds of publicity opportunities available to the station. A news conference, reception, and appearances in public places are possible publicity vehicles. The celebrity may agree to be interviewed on the station and to tape a promotional announcement. Many other events can be arranged with the visitor's cooperation.

Screenings

Many television stations invite newspaper reporters and media critics to view programs before the air date so that they may review them in their publications. Stations hope that the resulting articles will be positive and attract audience. Again, a press kit usually is prepared and distributed to those attending the screening.

Other kinds of events may be organized to capture media attention and publicity. Not all succeed, and that is one of the shortcomings of publicity as a method of audience promotion. The station has no control over the use of promotional materials delivered to the media or over whether reporters and photographers will attend a news conference. Screenings may result in negative comments or reviews and may prove damaging to the station's hopes. Usually, there is media interest in celebrity visits, though the focus of reporters and photographers may be on the celebrity exclusively and the station may not even rate a mention.

Publicity does have several advantages. Program listings are consulted and listening or viewing decisions are made as a result. Stories and photographs about the station in newspapers keep the station's call letters and frequency or channel number before the public. Comments on, or reviews of, programs attract public attention to the station, and the promotional benefits of publicity are achieved at little financial cost to the station.

Occasionally, a station reaps major publicity benefits unexpectedly. That was the case for a Baltimore station after the Baltimore Orioles began the season with ten straight losses. A disc jockey vowed to stay on the air until they won their first game. That happened 258 hours later. During that time, the vigil was covered, and the station mentioned, by the three major broadcast TV networks, CNN, ESPN, the wire services, every major radio network, and hundreds of newspapers in this country, and by media around the world. That is the kind of publicity that money cannot buy!

A station can take steps to ensure publicity. At the least, the promotion and marketing director should initiate a media relations program with noncompeting media, especially the local newspaper. Establishing and maintaining contacts with entertainment reporters and with city, business, feature, and lifestyle editors can produce continuing benefits. They will result in a heightened awareness of the reporters' and editors' priorities and information interests and enable the station to satisfy them with news releases and ideas for stories. Joint sponsorship of charity or public service events with another medium provides an additional vehicle for favorable publicity.

Public Relations   As indicated earlier, the term "public relations" covers essentially everything that affects how people perceive the station. Perceptions may be influenced by something as basic as the way a secretary answers the telephone or the carefully planned involvement of the station and its staff in a community fund-raising activity.

The principal publics with which a station tries to develop good relations are listeners or viewers and potential audiences. Influential publics, such as government leaders and leaders of community groups, also are important. Since advertisers also may be listeners or viewers, their perceptions of the station must not be ignored.

In striving to develop relationships with its publics, a station can do much to ensure that it will be regarded as a responsible, trusted, and valuable member of the community. For that reason, all employees must understand their role in the effort and must be encouraged, in all their dealings with the public, to act in ways that reflect well on the station.

At most stations, activities are planned to support the public relations effort. Opportunities abound, but the following are among those used most often:

Speakers' Program
Station executives and other staff members give talks to classes in schools and colleges and to community organizations.

Public Appearances
Station employees, especially radio personalities and television news anchors and reporters, appear at events in the community, such as charity fund raisers, shows, and exhibitions.

Participation in Community Organizations
Many stations encourage their employees to become members of organizations and clubs and to serve as officers. Many support their participation in fund-raising or other activities of charitable and service groups.

Open House
The public is invited to visit and tour the station and to meet with members of the staff. Appropriate occasions might include the station's anniversary, an addition to the building, or the installation of new equipment.

Awards
Awards won by the station and its staff are displayed prominently in the station.

Sponsorships

Many stations sponsor student scholarships and awards for citizens who have made significant contributions to the community. Other opportunities for sponsorships include sporting, educational, and cultural activities in the community, such as youth sports teams, children's art exhibitions, and concerts.

The activities described above are indications of the kinds of planned public relations efforts by many stations. However, the list is by no means exhaustive. Each station should consider ways in which it can play a role in the life of its community. The result can be a better community and heightened public awareness, as well as enhanced public perceptions of the station.

Promotions
Promotions refer to efforts by the station to promote itself to the public directly rather than through other mass media. When a station uses its own air to promote its image or programming, it is engaging in what is known as *on-air promotion*. *Off-air promotion* describes those promotion activities carried out directly with the public off the air, such as through the distribution of giveaways and advertising specialties on which the station's logo is displayed.

On-Air: Radio
Since a radio station determines how it will use its air time, promotional announcements, called *promos*, and other on-air promotions may be scheduled frequently, and may cover a wide range of programs, personalities, or station activities and achievements.

Format is a major factor in on-air promotion. Most stations with a music format draw attention to music content and personalities. Stations with a news format are likely to stress the range of news and information services provided. A talk station may emphasize personalities and issues.

Through its on-air promotions, a radio station strives to keep its call letters and frequency in the forefront of the listener's mind, to remind regular listeners and inform those sampling the station of its programming, and to point to the benefits of listening. Most stations also use their air extensively to promote their image through image promotion announcements or by including their slogan with other promotional announcements. The following are examples of ways in which radio stations use announcements to promote themselves on the air:

Identification Announcements
The Federal Communications Commission requires stations to identify themselves hourly by call letters and city of license. Stations may include promotional material in their ID announcements, and frequently they do so with a musical jingle.

Slogan
Stations that have a slogan often use it in their FCC-required station identification announcements and with other promotional announcements during appropriate programs. A station whose slogan emphasizes its community role, for example, may use it with time checks, traffic and weather reports, and with news and sports programs.

Format
Station format promos are useful in identifying for listeners ways in which the station fulfills their desires, and may be scheduled at any time.

Programs

Individual program announcements permit the station to promote programs, as opposed to format. Stations may use them for the program of a particular personality, a special, or a sports or interview program, for example.

News

Obviously, news is programming. For some stations it is the format. However, stations with a music format often separate news from other promotion. In addition to emphasizing the news programs themselves, many announcements draw attention to the news team, the speed and accuracy of their news gathering and reporting, and their awards.

Personalities

People, as well as programs, are a part of most stations' promotion efforts. Station personalities, such as disc jockeys, interviewers, and sports anchors are among those who may be promoted.

Contests   Many stations have concluded that one of the most effective ways of attracting attention and listeners is through contests. Their conclusion is not surprising, in view of the lengths to which some people will go to win a prize.

Contestants have eaten live worms and a precooked leather football for Super Bowl tickets, and goldfish for concert tickets. They have buried themselves underground and changed their names legally for cash. At a marriage ceremony on a busy street corner, the groom dressed as a prisoner, complete with ball and chain, and the bride wore a police uniform to show who would be boss in the union. Why? That is what they said they would do if they won a station's "How Far Would You Go for a Trip To Jamaica?" contest.

It is not necessary to require or expect such extreme behavior. Contests may take many forms, as illustrated by the following examples:

- A Fruita, Colorado, station ran a Colorado trivia contest. Each week, winners' names were entered in a grand prize drawing. The prizes were products made in the state and included sleeping bags, leather shoes, fishing rods, and state lottery tickets.

- A life-size figure of Elvis was placed in different locations by a Beacon, New York, station in its "Find Elvis" contest. Participants mailed in their answers and the winners were chosen randomly from correct entries. The prizes were the book *Is Elvis Alive?* and Elvis albums.

- Grandparents Day is observed by a St. Louis station with a "St. Louis Grandparent of the Year" contest. Entrants write a short letter telling why their grandparent should be selected. The prize, a one-week trip to Hawaii, goes to the winning grandparents.

- Dogs are the big winners in the annual "Halloween Dog Costume" contest sponsored by a Des Moines station. The categories are largest dog, scariest dog, dog and owner that look most alike, best celebrity look-alike dog, and best overall costumed dog. The "top dog" receives a year's supply of dog food, and category winners receive a bag of food. The owner of the top dog is treated to a weekend in Kansas City.

The large number of stations that conduct contests suggests that they are a very effective promotional tool. However, not every contest idea will lead to a surge in audience. Some never move beyond the idea stage because further consideration shows that they are lotteries, and the broadcasting of lottery information is a criminal offense in many states.

There are three elements of a lottery, and all three must be present if a promotion is to be considered an offense. They are *prize, chance,* and *consideration.* Obviously a prize is anything of value that a contestant may win. Cash, merchandise, trips, and services are examples of the prize element. Chance exists if the winners or the value of the prizes are determined, in whole or in part, by chance or lot. It is not a factor if the outcome rests on the skill of contestants or on the use of subjective standards, as in a beauty or talent contest. Of all the elements, consideration is the most difficult to define. Basically, it is the price a contestant must pay to take part, such as an entry fee or possession of an item for which payment had to be made. It also covers the expenditure of substantial time and effort by the contestant, such as listening to a long sales pitch or taking a test drive. To complicate the problem further, the interpretation of "substantial" differs from state to state.

The federal ban on the broadcasting of many kinds of lottery information, including promotions, was lifted by the Charity Games Advertising Clarification Act of 1988, which took effect in 1990. However, the act did not override state and local lottery regulations, and the promotion and marketing director must be familiar with those regulations before embarking on any contest that contains the three elements described.

Assuming that the contest idea raises no legal problems, consideration focuses on whether it has possibilities. Among the questions to be asked are these:

- Is it simple? In other words, will the rules be understood easily and will it be easy for people to participate?

- Is it involving? Does it have the potential to excite people and provide enjoyment directly for participants and indirectly for those not taking part?

- How will it affect programming? Can it be conducted without detracting from programs? Is it compatible with the station's sound?

- Is it appealing? Is the targeted audience likely to be attracted to the contest and the prizes to be won?

- How frequently must it be scheduled and how long must it last to attract the number of participants to make it worthwhile?

- What will it cost? What kinds of expenses will the station incur and will they be justified?

If a decision is taken to proceed, rules must be established and prizes determined and obtained. At this stage, FCC rules on licensee-conducted contests take effect.[3] They require that the licensee "shall fully and accurately disclose the material terms of the contest, and shall conduct the contest substantially as announced or advertised. No contest description shall be false, misleading or deceptive with respect to any material term."[4]

Although the material terms vary with the nature of the contest, they generally include the following:

How to Enter or Participate

The station must let people know exactly what they must do to be considered entrants. The contest rules should be stated in easily understood language and should be free of ambiguities. The airing of contest information on the station can provide regular listeners with the necessary details. If one of the aims is to boost audience, infrequent listeners and nonlisteners must be alerted and encouraged to tune in. Presumably, additional information vehicles will be required, and decisions will have to be made on which of them will reach targeted contestants most effectively and efficiently.

Eligibility

Who will and who will not be allowed to enter? Many stations routinely exclude employees and their families. The station may decide that others will not be eligible. For instance, if the grand prize is an automobile, persons who do not have a driver's license may be declared ineligible.

Entry Deadline

Deadline dates for the receipt of entries must be clear. This is particularly important if participants are required to mail them. Will they be dated by postmark or arrival at the station?

Prizes

The rules must indicate whether prizes can be won, when they can be won, the extent, nature, and value of the prizes, and the basis for their valuation. Prizes should not only be attractive but numerous enough to encourage participation. The station may provide them or arrange tradeouts for some or all of them with area businesses. Whatever their source, they must be described fairly and realistically. It would be hard to argue that "space available" plane tickets are part of a "dream vacation" or that "keys to a new car" is an accurate description if the car itself is not to be awarded. One of the biggest complaints from contest participants is the time they often have to wait to receive prizes. Accordingly, they should be available at the time winners are selected or shortly thereafter.

Selection of Winners

The rules must set forth when and how winners will be chosen. If entrants must telephone the station within a fixed period of time, attempts must be made to ensure that an open line will be available during that period. If the contest is designed to last for a designated period, care must be taken to avoid a premature end. This could happen, for instance, if the winner is the first person to submit the correct answer. If a tie is possible, a decision must be taken on a tie-breaking procedure.

The station should assign an employee to supervise the contest and to ensure that it runs smoothly. The person selected also will be responsible for guaranteeing compliance with the FCC's rules and other applicable regulations and laws. One station landed itself in trouble when it organized a "Roll in the Dough" contest. Scantily clad, honey-drenched contestants were required to roll around in 100,000 one-dollar bills to win the number that stuck to them. A total of $7,000 was awarded, but the station had to answer to the government for violating federal laws prohibiting the defacing of the currency.

The supervisor also should be charged with keeping contest records. This is especially important if individual prizes worth more than $600 are awarded, since details of the winners must be reported to the Internal Revenue Service.

On-Air: Television Like radio, television on-air promotion seeks to remind or inform the audience about the station to which they are tuned, the programs available, and the benefits to be gained. But there is an important difference.

By their emphasis on format and personalities, radio stations attempt to encourage listeners to stay tuned for considerable periods of time. Television stations would like to believe that people will switch to them and stay there. In reality, they tend to be attracted to specific programs. Accordingly, much of the effort is directed toward promoting individual programs or series and, for that reason, the scheduling of promos is important.

If the announcements are to be successful, they must reach those people who are most likely to view the programs being promoted. Since viewer tastes usually reflect preferences for types of programs, it is common to promote news or information programs before, during, or after similar programs. The same goes for situation comedies, game shows, drama, and other program types.

The frequency of program promos is also important. The goal should be to ensure that all those who might tune in are exposed to the announcement at least once.

Among the most common methods used by television stations to promote their image or programs are the following:

Identification Announcements
Stations may identity themselves aurally or visually at the required hourly intervals. In practice, of course, most announcements regularly combine audio and video and often link call letters and city of license with the station's logo or slogan.

Slogan
Use of the slogan can be an effective way of promoting the station's image, whether used alone or in combination with other program promos. Many network-affiliated stations adopt the network slogan and add their call letters and channel number.

Programs
Entertainment: The most common method of promoting entertainment programs is with a film or tape clip. Use of a *specific promo,* one that comprises a scene from the next program in a series, is more effective than a *generic promo,* which emphasizes the series rather than any single program.

Movies: Use of clips is a common device to promote movies. Stations usually look for the strengths of individual movies for the promotional emphasis. Stars, the plot, awards won by the movie, or the comments of critics are among the items that may be promoted.

Information: Clips from films or taped information programs may be especially desirable if they include a clash of opinion or a heated exchange. If a well-known person is to be interviewed, the emphasis may be on the personality rather than the content.

Local News: Local news is a major element in the budget of most television stations and may be the only locally produced program broadcast daily. It also plays a major role in the community's perceptions of the station. For these reasons, most stations place high priority on local news promotion. Among the emphases of news are generic promos, such as the anchors and reporters, the speed and accuracy of the station's news gathering and reporting, awards won for news coverage, and a slogan used by the news department. Specific promos are used to highlight stories that will be included in a particular newscast.

Many stations air audio promos under the closing credits of programs, urging viewers to stay tuned for the program that follows or to join the station again for a program with similar appeal later that day or on following days.

A station's own air has the potential to be a most valuable promotional tool. Its potential will not be realized, however, if the promotion department has access only to those times that cannot be sold to advertisers. Station management must make a commitment to use air time in the same way clients use it: to sell something. In this case, the station is selling its image and programs.

Since promos must be scheduled to reach targeted demographics, the department must request *fixed-position promotions*, which, by definition, cannot be bumped. A contract is signed with the sales department listing promo length and the specific time or daypart in which it will air. For internal accounting purposes, the promotion department is billed like any other client. Of course, times that have not been sold to clients still may be available for use by the department at no charge.

Obviously, all programs cannot be promoted on a regular basis. Priorities must be established, and that is done in consultation with the general manager, program and/or news director, and sales manager. As noted earlier, news has an ongoing priority at most stations affiliated with the three major networks because of its dominant impact on the station's image. At both affiliated and independent stations, high-cost syndicated programs must be given preference if they are to attract enough viewers to justify the price charged to advertisers to recoup the investment and generate a profit. Finally, scheduling should permit the kind of rotation that ensures adequate exposure without the kind of repetition that would prove annoying to viewers.

Off-Air Promotions   On-air promotions permit radio and television stations to reach people who happen to be listening or viewing. Off-air promotions can draw the attention of a wide range of people to the station.

Stations use a variety of means to promote themselves directly to the public off the air. Some, such as the sponsorship of live shows or remote broadcasts, are used by stations intermittently. Many, however, are carried out on a continuing basis in both radio and television. They include the following:

Bumper Stickers

Size limitations are more than offset by the fact that stickers are seen daily by large numbers of people. Usually, they contain the logo. Often, they include the station's slogan or promotion for a particular program.

Advertising Specialties

This term refers to a wide range of items bearing the station's logo and any other promotional material the station feels appropriate. Included in this category are pens, pencils, ashtrays, coffee mugs, T-shirts, and a host of similar items that are used regularly and are likely to be seen by persons other than the user.

Mail

Direct-mail promotions occasionally are used for special programs, though the cost is a deterrent to many stations. Some stations eliminate the mailing costs by including the promotion with bills, statements, or advertising matter sent out by companies sponsoring the programs.

Plastic Cards

Cards, similar to credit cards, are distributed by many stations and permit holders to enjoy special buying or use privileges with area merchants.

Record Sheets

Many radio stations publish weekly compilations of the top-selling recordings in their format and distribute them through music stores.

Station Publications

More and more stations are producing magazines or newsletters containing a variety of information about the station and its personnel. Many stations distribute them free through area stores and defray the publishing costs through the sale of advertising space in the publication.

Station Website

The newest off-air method, the Website offers round-the-clock promotion opportunities. It permits the dissemination of a variety of information about the station and its personalities, programming, and other activities, as well as links to other relevant sites.

Techniques of effective Website construction are still evolving. Many stations are exploring ways of making the site more attractive to visitors. They are discovering that the content must be displayed in a visually pleasing manner. To keep it fresh and to encourage return visits, it must be updated regularly and new sections must be added. Many stations are taking advantage of the interactive quality of the online medium to encourage audience involvement by inviting users to E-mail their thoughts on a range of station activities and on-site content they would find useful. However, if stations are to enjoy the full benefits of this increasingly important promotion tool, they must inform audiences and others of its existence. For that reason, frequent on-air reference to it is vital. In addition, the site address should be listed in all printed station materials, print and television advertising or promotion, and in appropriate off-air vehicles.

Stations are also learning that the site must not become a dumping ground for any and all information. Users' time is limited and an effort must be made to include only content that they will find beneficial. Among the items that may be appropriate for all stations are

- basic station information, such as call letters, channel number or frequency, E-mail address, and telephone number
- program schedules
- biographies and photographs of on-air talent
- details of awards won recently by the station and its employees
- special events in which the station is involved
- station history

Radio stations also may find it desirable to provide contest details. Those with a music format may use it for new music information and local concert announcements. Television stations may wish to include online versions of on-air promos, as well as excerpts from programs and movies to be aired.

Stations that have not yet established a Web presence should be aware of the risks of venturing into waters that are still being charted.

They must ensure, for example, that they hold ownership of all Website content. That is especially important if the site is developed by an independent contractor. In the absence of a "Work for Hire" agreement, the contractor will own the intellectual property (i.e., copyright) in the site. As a result, the station could be prevented from making changes in the content, and an identical product could be sold by the contractor to the competition.

Care should also be exercised if a station employee constructs the site. Generally, intellectual property created by an employee is owned by the employer if it is within the "scope of employment." However, doubt arises if the employee volunteers to carry out the work because of a personal interest in computers. Accordingly, it is advisable to have an employee assign their rights in the site to the station.

No matter who develops the site, the station must be satisfied that clearances have been received to use the content that appears there. Otherwise, it may face legal liability. Agreements should state that material does not infringe on any copyright, trademark, patent, or other proprietary rights, and that it is not libelous, slanderous, or defamatory.

Obtaining clearances can be time consuming, since licenses have to be obtained for all content that is not created or authored by the station or an employee charged with that responsibility.[5] However, failure to do so may prove very costly. Under the No Electronic Theft Act ("NET Act"), unauthorized copying of copyrighted material is a *criminal* act if the material in question has a value of at least $1,000 — even if no profit is earned from its use. Penalties include a fine of up to $250,000 and up to five years in prison for "willful" infringement. Civil penalties for copyright violation reach up to $100,000 per occurrence.

To guard against copying by others or unwitting violation of someone else's trademarks, the station should clear and secure trademark rights to its identity (e.g., "Q-103") and positioning statement. The earlier they are obtained the better, since superior rights may be asserted against anyone who might be tempted to profit from the station's creative endeavors.

The station must also identify and register its *domain name*, or Internet address. A check with the registering body, the Internet Corporation for the Assigned Names and Numbers (ICANN), will determine if the planned name is still available. Stations whose Website is hosted by an Internet Service Provider (ISP) should register the domain name in the name of the station, not that of the provider. Such a step will permit the station to change providers and take the name with it.

Public Service   As noted in Chapter 4, "Broadcast Programming," a station should foster good relationships with the public. One of the most effective ways of attaining that goal is through public service. Conscientious effort will be rewarded with community gratitude and awards, favorable publicity, and the perception of the station as a responsible corporate citizen.

Success is achieved to a large extent by employee and station involvement in community activities. However, a station can enhance its identity by a commitment to public service on the air. Using air time for promotions designed to raise funds or goods for the needy, to encourage traffic safety, or to combat adult illiteracy are examples of ways in which service can be rendered.

Stations regularly carry public service announcements for government and nonprofit agencies. Their broadcast does not lead, necessarily, to a public perception of the station as a concerned member of the community. But combining them with a serious commitment to public affairs programming may produce the desired results. The programs must deal with issues of community concern or meet a community need, and must be aired at times when they are likely to be heard or seen by a significant number of people. Many stations satisfy the first requirement, but not the second.

SALES PROMOTION

Sales promotion seeks to encourage the purchase of time on the station by advertisers and advertising agencies, and often involves the promotion of the broadcast media, as well as the station, for advertising.

Advertisers are interested in getting their messages to the people most likely to use their products or services, and in the most economical way. Accordingly, sales promotion places heavy emphasis on the broadcast media's ability to reach targeted demographics at a competitive cost.

The strengths of the station may be promoted in terms of the *quantity* or *quality* of the audience. Quantity refers to the number of listeners or viewers, while quality denotes characteristics of the audience, such as age, gender, and socioeconomic status. The station may point to quantitative or qualitative strengths over its entire schedule, during periods of the day, or in particular programs.

The element of cost is used in comparison with competing stations as well as other media. The aim is to persuade the advertiser that the station can deliver the number or kinds of people desired in a cost-efficient manner. An effective sales promotion campaign is the result of careful planning based on the following considerations:

Campaign Purpose
Is the primary purpose to project station image or sell time? If the former, will it be attractive to the targeted advertisers? If the latter, will the focus be on particular programs or dayparts? What about the financial expectations?

Target Clients
Will the campaign be directed toward existing advertisers and time-buyers, potential new clients, or both?

Client Benefits
What benefits will the campaign stress? Demographics and the cost of reaching them? Exposure to potential new customers? Other benefits?

Promotion Methods
Which medium or media will be used to reach the clients? Will the station's own air be used? What about the possibility of a joint promotion with an advertiser or advertisers?

Content
What content will be suited best to the medium or media selected? Can it be prepared by station staff or will outside services be required?

Budget
What costs will be incurred? Can they be justified by anticipated new business?

Scheduling
During which quarter of the year will the campaign benefit the station most? Will that period match advertisers' needs?

Program Impact
Can the campaign be used to draw additional listeners or viewers to the station? Will it detract from programming?

Evaluation
Will the campaign be evaluated on the basis of dollars generated or will other criteria be used, also?

Promotion Methods

The targets of sales promotion efforts are those persons who make decisions about the purchase of advertising time. For the most part, that means advertisers themselves and media buyers in advertising agencies. The emphasis is on what the station can accomplish for the advertiser. The methods are the same as those used for audience promotion:

Advertising   The broadcast and advertising trade press is an effective means of reaching those who are influential in making time-buying decisions, and includes publications such as *Broadcasting & Cable, Advertising Age, Radio & Records*, and *Daily Variety*. Often, stations place additional advertisements in the trade publications of other professions so that they may directly reach decision-makers in businesses that advertise, or may be persuaded to advertise, on radio or television.

The content of the advertisements is determined by the purpose of the campaign. Some attempt to project the station's image. Others seek to sell time on the station. It is hoped that success with the first will influence decisions on the second. The important point is that all advertisements should attract the interest of the decision-makers and be tailored to meet their needs.

The purpose of the advertising will suggest those characteristics of the station to be highlighted. Image advertising may place particular emphasis on community involvement and resulting recognition received by the station through community awards. The theme of market leadership may be projected through ratings and station facilities.

Advertisements geared directly to the sale of time often point to ratings for particular programs. Ratings dominance in certain dayparts and with key demographics also may be stressed. Additional characteristics may include the station's coverage area, personalities, and merchandising plans.

Direct-mail advertising can be targeted to advertisers of particular kinds of products or services and draw attention to the station's strengths for those advertisers. Additionally, direct mail offers great flexibility in the number and format of sales promotion materials that can be distributed.

Trade press and direct-mail advertising permit stations to reach directly those who make decisions on the purchase of advertising time and reduce the amount of waste circulation. Other advertising vehicles, such as newspapers, billboards, and displays, are used to promote sales, even though the audience for them is not limited to time-buyers.

Publicity and Public Relations   The focus of sales publicity in newspapers and magazines is on those station activities and achievements likely to impress advertisers. Stories about ratings successes, awards won by the station or staff members, and favorable reviews of programs are examples of information that can be useful.

Public relations activity concentrates on personal contacts between station executives and sales personnel with the business community. Many stations require or urge membership in appropriate community and professional organizations and participation in community activities. A speakers' program allows station personnel to make presentations at meetings attended by people involved in business.

Promotions   One of the most basic and effective tools is the sales kit used by the local sales staff, the station representative, and advertising agencies. It provides information on the market and the station, and may be left behind after a sales call or mailed to potential clients.

With some modifications, many of the off-air promotions used in audience promotion can be beneficial in sales promotion. Bumper stickers can point to the station's advertising effectiveness. Advertising specialties can be selected from among those used most frequently by business persons. Ashtrays, coffee mugs, pens, pencils, calendars, and memo pads are examples.

Mailings to actual and potential time-buyers might include magazines or newsletters, with information on station sales activity, advertising news, explanations of advertising legislation, and a calendar of forthcoming special programs or events that the station will air or sponsor. Other examples of mailings are letters of thanks for business placed with the station and details of forthcoming advertising opportunities.

On an even more personal level, station sales staff promote sales by entertaining clients at meals or at sports, social, or cultural events. Many stations organize, especially for clients, sports or recreation activities such as golf or tennis tournaments. Television stations often arrange a party for advertisers to see excerpts from the fall season's program schedule.

Increasingly, the impetus for promotions is coming from the client, who teams with the station in a joint effort. Many advertising agencies make such activities a condition of the buy. In these so-called *value-added promotions*, the client receives from the station marketing assistance that exceeds the value of the spots purchased. However, these promotions can produce benefits for the station — and for the consumer, too.

Plastic cards are an example. The station produces and distributes the cards and airs announcements promoting their use to obtain discounts at the client's business. The client makes a spot buy in an amount that matches the value of the promotional time and offers the discounts. As a result, the station obtains revenue from the sale; the advertiser receives exposure beyond the time purchased and the improved in-store traffic that should result; and the card holders enjoy the discounts. Such promotions impress participating clients with the station's advertising effectiveness, and can be used as a persuasive tool with other clients or potential clients.

Mutual benefits can be achieved, also, through radio remote broadcasts from stores, malls, and other places of business. The joint sponsorship of live shows by stations and advertisers is another example, and appearances by radio and TV personalities at places of business can have similarly beneficial results.

Many other joint ventures are possible. However, they should be chosen carefully, and with an eye to their value as sales promotion tools.

A value-added promotion method practiced by some stations is *merchandising*. It involves services by the station to assist the advertiser, but the station receives no income, apart from that for the air time purchased.

In effect, the station is donating those services to the advertiser. For that reason, many stations reject merchandising entirely, but some stations use it to promote sales, especially if they are seeking a competitive edge against other stations or if their ratings are so low that additional sales incentives are necessary.

Among the more common methods of merchandising are these:

Point-of-sale signs, supplied by the station and located in the advertiser's store or place of business.

Displays in stores and shops. Again, the materials are provided by the station.

Newspaper and billboard advertisements for a program that the advertiser sponsors. The advertiser is named in the ads, but does not pay any of the advertising costs.

Appearances by station personalities at the advertiser's place of business, at no cost to the advertiser.

Remote radio broadcasts from the advertiser's business, with the station meeting the costs involved.

Public Service   A station's dedication to public service is no less important to its sales promotion than to its audience promotion efforts. The station that is perceived by advertisers as an important member of the community can reap financial benefits. Whether that perception is based on the involvement of the station and its staff in community activities or on its commitment to public affairs programming, the sales department has an important stake in the station's public service endeavors.

WHAT'S AHEAD?

The role of the promotion and marketing director has always been important. As competition for audiences and advertisers intensifies, it will become pivotal to the station's success in projecting an identifiable image that differentiates it from competing stations and other media.

In this new climate, stations are being required to move beyond traditional positioning statements to *brand positioning* or *branding.* In other words, implanting in consumers' minds a clear and unambiguous perception of what the station's product is, to whom it is directed, and the benefits it offers.

The branding imperative coincides with an era of reductions in audience size, especially for television stations, diminishing the impact of on-air promotions. As a result, increased attention will have to be paid to other promotional methods.

One that suggests itself is telemarketing. Even though some stations engage in it, most broadcasters have not pursued it or, at least, not as enthusiastically as many other businesses. An Arbitron study, for example, found that radio station promotion campaigns rarely target an important segment of the audience: at-work listeners. Sixty-five percent of respondents said they are more likely to listen to radio while at work than to read the newspaper (39 percent), surf the Internet (15 percent), or watch television (10 percent). However, only 5 percent of listeners surveyed reported that they had been called at work by a radio station to take part in a contest or other promotional activity.[6] The study's findings also indicate that the at-work audience is not targeted by other promotion methods.[7]

These results point to a valuable opportunity for radio stations to market themselves more vigorously to an already receptive audience. That is especially true for stations whose formats are popular in the workplace — adult contemporary (the top choice), oldies, alternative rock, country, and album-oriented rock.[8]

The promotion and marketing director, in both radio and television, must recognize that at-work and at-home telemarketing can be a powerful tool and add its power to the existing promotional mix. By delivering a personal, one-on-one message, it can strengthen relationships with audiences and encourage sampling by others. It lends itself to contests among respondents and can be accomplished through employees, provided that they are trained in tele-marketing techniques. If it is determined that the station's human resources are inadequate to the task, an outside company can be engaged.

Whatever choice is made, the station must realize that consumers are bombarded by marketing calls. Accordingly, only one message should be included in the script and it should give them an incentive to listen to it and act on it. Furthermore, only calls that are likely to be productive should be made if unnecessary effort and expense are to be avoided.

The Internet offers an indispensable tool for promoting and marketing the station to both consumers and advertisers. Stations that have not yet explored and responded to its potential must move quickly if they are to remain competitive. Some of the advantages that can be enjoyed through Webcasting, a Website, and E-mail were described earlier. Together, they constitute an unprecedented opportunity to forge stronger bonds with existing audiences and attract new ones.

The benefits of the Internet to stations of all sizes and in all markets are many. The online medium is more affordable and cost-effective than traditional off-air media. Its permanent accessibility and its capacity to offer in-depth and tailored information permit the station to expand considerably its range of services. The addition of audio and video to text can enhance its impact and accomplish multiple impressions through return visits. It also facilitates database building and market research.

Its significance has been summarized in this way:

> With its advanced technology, the Internet offers the content depth of libraries, the storytelling impact of audio and video, the interactivity of computer games, the searchability of computer databases, the connectivity of the worldwide telephone system, the personal targeting of direct mail — in all, the power of a fully integrated marketing media combining content, computing, and communications.[9]

The promotion and marketing director cannot afford to underestimate the part that the Internet can play in the increasingly crowded media marketplace.

SUMMARY

Broadcast promotion and marketing refers to those activities through which a radio or television station attempts to promote its own interests. In many stations, the task is assigned to a promotion and marketing department, headed by a director who answers directly to the general manager.

The director assists in the development of a promotion plan, which identifies the station's competitive strengths and weaknesses, and sets forth a course of action to capitalize on strengths and correct weaknesses. Carrying out the plan is the director's responsibility and involves the creation, planning, implementation, and evaluation of audience and sales promotion campaigns.

The promotion and marketing director should have knowledge of marketing, promotion methods, research, professional services, and applicable laws and regulations. Professional skills in writing and production, developing and operating a Website, and planning and evaluating promotion campaigns are also desirable. Adaptability, cooperation, and creativity are among the necessary personal qualities, and they should be combined with the administrative ability to run the department

Audience promotion seeks to maintain and increase the station's audience. Usually this is accomplished by projecting to listeners or viewers an image of the station (image promotion) and by promoting the station's content (program promotion).

Sales promotion is targeted toward those who make decisions on the purchase of advertising time, usually advertisers themselves and media buyers in advertising agencies. Promotion activities may be designed to project the station's image or to sell time to clients.

Even though the targets and goals of audience and sales promotion may differ, most stations use four principal methods for both: advertising, publicity and public relations, promotions, and public service.

The most commonly used advertising media for audience promotion are newspapers, outdoor, transit, and broadcast. Sales promotion relies more heavily on trade press and direct-mail advertising, though other media are used.

Many stations consider publicity to be "free" advertising, since they receive promotional benefits at little or no financial cost. Accordingly, they provide newspapers with news releases, photographs, press kits, and program listings for possible use. Publicity events, such as news conferences and TV program screenings, also are organized for coverage by other media.

Public relations is a broad term covering essentially anything that may influence people's perceptions of a station. Most stations attempt to influence perceptions through planned efforts. Speeches, public appearances, participation in community organizations, awards, and sponsorships are examples of audience promotion activities. In sales promotion, the public relations effort focuses most frequently on personal contacts between station executives and sales staff and members of the business community.

Promotions are attempts to promote the station directly to audiences and advertisers both on and off the air. Typical radio on-air audience promotions include ID announcements, format, program, news and personality promos, and contests. Television on-air promotions are characterized by promos for individual programs or series. In both radio and television, the station's Website is an increasingly important means of off-air promotion. Others include bumper stickers, advertising specialties, and direct mail.

Sales promotions include the sales kit, mailings to advertisers, and advertising specialties. Entertaining clients and potential clients is a widespread practice. Increasingly, stations are engaging in joint marketing efforts with advertisers in value-added promotions.

Public service is important both in audience and sales promotion. In general, it is characterized by close identification with the community through station and staff involvement in community activities and through relevant public service promotions and announcements and public affairs programming.

Brand positioning is becoming an imperative in these times of intense competition. To accomplish it successfully, stations will have to explore more aggressive promotion methods, including a serious commitment to telemarketing and enhanced utilization of the Internet.

CASE STUDY: RADIO

Cumberland Place Mall, located in a city of more than 300,000 in the Southwest, will celebrate its tenth anniversary in August.

You are promotion director of Q-106, the market's top adult contemporary station. You receive a call from Janet Turner, the mall's newly appointed marketing director. She wants to know if you would be interested in a joint promotion to mark the anniversary. You ask what she has in mind.

She tells you that she plans a free concert in the mall's parking lot. You have reservations. August is a very hot month and residents usually don't venture far from air conditioning.

Janet has an answer. "I'm going to book 'The Namesakes.' You know how popular they are." It's true. The rock group is very popular and draws big crowds when it plays in area clubs.

You ask for time to consider the idea. A couple of days later, you call and tell her to "count us in." After all, Cumberland Place is a major account.

The mall will make a $5,000 advertising buy on your station and will supply ten $100 gift certificates from mall merchants as door prizes. Those who attend will register, and the prizes will be awarded at intervals throughout the evening. You will give the event heavy on-air promotion and broadcast a remote from the concert, scheduled to start at 7:00 P.M. and run until the mall's closing time at 10:00 P.M.

To Janet's dismay, only a handful of people are in the parking lot at 7:00 P.M. The temperature is 98 degrees. As the evening progresses, more people arrive. You estimate the crowd at 180 before concertgoers begin to drift away.

Exercises

1. To what do you attribute the low turnout?

2. What lessons did you learn from the experience?

3. What idea would you have originated to capitalize on the anniversary? What results would you expect?

CASE STUDY: TELEVISION

You are promotion and marketing director of an ABC affiliate in a medium market in the Southeast. Your 6:00 P.M. newscast is strong. You are trying to build audience for your Monday through Friday 5:00 and 5:30 P.M. news programs and gain ground on the NBC affiliate, whose local news is ranked first in both time slots.

The final episode of a very popular and long-running network situation comedy will air on May 14, right in the middle of your next ratings period. The timing appears perfect. You reach agreement with WZYX-FM for a joint promotion. The station is first in the market among persons 12+ with its country music format. Here is how it will work.

Starting on April 14, you will give answers every day to two trivia questions about the sitcom, one in the 5:00 P.M. and the other in the 5:30 P.M. newscast. The following day (Mondays for the Friday questions), the disc jockeys on the radio station's top-rated morning show will pose the questions between 7:00 and 8:00 A.M. The first person to answer the questions correctly each day will be entered in the grand prize drawing on May 15. The prize is impressive — round-trip airline transportation for two to New York City, a three-day stay in a first-class hotel, $500 in spending money, and an invitation to attend the taping of a network soap opera.

During the promotion's run, you air promos featuring the two disc jockeys in all your newscasts. The radio station's promos are broadcast in morning drive Monday through Friday. Both promos invite viewers to "Watch, Listen, and Win."

When you receive the ratings book, you are disappointed. There is no change from year-ago numbers for the two newscasts. And there has been a drop from the February book.

Exercises

1. How realistic was your idea?

2. If you remain convinced that it made good sense, where could the problem lie?

3. The radio station seemed to be an excellent choice for a joint promotion. Do you still think so? Why, or why not?

4. You believed that the grand prize was a sure audience-builder. How attractive do you think it was to the audience you hoped to attract to your newscasts?

5. If a similar opportunity presents itself again, what will you do differently? Why?

NOTES

1. Different titles are used for the head of the department responsible for promotion and marketing. They include promotion manager, marketing director, director of creative services, and director of advertising, promotion, and publicity.

2. Just as the title of the head of the department differs from station to station, so does the name of the department.

3. The FCC defines a contest as a "scheme in which a prize is offered or awarded, based upon chance, diligence, knowledge, or skill, to members of the public."

4. 47 *CFR* 73.1216.

5. Content for which a license may have to be sought includes music, video, still images and graphics, and text. The American Society of Composers, Authors, and Publishers (ASCAP), Broadcast Music, Inc. (BMI), and the Harry Fox Agency license most music or can advise how and where to obtain a license. For video, contact should be made with the television station or network that aired it. Production companies are the most logical starting point for movie clips. To license still images, organizations in which the photographer may hold membership are a useful source. The most prominent are the Picture Agency Council of America, American Society of Media Photographers, and American Society of Picture Professionals. The Graphic Artists Guild should be able to supply infor-

mation for work by a graphic artist. For text, the publisher or the author's literary agent are the most appropriate contacts.

6. Donna Petrozello, "Radio Missing 'At-Work' Opportunities," *Broadcasting & Cable*, September 27, 1997, p. 31.

7. Only 8 percent of those surveyed reported receiving a fax at work from a station and only 12 percent a letter.

8. Petrozello, *op. cit.*

9. William J. Comcowich, "Marketing on the Internet," *NAB MultiMedia News*, Winter, 1996, p. 19.

ADDITIONAL READINGS

Balon, Robert E. *Radio in the '90s: Audience Promotion and Marketing Strategies.* Washington, DC: National Association of Broadcasters, 1990.

Contests, Lotteries and Casino Gambling: What You Don't Know May Get You in Trouble. Washington, DC: National Association of Broadcasters, 1996.

Eastman, Susan T., and Robert Klein. *Promotion and Marketing for Broadcasting and Cable,* 2nd ed. Prospect Heights, IL: Waveland Press, 1991.

Guidelines for Radio: Best of the Best Promotions—III. Washington, DC: National Association of Broadcasters, 1994.

MacDonald, Jack, and Curtis R. Holsopple. *Handbook of Radio Publicity and Promotion,* 3rd ed. Blue Ridge Summit, PA: TAB Books, 1990.

Money Makers II: Sales Promotions from the Hundred Plus Television Markets, 2nd ed. Washington, DC: National Association of Broadcasters, 1996.

Roberts, Ted E. F. *Practical Radio Promotions.* Boston: Focal Press, 1992.

7 BROADCAST REGULATIONS

This chapter surveys broadcast regulation and focuses on

☐ the post-1996 regulatory framework

☐ FCC license application and reporting requirements

☐ FCC policies pertaining to ownership, programming, announcements, commercials, and operating requirements

Historically, broadcasting has been the most heavily regulated mass medium. Broadcast regulation was based upon concepts of "public interest" and scarcity, which meant, simply, that there were more applicants for licenses than there were available frequencies. In the 1980s, a deregulation frenzy swept the federal government, and the "scarcity" rationale for regulation was declared by the Federal Communications Commission to be no longer valid.

In the early 1990s, the relaxation of formal broadcast regulation continued. Ownership rules were changed in 1991 to permit duopoly, the common ownership of more than one station in the same class of service in the same market. Other long-standing FCC rules, such as the Financial Syndication Rules (Fin-Syn) and the Prime-Time Access Rule (PTAR), were eliminated. And then, in February 1996, the Congress enacted. and the President signed, the Telecommunications Act of 1996.[1]

This new law was a sweeping revision of the 1934 Communications Act. However, its principal long-term impact will probably be upon the ownership face of the industry. The law should more appropriately be called the "Consolidation Act of 1996," because it has permitted concentration of electronic media ownership at the national and local levels.

BACKGROUND

During the early days of broadcasting, there were very few rules to follow. Anyone who wanted to transmit a broadcast signal on any frequency could do so, thus creating a jamming effect on frequencies carrying more than one station.

After years of discussion and compromise among all factions involved in this growing industry, Congress passed the Radio Act of 1927. The act provided for the formation of a Federal Radio Commission (FRC), comprising five persons appointed by the President, one of whom would be selected as chairman. The FRC was to oversee broadcasting on a trial basis for one year. At the end of the year, its term was extended and it continued in effect until 1934.

It soon became apparent that broadcasting needed a new and more comprehensive regulatory agency. In February 1934, President Franklin D. Roosevelt sent to Congress a proposal to create an agency to be known as the Federal Communications Commission (FCC) and to bring all means of electronic communication under the jurisdiction of this one agency. The Commission would be composed of seven members appointed by the President, with the advice and consent of the Senate. One member would be designated as chairman by the President.

Today, the FCC is a five-member body, but that is not the only change. Under Chairman Mark Fowler (1981–1987), the Commission embarked on a program of industry deregulation. His successor, Dennis Patrick (1987–1989), accelerated the trend, culminating with the elimination of the Fairness Doctrine.[2] That decision put the FCC into bad standing with Congress, which had already been legislating to fill the regulatory void caused by commission policy changes.

After George Bush became president in 1989, he appointed as FCC chairman Alfred Sikes, former head of the National Telecommunications and Information Administration. Sikes successfully mended congressional fences. He worked to revise certain archaic rules, such as the financial syndication regulations and, at the same time, he pioneered new concepts, like the entry of telephone companies into video. Sikes also undertook some technology-based initiatives, such as high-definition television (HDTV) and digital audio broadcasting (DAB). He was an activist chairman who perpetuated market-place regulation and charted many new waters. Sikes resigned on January 19, 1993, one day before Bill Clinton assumed office.

President Clinton appointed Commissioner James Quello as acting chairman. He served until Clinton nominee Reed Hundt was sworn in as chairman later that year. Chairman Hundt's FCC was often bogged down in internal conflict. He did initiate efforts to reintroduce some elements of licensee responsibility in the wake of deregulation. One of his successful undertakings was in the area of children's television content and reporting rules. Early in President Clinton's second term, Hundt resigned and was replaced by former FCC General Counsel William Kennard.

THE ROLE OF BROADCAST REGULATIONS

The FCC, the Broadcaster, and the Public Interest

When broadcasting emerged, it was recognized as having an obligation to serve the public interest. This phrase, along with convenience and necessity, was included in the Communications Act for specific reasons, not the least of which was to give the Federal Communications Commission maximum latitude to use its own judgment in matters relating to commercial broadcasting. Section 303 of the Communications Act, for example, begins: "Except as otherwise provided in this Act, the Commission from time to time, as public convenience, interest or necessity requires shall . . ." This section goes on to list nineteen functions, ranging from the power to classify radio stations to the power to make whatever rules and regulations the FCC needs to carry out the provisions of the act. The term "public interest" similarly occurs in the crucially important sections dealing with granting, renewing, and transferring licenses.

The public interest has been discussed and defined by Congress, broadcasters, and the public for so long that its meaning has become whatever a person wants it to be. This is especially true of broadcasters, since they are ultimately the ones who determine what the public interest means, at least for their audiences. The real burden of definition must come from the Commission, but even the Commission has granted leeway to licensees, since they are in daily contact with their audiences and obtain feedback from them, thereby being able to gauge what is in their best interests. The Commission does believe that it is in the public interest for stations to carry programs dealing with community issues and problems.

The whole topic of what is and what is not public interest is once again under review. Following the Red Lion Supreme Court decision in 1969[3] upholding the constitutionality of the Fairness Doctrine, many broadcast regulations were based upon the scarcity rationale. It was scarcity that allowed for different First Amendment standards for the print and electronic media businesses. In its 1987 decision eliminating the Fairness Doctrine, the FCC decided that scarcity of viewpoint sources no longer existed, which left only the concept of public interest as a basis for regulations. In the future, decisions on the public interest would be made on a case-by-case basis.

Other Regulatory Agencies

Broadcast regulation does not come entirely from the Federal Communications Commission. Of all the regulatory agencies, probably the one that has the greatest impact on broadcasting, other than the FCC, is the Federal Trade Commission (FTC).

Deregulation by the FCC has further enhanced the importance of the FTC. In 1986, the FCC eliminated many of its rules on station business practices, including fraudulent billing and contests. The terminated regulations were characterized as "unnecessary regulatory underbrush," which duplicated other federal and state laws. Much of the responsibility abdicated by the Federal Communications Commission was absorbed by the Federal Trade Commission.

The FTC is the primary agent of the federal government that regulates advertising. Its general mandate is to guard against unfair and deceptive advertising in all media. Broadcasters, or rather the companies that advertise on broadcast facilities, are the main target of this agency, since the broadcast media are a mass-advertising funnel that reaches out to almost the entire population. Because the agency was created under the authority of Congress to regulate interstate commerce, products or services must be sold in interstate commerce, or the advertising medium must be somehow affected by interstate commerce before the FTC can intervene. Since the FTC is charged with policing unfair or deceptive advertising, the terminology needs to be defined.

Deceptive Advertising   There are four considerations in deciding whether an advertisement is deceptive:

- The meaning of the advertisement must be determined. In other words, what promise is made?
- The truth of the message must be determined.
- When only a part of the advertisement is false, it must be determined whether the false part is a material aspect of the advertisement; that is, is it capable of affecting the purchasing decision of the consumer?
- The level of understanding and experience of the audience to which the advertisement is directed must be determined.[4]

Two cases will help explain these concepts. In the early 1970s, a spokesman for Chevron F-310 gasoline additive in advertisements claimed he was standing in front of the Standard Oil Research Laboratories when, in fact, he was standing in front of a county courthouse. Was this deceptive advertising? The FTC said no — that the location of a spokesman is irrelevant to a consumer making a purchasing decision.[5]

On the other hand, Standard Oil of California was ordered to stop claiming that its Chevron gasolines with F-310 produce pollution-free exhaust. The Commission banned television and print advertisements in which the company claimed that just six tankfuls of Chevron will clean up a car's exhaust to the point that it is almost free of exhaust-emission pollutants.[6]

Other agencies, both state and federal, also are involved in the regulation of advertising. The advertising industry itself has industry-sponsored groups that are active in resolving complaints against advertisers. The National

Advertising Division (NAD) of the Council of Better Business Bureaus and the National Advertising Review Board (NARB) are two examples.

Consumers, as a whole, have little or no influence when it comes to policing false advertising. For the most part, all they can do is report it to the regulatory agencies.

Besides the FTC, the advertising business is touched by at least thirty-two federal statutes, including the Federal Drug and Cosmetic Act, Consumer Credit Protection Act, Copyright Act, and Consumer Products Safety Act.

The FTC's ascendancy to fill the regulatory void left by the FCC has not been limited to advertising matters. In a significant decision on FCC must-carry rules, a federal court adopted an FTC report that concluded that the absence of the rules would not be harmful to local broadcasting.[7]

Other federal agencies and executive departments have also stepped into the power vacuum left by FCC deregulation actions. One such example is the Department of Justice. It has become especially active since passage of the 1996 Telecommunications Act. As noted above, the act allowed expanded electronic media ownership consolidation nationally and locally. Since then, the department has been investigating on a case-by-case basis the extent to which legally permitted consolidation also concentrates on radio advertising revenue. Such examinations have extended to situations where in-market concentration leads to dominance in a particular format. Another is the National Telecommunications and Information Administration (NTIA), which is located in the Commerce Department and is the White House policy office on telecommunications.

APPLICATION AND REPORTING REQUIREMENTS

One day, perhaps, both federal income tax and broadcast station forms will be simplified. Until that happens, the forms will continue to be cumbersome. The broadcast industry is full of forms: for a construction permit to build a radio or television station, for a broadcast license renewal, and so on.

To begin the process of establishing a new broadcast station, an individual, partnership, or corporation must meet certain criteria. They include the following:

- The licensee must be a U.S. citizen.
- The licensee must be of good character.
- The licensee must have substantial financial resources to establish and maintain the station.
- The licensee must have the technical ability to operate the station according to FCC regulations.[8]

Applicants requesting to construct a new facility or make changes in an existing AM, FM, or TV facility must use FCC Form 301 (see Figure 10.10). In the event an applicant cannot complete construction within the time permitted, an extension of the construction permit or replacement of an expired construction permit must be requested. FCC Form 307 should be used for this purpose. The application must contain a specific and detailed statement showing that failure to complete the construction was due to causes beyond the control of the applicant.

Once the construction is completed, it is necessary to apply for a license using FCC Form 302. Applicants must show compliance with all terms, conditions, and obligations set forth in the original application and construction permit. Upon completion of the construction, the permittee may begin program tests upon sending a notice to the FCC.

Prior to September 1998, during the period of operation, all stations were required to file with the FCC an annual employment report form, FCC 395-B (see Figure 3.2), on or before May 31 of each year. The employment data filed were to reflect figures from any one payroll period in January, February, or March. The same payroll period had to be used each year. The FCC used the reported data to monitor compliance with its EEO regulations.[9]

In addition, stations had to file at license renewal time an equal employment opportunity report form, FCC 396 (see Figure 3.3). The report was required to determine whether or not the station's personnel composition reflected that of the community of license. Stations with fewer than five employees were exempt from filing the form.

As noted in Chapter 3, "Human Resource Management," the FCC suspended in September 1998 the requirement that stations file the two forms in the wake of a court ruling that threw out the Commission's broadcast affirmative action requirements.[10] Chairman Kennard announced that a proposal for new rules would be issued, and he urged broadcasters to voluntarily file EEO data with the Commission.

In 1993, the FCC intensified its employment reporting rules by requiring a midterm license report on television stations' employee composition. For a detailed discussion of the Commission's equal employment opportunity reporting regulations, see Chapter 3.

The FCC requires each commercial broadcast licensee to file an ownership report (FCC Form 323) once a year, on the anniversary of the date that its renewal application must be filed.

Sports and network affiliation agreements must be in writing, and single copies of all local, regional, and national network agreements must be filed with the FCC within thirty days of execution.

Deregulation has ended the need to file with the FCC notification of radio and television station programming changes. To replace previous program ascertainment requirements, the Commission requires only that stations place in their public file quarterly a list of five issues and programming related to those issues. The quarterly lists must be in the file by January 10, April 10, July 10, and October 10, respectively, each year. See Figure 7.1 for an illustration of what a typical station quarterly issues and/or programs list might look like. Note that the list should reflect the station's "most significant programming treatment" of community issues and needs. The programming need not be locally produced.

Broadcast licenses are not issued on a permanent basis and must be renewed on a regular timetable. All licensees, except those TV and noncommercial stations selected to complete the long-form audit, must file the simplified renewal application form, FCC 303-S (Figure 7.2). It must be filed every eight years by television and radio stations, on or before the first business day of the fourth month prior to the expiration of the existing license.[11] Please note that the short-form "postcard" renewal is a short form no longer.

Figure 7.1 *Sample quarterly issues/programs list. (Source: Fisher Wayland Cooper Leader & Zaragoza L.L.P. Used with permission.)*

QUARTERLY ISSUES/PROGRAMS LIST

There follows a listing of some of the significant issues responded to by Station (Call Sign), (City of License), (State of License), along with the most significant programming treatment of those issues for the period _____ to _____. The listing is by no means exhaustive. The order in which the issues appear does not reflect any priority or significance.

Description of Issue	Program/Segment	Date	Time	Duration	Narration of Type and Description of Program/Segment
(1) Elimination of the Federal payment to the District of Columbia	"D.C. This Week"	Sunday Jan. 7	12:00 p.m.	30 minutes	Round table discussion with Derek Maginty, DC commentator for WAMU(FM), Mark Plotkin, host of "DC Politics Hour," WAMU(FM), Eleanor Holmes Norton, DC Delegate to Congress and Mayor Marion Barry on various proposals rumored to exist to eliminate the federal payment to the District of Columbia.
(2) Elimination of the Federal payment to the District of Columbia	Special News Coverage of Press Conference	Monday Jan. 8	10:00 a.m.	15 minutes	Station interrupted its regularly scheduled programming to cover the press conference called by Representative Tom Davis, Chair of the Subcommittee on the District of Columbia on his proposal to eliminate the Federal payment to the District of Columbia while at the same time picking up the cost of the city's Medicaid program.
(3) Elimination of the Federal payment to the District of Columbia	11 O'Clock News	Monday Jan. 8	11:00 p.m.	2 minutes	Interview with D.C. financial control board chair Andrew Brimmer regarding the board's reaction to the Davis proposal.
(4) Elimination of the Federal payment to the District of Columbia	News feature following noon and 6 p.m. news	Mon-Fri Jan. 8-12	12:25 p.m. 6:25 p.m.	5 minutes each part	Examination of the amount of federal property located in the District of Columbia versus the amount of the Federal payment; comparison with other local jurisdictions' Federal property presence; examination of the escalating costs of funding the Medicaid program in the city; other financial aid being discussed for the city; wrap-up segment.
(5) Elimination of the Federal payment to the District of Columbia	Editorial	Monday Jan. 15	10:30 a.m.	2 minutes	Regardless what solutions are chosen by Congress, the time for action is quickly passing if the city is to survive.

Figure 7.2   *Excerpt from FCC Form 303-S.*

SECTION III: TO BE COMPLETED BY COMMERCIAL AND NONCOMMERCIAL AM, FM and TV APPLICANTS ONLY

1. Have the following reports been filed with the Commission:

    (a) The Broadcast Station Annual Employment Reports (FCC Form 395-B), as required by 47 C.F.R. Section 73.3612?   ☐ Yes   ☐ No

    ☐ Exhibit No.

    If No, attach as an Exhibit an explanation.

    (b) The applicant's Ownership Report (FCC Form 323 or 323-E), as required by 47 C.F.R. Section 73.3615?   ☐ Yes   ☐ No

    If No, give the following information:

    Date last ownership report was filed: _____

    Call letters of station for which it was filed: _____

2. Has the applicant placed in its public inspection file at the appropriate times the documentation required by 47 C.F.R. Section 73.3526 and 73.3527?   ☐ Yes   ☐ No

    If No, attach as an Exhibit a complete statement of explanation.

    ☐ Exhibit No.

3. **FOR COMMERCIAL AM, FM AND TV APPLICANTS ONLY:**

    Is the station currently on the air?   ☐ Yes   ☐ No

    If No, attach as an Exhibit a statement of explanation, including the steps the applicant intends to take to restore service to the public.

    ☐ Exhibit No.

4. **FOR COMMERCIAL AND NONCOMMERCIAL TV APPLICANTS**

    Attach as an Exhibit a summary of written comments and suggestions received from the public, if any, that comment on the station's programming and characterize that programming as constituting violent programming.

    ☐ Exhibit No.

5. **FOR COMMERCIAL TV APPLICANTS ONLY:**

    (a) For the period of time covered by this report, has the applicant complied with the limits on commercial matter as set forth in 47 C.F.R. Section 73.670? (The limits are no more than 12 minutes of commercial matter per hour on weekdays, and no more than 10.5 minutes of commercial matter per hour during children's programming on weekends. The limits also apply pro rata to children's programs which are 5 minutes or more and which are not part of a longer block of children's programming.)   ☐ Yes   ☐ No

    (b) If No, submit as Exhibit a list of each segment of programming 5 minutes or more in duration designed for children 12 years old and under and broadcast during the license period which contained commercial matter in excess of the limits. For each programming segment so listed, indicate the length of the segment, the amount of commercial matter contained therein, and an explanation of why the limits were exceeded.

    ☐ Exhibit No.

Figure 7.2 *Continued*

FOR COMMERCIAL TV APPLICANTS ONLY

6. <u>For the license period prior to September 1, 1997,</u> attach as an Exhibit a summary of the applicant's programming response, nonbroadcast efforts and support for other stations' programming directed to the educational and informational needs of children 16 years old and under, and reflecting the most significant programming related to such needs which the licensee has aired, as described in 47 C.F.R. Section 73.3526(a)(8)(iii).

Exhibit No.

7. <u>For the period from September 1, 1997, to the filing of the applicant's license renewal application,</u> state the average number of hours of **Core Programming** per week broadcasts by the station. See 47 C.F.R. Section 73.671(c).

   Does the licensee identify each **Core Program** at the beginning of the airing of each program as required by 47 C.F.R. Section 73.673? ☐ Yes ☐ No

   Does the licensee provide information identifying each **Core Program** aired on its station, including an indication of the target child audience, to publishers of program guides as required by 47 C.F.R. Section 73.673? ☐ Yes ☐ No

8. Complete the following for each **Core Program** that you aired on or after September 1, 1997, that meets the definition of **Core Programming**, including **each** composite element of such programming. Complete chart below for each **Core Program**. (Use supplemental page for additional programs.)

Title of Program:			Origination		
			Local	Network	Syndicated
Days/Times Program Regularly Scheduled:	Total times aired	Number of Preemptions	If preempted and rescheduled, list date and time aired.		
			Dates	Times	
Length of Program: (minutes)					
Age of Target Child Audience: from _____ years to _____ years.					
Describe the educational and informational objective of the program and how it meets the definition of Core Programming.					

Figure 7.2 *Continued*

9. Complete the following for each **Non-Core Educational and Informational Programs** that you aired on or after September 1, 1997, that is specifically designed to meet the educational and informational needs of children ages 16 and under, but does not meet one or more of the composite elements of the definition of **Core Programming**. See 47 C.F.R. Section 73.671. Complete chart below for each additional such educational and informational program. (Use supplemental page for additional programs.)

Title of Program:			Origination		
			Local	Network	Syndicated
Days/Times Program Aired:	Total times aired	Number of Preemptions	If preempted and rescheduled, list date and time aired.		
			Dates		Times
Length of Program: (minutes)					
Age of Target Child Audience (if applicable): from ____ years to ____ years.					
Describe the program.					
Does the program have educating and informing children ages 16 and under as a significant purpose?			☐ Yes		☐ No
If Yes, does the licensee identify each program at the beginning of its airing consistent with 47 C.F.R. Section 73.673?			☐ Yes		☐ No
If Yes, does the licensee provide information regarding the program, including an indication of the target child audience, to publishers of program guides consistent with 47 C.F.R. Section 73.673?			☐ Yes		☐ No

10. List **Core Programs**, if any, aired by other stations that are sponsored by the licensee and that meet the criteria set forth in 47 C.F.R. Section 73.671. Also indicate whether the amount of total **Core Programming** broadcast by another station increased.

Name of Program	Call Letters of Station Airing Sponsored Program	Channel Number of Station Airing Sponsored Program	Did total programming increase?	
			☐ Yes	☐ No
			☐ Yes	☐ No
			☐ Yes	☐ No

For each **Core Program** sponsored by the licensee, complete the chart below.

Title of Program:			Origination		
			Local	Network	Syndicated
Days/Times Program Regularly Scheduled:	Total times aired	Number of Preemptions	If preempted and rescheduled, list date and time aired.		
			Dates		Times
Length of Program: (minutes)					
Target Child Audience: from _____ years to _____ years.					
Describe the educational and informational objective of the program and how it meets the definition of **Core Programming**.					

Figure 7.2 *Continued*

11. Does the licensee publicize the existence and location of the station's Children's Television Programming Reports (FCC 398) as required by 47 C.F.R. Section 73.3526(a)(8)(iii)?

☐ Yes   ☐ No

If No, attach as an Exhibit a statement of explanation, including the specific steps the applicant intends to implement to ensure compliance in the future.

Exhibit No.

12. Include as an Exhibit any other comments or information you want the Commission to consider in evaluating your compliance with the Children's Television Act. This may include information on any other non-core educational and informational programming that you aired or plan to air, or any existing or proposed non-broadcast efforts that will enhance the educational and informational value of such programming to children. See 47 C.F.R. Section 73.671, NOTE 2.

Exhibit No.

NOTE: Where applicable, applicants in responding to Questions 6, 8, 9 and 10 may submit or incorporate by reference any previously filed FCC Form 398s setting forth the information sought to be elicited in FCC Form 303-S.

WILLFUL FALSE STATEMENTS MADE ON THIS FORM ARE PUNISHABLE BY FINE AND/OR IMPRISONMENT (U.S. CODE, TITLE 18, SECTION 1001), AND/OR REVOCATION OF ANY STATION LICENSE OR CONSTRUCTION PERMIT (U.S. CODE, TITLE 47, SECTION 312(a)(1)), AND/OR FORFEITURE (U.S. CODE, TITLE 47, SECTION 503).

I certify that the statements in this application are true, complete, and correct to the best of my knowledge and belief, and are made in good faith.

Name of Licensee	Signature
Date	

The short-form renewal was a product of deregulation and consisted of only eight questions. However, the simplicity has begun to fade, and the form is growing. In response to the Children's Television Act of 1990,[12] the FCC added a ninth question for all television renewal applicants. It requires a summary of the applicant's children's programming activity and its compliance with commercial content restrictions. It applies to all television renewal applicants whose license expired after June 1, 1992. Other questions have been added since then, and part of the current form is displayed as Figure 7.2.

Licenses that are in good standing may be sold and transferred by licensees to third parties with the consent of the FCC. To obtain consent, the seller and buyer must file FCC Form 314 (see Figure 10.8) with the Commission's Mass Media Bureau.

OWNERSHIP POLICIES

Simply put, the ownership rules govern who can own what, and where. They include limitations on numbers and kinds of stations that can be commonly owned in a market and on the total number that can be owned in the country as a whole by a single person or entity. Another ownership consideration has to do with the length of time a station must be held by an owner before it can be sold. Cross-ownership rules exist for newspaper-broadcast combinations.

Deregulation's largest impact on changing the face of the broadcast industry has resulted from the relaxation of the ownership rules. The oldest and best known was the duopoly rule, which was designed to prevent a single person or entity from owning more than one station in a market providing the same class of service. Consequently, no individual or company could own more than one AM, one FM, or one TV station in the same service area. This media-concentration rule served its purpose for many years. But the decline of AM's competitive position in particular, and of radio's profitability in general, led to its reexamination.

On September 16, 1992, a new duopoly rule became effective. The change allowed a single party to have up to three radio stations in the same market in markets with fewer than fifteen stations. However, the three commonly owned stations could not exceed 50 percent of the total number of stations in the market. No more than two of the three stations could be the same class of service (AM or FM). In markets with fifteen or more stations, a single entity could own up to four stations, no more than two of which could be AM or FM. In those markets, there was an additional requirement: The combined audience share of the commonly owned stations could not exceed 25 percent.

Before the implementation of the new local ownership rules, many operators who were experiencing financial or competitive strain had entered into local marketing agreements (LMAs). Under an LMA, a station sells all or some of its weekly broadcast schedule to another station in the market, which uses the air time to broadcast content, including commercials, over the selling station. When the new duopoly regulations were adopted, they were accompanied by a new LMA requirement. It said that if an LMA exceeded 15 percent of the selling station's weekly broadcast schedule, that station had to be counted as an owned station for the station buying the time. For example, if FM station A bought more than 15 percent of the time of FM station B, FM station A could own no other FM station in the market because two was the limit in the same class of service.

The ownership rule changes also affected the limits for the number of stations that could be owned nationwide by a single party. The 1992 multiple ownership rules increased the radio levels to eighteen AM and eighteen FM stations, and a further increase to twenty AM and twenty FM stations was permitted thereafter.

The television multiple-ownership limit of twelve was unaffected by the 1992 changes. However, the television rule depended upon the percentage of TV households reached nationally by commonly owned stations, with the upper limit being 25 percent. Therefore, if a company owned five television stations that covered 25 percent of the television households in the United States, it could not own any more. Special variations of the rule allowed UHF stations to count for only one-half of television market households in calculating the 25 percent.

The change in local ownership rules continued in the 1996 Telecommunications Act. Now, the changes became dramatic.

Multiple ownership limits for radio nationwide were eliminated completely. By 1998, there were publicly traded companies that owned hundreds of commercial radio stations each. Such companies included Clear Channel and Chancellor.

The local-level ownership rules for radio changed as well. Limits were set according to market size and class of service. The 1996 local radio ownership concentration rules are as follows:

Commercial Stations in Market	Single Owner Limit (Own, Operate, or Control)
45 plus	Up to 8, no more than 5 in the same class of service
30–44	Up to 7, no more than 4 in the same class of service
15–29	Up to 6, no more than 4 in the same class of service
14 and less	Up to 5, no more than 3 in the same class of service — but a single owner cannot own more than 50 percent of the total number of commercial stations in the market [13]

The television rules were changed more modestly under the 1996 act. National ownership levels were removed, as they were in radio. However, there is a cap of coverage of 35 percent of U.S. TV households. Once that limit is reached, no additional stations may be purchased, whatever the number of stations currently owned.

The 1996 law permits the FCC to issue waivers to allow common ownership of radio and television stations in the same market. The FCC prohibition on duopoly ownership of TV stations in the same market remains, but the 1996 law ordered the Commission to study the matter. Existing restrictions against daily newspaper ownership of electronic media servicing all or part of the same market continue, but have been under FCC review.

Prior to the 1996 law, the FCC eliminated what was known as the "three-year rule." It had required broadcasters who acquired a station to operate it for three years before being allowed to sell it. Now, there is no holding period for existing stations. However, a one-year holding period is required for newly built stations. The end of the rule led to a flurry of station transactions and brought new investors and new types of financing into the industry.

The combination of the changes in the ownership rules and the abolition of the three-year rule resulted in innumerable mergers, corporate takeovers, and leveraged buyouts.

PROGRAMMING POLICIES

Programming policies cover a broad area of station activity. Here, the focus is on those of particular significance to station management.

Political Broadcasts

Enforcement of federal laws and FCC regulations pertaining to political advertising has become a particular emphasis with the FCC. There is obviously a great deal of interest in this topic by office holders and office seekers. Congressional pressure has led to political rate audits, and the Commission is authorized to levy fines for violations of the political rules. Former candidates have also sued broadcast stations for alleged overcharges. Who is allowed access to the airwaves, when, and at what rate are critical questions. Ignorance or informed noncompliance can be expensive and career-ending. FCC attorneys advise their clients to issue political advertising policy statements and to maintain a station political advertising checklist. (see Figure 7.3.) Now, on to the specifics of the laws and regulations.

The "equal opportunities" provision of Section 315 of the Communications Act is commonly (and incorrectly) referred to as the "equal time" provision. It allows broadcasters to permit a legally qualified candidate for public office to "use" a station's facilities, but they must afford equal opportunities to all other opposing legally qualified candidates for that office, provided a request for equal opportunities is made within seven days of the first prior use.

The use of a broadcast facility by a candidate is defined as any appearance on the air by a legally qualified candidate for public office, where the candidate either is identified or is readily identifiable by the listening or viewing audience. Appearances by candidates in the following types of broadcasts are not considered "uses" and therefore are exempt from the provision:

- bona-fide newscasts
- bona-fide news interviews
- bona-fide news documentaries (if the appearance of the candidate is incidental to the presentation of the subject or subjects covered by the news documentary)
- on-the-spot coverage of bona-fide news events (including but not limited to political conventions and activities incidental thereto)

Figure 7.3 *Sample political advertising checklist. (Source: Fisher Wayland Cooper Leader & Zaragoza L.L.P. Used with permission.)*

POLITICAL ADVERTISING CHECKLIST

Name of Candidate: _____

Office Being Sought: _____

Person Ordering Advertising: _____

Relationship to Candidate: _____

Person to Whom Disclosure Is Given: _____

Date   **Item**

___   Candidate has been determined to be "legally qualified."

___   Candidate's announcement constitutes a "use," *i.e.*, candidate personally appears on the spot and is identifiable.

___   Candidate's announcement contains proper sponsorship identification.

___   Candidate has provided NAB form or other written statement of agency authorization to place advertising on behalf of candidate.

___   Candidate has been provided with:

    --   XXXX-TV Statement of Policy on Political Advertising; and

    --   XXXX-TV Station Rate Information

___   Campaign Committee has provided list of officers and directors.

Date: _____   _____
                                                    Salesperson

In response to petitions from the National Association of Broadcasters and others, the FCC authorized broadcasters to sponsor political debates. In 1987, the debate exemption was expanded to cover candidate-sponsored debates.[14] In both cases, even if all competing candidates do not appear on the debate, the broadcast will be exempt from the equal opportunities requirements, provided the debate has genuine news value and is not used to advance the candidacy of any particular individual. Also, taped debates need not be aired within 24 hours of their occurrence to qualify for exemptions, as long as they are broadcast currently enough so that they are still bona-fide news.

Specifically, licensees now may air in-studio debates featuring only the most significant candidates. Minor candidates are not entitled to request other air time if they are not invited to appear.

In 1991, the Section 315(a)(4) exemption was expanded to include a situation in which a local television station dedicated an hour of time to be shared equally by the two major presidential candidates for separate thirty-minute presentations. Although not technically a debate, it did qualify for the use exclusion.[15]

If a broadcast constitutes a "use" of a station by a legally qualified candidate for public office, Section 315 of the Communications Act prohibits a station from censoring the broadcast content, directly or indirectly. This "no censorship" provision bans a station from refusing to broadcast a "use" by a candidate or any person connected with the content or format of the broadcast. Thus, even if the proposed broadcast contains libelous statements, the station is prohibited from rejecting it. For this reason, the U.S. Supreme Court has exempted broadcasters from liability under state libel and slander laws for any defamatory material contained in such a broadcast use.

Under Section 312(a)(7) of the Communications Act, broadcasters are required to allow "reasonable access to or to permit purchase of reasonable amounts of time for the use of a broadcasting station by a legally qualified candidate for Federal elective office on behalf of his candidacy." In 1971, the FCC ruled that each licensee has a public interest obligation to make the facilities of its station "effectively available" to all candidates for public office. It was assumed that this rule would be considered in a case-by-case manner.

Comparisons between the requirements of Sections 315 and 312(a)(7) always seem to cause confusion. It can best be avoided by remembering that, under Section 315, a broadcaster has no obligation to political candidates unless one of them has been allowed to use the broadcast facility. Section 312(a)(7), on the other hand, requires a broadcaster to provide time to candidates for federal elective office. Section 315(b)(1) and (2) of the 1934 act set standards for rates to be charged to political candidates. The following paragraphs summarize the rate advice one law firm provides to its clients:

Pre-election Period and Lowest Unit Charge

For "uses" broadcast during the forty-five days before a primary or primary runoff election and sixty days before a general election (including election day), you may charge candidates no more than your "lowest unit charge" for the same class (rate category) of advertisement, the same length of spot, and the same time period (daypart or program). The candidate must be sold spots at the lowest charge you give to your most favored advertiser for the same class, length of spot and time period. If your lowest unit charge is commissionable to an agency, you must sell to candidates who buy direct at a rate equal to what the station would net from the agency buy. This agency rule does not apply to spots sold by a station's national rep firm.

Candidates get the benefit of any volume discounts you offer to other advertisers even if they purchase only one spot. Thus, if you charge $20 for a single one-minute spot and $150 for ten one-minute advertisements (or $15 per ad), you may charge a candidate only $15 for a one-minute ad even if the candidate buys only one spot. However, you can offer legally qualified candidates an additional volume discount from the lowest unit charge for purchases that do not qualify for the volume discount, but you must make the volume discount available on a non-discriminatory basis to all candidates.

Any station practices that enhance the value of advertising spots must be disclosed, and must be made available to candidates. These include, but are not limited to, discount privileges that affect the value of the advertising, such as bonus spots, time-sensitive make goods, preemption priorities, and other factors that enhance the value of the advertisement. Under the rules, if you have provided any commercial advertiser with even a single time-sensitive make good for the same class of spot during the preceding year, you must provide time-sensitive make goods for all candidates before the election.

Who is Entitled to the Lowest Unit Charge?

Only "uses" by legally qualified candidates for public office are entitled to the lowest unit charge. The candidate must appear personally in the spot by voice or image, and the appearance must be in connection with his or her campaign. If the owner of the general store runs for sheriff, he or she is not entitled to the lowest unit charge for spots promoting the store's weekly specials.

A demand for equal opportunities can change this. A candidate making a valid equal opportunity claim in response to his or her competitor's spots will be entitled to the same rate the competitor paid, and may use the time any way he or she sees fit. If the candidate he or she is responding to got the lowest unit charge, he or she gets it too, by operation of the equal opportunities provision.[16]

In addition to all the other requirements, broadcasters have an affirmative obligation to discover who is behind nominal sponsoring organization of political advertising.

All of these matters, including "issues" advertisements, are now subject to Congressional and Department of Justice examination.

Fairness Doctrine

The Fairness Doctrine required broadcasters to devote time to coverage of "controversial issues of public importance" and to make sure that such coverage was not grossly out of balance. In other words, reasonable opportunity was to be afforded for presentation of contrasting views. It was left to broadcasters to decide what issues were controversial and how to treat them on the air.

After calling the Fairness Doctrine the *sine qua non* for broadcast license renewal in 1974, the FCC declared it unconstitutional and essentially unenforceable in 1987.[17] Subsequent to its repeal, Congress each session, until 1993, annually passed a law to codify the doctrine. Since the Republicans took over Congress in 1995, there has been no such effort and the FCC has shown little interest, despite White House signals. With the fragmentation of the radio audience and the emergence of new commercial television networks, it is unlikely it will be back.

Children's Programming

The FCC began a study of children's television programming in the early 1970s. In 1974, it issued a Children's Television Report and Policy Statement. The Commission stated that television stations would be expected to provide diversified programming designed to meet the varied needs and interests of the child audience. It said that television stations should provide a "reasonable amount" of programming designed for children, intended to educate and inform, not simply to entertain.

On December 22, 1983, the FCC adopted a report and order terminating its thirteen-year inquiry into this kind of programming. While reaffirming the obligations of all commercial broadcast television stations to serve the special needs of children, it rejected the option of mandatory programming requirements for children's television by a three-to-one vote. As a result, broadcasters could justify their inattention to such programming based upon alternate children's programming available in the market on public television or cable.

Citizens' groups were outraged by the perceived FCC abandonment of the licensee's obligation to children's programming. Their unhappiness was intensified by the Commission's 1984 elimination of commercial guidelines for children's programming.

In 1990, activists succeeded in their efforts to restore commercial limits and licensee program obligations for children, and the Children's Television Act passed. President Bush signed the law and, in 1991, the FCC adopted regulations implementing the act, which went into effect in 1992.[18]

As administered by the FCC, the act no longer allows broadcasters to satisfy their children's programming obligation by relying on what is available on cable and public television. Children's programming was defined as those "programs originally produced and broadcast primarily for an audience of 12 years old and under."[19] Broadcasters' compliance with the program requirements would be examined at license renewal time. The law also reimposed limitations on commercials in children's programming: 12 minutes per hour on weekdays and 10.5 minutes on weekends.

Under regulations adopted by the FCC to implement the 1992 law, television stations had to report quarterly in their public inspection file their compliance with the commercial limits requirements. In addition, TV stations were to keep an annual list of programming and other efforts geared to meet the educational and informational needs of children.

FCC experience under the new regulations was not good. Fines for exceeding the commercial limits were sizable and frequent. The anticipated children's programming upgrade and improvement did not occur.

After four years of experimentation under the Children's Television Act, the FCC in 1996 issued new rules and new reporting requirements. The Telecommunications Act required TV stations to air at least three hours per week of "core" children's programming. That is defined as programming designed to educate and inform children. It must air on a regularly scheduled basis weekly during the hours of 7:00 A.M. to 10:00 P.M. Such programming must be at least 30 minutes in length.

To monitor compliance with its new rules, the FCC also introduced FCC Form 398, which television stations must complete on a quarterly and annual basis. It requires the reporting television station to have a named children's programming liaison and to report performance for the quarter just ended and plans for the quarter coming up. The station must also notify the public of the existence of Form 398 and collect public comments on its children's programming.

Prime-Time Access Rule

The prime-time access rule (PTAR) required that network-owned or network-affiliated television stations in the fifty largest markets present no more than three hours of network or off-network programs, other than feature films or, on Saturday, feature films, during prime-time hours (7:00 to 11:00 P.M. Eastern and Pacific time, and 6:00 to 10:00 P.M. Central and Mountain time). Exceptions were made for network news, public affairs or documentary programs, and programs designed for children. The PTAR was repealed by the FCC effective August 30, 1996.[20]

Financial Syndication Rules

When the FCC adopted the PTAR in 1971, it also enacted a financial syndication rule. It prohibited networks from ownership and distribution (syndication) of prime-time entertainment programs that they exhibited. The restriction was justified on the grounds that the networks enjoyed up to a combined 90 percent share of audience and had program dominance. But things changed a lot in the following twenty years, and network audiences plunged to just over a 60 percent share. In 1990, the FCC attempted to modify the original rules to grant networks some ownership and distribution rights. Subsequently, the courts, on network petition, found the new FCC rules unreasonable. Responding to a blistering court opinion, the Commission largely abandoned the 1971 rules early in 1993.[21] The formal end came in 1995.[22]

Obscenity, Indecency, and Profanity

The U.S. Criminal Code forbids the utterance of "any obscene, indecent, or profane language by means of radio communication."[23] The problem, as it pertains to programming, is the definition of what is obscene or indecent.

The prevailing standard for obscenity was adopted by the U.S. Supreme Court in its 1973 resolution of Miller v. California. The Court's three-part test is: (1) whether the average person, applying contemporary community standards, would find that the work, taken as a whole, appeals to prurient interests; (2) whether the work depicts or describes in a patently offensive way sexual conduct specifically defined by applicable state law; and (3) whether the work lacks serious literary, artistic, political, or scientific value.

After the Miller case, the FCC standard for indecency was the "seven dirty words" test announced in the Pacifica case involving George Carlin.[24] That changed in 1987, when the FCC issued a new indecency standard.[25] It is now defined as "language or material that depicts or describes, in terms patently offensive as measured by contemporary community standards for the broadcast medium, sexual or excretory activities or organs." Contemporary community standards, said the FCC, were meant to be those of the average broadcast viewer or listener.

The 1987 indecency standard has been a problem from its inception. There have been three major points of contention: What was prohibited? When was it prohibited? How much would violations cost? The standard itself has been upheld by court decisions in the face of claims that it is vague and indefinite.[26]

Enforcement hours have been another story. Originally, the FCC proposed a "safe harbor" when adult programming might be broadcast. That time period was identified as the hours of midnight to 6:00 A.M. For a time, under a congressional mandate, the Commission extended the coverage of its indecency rule to 24 hours a day. However, the courts repeatedly refused to allow the FCC limitations. The issue was finally resolved in 1995 when the U.S. Court of Appeals for the D.C. Circuit ruled that the FCC could permit the broadcasting of indecent material between the hours of 10:00 P.M. and 6:00 A.M. [27]

In addition to establishing safe harbor hours for adult content, the FCC, as noted in Chapter 4, "Broadcast Programming," has developed a voluntary ratings system to alert viewers to adult content, indecency, and violence in television programming.

Unlike obscenity, indecency is protected First Amendment speech. It is regulated under the nuisance theory of law, which says that it is subject to the time of day. Courts have approved the curtailment of indecency at times when children might be expected to be in the audience. The safe harbor debate has been about what those hours are. The final major enforcement wrinkle is the amount of an FCC fine. Under current forfeiture schedules, the basic one-time indecency fine is $7,000. Sanctions can increase to a limit of $250,000 for a continuing violation. Many of the cash penalties imposed so far have been against New York "shock jock" Howard Stern. His show is syndicated nationally, and the FCC has been fining both the originating and carrying stations. Stern's employer, Infinity, has paid about $1.7 million in fines[28] and has had FCC approval of station acquisitions threatened.[29]

Indecency has been, and will be, a major initiative for the FCC. Litigation is costly, and broadcasters who cannot afford to fight for perceived First Amendment principles would be well advised to be cautious in observing a less-than-definite standard.

Violence

Violence is, and has been, an area of industry self-regulation. While threatening regulation, the FCC knows very well, given its problems with indecency, that program content regulations are difficult to enforce. From time to time, members of Congress, like former Senator Paul Simon, have threatened legislation. However, each time the industry has escaped.

The most recent serious threat was resolved when the FCC adopted a table of voluntary program ratings (see Appendix A, "TV Parental Guidelines") designed to alert viewers to program content. Compliance with the ratings by program exhibitors has not been universal.

In addition to the ratings initiative, there was also an agreement by the television networks to pay for an ongoing independent study of the level of violence in television programming. The agreement followed threats of FCC regulation and Congressional legislation.

Racial Slurs

Shock jocks are not new to the airwaves, but the audience fragmentation of the 1990s and the success of Howard Stern have led to a shock jock breakout from East to West. More and more air hosts are pushing the envelope of acceptable standards for program content. Complaints about problem content are no longer limited to indecency. The 1990s have seen an increasing number of allegations of racism.[30]

The FCC has been confronted with the problem of racial comments in the past. Its policy has been to rely on industry self-regulation, and it has no fine or forfeiture for such comments. The Commission's position is that federal law does not prohibit them. Indeed, the U.S. Supreme Court has decided that hate speech is protected First Amendment activity.[31]

In one case, the FCC was asked to halt the sale of a Washington, D.C. radio station to a company that employed a disc jockey who allegedly made racially insensitive comments on the air. In a petition filed to block the sale, the African American Business Association said that the sale would create a hostile environment for Blacks working at the station.[32]

While a search is under way to find a solution to this emerging problem at the national level, the current remedial approach appears to rely on the amount of pressure that can be brought against management by community groups. In one instance, community pressure was joined by a withdrawal of advertising support for the offending program, and station management elected to suspend and then fire the disc jockeys.[33] In 1998, five years after their dismissal, the disc jockeys were hosting a successful nationally syndicated morning show in the same market. Where dictates of good taste do not govern an air host's behavior, perhaps concern about occupational longevity would be an appropriate guiding principle. But, obviously, it does not always work.

On-the-Air Hoaxes

The electronic media industry has a legacy of spoofs and hoaxes dating back to the famous 1938 "War of the Worlds" broadcast by Orson Welles. His elaborate radio production describing an invasion by men from Mars caused a panic.

The late 1980s and early 1990s saw a new rash of incidents, perhaps another by-product of audience fragmentation. One, in St. Louis, resulted in a substantial FCC fine. In that case, a disc jockey for KSHE-FM aired a Civil Defense alert for impending nuclear attack.[34] The fact that it occurred in the midst of the Gulf War only intensified audience reaction.

Responding to this and other complaints, many involving false reports of crimes, the FCC issued a new hoax rule in 1992. It forbids the broadcast of false information concerning a crime or catastrophe if (1) the information is known to be false; (2) it is foreseeable that the broadcast will cause substantial public harm; and (3) broadcast of the information does, in fact, directly cause substantial harm.[35] The basic FCC one-time fine for knowingly broadcasting a hoax is $7,000.

Lotteries

There has been a long-time FCC requirement that prohibits stations from broadcasting any advertisement or information concerning a lottery. As noted in Chapter 6, "Broadcast Promotion and Marketing," there are three elements to a lottery: prize, chance, and consideration. The prize must consist of something of value. Chance means that skill will not improve a player's chance of winning. Consideration means that the contestant has to provide something of value to participate. Listen- or watch-to-win requirements by many stations are not deemed to be consideration.

Many states have lotteries that use the electronic media to promote and disseminate information, but there was some concern that the FCC lottery prohibition would prevent broadcasters from airing lottery spots and news. To remedy the situation, Congress passed a law stating that the lottery rule should not apply to "an advertisement, list of prizes, or information concerning a lottery conducted by a state . . . broadcast by a . . . station licensed to a location in that state or adjacent state which has a lottery."[36]

Congress revisited the lottery question in 1988 when it passed the Charity Games Advertising and Clarification Act. The FCC implemented the law in 1990.[37] In essence, the new rules created further exemptions to the general lottery prohibition. Basically, lotteries for tax-exempt charities, governmental organizations, and commercial establishments running an occasional lottery may be advertised now. To qualify, however, the lottery and its advertising must be legal under state law.

The FCC does have a fine for noncompliance with the lottery rule: $4,000 per occurrence. This is one area in which broadcasters may need local legal advice before proceeding.

In recent years, questions have arisen about the ability of broadcasters to carry commercials for casinos which have sprung up around the country. Initially, the FCC reasoned that, under the lottery prohibition of the United States Code,[38] they could not. There has been a series of cases on the topic and, in 1998, the Supreme Court refused to review a decision of the Ninth Circuit U.S. Court of Appeals that found the FCC's gambling prohibition unconstitutional.[39]

The FCC has said that it will enforce its gambling casino advertising prohibition in those states not affected by the decision, absent a court order. Apparently, gambling advertising will be legally contested state-by-state.

Other Regulations

The deregulation era has seen the termination of many regulations, some of long standing. Most were eliminated in the Commission's "regulatory underbrush" proceedings in the 1980s, which allowed other federal agencies, like the FTC, to enter the regulatory void. Among the FCC regulations discontinued were those pertaining to

- double billing
- distortion of audience ratings
- distortion of signal coverage maps
- network clipping
- false, misleading, or deceptive advertising
- promotion of nonbroadcast business of a station[40]

Obviously, many rules remain in effect. Two that bear mention are rules regarding contests and phone conversations. The FCC has a strict contest rule.[41] As noted in Chapter 6, "Broadcast Promotion and Marketing," it requires the following:

- A station must fully and accurately disclose the material terms of the contest (prizes, eligibility, entry terms, etc.).
- The contest must be conducted substantially as advertised.
- Material terms of the contest may not be false, misleading, or deceptive.

As applied by the FCC, failure to mention a relevant fact can be as serious as making a false statement. For example, advertising a resort stay as a contest prize must include information that transportation is not included if it is not.

FCC phone conversation rules also survived the "underbrush" proceedings. Simply stated, persons answering the phone must grant permission before their voice is put on the air live or prior to recording it for later broadcast.

ANNOUNCEMENTS

As used in broadcasting, the word "announcement" has a multitude of meanings and just as many regulations to cover them.

If a broadcast station or network airs a program that relates to an element of time that is significant, or if an effort is made by the program content to create the impression it is live, an announcement must be made stating that the program is either taped, filmed, or recorded.

A good example might be ABC-TV's "The Day After," which dealt with the time in which we live and the fear of World War III and a nuclear holocaust. The program was done in such a way that it seemed that the action was taking place live. The producers included messages at the beginning and end of the program that it was a taped dramatization.

Broadcast stations are required to identify themselves at the beginning of daily operations and at the end of operations for that day. In other words, stations must start and end their broadcast day with station identification announcements. They are also required to air a station identification hourly, as close to the hour as feasible at a natural break in the programming. Television stations may make their station identifications either visually or aurally.

When a station broadcasts any material for which it receives compensation, it must identify the person or group sponsoring the broadcast. Compensation refers to money, services, or other valuable consideration. Sponsorship identification remains a problem, particularly in children's shows where the station receives the program from a distributor in exchange for air time.

Disregarding the sponsorship identification rule has landed some stations in trouble for payola, the practice whereby recording company representatives have secretly rewarded disc jockeys for playing and plugging certain records. Payola is one FCC policy that has not been a casualty of deregulation. Indeed, in 1988, the Commission issued a statement reemphasizing the importance it attaches to payola policies.

Similarly, the sponsorship identification rule also applies to "plugola." Plugola is the on-the-air promotion of goods or services in which someone selecting the material broadcast has an undisclosed financial interest.

In broadcasting, there is a type of announcement referred to as a "teaser" or "come-on" spot. This announcement may consist of catchwords, slogans, symbols, and so forth. The intent is to arouse the curiosity of the public as to the identify of the advertiser or product to be revealed in subsequent announcements. The FCC has ruled that, even though the final advertisement in a campaign fully identifies the sponsor, the law requires that each teaser announcement reveal the identity of the sponsor.

When concert promotions are carried on a station and it receives some type of valuable consideration in return, the station must make this fact known. Concert-promotion television announcements for which consideration has been received must be logged as commercial announcements.

Finally, there are public service announcements. These are announcements provided by the station without charge and include spots that promote programs, activities, or services of federal, state, or local governments (e.g., sales of savings bonds), or the programs, activities, or services of nonprofit organizations (e.g., Red Cross, United Way), or any other announcements regarded as servicing community interests. Here, the station must identify the group on whose behalf the PSA is being aired.

COMMERCIAL POLICIES

Commercial broadcasting in the United States operates in a free-enterprise system. Profit is the motivating factor, and it comes from a station's success in generating revenue from advertisers.

The public interest should be the primary consideration in program selection. However, as part of the deregulation of radio and television, the FCC has eliminated all program-length commercial restrictions. The rationale is the belief that audience selection and other marketplace forces will be more effective in determining advertising policies that best serve the public.

On the other hand, the Commission continues to prohibit the intermixture of commercial and programming matter. The Commission's basic concern is whether a licensee has subordinated programming in the public interest to commercial programming, in the interest of salability. The selection of program matter that appears designed primarily to promote the product of the sponsor, rather than to serve the public, will raise serious questions as to the licensee's purpose. But the fact that a commercial entity sponsors a program that includes content related to the sponsor's products does not, in and of itself, make a program entirely commercial.

If the program content promotes an advertiser's product or service, one key question the Commission will ask is on what basis the program material was selected. If the licensee reviews a proposed program in advance and makes a good-faith determination that the broadcast of the program will serve the public interest and that its information or entertainment value is not incidental to the promotion of an advertiser's product or service, the program will not be viewed as a program-length commercial. To avoid any possible questions by the FCC, care should be taken to separate completely the program's content and the sponsor's sales messages.

Another commercial policy deals with "subliminal perception." Briefly, this pertains to the practice of flashing on a television screen a statement so quickly that it does not register with the viewer at a conscious level, but does make an imprint on the subconscious. For instance, if a station or network were to flash on the screen the words "Buy Coke" every 10 seconds throughout a program, in all probability the viewer would have a strong desire to buy a Coke by the end of the program. It is quite obvious why this type of advertising is illegal.

For years, radio and television broadcasters have been accused of "cranking up the gain," so to speak, on their commercials. Whether the commercials are louder than the program itself has to be determined on an individual basis. The FCC requires that stations take appropriate measures to eliminate the broadcast of objectionably loud commercials.

The sale of commercial time is the lifeblood of the broadcasting industry. However, there may be times when a licensee does not want to sell time to an individual or group. The courts have held that broadcast stations are not common carriers and may refuse time for products or services they find objectionable. The licensee also may refuse to do business with anyone whose credit is bad.

Whether stations should be required to sell time for opinion or editorial advertising was an open question until 1973, when the Supreme Court upheld the principle of licensee discretion. Care should be taken to note the exceptions to the general rule. First, it is obvious that stations cannot refuse to sell time to a political candidate in response to a valid Section 315 equal opportunities request. Second, the antitrust laws make it illegal for a station to refuse advertising if the purpose of the refusal is to monopolize trade or if the refusal is part of a conspiracy to restrain trade.

Prior to the Commission's "postcard renewal" and deregulation proceedings, license renewal applicants were required to state the maximum amount of commercial matter they proposed to allow in any 60-minute period. Currently, there is no rule that limits the amount of commercial material that may be broadcast in a given period of time.

Restrictions placed on commercials in children's programs included commercial limits, separation of program and commercial matter, excessive promotion of brand names, and false advertising. The FCC had eliminated commercial limits in its deregulation of television, but a federal court found that it had inadequate justification to do so. As noted earlier, the Children's Television Act of 1990 reimposed commercial limits of 12 minutes per hour on weekdays and 10.5 minutes per hour on weekends. The act also directed the FCC to reexamine the question of program-length commercials with respect to children's programming. In a 1992 proceeding convened to implement the act, the Commission defined such a commercial as a "program associated with a product in which commercials for that product aired."

OTHER POLICIES

Public Inspection File

All broadcast stations must keep certain documents and information open to public inspection at "the main studio of the station, or any accessible place" in the community of license during regular business hours. Public inspection file content must now be retained for the entire license term of eight years. In addition to permitting on-site inspection, stations must make photocopies of public file contents available upon receiving telephone requests for such contents. Under public file rules adopted by the FCC in mid-1998, stations may maintain all or part of their public file in a computer database rather than in paper files.

Set forth below is a summary of the contents of the public inspection file required under the new rules. Except where noted, the requirements apply to both commercial and noncommercial stations.

Authorizations: A station's current authorization (license and/or construction permit) and any documents that reflect a modification of or condition on the authorization.

Applications: All applications filed with the FCC and related materials, including information about any petitions to deny the application served on the applicant. These are retained as described above.

Citizen Agreements: All written agreements with citizens groups, which must be retained for the duration of the agreement, including any renewals or extensions.

Contour Maps: A copy of any service contour maps submitted with any application filed with the FCC, together with other information in the application showing service contours, main studio, and transmitter site locations. This information is retained as long as it is current and accurate.

Ownership Reports: The most recent complete ownership report filed with the FCC, any statements filed with the FCC certifying that the current report is accurate, plus any related material. Copies of the contracts listed in the report or an up-to-date list of those contracts is also required. Copies of contracts must be made available within seven days if the latter option is chosen.

Political File: No changes. All requests for time that a station receives from a candidate for public office, and a description of how the station responded to the request. These are retained for two years.

Annual Employment Reports: A copy of all annual employment reports filed with the FCC and related material. These are retained for the entire license term.

The Public and Broadcasting: A copy of the revised manual (when it becomes available).

Public Correspondence: A copy of all written comments and suggestions received from the public, including E-mail communications, regarding the station's operation, unless the writer requests the correspondence not be made public, or the licensee believes that it should be excluded from the file based on its content (for example, defamatory or obscene letters). E-mail correspondence may be retained as described above. (Note that this requirement does not generally apply to noncommercial stations, but such stations may choose to retain letters from the public regarding violent programming. All TV stations are required to file with their license renewal applications summaries of any letters received regarding violent programming.)

Material Related to an FCC Investigation or Complaint: Material that has a substantial bearing on a matter which is the subject of an FCC investigation or a complaint to the FCC about which the applicant, permittee, or licensee has been advised. This is retained until the FCC provides written notification that the material may be discarded.

Issues/Programs Lists: The quarterly list of programs that have provided the station's most significant treatment of community issues during the preceding three-month period. Each list should include a brief narrative describing the issues to which the station devoted significant treatment and the programs (or program segments) that provided this treatment, including the program's (or segment's) title, time, date, and duration. These are due on January 10, April 10, July 10, and October 10 of each year and must be retained for the entire license term.

Children's Commercial Limits: For commercial TV stations, quarterly records sufficient to substantiate the station's certification in its renewal application that it has complied with the commercial limits on children's programming. The records for each calendar quarter must be placed in the file no later than the tenth day of the succeeding calendar quarter (e.g., January 10, April 10, etc.). These are retained for the entire license term.

Children's Television Programming Reports: For commercial TV stations, the quarterly Children's Television Programming Report on FCC Form 398 showing efforts during the preceding quarter and plans for the next quarter to serve the educational and informational needs of children. This must be placed in the file no later than the tenth day of the succeeding calendar quarter (see above). These reports are kept separate from other materials in the public file and are retained for the entire license term.

License Renewal Local Public Notice Announcement: Statements certifying compliance with the local public notice requirements before and after the filing of the station's license renewal application. These are retained for the same period as the related license renewal application.

Radio Time Brokerage Agreements: For commercial radio stations, a copy of each time brokerage agreement related to the licensee's station or involving programming of another station in the same market by the licensee. Confidential or proprietary information may be redacted where appropriate. These are retained for as long as the agreement is in effect.

Must-Carry/Retransmission Consent Election: For TV stations, a statement of the station's election with respect to either must-carry or retransmission consent. In the case of noncommercial stations, a copy of any request for mandatory carriage on any cable system and related correspondence. These are retained for the duration of the period for which the statement or request applies.

Donors' Lists: For noncommercial stations only, a list of donors supporting specific programs. This is retained for two years.

Operating Requirements

The legal guidelines for operation comprise one of the most important policies for a broadcaster. In the early days of radio, broadcasting stations went on the air when they pleased and where they pleased. Adhering to an assigned frequency was of no concern. With the passage of the Communications Act of 1934, broadcasting became highly regulated. Despite deregulation of many areas of station activity, the FCC continues to monitor technical operations very closely.

When licensees are allocated a channel for broadcast purposes, in effect, they have entered into a contract. They must keep their signal on that channel and at the power allotted to them at all times. They are also required to run checks on their entire transmitting system and to note and retain the information gathered.

Licensees must observe FCC rules on the painting and lighting of towers, whether they own them or not. The Commission is now emphasizing observation of these rules and has an authorized $10,000 fine to deal with those who do not adhere to them. A similar initiative has been under way to ensure that all stations have Emergency Alert System equipment in operational order. The fine for a deviation is $8,000. Those stations with directional patterns must keep them within prescribed limits or be subject to a $7,000 fine.

Inspectors from one of the various FCC field offices arrive unannounced and inspect the station for violation of the Commission's engineering standards and other rules. After the inspection, the licensee will receive either (1) no notice at all, if the inspector determines that no violation exists; (2) a letter alerting the station that a problem does exist that could, if continued, result in a violation or prevent the station from performing effectively; or (3) an official notice of violation.

An important fact for all managers of broadcast stations to keep in mind is that, no matter how good their programs are, no matter how grandiose their facility may be, or how efficient their sales staff is, everything within their command is just as good as the technical staff that keeps the show on the air.

Fines and Forfeitures

Sections 503(b)(1) and (2) of the 1934 act authorize the FCC to levy monetary fines and forfeitures for violations of its regulations or certain federal statutes. Initial FCC authorization was for a fine of up to $2,000 for each individual violation and a total of $20,000 for continuing violations. In 1989, the limits were increased to $25,000 and $250,000, respectively. The justification for the increase was to provide strength to enforcement actions. In 1991, the Commission issued a fine and forfeiture schedule that set amounts for various categories of infractions. That basic menu was revised by the FCC in August 1993. Some of the relevant fines and forfeitures have been identified in various parts of this chapter. For a review of the violation classifications and the base fine for each, see Figure 7.4.

Regulatory Fees

The Omnibus Budget Reconciliation Act of 1993 requires the Federal Communications Commission to assess regulatory fees. These "user fees" are separate and distinct from application fees, which were authorized in 1987.

Figure 7.4 *Base amounts for FCC forfeitures.*

Violation	Fine
Construction or operation without authorization	$ 10,000
Unauthorized substantial transfer of control	8,000
Violations of rules relating to distress and safety frequencies	8,000
False distress communications	8,000
Violation of alien ownership rule	8,000
Failure to permit inspections	7,000
Interference	7,000
Failure to respond to Commission communications	4,000
Exceeding authorized antenna height	5,000
Exceeding power limits	4,000
Unauthorized emissions	4,000
Using unauthorized frequency	4,000
EAS equipment not installed or operational	8,000
Transmission of indecent/obscene materials	7,000
Violation of political rules	9,000
Fraud by wire, radio, or television	5,000
Violation of children's television requirements	8,000
Failure to engage in required frequency coordination	4,000
Failure to comply with prescribed lighting/marking	10,000
Unauthorized discontinuance of service	5,000
Use of unauthorized equipment	5,000
Construction or operation at unauthorized location	4,000
Violation of main studio rule	7,000
Violation of broadcast hoax rule	7,000
Failure to file required forms or information	3,000
Violation of public file rules	10,000
Violation of sponsorship ID requirements	4,000
Violation of requirements pertaining to broadcasting of lotteries or contests	4,000
Broadcasting telephone conversations without authorization	4,000
Failure to make required measurements or conduct required monitoring	2,000
Failure to provide station identification	1,000
Unauthorized pro forma transfer of control	1,000
Failure to maintain required records	1,000

The amount of the fee depends on the class of license held by a broadcaster. Collection commenced on April 1, 1994, and the Commission can levy a late fee of up to 25 percent. Regulatory fees for radio depend on category and range from an annual fee of $200 to a top of $2,000. There are also fees on AM and FM construction permits. Television fees vary with VHF or UHF allocation and market size. For an idea of how the fees are calculated, please see Figure 7.5.

Figure 7.5   *Fiscal 1997 FCC regulatory fee schedule. (Source: Fisher Wayland Cooper Leader &*
Zaragoza L.L.P. Used with permission.)

Fee Category	Annual Regulatory Fee
TV (47 CFR Part 73) VHF Commercial	
Markets 1-10	35,025
Markets 11-25	28,450
Markets 26-50	18,600
Markets 51-100	9,850
Remaining Markets	2,725
Construction Permits	4,800
TV (47 CFR Part 73) UHF Commercial	
Markets 1-10	16,850
Markets 11-25	13,475
Markets 26-50	8,750
Markets 51-100	4,725
Remaining Markets	1,350
Construction Permits	2,975
Satellite Television Stations (All Markets)	950
Construction Permits — Satellite Television Stations	345
Low Power TV, TV/FM Transistors & Boosters (47 CFR Part 74)	220
Broadcast Auxiliary (47 CFR Part 74)	25
Cable Antenna Relay Service (47 CFR Part 78)	65
Cable Television Systems (per subscriber) (47 CFR Part 76)	.54
Interstate Telephone Service Providers (per revenue dollar)	.00116
Earth Stations (47 CFR Part 25)	515
Space Stations (per operation station in geosynchronous orbit) (47 CFR Part 25) also includes Direct Broadcast Satellite Service (per operational station) (47 CFR Part 100)	97,975
Low Earth Orbit Satellite (per operational system) (47 CFR Part 25)	135,675
International Bearer Circuits (per active 64KB circuit)	5
International Public Fixed (per call sign) (47 CFR Part 23)	310
International (HF) Broadcast (47 CFR Part 73)	390

Figure 7.5   *Continued*

Fee Category	Annual Regulatory Fee
PMRS (per license) (Formerly Land Mobile — Exclusive Use at 220–222 MHz, above 470 MHz, Base Station and SMRS) (47 CFR Part 90)	10
Microwave (per license) (47 CFR Part 101)	10
Interactive Video Data Service (per license) (47 CFR Part 95)	No Fee
Marine (Ship) (per station) (47 CFR Part 80)	5
Marine (Coast) (per license) (47 CFR Part 80)	5
General Mobile Radio Service (per license) (47 CFR Part 95)	5
Land Mobile (per license) (all stations not covered by PMRS and CMRS)	5
Aviation (Aircraft) (per station) (47 CFR Part 87)	5
Aviation (Ground) (per license) (47 CFR Part 87)	5
Amateur Vanity Call Signs (per call sign) (47 CFR Part 97)	5
CMRS Mobile Services (per unit) (47 CFR Parts 20, 22, 24, 80, and 90)	.24
CMRS Messaging Services (per unit) (47 CFR Parts 20, 22, and 90)	.03
Multipoint Distribution Services (per call sign) (47 CFR Part 21)	215
Radio — AM and FM (47 CFR Part 73)	
Group 1	2,000
Group 2	1,800
Group 3	1,600
Group 4	1,400
Group 5	1,200
Group 6	1,000
Group 7	800
Group 8	600
Group 9	400
Group 10	200
AM Construction Permits	195
FM Construction Permits	950

DEALING WITH COMPLAINTS

For the most part, stations only receive complaints when an individual or group is angry about a program, a news report, a commercial, an editorial, or something technical like "your darn station is coming in on my toaster."

However, some people complain not only to stations but to the FCC. It disposes of most complaints by sending a letter to the complainant without ever contacting the broadcast station in question. For complaints involving political broadcasts or questions of access, the Commission encourages good-faith negotiations between licensees and persons who seek broadcast time or have related questions. In the past, such negotiations often have led to a disposition of the request or questions in a manner that is agreeable to all parties.

In general, the Commission limits its interpretive rulings or advisory opinions to cases in which the specific facts in controversy are before it for decision.

Written complaints to local stations must be kept in the public file, and the management should act or react to the complainant as soon as possible. Radio and television station operators are in a business where the image of the station must be a positive one or the audience may simply turn the dial or shut the TV or radio off. Good public relations are important ingredients in the management of any electronic media system.

With deregulation and some of the controversies that have ensued, the question now is what further changes, if any, will take place in the regulations and the agencies that enforce them. If the broadcast industry accepts the responsibility of self-regulation, deregulation may continue.

Accordingly, deregulation brings additional responsibilities for the broadcast manager. Some management decisions, especially in the area of programming, will have to be looked at in a different light without the federal regulations to guide the industry. The results of this new freedom within what was a heavily regulated business will come with time. If the industry does not take advantage of deregulation, it will find the old regulations being imposed once again. It is going to take time to determine whether or not broadcasters are willing to seize the opportunity to function in an environment similar to that of the print media. Responsible management will be the key.

WHAT'S AHEAD?

Broadcast and cable regulation are very sensitive to the political climate. It is hard to anticipate exactly what the future political environment will be. The changes that have occurred since the last edition of this book in 1995 have been momentous, but have not altered the basic deregulatory trend begun in 1981.

However, there is now some discussion of a reexamination of a licensee's role as a public trustee of the broadcast spectrum. The government's success in auctioning off some spectrum has established that it carries significant monetary value. And if broadcasters are to continue to get to use it at a nominal cost, some level of public responsibility will be expected in exchange.

In recent years, the FCC has enacted children's television programming requirements, and the political rules are being discussed. Consolidation has produced mega-public companies whose value and earnings are displayed on a regular basis.

As owner-operator broadcasting goes the way of the family farm, it is not unreasonable to foresee a day when the consolidated companies will be held to the high standards of public service that many earlier broadcasters set for themselves.

Should this forecast be correct, we might well see a day when some degree of reregulation occurs. When deregulation began, the FCC captured its spirit in a postcard license renewal form. Since then, the form has grown to a ten-page document. Perhaps that transition itself is the best demonstration of the fact that the bottom of the deregulation curve has been passed and that we are on our collective way up the other side.

SUMMARY

Traditionally, broadcast regulation has been based on the principles of the public interest and scarcity. The public interest remains intact. However, the Federal Communications Commission has effectively removed scarcity as a rationale.

The FCC was established by the Communications Act of 1934. It is the agency charged with regulating the electronic media but, in recent years, embarked on a program of industry deregulation. The Telecommunications Act of 1996 escalated further deregulation and electronic media consolidation. The new law has increased the participation of other arms of the federal government, like the Department of Justice, in communication regulation. Another agency, the Federal Trade Commission, polices advertising in broadcasting and other media.

Would-be and actual station licensees are required to file a large quantity of information with the FCC. Forms must be submitted to request authorization to construct a station and to obtain a license to operate. The Commission also requires submission of ownership reports and license renewal forms.

Despite deregulation, the FCC retains and continues to enforce many policies. There are restrictions on the numbers and kinds of stations that can be owned by one person or entity in a single community and nationwide. Programming policies cover, among other content, political broadcasts, and the use of obscenity, indecency, and profanity.

Stations are required to maintain for public inspection a file containing copies of all applications to the FCC, ownership and employment reports, details of programs broadcast in response to community issues, and other information. They also must comply with operating requirements set forth in their license.

In this new era, broadcasters must show that they can operate responsibly without close regulation. If they do not, a reimposition of at least some of the terminated policies is likely.

CASE STUDY

KXXX is an AM station in the Midwest and is a "must buy" for any political candidate. The station has sizable ratings in all demographics. It does not need or want political business. It is now the political season and the incumbents and wanna-bes are in full flower.

Of particular interest in the state this year is the election for governor. KXXX has refused to sell time to any candidate in either the primary or the general election. But the station did broadcast live a debate between the two major party candidates. A third-party candidate, Tom Steel, who was unable to be present at the broadcast debate, is demanding that the station sell him commercial time.

It is now forty-five days before the general election. KXXX refuses to sell or give time to Steel. He files a 315 "equal opportunity" complaint with the FCC claiming that the broadcast debate between the major party candidates constituted a 315 "use" mandating that he get equal time.

Exercises

1. Does KXXX have any obligation to sell or give time to Steel under Section 315 of the 1934 Communications Act? Why or why not?

2. If not under Section 315, can Steel make any claim under Section 312(a)(7) of the 1934 act?

3. If you or the FCC determine that there was, in fact, an obligation to sell to Steel, what rate would the station be required to offer him for Monday through Friday morning drive time?

CASE STUDY

KILS is owned by a multiple radio station operator and it has a complex ownership and financial structure. The annual 323 ownership report is 100 pages long. The station has not been performing especially well. It has a staff of six persons — one clerical, one in programming, and four in sales. The clerical person is the business manager. She does the log and is also the receptionist.

Recently, to improve its prospects, KILS changed its format to classic rock and canceled its old program supplier. Unfortunately, the new music was not ready on time, so the manager decided to play a single record by Joan Jet to get attention to the format change and to buy time. The song was played 24 hours a day for seven straight days.

The complaints poured in by phone, fax, and mail — hundreds of them. At one point, the police were called and pickets showed up outside the station. In an effort to file a complaint with the FCC, one especially crazed listener called in to the receptionist and demanded that the station photocopy and mail to her everything in the station's public file, back to the date the station went on the air. At the time of the complaint, KILS was in the seventh year of an eight-year license. It went on the air in 1971.

Citing lack of personnel and funds to comply with the listener's request, the station refused. The listener proceeded to file a complaint with the FCC.

Exercises

1. Must a station maintain a public file and comply with a phone request to provide documentation contained in it?

2. If a public file is required, what items should be in it?

3. If required, for what period must documentation be retained in a public file?

4. Under existing FCC rules, did KILS have any alternative to the phone request to photocopy and mail the documents to the listener?

NOTES

1. Telecommunications Act of 1996, Pub. L. 104–104, Feb. 8, 1996, 110 Stat. 56.

2. Syracuse Peace Council, 2 FCC Rcd. 5043, 1987.

3. Red Lion Broadcasting Co. v. Federal Communications Commission, 395 U.S. 367, 1969.

4. Don R. Pember, *Mass Media Law*, p. 471.

5. *Ibid.*, p. 470.

6. *Ibid.*, p. 476.

7. Century Communications Corporation v. Federal Communications Commission, 835 F2d 292, 1987.

8. 47 *USC* 308(b).

9. 47 *CFR* 73.2080 (b) and (c).

10. Lutheran Church-Missouri Synod v. FCC, D.C. Cir. No. 97–116 (April 14, 1998).

11. The 1996 Telecommunications Act changed the license term to eight years for both radio and television stations. Prior to that, the television term was five years and the radio term was seven years.

12. 47 *USC* 303(a), 303(b), and 394.

13. 47 *CFR* 73.3555.

14. WCVB-TV, 63 RR 2d 665, 1987.

15. In King Broadcasting Co., 6 FCC Rcd. 4998, 1991.

16. *Political Broadcasting Advisory*, Fisher Wayland Cooper Leader & Zaragoza L.L.P., January 1998, p. 7.

17. Meredith Corp. v. Federal Communications Commission, 809 F2d 863, 1987; Syracuse Peace Council, 2 FCC Rcd. 5043, 1987.

18. In the Matter of Policies and Rules Concerning Children's Television Programming, 6 FCC Rcd. 2111, 1991.

19. *Ibid.*

20. Review of The Prime Time Access Rule, 10 FCC Rcd. 5672 (1995).

21. "Networks Victorious in Fin-Syn Fight," *Broadcasting & Cable*, April 5, 1993, p. 7.

22. Syndication and Financial Interest Rules, 10 FCC Rcd. 12165 (1995).

23. 18 *USC* 1464.

24. Federal Communications Commission v. Pacifica Foundation, 438 U.S. 726, 1978.

25. New Indecency Enforcement Standards to Be Applied to All Broadcast and Amateur Radio Licenses, 2 FCC Rcd. 2726.

26. Action for Children's Television v. Federal Communications Commission, 852 F2d 1332, 1988.

27. Action for Children's Television v. Federal Communications Commission, 58 F3d 654.

28. Sagitarrius Broadcasting Corp. (Settlement Agreement), 10 FCC Rcd. 12245 (1995).

29. "Stern Warning: FCC Delays Station Sales," *Broadcasting & Cable*, January 10, 1994, p. 62.

30. "Disc Jockeys Air Racial Diatribe," *St. Louis Post-Dispatch*, May 11, 1993, p. 1.

31. R.A.V. v. City of St. Paul, Minnesota, 112 S. Ct. 2538, 1992.

32. "Infinity, Stern Hit with Racism Complaint," *Broadcasting & Cable*, November 22, 1993, p. 36.

33. "Steve & D.C. Suspended," *St. Louis Post-Dispatch*, May 13, 1993, p. 1.

34. Letter to KSHE-FM, 6 FCC Rcd. 2289.

35. Broadcast Hoaxes, 70 RR 2d 1383, 1992.

36. 18 *USC* 1307(a) (2).

37. Broadcast of Lottery Information (Charity Games), 67 RR 2d 996, 1990.

38. 18 *USC* 1304.

39. Valley Broadcasting Co. v. United States 107 F. 32. 1328 (9th Cir. 1997).

40. T. Barton Carter, Marc A. Franklin, and Jay B. Wright, *The First Amendment and the Fifth Estate*, pp. 393–394.

41. 47 *CFR* 73.1216.

ADDITIONAL READINGS

Creech, Kenneth C. *Electronic Media Law and Regulation*. Boston: Focal Press, 1993.

Devol, Kenneth S. (ed.). *Mass Media and the Supreme Court*, 4th ed. New York: Hastings House, 1987.

Holsinger, Ralph L., and Jon Paul Dilts. *Media Law*, 3rd ed. New York: McGraw-Hill, 1994.

Kahn, Frank J. (ed.). *Documents of American Broadcasting*, 4th ed. Englewood Cliffs, NJ: Prentice-Hall, 1984.

NAB Legal Guide to Broadcast Law and Regulation, 3rd ed. Washington, DC: National Association of Broadcasters, 1988.

Zelezny, John D. *Communications Law: Liberties, Restraints, and the Modern Media*. Belmont, CA: Wadsworth, 1993.

8

MANAGING THE CABLE TELEVISION SYSTEM

This chapter considers cable TV management by examining

☐ franchising and refranchising procedures

☐ managerial functions and responsibilities, with special attention to programming, economics, and promotion

☐ the regulatory environment in which cable systems operate

While Guglielmo Marconi was working toward his dream of a telegraph system without wires, he would have laughed at the irony that, less than a century later, telecommunications *with* wires would again be all the rage. To Marconi and other electrical tinkerers of the early twentieth century, it was a great goal to one day be able to send messages over long distances without the need of wires. These electronic pioneers brought us radio and, later, television. All the while, the fact remained that many more messages could be sent — much more clearly — through cable than could be broadcast over the airwaves. While Marconi might have laughed, broadcasters are not amused. Cable is a major competitor, siphoning off audiences, revenues, and programming from conventional television broadcasters.

As the twentieth century moved to a close, more than 11,000 cable systems passed almost 97 percent of the nation's 98 million television households.[1] Cable penetration totaled 67 percent of those homes, yielding almost 66 million subscribers.[2] Of that number, 48 million, or 74 percent, also subscribed to pay-cable services.[3]

In the ten years from 1987–88 to 1996–97, audience shares for basic cable networks more than doubled, from 15 percent to 36 percent of all TV households.[4] In contrast, shares for broadcast network affiliates dropped sharply, from 61 percent to 43 percent.[5]

Cable's strength as a competitor for advertising revenues was also demonstrated during the period. Total cable revenues increased dramatically, from just over $1 billion annually to more than $7.8 billion.[6] Original productions, combined with the purchase of successful off-network programs, added to cable's growing popularity.

As they look to the future, cable companies are contemplating ways of consolidating their profitability. Many have already begun the process of transforming themselves from program purveyors to suppliers of a full range of communications services.

THE FRANCHISING PROCESS

Anyone considering a career in cable television should be familiar with the basis of cable operation: *franchising*. The franchise agreement provides the cable system with authorization to utilize public rights-of-way in conducting business, and establishes the terms and conditions under which this can be done. The franchise is to cable what the license is to broadcast stations.

In the beginning, the process was an area of shared responsibility between local and federal governments. Local governments issued the franchise because of the uses cable systems made of city streets and other rights-of-way. The Federal Communications Commission set standards for the provisions franchises should include.

This structure of dual responsibility was confusing and ripe for abuse. Revenue-starved cities placed many demands on potential cable operators as preconditions to franchise issuance. This was true, particularly, when an exclusive franchise was at stake. In their zeal to win, competing companies made promises that were neither practical nor affordable. Bribery of officials to obtain lucrative franchises was not unknown. No one was happy — neither the local governments nor the operators.

It was in this climate that Congress enacted the Cable Communications Policy Act of 1984. The act continued the requirement that operators obtain a franchise. Franchising authority remained with local governments, and they determined the franchise term.

However, limitations were imposed on what a government could demand before granting a franchise. Cities could require franchisees to offer broad categories of programming (e.g., for children), but were not permitted to specify carriage of particular networks or services to satisfy the requirement. They could also include in the franchise agreement a provision that channel space be allocated for public, educational, or governmental access, so-called "PEG" channels. Systems with thirty-six or more channels had to provide space for *commercial leased access*; in other words, channels available for lease by persons unrelated to the cable company.

The 1984 law provided that the franchise authority might grant one or more franchises within its jurisdiction. Companies that overpromised in their eagerness to obtain a franchise could receive relief upon adequate showing of an inability to comply. Cities were entitled to collect a franchise fee from cable operators. However, it could not exceed 5 percent of the cable system's gross revenue for any twelve-month period. The act also freed systems from franchise authority rate regulation.

The history of experience under the 1984 act was not one of success. Basic provisions of the law were challenged in court by the cable industry itself. One such provision was that which allowed franchise authorities to award exclusive franchises.[7] Deregulated cable rates exploded. The twin pressures of litigation and consumer reaction forced Congress to reexamine cable regulation. It did so, and passed the Cable Television Consumer Protection and Competition Act of 1992. The major impact of the new law on franchise requirements was a prohibition on the granting of exclusive franchises. The law imposed many new obligations on franchisees and ended the "deregulation" of cable. Basic requirements of the law are reviewed in the regulation section later in the chapter.

FRANCHISE RENEWAL

As noted earlier, cable franchises are issued by local governments, not the FCC. Unlike broadcast licenses, cable franchises have no universally fixed term. Each local authority sets the term of the franchise or franchises within its jurisdiction. Before 1984, there were no universal rules for the procedure or for criteria to be applied in franchise renewals. Cable operators wanted the security that the FCC license afforded broadcasters. Broadcast licensees had a "renewal expectancy." In other words, if they had rendered "substantial past meritorious service to the public" during their license term, they expected that the license would be renewed. On the other hand, the absence of renewal standards in the cable industry had become an impediment to investment.

The Cable Communications Policy Act of 1984 addressed cable operator renewal concerns. The act set national renewal standards, but left the administration of those standards to local franchise authorities. It also established specific timetables and criteria for renewal. Cable operators may initiate the renewal procedure by submitting written notice to their franchise authority. Any operator seeking renewal is entitled to a public hearing at which its past performance can be evaluated and the future cable-related needs of the community considered. The hearing must be held within a six-month period, beginning no later than thirty months before the expiration of the franchise. At the conclusion of this evaluation, an operator may submit a renewal proposal. The franchise authority has a fixed period within which to accept it, or indicate its preliminary determination that the franchise should not be renewed.[8]

Denial of a renewal proposal must be based on one or more of the four factors examined at such a proceeding, which considers whether

- the cable operator has substantially complied with the material terms of the existing franchise and with applicable law;

- the quality of the operator's service, including signal quality, response to consumer complaints, and billing practices, but without regard to the mix or quality of cable services or other services provided over the system, has been reasonable in light of community needs;

- the operator has the financial, legal, and technical ability to provide the services, facilities, and equipment as set forth in the operator's proposal; and

- the operator's proposal is reasonable to meet the future cable-related community needs and interests, taking into account the cost of meeting such needs and interests.[9]

The relative security afforded a cable operator by the law should not lead to laxity about the renewal process, however. Even though most franchises are granted for ten to fifteen years, many operators recommend an early start on preparing the new proposal.

If the franchisee has performed well during the franchise term, the task of obtaining renewal may not be too difficult. Nonetheless, the need to plan is extremely important. It should include identifying and resolving potential problems, striving to respond to community needs and desires for programming, and determining whether or not the system should be upgraded or expanded. With an eye toward renewal, many systems operated by multiple system operators (MSOs) sample customer attitudes in their monthly program guide.

Sensitivity to subscribers' needs is essential. An operator who is not prepared will run into difficulties during the refranchising procedures. It is important to let the public know what has been accomplished and what is planned.

Presentations before the local governmental authority must be professional. Information must be accurate and displayed in a form that can be read and understood easily. Keeping files on complaints, no matter how minute, as well as complimentary correspondence, also will be of value.

Once the franchise has been renewed, full attention returns to day-to-day operations.

ORGANIZATION

Like a broadcast station, a cable television system is organized according to the major functions that must be carried out to ensure successful operation. While differences exist in organizational structure, the functions are similar and are allocated to departments. The following departments are found in many systems:

Government Affairs and Community Relations

These activities are often performed by only one person, with the title of director. Government affairs revolves around contacts with federal, state, and local elected officials, especially those who make up the franchising authority. The planning and execution of public relations campaigns designed to create and maintain a favorable image in the franchise area are the focus of community relations.

Human Resources

A manager may be the only person charged with human resource responsibilities. They include recruiting and interviewing job applicants, orienting new employees, developing and implementing employee training and evaluation programs, and processing benefits.

Business Operations

A director supervises the work of personnel in this department, which has responsibility for processing revenues and expenditures, handling collections, and computer operations.

Advertising Sales

The sale of local availabilities in advertiser-supported networks is a major responsibility of this department, headed by a manager. Many systems also sell classified advertising and spots on local origination channels.

Technical Operations

A director is charged with responsibility for this department, which engages in a variety of tasks. They include maintenance and operation of the headend (i.e., the facility that receives, processes, and converts video signals for transmission on the cable) and trunk and feeder cables; maintenance of the standby power supply; testing and adjustment of signal strength; installation and repair of drop cables and hookups to cable boxes and videocassette recorders; planning and construction of extensions to the cable system in new subdivisions and apartment complexes; and the dispatch of technicians. The director is assisted by supervisors with expertise in the different operational areas.

Marketing

A marketing director heads this department. Its major responsibilities are the sale of the system's program services to subscribers, and the planning and execution of advertising and promotion campaigns in furtherance of that goal. The department engages in market analyses to assess customer preferences and potential, determines the packaging of services and their price structure, and conducts door-to-door and telemarketing sales campaigns.

Figure 8.1   *Organization of a cable television system.*

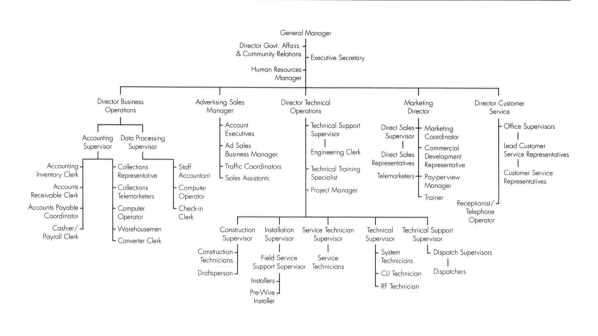

Customer Service

This department, headed by a director, deals with all customer service and repair calls, inquiries, and complaints.

The number and organization of employees is influenced by the size of the system and by its status as a single entity or part of a multiple system operation. Management preferences also play a role in system organization, and scores of variations exist. Figure 8.1 shows how a system may be organized. It is headed by a general manager (GM).

The GM directs and coordinates all system activities to ensure efficient and profitable operation within the framework established by federal law and the local franchise agreement. In particular, the general manager

- supervises and coordinates, directly or through subordinates, all personnel

- directs, through subordinates, employee compliance with established administrative policies and procedures, safety rules, and governmental regulations

- examines, analyzes, and establishes system directions and goals

- prepares and directs procedures designed to increase efficiency and revenues and to lower costs

- prepares, implements, and controls the budget

- approves requisitions for equipment, materials, and supplies, and all invoices

- represents the system to local government, business, the media, and other groups

As in a broadcast station, each department is unique. However, there are major differences. The cable company sends its signals through wires; the broadcast station through the airwaves. In broadcast, advertisers are the primary market. In cable, the audience is the market and the system's financial success is tied closely to the number of subscribers it can attract and the number of services they purchase.

These realities impose on cable managers an obligation to ensure that the technical quality of the signal is of the highest caliber. Viewers will continue to subscribe as long as they feel they are receiving value for their money. If they do not, the system will experience subscriber disconnects, or *churn*. Accordingly, the marketing and technical staffs must cooperate closely, since the retention and addition of subscribers depend heavily on a signal that is technically acceptable when delivered to the home. The system manager must pay close and constant attention to those two areas of activity. They are the very foundation upon which the company survives.

The general manager must know what is happening in every department. This can be accomplished through regular meetings with department heads. Such meetings also provide an effective method of solving problems before they become crises.

Cable managers must be sensitive to the needs of their employees. Getting to know the staff, being receptive to their problems and ideas, and keeping an open-door policy will be beneficial in the smooth and effective running of the operation. Apathy and discontent also may be avoided as a result.

PROGRAMMING

The programming challenge for cable system operators has never been greater. The explosion of available program services has continued unabated. New federal laws require operators to carry certain local broadcast stations.[10] Old federal laws permit or require that channels be provided for mandatory access, like PEG access, and for lease by third parties. Franchise agreements may require still other channel dedication for services such as local origination.

Technological advances, including video compression and fiber optics, are rapidly expanding program choices and channel capacity. Interactive services, like video-on-demand and pay-per-view, are now part of the program mix.

Management must make program selections that satisfy subscribers' demands for choice and value while maximizing system revenue.

Essentially, system programming is of two types: voluntary and involuntary. Voluntary operator program choices include distant broadcast signals, advertiser-supported satellite networks, premium satellite services, and special programming, such as pay-per-view. Involuntary programming may include local broadcast stations under the must-carry rules, PEG mandatory access, leased access, and local origination.

Once chosen, programming must be paid for. Most voluntary programming requires payment; most involuntary programming does not. System operators pay for programming in two ways. The first is a requirement of federal law. In 1976, Congress enacted a comprehensive copyright law that required cable systems to pay semiannual fees for the carriage of some television stations. Copyright fees are not owed for carriage of local stations under must carry.

However, a compulsory fee set by law is required to carry distant commercial stations, including superstations. Amounts owed are a statutory percentage of subscriber receipts and range from just under 1 percent to a maximum of 3.75 percent. Actual sums depend on the number of distant signals carried and the date of their introduction into the schedule by the cable system.

In addition to the copyright payment, most voluntary program selections involve a payment directly to the program supplier. Such payments normally are calculated on a per-subscriber basis and are influenced by system size, since volume discounts are offered. There may be surcharges for some networks, especially those that offer professional sports, such as ESPN and TNT. In those instances, the programmer passes along to the cable system part of the substantial rights fee for such programming. However, many advertiser-supported cable networks allow systems to sell local advertising in network programming. This local revenue generation helps to offset the programming cost.

Costs for noncommercial premium channels, like HBO, are far different. Payments are also set on a monthly, per-subscriber basis, but the amounts are much higher than for commercial, advertiser-supported networks. Again, volume discounts are offered. Obviously, no commercial offset for local system revenue generation is possible. Consequently, subscriber charges for premium channels are also much higher than those for basic sources.

Some program decisions result in payments to the cable system. Home shopping networks, for example, pay local systems a percentage of gross product sales generated in the system's franchise area. New networks often provide systems with financial marketing support to assist their launch in the community. The sums are not large, but may amount to several thousand dollars.

It has been emphasized that the audience is the major customer of cable television and provides its principal financial support. For that reason, an important economic consideration in all programming decisions is the anticipated impact on subscriptions. A major goal in program selection is the addition of subscribers and the minimizing of disconnects. Decisions to accomplish those goals will rely on the operator's familiarity with the composition and program preferences of the community and of subscribers and nonsubscribers.

The operator's expertise in program selection is very important. It was noted earlier that cable systems pass almost 97 percent of the nation's television households, but that only about 67 percent of those homes subscribe. Attractive program choices must be available to convert some of the nonsubscribing homes to subscribers.

Recognizing the potential and limitations of the system's technology, legal obligations contained in federal law and the franchise agreement, and the need to maximize audience appeal and ensure a profit, the operator proceeds to program the available channels. Typically, the services provided include the following:

Local Origination and Access Channels
Many systems are required by the franchise agreement to produce programs for carriage on local origination, or community, channels. Time, temperature, and newswire displays, round-table discussions, and local sports are examples. Some also use the channel for community bulletin boards and program previews. In all cases, operators control the content.

The agreement also may require that channels be reserved for public, educational, and governmental access. This programming is produced by persons outside the cable company and often includes discussions, credit and noncredit courses, and meetings of local government bodies.

As noted earlier, some systems are required to offer leased access to individuals or groups. The content varies widely, reflecting the interests and goals of the leasing parties.

Most systems add audio to the service mix. Local radio stations are an example. Many also carry digital audio programming with several dozen channels of specialized music. Digital Music Express (DMX), for instance, offers thirty different music formats in CD-quality sound, with neither commercials nor announcers.

Local, Over-the-Air Broadcast Stations

The 1992 act reimposed must-carry rules on the cable industry.[11] Simply put, must carry requires a cable system to carry the commercial and noncommercial stations in its area. Under the law, broadcasters were required to choose between must carry or retransmission consent before October 6, 1993. Retransmission consent is a legal alternative to must carry. If a station elected retransmission consent, that amounted to a must-carry waiver. Under retransmission consent, broadcast stations could not be carried on a cable system without their consent. If a station and system could not reach a retransmission agreement, the system was free to drop the station in question.

The 1992 law considerably reduces programming discretion by a cable operator with respect to local television stations. More detail on the specifics of must carry may be found in the regulation section later in the chapter.

Distant Broadcast Stations

So-called "superstations," such as WGN (Chicago) and WWOR (New York), offer entertainment and sports programming that may not be available from other sources. The system pays to the stations a small, monthly subscriber fee. As noted earlier, copyright fees may be substantial if several distant stations are included in the channel lineup, particularly if they have been added since 1981, when new FCC rules went into effect.

Basic Cable Networks

Operators have dozens of satellite-delivered networks from which to choose. Some target a narrow audience with specialized content, while others seek a broader audience with more diverse programming (see Figure 8.2). Together, the networks provide a range of programming, and their selection will reflect the operator's perceptions of the interests and needs of the community and its subgroups. Compensation arrangements for system carriage of these mostly advertiser-supported networks were reviewed earlier in the chapter.

Pay-Cable Networks

These networks (see Figure 8.3) offer commercial-free entertainment for a monthly subscriber fee, part of which is retained by the cable company. As a result, these so-called "premium" channels are a high economic priority for operators.

Figure 8.2 *Selected basic cable networks and their content.*

Name	Content
A&E Television Network	Original biographies, mysteries, literary adaptations, documentaries
AMC (American Movie Classics)	Fifty years of Hollywood's greatest films
C-SPAN (Cable Satellite Public Affairs Network)	Live coverage of the House of Representatives, Congressional hearings, National Press Club speeches, federal judiciary, books, the next presidential election, public policy events, viewer call-in
CNBC	Business, money, and talk programming
CNN (Cable News Network)	Major breaking stories, business, weather, sports, special interest reports
Discovery Channel	Informative entertainment about nature and the environment, science and technology, history, adventure, and the people who share our world
ESPN	Sports events, special events and series, news
Fox Family Channel	Original movies and series, classic movies, westerns, comedies, children's programming, music specials
Headline News	National and international stories, consumer, sports, and entertainment news, extended weather forecasts, in 30-minute blocks
Learning Channel, The (TLC)	History, science, human behavior, and lifestyles, combined with preschool and "how-to" programs
Lifetime Television	Original movies, specials, series, parenting and lifestyle information, public awareness campaigns, all directed toward women
MTV: Music Television	Contemporary stereo music and pop culture
Nickelodeon/Nick at Nite	News and entertainment for children/classic TV programs for the people who grew up with television
QVC	Home shopping, offering a range of products to viewers
TBS Superstation	Movies, sports, comedies, original programming
TNN: The Nashville Network	Original concert specials and series, music videos, entertainment news and interviews, live variety, country lifestyle information, sports
TNT (Turner Network Television)	New and vintage motion pictures, original films, children's programming, sports, special events
USA Network	Original series, movies, specials, sports, and programming for women, children, teens, and adults
VH-1 (Music First)	Current and classic music videos, music-based series and movies, original concerts, special events, news and interviews
Weather Channel, The	Local, regional, and national weather forecasts, travel forecasts, severe weather coverage

Some systems are using channel space for their own newscasts and for system-purchased syndicated programming, previously the exclusive domain of network affiliates and independents. Those with the necessary technology are reserving channels for pay-per-view (PPV) programming, permitting subscribers to select special programs, such as sports or entertainment specials, for which they are

Figure 8.3   *Selected pay-cable networks and their content.*

Name	Content
Bravo Cable Network*	American and international films, performing arts, profiles, interviews, music
Cinemax	Box office hit movies
Disney Channel, The*	Original series, movies, specials, combined with timeless classics
Encore	Hit movies from the 1960s, 1970s, and 1980s
Flix	Popular movies from the 1960s into the 1990s
HBO (Home Box Office)	Box office hits, original movies, comedies, documentaries, series, music, sports, family programming
Movie Channel, The (TMC)	Movies of all genres and from all decades
Showtime	Theatrical films, original movies and series, boxing, family entertainment
STARZ!	First-run movies, film festivals
Sundance Channel	New independent films

*May be offered on expanded basic by some systems

Figure 8.4   *Selected pay-per-view cable networks and their content.*

Name	Content
Action Pay Per View	Independent action, sci-fi, and thriller movies
Adam & Eve Channel, The*	Adult films
AdulTVision	Adult-themed movies
Cable Video Store (CVS)	Hollywood movies
Playboy TV*	Adult entertainment
Spice*	Adult films
Viewer's Choice	Eleven-channel multiplex offering the latest Hollywood films and special musical and live sporting events

*May be offered as a premium channel by some systems

billed separately. Individual systems may contract for the rights to carry a pay-per-view event or to acquire programs from one of several national PPV services (see Figure 8.4) under a fee-splitting arrangement. Although PPV results have been somewhat disappointing to date, industry professionals predict significant growth. Still other channels are being dedicated to the emerging video-on-demand market, which may become a significant revenue source.

Programming is a key contributor to successful operation. Without appealing programs, there would be no subscribers. Without subscribers, there would be no system. Providing a balanced program service at an acceptable cost is a continuing challenge.

Tiering

Once the operator has made all the programming choices, attention will turn to marketing the selected products. Historically, cable systems have bundled certain categories of programming together for sale to potential subscribers. That practice is known as *tiering*. Typically, the subscribers' fee structure is tied to the tiers, and the total monthly charge depends on the options chosen.

There has always been a relationship between tier structure and government regulation, both federal and local. The best current example of the relationship is the massive change in tiering that resulted from the Cable Television Consumer Protection and Competition Act of 1992. The law requires cable systems to establish a separate *basic tier* and specifies what must be included in it.[12] The minimum requirements include all must-carry stations, distant television stations carried by the system, excluding superstations, home shopping stations,[13] and mandatory access channels. Rates for this government-mandated tier are regulated by the local franchise authority. Details of rate regulation appear later in the chapter.

The basic tier requirement, and the rate control that went with it, caused a significant realignment of the structures that existed before the 1992 law. Operators had to create a new home for those program sources which were subject to price increases or surcharges. Because of government-imposed basic rate control, operators could no longer easily pass along to subscribers program costs for existing sources or for new sources.

As a consequence, most of the nation's 11,000 systems have established some form of expanded basic tier. *Expanded basic*, or *expanded service*, as some call it, usually includes the non-must-carry, nonpremium services that existed previously in the old basic tier. Here are found primarily the advertiser-supported cable satellite networks. Typical expanded basic offerings would include CNN, USA, MTV, and A&E, for example.

The new tiering plans also have a premium level beyond the expanded basic service. At this level are positioned the standard, premium noncommercial program services. Such offerings might include HBO, Showtime, Cinemax, The Movie Channel, and The Disney Channel. These premium channels may be subscribed to on an individual or package basis.

Figure 8.5 reflects the tiering structure used by one operator. It shows that the system has four tiers of bundled programming: limited basic, expanded service, value pack, and entertainment pack. It also offers bundled and unbundled premium services, together with pay-per-view movies and events on its "home theater" channels.

Tiering structure has been acutely sensitive to the presence or absence of government regulation. The longevity of the current tier concept will depend, in large part, on the continuation of the present regulatory model.

Figure 8.5   *Tier structure of a cable television system.*

Limited Basic

2	WGN (WB), Chicago	8	Headline News
3	Education & Government	9	WELF (Ind), Dalton
4	WRCB (NBC), Chattanooga	10	WTVC (ABC), Chattanooga
5	WTCI (PBS), Chattanooga	11	WDSI (Fox), Chattanooga
6	WFLI (UPN), Cleveland	12	WCLP (PBS), Chatsworth
7	TBS Superstation	13	WDEF (CBS), Chattanooga

Expanded Service

14	CNN	39	Home Shopping Network
15	USA	40	Knowledge TV
16	ESPN	41	The Learning Channel
23	Sneak Prevue	42	fX
25	MTV	43	Odyssey
26	A&E	44	Prevue Guide
27	TNN	45	CMT
28	Nickelodeon	46	Lease Channel
29	Lifetime	57	Black Entertainment TV
30	VH1	58	TV Food Network
31	Fox Family Channel	59	Fox News
32	The Weather Channel	60	Fit TV
33	Fox Sports South	69	Shop at Home
34	Cartoon Network	70	Outdoor Life
35	E!	75	Sneak Peek
36	Game Show Network	76	C-SPAN
37	CNBC	77	C-SPAN 2
38	QVC		

Value Pak

17	TNT	20	Discovery Channel
18	TV Land	21	Animal Planet
19	American Movie Classics	22	Home & Garden TV

Entertainment Pak

47	ESPN 2	52	Sci-Fi Channel
48	Turner Classic Movies	53	Court TV
49	Comedy Central	54	The History Channel
50	MOVIEplex	55	Bravo
51	The Golf Channel	56	Z Music

Premium Pay Services

61	Showtime	80	HBO
62	The Movie Channel	81	HBO Plus
63	Cinemax	82	HBO Family
64	The Disney Channel		

Pay-Per-View

65	Home Theater	72	Home Theater
66	Home Theater	73	Home Theater
67	Home Theater	74	Home Theater
68	Home Theater		

ECONOMICS

In the 1990s, the number of basic subscribers rose by about 25 percent, from 52 million to almost 66 million.[14] The increase in pay-cable subscribers was almost as dramatic, up from 39 million to 48 million.[15] With these impressive gains, cable operators are focusing increasingly on the marketing of their services and the sale of time to advertisers.

Revenues

Monthly subscriber fees account for 81 percent of cable television revenues.[16] Basic rates, which averaged $26.48 in 1997,[17] make up 66 percent of fee revenue,[18] with the remainder coming from pay services, with an average rate of $8.00 a month.[19]

It is the responsibility of the system's marketing department to recruit subscribers. Figure 8.6 illustrates how the marketing process works for the program services listed in Figure 8.5. Subscribers pay a flat fee to receive all the programming in the limited basic tier. A higher fee provides subscribers with all the programming in the basic tier and the expanded service tier. An additional fee is required for the value pack. Note that the system markets all three tiers in what it calls "preferred service." However, it offers no discounts. The cost is the total of the three priced individually. A still higher price is charged to subscribers who wish to receive the ten services in the entertainment pack. Premium services may be purchased individually, except for the three HBO channels. Four of the offerings carry the same price tag. The cost of the home theater channels varies according to the movie or event ordered.

One technique formerly employed by cable system marketers is no longer available. Before the 1992 cable law, subscribers were required to buy through one tier to get to the next. For example, they had to purchase expanded basic to obtain premium services. The law prohibits buy-through requirements, except for the government-mandated basic channels.

A cable system's revenues are not limited to regular video program services. Pay-per-view and digital audio also contribute to an operator's gross revenue.

Installation, reconnect, and change of service charges, together with equipment rental (e.g., remote controls, addressable converters), add incremental income.

If revenues are to be enhanced, cable managers must continue to pay close attention to subscriber needs and provide prompt, efficient, and courteous service. One study of almost 1,800 subscribers and nonsubscribers concluded that good service equates with good value and poor service with poor value, regardless of the rates charged.[20]

Many systems have installed telephone automatic response units (ARUs) so that questions may be channeled directly to the appropriate information source. Allied with computers, the units permit subscribers to check their account balance and the date and amount of their last payment, order special movies or events, report a service problem, confirm or reschedule a service or installation appointment, and receive general information.

Important as technology is, its contribution may be limited by the personnel assigned to it. Accordingly, customer service representatives (CSRs) must

Figure 8.6 *Tier pricing structure of a cable television system.*

Limited Basic	6.45
Expanded Service	16.78
Value Pak	4.85
Preferred Service (Limited Basic, Expanded Service, Value Pak)	28.08
Entertainment Pak	4.95
Showtime	11.00
The Movie Channel	11.00
Cinemax	11.00
The Disney Channel	11.00
HBO, HBO Plus, HBO Family	12.50
Home Theater	*

*Prices vary with movie or event

be trained in its use and must understand the importance of customer satisfaction. A dissatisfied customer may mean one fewer subscriber and a lost revenue source. Telemarketing assistants must be informed, but not aggressive and dictatorial.

Similarly, company employees who come face-to-face with customers and prospective customers must be knowledgeable and skilled in human relations. Installers and service technicians must be aware of the subscriber's needs, take appropriate steps to avoid damage to property, and be tolerant in explaining and responding to questions about the operation of cable in the home. Door-to-door sales representatives must be suitably dressed and act in a professional manner.

The importance of cable to subscribers is exemplified when a storm or other event interferes with service. Typically, the system's telephone lines are jammed with calls and the temperament of the CSRs is put to the test. Patience and a sympathetic attitude can do much to disarm customers' annoyance and to reassure them that the problems are being resolved. On such occasions, however, frankness is mandatory. Only realistic estimates of service resumption time should be given. If wild and unsubstantiated guesses are made and not fulfilled, annoyance will grow into anger and, possibly, more lost customers and revenue.

Advertising is becoming an increasingly significant revenue source. Between 1990 and 1997, local and spot sales more than tripled, to $1.9 billion, and accounted for 25 percent of all cable advertising revenue.[21]

Multiple system operators have been especially aggressive in developing this revenue source. Often, they interconnect individual systems in contiguous geographic areas to deliver more homes to advertisers. Some large metropolitan systems owned by different operators may interconnect for the purpose of marketing local and spot announcements.

Cable has several advantages for advertisers. It attracts audiences that are characterized as better-educated and more affluent than the average TV viewer. The special-appeal programming of many basic networks permits the targeting of specific demographics, much like radio. In addition, time is less costly than on a broadcast television station. However, the quality of ads produced only for cable often is inferior, and the automated hardware to run them is expensive and often unreliable.

Figure 8.7 *Cable TV system rate card.*

	6am-12am Rotator	6pm-12am Rotator	6pm-12am Fixed Position	6am-6pm Rotator	6am-6pm Fixed Position
CNN USA ESPN Discovery Lifetime	$25	$50	$60	$18	$34
TNT TNN Learning Ch. Headline News Nickelodeon	$22	$40	$46	$16	$28
A&E MTV VH-I FX HGTV Family FOX Sports So.	$18	$34	$38	$12	$24
BET CNBC E! CMT Weather Outdoor Life Food Network	$12	$22	$30	$10	$18

Weather Channel Crawl:
$125 per week (Monday - Sunday)
280 Characters

Prevue Guide Crawl:
$100 per week (Monday - Sunday)
240 Characters

Time is sold on local origination channels and on many basic networks. The majority of networks make available for local sale two minutes every hour. CNN and TNT, however, make available three minutes.

Figure 8.7 shows the rate card for a system offering rotating schedules in three dayparts and fixed-position schedules in two. The rates are for 30-second spots. Sixty-second spots are sold at twice the 30-second charge. Note that a different rate applies to purchases of week-long crawls (data that moves across the screen) on The Weather Channel and the Prevue Guide Channel. A different pricing mechanism also is used for special packages and special programming.

The knowledge, skills, and personal qualities of the advertising sales manager and the account executives, and the sales tools necessary for success, are similar to those required of their broadcast counterparts, described in Chapter 5, "Broadcast Sales."

Historically, cable systems have not been preoccupied with ratings. What was important was that subscribers signed up and enjoyed their viewing experiences enough to continue their subscription. Now that advertising is becoming a more important revenue source, systems are more ratings-conscious. To assist them, Nielsen has developed the Nielsen Homevideo Index (NHI), which measures audiences for basic and pay services. The company also undertakes specially commissioned studies for operators.

Reliable audience information is a necessity if local ad sales are to continue their growth and operators are to make informed decisions in selecting programs with appeal to audiences and to the advertisers that seek them.

Expenses

In addition to paying regular taxes, cable television systems are required to hand over to the franchising authority up to 5 percent of their revenues and, in some cases, channel capacity for public, educational, and governmental use.

The cost of laying cable averages between $30,000 and $35,000 per mile. This is a substantial investment for a business that must share its revenues with the community. The investment becomes even larger if the cable company has agreed in its franchise to originate local programming and has to equip a production facility.

Many of the system's operating expenses are similar to those of a broadcast station: salaries, commissions, employee benefits, payroll taxes, utilities, supplies, programming, travel, and communication. Major differences are the franchise fees described above, maintenance and repair of miles of cable and associated equipment, and pole rental. Principal expense items are listed in Figure 8.8.

Like the broadcast manager, the cable manager faces a difficult task in trying to increase revenues and control costs in a very competitive marketplace. Consumers have many options in spending their entertainment and information dollars. Likewise, businesses have a choice of vehicles for marketing their products and services. Careful attention to the needs of both groups, and appealing and economically attractive responses, are imperative.

Figure 8.8   *Cable TV system expense items.*

Technical salaries	Utilities
Technical overtime	Vehicles
Office salaries	Equipment repairs
Office overtime	Production
Marketing salaries	Advertising and marketing
Marketing commissions	Office supplies
Contract labor—marketing	Postage
Employee training	Telephone—base rate
Employee benefits	Telephone—long distance
Payroll taxes	Insurance
Installations	Legal and consulting
Contract labor—technical	Publications and subscriptions
Maintenance	Travel
Operating supplies	Bad debt
Converter maintenance	Janitorial/building
Pole rental	Property and general taxes
Basic programming	Data processing
Pay-cable programming	Franchise fees
Pay-per-view	Copyright fees
Program guide	Charitable contributions
Subscriber billings	Association dues

PROMOTION

Cable promotion has begun to reflect the maturity of the business itself. The original elements are still there, to be sure. Systems continue to use direct mail, door-to-door, and on-the-air solicitations, but other techniques are being employed as well. Principal among them is over-the-air television. Local TV stations once were reluctant to accept cable advertising, since the two were seen to be in direct competition for audiences. For the most part, that reluctance is gone and systems, individually or as part of an area marketing group, use broadcast television extensively. The results are impressive. People who watch television are, after all, a logical market for cable systems.

Radio is attractive, too. It is cost-effective, and advertising can be targeted to the unique formats and demographics of stations.

Newspaper is used successfully, particularly to feature coupons for a premium service at an introductory rate and with no installation cost. Program listings in the newspaper's television program supplement, in cable guides, and in *TV Guide* also are forms of valuable promotion.

Most systems use a monthly program guide to carry listings and interest subscribers in upgrading their service. Some employ a basic channel, called a "barker channel," to promote premium services and pay-per-view.

Promotion costs can often be offset by co-op money from the national cable networks, and system managers need to know how to access such funds.

Promotion sophistication for the system will increase as the battle for subscribers and advertisers continues to intensify. As a result, it will become a critical skill for cable management.

REGULATION

Since its inception, cable has been an irritant to the Federal Communications Commission. To begin with, it was not an area of federal prerogative. Regulatory responsibility has always been shared with local authorities, whose streets and rights-of-way are essential for a cable system's operation.

The giant cable industry of today was not even contemplated when the 1934 Communications Act was written. Consequently, federal regulation of cable was done on an as-needed basis by the FCC. Courts and the FCC, alike, wrestled with rationales for tying regulation into the framework of the act. The commission's jurisdiction was confined to system operational matters; franchising was left to local authorities.

The initial FCC cable regulatory motivation was to protect licensed television broadcasters from the perceived threat of cable. The threat took two forms: first, cable's ability to reduce locally licensed stations' audiences and revenues by importing out-of-market signals; and second, its retransmission of expensive local broadcasters' programming without compensation.

As noted above, the FCC first attempted to deal with its cable concerns under imputed authority derived from the 1934 act. By 1984, cable had grown to the point that it was able to demand, and receive, explicit regulatory status from Congress. That law was the Cable Communications Policy Act of 1984, which deregulated cable. However, industry stewardship of its deregulated status was not successful in the eyes of many consumers and Congress. In response, Congress passed the Cable Television Consumer Protection and Competition Act of 1992.

To combat the first threat, the importation of out-of-market signals, the FCC enacted signal carriage rules. They took three forms: *must carry, network nonduplication,* and *syndicated exclusivity.* The second problem, noncompensation to local broadcasters, was addressed to some degree by Congress in the Copyright Act of 1976.

All the signal carriage rules of the FCC have had many reincarnations, but none more than the must-carry rules. As noted earlier, must carry requires a cable system to carry the commercial and noncommercial television stations in its area. These long-standing rules were struck down on First Amendment grounds in two court decisions in the mid-1980s. Broadcasters' attempts to restore them were finally achieved in the 1992 act, but they were challenged in the courts. In 1997, however, the Supreme Court upheld their constitutionality in a 5–4 decision.

The 1992 must-carry rules apply to carriage of both commercial and noncommercial television stations. The principal requirements are as follows:

- Systems with more than 12 channels must set aside up to one-third of their channel capacity for local signals.

- Home shopping stations are entitled to must carry, as are qualified low-power television (LPTV) stations.

- Systems with 12 or fewer channels must carry 1 local noncommercial station; systems with 13 to 36 channels may be required to carry up to 3 local noncommercial stations; and systems with more than 36 channels may be required to carry more than 3 local noncommercial stations if the programming of the additional stations does not substantially duplicate the content of the other stations.

As noted earlier, the 1992 law allows stations to select a retransmission consent option in lieu of must carry. Stations that opt for retransmission consent must negotiate with local cable systems for channel position and compensation. If the negotiations are unsuccessful, a local station might end up with no system carriage at all for three years.

A second FCC signal carriage rule is network nonduplication or network exclusivity. It prohibits a cable system from carrying an imported network affiliate's offering of a network program at the same time it is being aired by a local affiliate.

The third significant carriage rule involves syndicated program exclusivity, known as "syndex." Prior to 1980, the FCC protected a local station's syndicated programs against duplication in the market from distant signals imported by cable systems. In 1988, the commission reinstituted the rule, but delayed its implementation until January 1, 1990. The new rule allows a local station with an exclusivity provision in its syndicated program contract to notify local cable systems of its program ownership. Once notified, the system is required to protect the station against duplication from imported signals, including those of pay and nonpay cable networks transmitted by satellite.

The other principal FCC concern about the emerging cable industry was the question of compensation of broadcasters for retransmission of their signals by cable. The controversy finally was resolved in 1976, when a new copyright law was passed. Under the law, cable TV was to pay royalties for transmission of copyrighted works. These revenues were in the form of a compulsory license paid to the registrar of copyrights for distribution to copyright owners.

According to the provisions of the law, cable operators must pay a copyright royalty fee, for which they receive a compulsory license to retransmit radio and television signals. The fee for each cable system is based on the system's gross revenues from the carriage of broadcast signals and the number of *distant signal equivalents*, a term identifying non-network programming from distant television stations carried by the system.

The law requires a cable operator to file semiannually a statement of accounts. Information in this report includes the system's revenue and signal carriage, as well as the royalty fee payment.

The law also established a now-abolished Copyright Royalty Tribunal (CRT), composed of five commissioners, to distribute the royalty fees and resolve disputes among copyright owners and to review the fee schedule in 1980 and every five years thereafter. The CRT administered three funds: (1) the basic royalty fund; (2) the 3.75 percent fund established to compensate copyright owners for distant signals added after June 24, 1981; and (3) the syndex fund. Claims against the funds, totaling more than $100 million annually, are made by broadcasters, the Motion Picture Association of America, sports organizations, and the Public Broadcasting Service. Changes in the funds administered and the amounts collected have occurred as the FCC and Congress have altered the signal carriage rules. The abolition of the CRT had no effect on copyright fees owed, or on cable system reporting requirements.

The 1992 cable law did much more than restore must carry. Essentially, it reregulated cable. Of special significance was the act's reintroduction of rate regulation, which had been abolished in 1986. The period of deregulation saw an explosion of system rates, with resulting pressure on Congress by angry subscribers.

In accordance with the law, the FCC in 1993 established rate regulations for implementation by local franchise authorities. The basic tier must be available separately. Before regulating basic rates, a franchise authority must obtain FCC certification. If certification is denied or revoked, the commission will regulate directly the rates for the system's basic tier.

The 1992 act sets forth criteria for determining whether or not rates are reasonable. Costs include programming, franchise fees, and taxes. Revenues include subscriber fees and advertising. A reasonable profit is allowed. The determination of reasonable rates is decided, in part, on basic rates for systems with competition. If a cable system wishes to raise basic rates, it must give the franchise authority thirty days' notice. Under the Telecommunications Act of 1996, basic rate regulation was scheduled to be eliminated in 1999.

Expanded basic rates can be regulated under the "bad actor" concept. For 180 days after April 4, 1993, franchise authorities or subscribers could file complaints with the FCC about unreasonable rates. After that date, expanded basic rates could be challenged only when they were increased. Rates for premium channels and pay-per-view are not regulated.

WHAT'S AHEAD?

The future of cable can be summed up in one word: competition. It will come from many directions — DBS, wireless cable, telephone and utility companies, and others. Indeed, any business with a fiber network in place may emerge to challenge cable systems that formerly enjoyed a virtual monopoly.

DBS may be an especially strong foe. Attracted by low-cost dishes and the possibility of local station carriage, subscribers are expected to more than double by 2004.[22] That would result in a television household penetration of 18 percent, compared to 8.7 percent in 1998.[23] Similarly, the number of subscribers to telco-owned (i.e., owned by a telephone company) cable systems is projected to rise, from 250,000 in 1998 to four million in 2004.[24] During the same period, cable is expected to experience a reduction in the number of new subscribers and a drop in its TV household penetration from 66 percent to 64.5 percent.[25]

Nonetheless, cable operators are not ready to throw up their hands. In fact, media investment analysts anticipate continuing cable prosperity into the early years of the twenty-first century, sparked by some of the same technologies that have resulted in the intensified competitive environment in which the industry finds itself. Among the areas they expect to produce growth are rate hikes and new subscribers, especially to premium channels, revenue from pay-per-view events, and sales of emerging services in telephone and data links.[26]

Despite the fact that the anticipated headlong rush of cable companies into the telephone business has not materialized, several MSOs (multiple system operators) have launched cable telephony services. Some have gone further and have begun the transition to full-service providers, offering a package of bundled services that includes video, voice, and data.

Their confidence may be well-founded. A survey by The Strategis Group revealed that nearly 80 percent of households would subscribe to combinations of communications services from a single provider at the services' current cost. The highest preference was for a local and long-distance telephone combination (32 percent). However, preference was also shown for combinations of local phone and cable (29 percent), long-distance and cable (27 percent), and local phone, long-distance, and cable (23 percent).[27]

Cable can also take heart from the exploding interest in the Internet and the desire for high-speed access to it. Eight-five percent of cable subscribers told pollsters that they were interested in leasing cable modems from their local system. Nearly half of them said that they were extremely interested.[28]

Undoubtedly, many cable operators who have not yet embarked on the path to full-service will follow the industry leaders. Satisfying consumer price and service expectations will be among the challenges they will confront.

Meeting them will not be easy. A 1998 cable/satellite TV customer satisfaction study by J. D. Power and Associates noted that satellite services outranked cable operators by an average of 29 points. Among the categories rated were: ease of operation, cost, ease of installation, program selection, ease of getting service problems solved over the phone, and ability to get a serviceman to come to their home.[29] The study's findings also raise questions about subscriber loyalty. Fewer than one in eight respondents said they would consider switching providers in the next year. However, among those who would consider a change, the majority were cable subscribers.[30]

SUMMARY

Cable is hardwired and requires rights-of-way over and under city streets to gain access to viewers' homes. Because of this unique requirement, cable systems are licensed by local governments. The licenses are called franchises, and they have to be renewed at intervals set forth in the franchise agreement.

Cable television systems are run by general managers, who answer to ownership. Reporting to the general manager are the heads of departments with clearly identified responsibilities. Usually, they include government affairs and community relations, human resources, business operations, advertising sales, technical operations, marketing, and customer service.

Programming decisions take into account technological, legal, and audience-appeal and associated economic factors. Program sources include local origination and access channels, local and distant over-the-air television stations, and basic and pay-cable networks. Many systems also offer special programs on a pay-per-view (PPV) basis. Typically, program services are bundled into tiers and are priced accordingly.

Initially, cable revenues consisted almost entirely of monthly subscriber fees. As the industry has matured, it has developed other revenue sources, including the sale of local advertising and pay-per-view services. Operating expenses are similar to those of broadcast stations, but with some notable differences. Systems must pay to the local franchise authority a franchise fee of up to 5 percent of their gross revenues. They are also required to meet the cost of maintaining and repairing miles of cable and allied equipment, and of renting poles on which to string the cable.

Promoting the varied program services available is a high priority in attracting and retaining subscribers. Among the most effective promotional tools are door-to-door and direct-mail marketing, local television and radio stations, newspapers (especially the television program supplement), and the system's own channels.

Cable systems are required to carry, or obtain retransmission consent from, local commercial and noncommercial television stations. Local stations are protected against direct cable competition by network nonduplication and syndicated exclusivity rules. Many systems also have to provide access channels.

New competitors are entering the video distribution marketplace, and they will pose major challenges to the cable industry. In turn, cable operators will seek to attract subscribers to a range of communications services.

CASE STUDY

Janet Thornton is the newly-appointed marketing director of a 73,000-subscriber MSO cable system in a top-100 television market in the Midwest.

One of her first responsibilities is to review the basic cable subscriber count for the past five years and to recommend to general manager Blake Newsome ways of boosting the number. She is appalled to discover that annual churn averages 25 percent. She is confident that she can do better.

Janet proposes a promotion that will run from Thanksgiving through December 20. It will offer free installation to all who donate a new toy with a retail value of at least $5.00. The toys will be delivered to residents at the local children's home on Christmas Eve. Blake gives her the go-ahead.

The initial response suggested that she had scored a big success. Toys flooded in. A total of 3,870 subscribers were added, a staggering 47 percent of the number for the entire year.

During the following twelve months, Janet's reputation began to suffer. Churn increased and, at year's end, stood at 34 percent. Twenty percent were subscribers who had signed up during the promotion.

Exercises

1. How would you account for the higher-than-average churn rate?

2. Why did such a large percentage of the new subscribers churn during the first twelve months?

3. How might Janet have protected against the high number of disconnects?

4. What lessons may be drawn from Janet's experience?

NOTES

1. *Cable Television Developments,* Spring, 1998, p. 1.

2. *Ibid.*

3. *Ibid.,* p. 3.

4. *Ibid.,* p. 5.

5. *Ibid.*

6. *Ibid.,* p. 9.

7. City of Los Angeles v. Preferred Communications, 106 S.Ct. 2034, 1986.

8. 47 *USC* 546.

9. 47 *USC* 546(c)(1)(A-D).

10. 47 *USC* 534, 535.

11. *Ibid.*

12. 47 *USC* 543.

13. Kim McAvoy, "Home Shopping Gets Must Carry," *Broadcasting & Cable,* July 5, 1993, p. 8.

14. *Cable Television Developments,* Spring, 1998, p. 2.

15. *Ibid.,* p. 3.

16. *Ibid.,* p. 8.

17. *Ibid.,* p. 3.

18. *Ibid.,* p. 8.

19. *Ibid.,* p. 3.

20. "Service Showing," *Broadcasting,* February 5, 1990, p. 86.

21. *Cable Television Developments,* Spring, 1998, p. 9.

22. *Cablevision Blue Book,* Vol. VII (Spring/Summer, 1998), p. 8.

23. *Ibid.*

24. *Ibid.,* p. 10.

25. *Ibid.,* p. 8.

26. Donna Petrozzello, "Cable Up, Broadcast Down," *Broadcasting & Cable,* September 21, 1998, p. 15.

27. *Cablevision Blue Book,* Vol. VII (Spring/Summer, 1998), p. 36.

28. *Ibid.,* p. 41.

29. Donna Petrozzello, "DBS Tops J.D. Power Survey," *Broadcasting & Cable,* September 14, 1998, p. 48.

30. *Ibid.,* p. 50.

ADDITIONAL READINGS

Bartlett, Eugene. *Cable Communications: Building the Information Infrastructure.* New York: McGraw-Hill, 1995.

Bone, Jan. *Opportunities in Cable Television.* Lincolnwood, IL: VGM Career Horizons, 1993.

Crandall, Robert W., and Harold Furchgott-Roth. *Cable TV: Regulation or Competition?* Washington, DC: Brookings Institution, 1996.

Eastman, Susan Tyler, and Douglas A. Ferguson. *Broadcast/Cable Programming: Strategies and Practices,* 5th ed. Belmont, CA: Wadsworth, 1997.

Eastman, Susan Tyler, and Robert Klein. *Promotion and Marketing for Broadcasting and Cable,* 2nd ed. Prospect Heights, IL: Waveland Press, 1991.

Fenneran, William B., and Richard E. Wiley (eds.). *The Cable Television Consumer Protection and Competition Act of 1992: What Does It Mean?* Englewood Cliffs, NJ: Prentice Hall, 1993.

Fuller, Linda K. *Community Television in the United States: A Sourcebook on Public, Educational, and Governmental Access.* Westport, CT: Greenwood Press, 1994.

Howard, Herbert H., Michael S. Kievman, and Barbara A. Moore. *Radio, TV, and Cable Programming,* 2nd ed. Ames, IA: Iowa State University Press, 1994.

Johnson, Leland L. *Toward Competition in Cable Television.* Cambridge, MA: The MIT Press, and Washington, DC: American Enterprise Institute for Public Policy Research, 1994.

Parsons, Patrick R., and Robert M. Frieden. *The Cable and Satellite Television Industries.* Boston: Allyn & Bacon, 1998.

Smith, F. Leslie, Milan Meeske, and John Wright. *Electronic Media and Government: The Regulation of Wireless and Wired Communication in the United States.* White Plains, NY: Longman, 1995.

Understanding Broadcast and Cable Finance: A Handbook for the Non-Financial Manager. Washington, DC: National Association of Broadcasters, 1994.

Vane, Edwin T., and Lynne S. Gross. *Programming for TV, Radio, and Cable.* Boston: Focal Press, 1994.

Warner, Charles, and Joseph Buchman. *Broadcast and Cable Selling,* 2nd ed. updated. Belmont, CA: Wadsworth, 1993.

9 PUBLIC BROADCAST STATION MANAGEMENT

This chapter is devoted to that area of noncommercial broadcasting known as public broadcasting. It examines

☐ **the organization and framework of public broadcasting in the United States**

☐ **the major management functions performed by public broadcasting executives**

☐ **the challenges facing public broadcasting today and the management tools available to meet them**

☐ **the differences and similarities in operations between commercial broadcasting and public broadcasting**

Noncommercial educational broadcasting accounts for approximately 16 percent of total radio stations and about 23 percent of total television stations operating in the United States today.[1] Despite these significant percentages, most broadcast professionals and broadcast students know little about the intricacies of educational broadcasting.

Within the category of noncommercial broadcasting there is a subcategory known as public broadcasting, which encompasses those broadcasters who meet the minimum operating requirements established by the Corporation for Public Broadcasting to qualify for federal funding.

Public broadcasting represents a specialized area of over-the-air broadcasting with its own unique concepts and principles. In public television, for example, unlike its commercial counterpart, the emphasis is not on generating mass audience numbers per program, but on the cumulative weekly audience. That is true because programs seek to respond to the content preferences of diverse audiences. Accordingly, calculation of the number of different people or households viewing over the course of a week is a more realistic measure of program appeal than the number tuned to a particular offering. Public radio is largely format-based, as is commercial radio. However, public radio formats are somewhat different in that they possess more limited audience appeal. The emphasis is to increase time spent listening (TSL) by the audience. Commercial broadcasting sells the audience to advertisers; advertisers are the market. In public broadcasting, the audience is the market and public stations depend, increasingly, on direct audience financial support. Accordingly, revenue sources for public broadcasting and commercial broadcasting are very different. So are expenses. National TV networks still pay commercial stations some amounts to carry their programs, but public stations must pay for their programming.

There is one major similarity between public and commercial broadcasting, however, and that is the bottom line. Commercial stations operate for profit and must be expense- and revenue-conscious. Public stations, while nonprofit in nature, are financially accountable and must conform expenses to anticipated revenue generation. This is especially true in these days of significantly diminished governmental funding.

THE STRUCTURE OF PUBLIC BROADCASTING

The origins of the current structure in public broadcasting date to the 1967 report of the Carnegie Commission on Educational Television. Many of its recommendations to enhance the viability of noncommercial educational broadcasting were enacted into law by the Public Broadcasting Act of the same year, which created the Corporation for Public Broadcasting (CPB).

Distribution services for programs were added in 1969 to 1970, when the CPB and some noncommercial stations formed membership corporations. The television vehicle was named the Public Broadcasting Service (PBS), and the radio organization was called National Public Radio (NPR). Both of these entities provide member stations with various program options and services, which will be discussed in greater detail later in the chapter.

As a result of these developments, a three-level structure emerged:

1. local noncommercial educational radio and television stations licensed by the Federal Communications Commission

2. the Corporation for Public Broadcasting, which is primarily a funding mechanism

3. PBS and NPR, membership corporations

TELEVISION

By the late 1990s, 368 noncommercial television stations were on the air, of which 125 were VHF and 243 UHF.[2] Of these, approximately 172 licensees, operating 349 stations, belonged to the Public Broadcasting Service.[3] The licensees, some of which operate more than one station, may be divided into four distinct categories:

Community stations are operated by nonprofit community corporations created to build and run them. Most stations are located in large cities and have a significant dependence upon community support. Some are major program production centers.

University stations arose as a natural consequence of the educational mission of their sponsoring institutions. Historically, they have relied less on viewer support than community stations, and some operate as program origination sources for other public stations. University stations are the second largest group of licensees.

Local authority licensees, primarily public schools, are instructional in nature. As a consequence, the bulk of their programming is instructional. They rely on the audience for some degree of financial support. The number of local authority licensees has declined over the years.

State agencies have been created by law in about half of the states to operate statewide networks of public stations that are heavily involved in program production, both for instruction and for general audiences. State agencies operate the largest number of noncommercial television stations in the United States.[4]

Organization and Personnel

The size and structure of a public television station depend on market size, the type of licensee, and the programming it offers to the public. Stations are organized into various departments performing specific functions. Figures 9.1 and 9.2 depict the structure of a university licensee, Southern Illinois University in Carbondale, Illinois, and a community corporation, KPTS, which operates a television station in Wichita, Kansas. Department heads report to a general manager or station manager, who is responsible for the overall operation. Note that community corporations may be organized somewhat differently from other licensees because of their generally larger size and, in some instances, their role as a national production center.

Figure 9.1 *Organizational chart of a university licensee, Southern Illinois University, Carbondale, Illinois. (Used with permission.)*

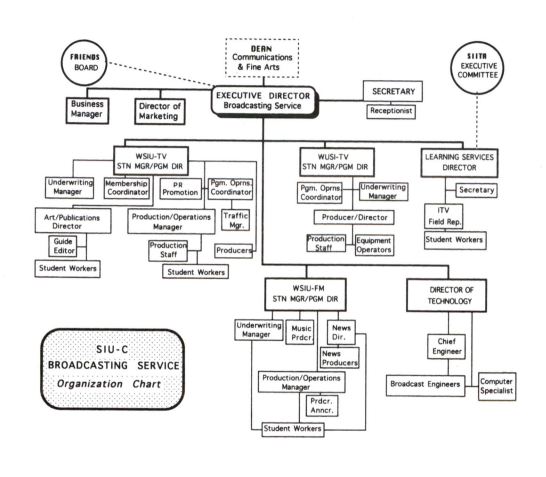

The level to which the general manager reports varies according to the type of licensee operating the station. Community stations generally have a broad-based community board of directors to which the manager is responsible. In university stations, the manager usually reports to a designated university official. Public school station managers deal with the superintendent of schools or the school board. In the case of state-operated stations, the upper-level structure is an entity created by state law. Whatever the nature of the licensee or structure, the manager is accountable to a higher authority, and that authority determines the degree of autonomy the local manager has.

Figure 9.2 *Organizational chart, KPTS-TV, a community corporation licensee in Wichita, Kansas. (Used with permission.)*

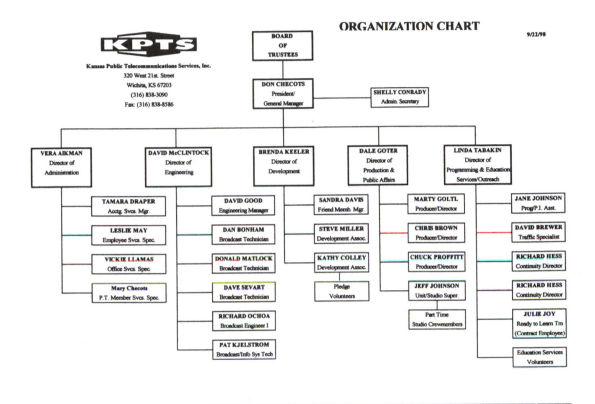

Management Tasks

The responsibilities of the public broadcast manager are concentrated in eight primary areas. Through an examination of each, it will be possible to develop an appreciation of the challenges the public television executive faces and the tools available to meet them. The review of management tasks will also offer an opportunity to compare and contrast public and commercial television. The main management functions of the public television executive are as follows:

- financial
- programming
- promotion
- research
- cable relations
- community relations
- engineering
- administration

Financial: Revenues   If there is a top priority for public broadcast management, it is revenue. For years, the base of financial support for public television, whatever the type of licensee, has been governmental. In the 1990s, the reliability of that support came into question. In 1995, the Republican party replaced the Democratic party as the Congressional majority in the House of Representatives and the Senate. It was the first time in forty years that both houses of Congress had been in Republican hands.

The Republicans had several marquee issues on their 1995 agenda, one of which was the elimination or reduction of federal financial support for noncommercial public radio and television.

This legislative initiative triggered an intense grassroots lobbying effort on behalf of public broadcasting. Federal financial support, though reduced, was not eliminated. While the reduction, not counting inflation, has not been that dramatic, it has really hurt.

In 1994, the Corporation for Public Broadcasting distributed $275 million in federal monies to public television and radio stations.[5] The 1997 figure was $229 million.[6]

The crisis could not have come at a worse time, because the 1990s also saw increased competition for audiences and funds. In the late 1990s, a new financial problem appeared in the form of the FCC-mandated conversion to DTV. Estimates of the costs of this project vary, but the figure per television station will be in the millions of dollars. As will be noted in the next section, some federal support for equipment does exist, but it always has.

Public television stations need funds to operate. Since they are noncommercial, the sale of time to advertisers is precluded. Principal sources of funding are as follows:

- federal government
- state and local governments
- audience
- underwriting
- other

Federal Government   The financial base of most public television stations is provided by an annual Community Service Grant (CSG) from the Corporation for Public Broadcasting. Only one CSG is permitted per licensee. To qualify for a grant, each public station must file an annual Certification of Eligibility (see Figure 9.3). Basic requirements are that the station be full-power with a noncommercial educational license; that it operate at least 3,000 broadcast hours per year; that it have a minimum full-time professional staff of ten; and that it have nonfederal financial support of at least $650,000 a year.[7] Stations must also file an annual financial report, a Station Activities Survey, and an Offer and Acceptance with the Corporation for Public Broadcasting.

After receiving the certification, the CPB determines the amount of the grant per station and assigns a CSG factor to the station. The factor is also used to calculate PBS membership and regional network fees.

Figure 9.3 *Television Community Service Grant Certification of Eligibility, KPTS-TV, Wichita, Kansas. (Used with permission.)*

Station Code	T05300	Station	**KPTS-TV**
City	Wichita	State	**KS**

CORPORATION FOR PUBLIC BROADCASTING

APPLICATION FOR A
FISCAL YEAR 1998 TELEVISION COMMUNITY SERVICE GRANT
AND INTERCONNECTION GRANT

Kansas Public Telecommunications Service, Inc.
(Licensee Name)

through its authorized officials, hereby applies for a Corporation for Public Broadcasting (CPB) Television Community Service Grant ("CSG") and Interconnection Grant. The eligibility data contained in the pages attached, together with the relevant financial data contained in the applicant's response to the CPB Annual Financial Report for Fiscal Year 1996 are expressly made a part of this Application. The grant amounts have been determined by distribution formulas approved by the CPB Board of Directors. Applicant agrees to these grant computations and understands that the amounts offered are subject to decreases. Applicant certifies that the licensee and its station meet or exceed each of the criteria for grant eligibility as stated in the attached "Fiscal Year 1998 Television Community Service Grant Certification of Eligibility" and certifies the accuracy of all of the data and information provided in that Certification of Eligibility.

CSG Amount: $ 377,063

CSG Grant Spending Period:
October 1, 1997 through September 30, 1999

Interconnection Grant Amount: $ 12,310

Interconnection Spending Period
October 1 1997 through September 30, 1998

(SPECIAL NOTE: The amounts offered represent the combined grant amounts for all CPB-supported television stations licensed to the above referenced licensee.)

Make Check Payable To:
Kansas Public
Telecommunications Service, Inc.   **(Payee)**
(Payee will be the licensee unless the licensee authorizes an alternate in writing to CPB. If the CSG payment and Interconnection payment must be made by separate checks, please request in writing with a rationale to the address below.)

Authorized Official of Licensee: Must be authorized to sign binding grants/contracts for the licensee. Should be the same as that on the Offer and Acceptance, and Final Report.

Name: Don Checots

Title: President & General Manager

Signature: _(Authorized Official of Licensee)_

Mail Check To:

Station: KPTS

10/06/97
(Date)

Address: 320 West 21st Street N

Wichita, KS 67203-2499

Mail Complete Application To:

Attn: Vera Aikman
(Name)

Director of Administration
(Title)

**System and Station Development
Corporation for Public Broadcasting
901 E Street NW
Washington, DC 20004-2037**

General/Station Manager

Name: Don Checots

Title: President & General Manager

Phone: (316) 838-3090

Figure 9.3   *Continued*

**CORPORATION
FOR PUBLIC
BROADCASTING**

Station Code	T05300	Station	KPTS-TV
City	Wichita		KS
Licensee Name	Kansas Public Telecommunications Service, Inc.		

FISCAL YEAR 1998 TELEVISION COMMUNITY SERVICE GRANT CERTIFICATION OF ELIGIBILITY

NOTE: This document requires two different signatures: one for the licensee and one for the station. See bottom of form for clarification.

To help determine the station's eligibility for a Fiscal Year 1998 Community Service Grant, review the items below and check "Yes" or "No" for each criterion.

CRITERIA FOR GRANT ELIGIBILITY

The station and licensee specified above currently meet or exceed the following criteria:

	Yes	No	
a.	X	____	The station is operating as a full-power station under a noncommercial educational license granted by the FCC.
b.	X	____	The station had nonfederal financial support of at least $634,400 during FY 1997.
c.	X	____	The station has unrestricted access to studio and production facilities and regularly produces and broadcasts locally originated programming.
d.	X	____	The station broadcast 365 days during FY 1997, for a minimum of 3,000 hours.
e.	X	____	The station has a daily broadcast schedule devoted primarily to programming of good quality which serves demonstrated community needs of an educational, informational and cultural nature, within its primary signal area.

A program schedule designated to further the principals of particular religious philosophies does not meet the definition of this criterion.

Stations licensed to political organizations do not meet the definition of this criterion.

| f. | X | ____ | The station and its licensee comply in full with the Federal Communications Commission's regulations concerning equal employment opportunity (47 C.F.R. 73.2080). |
| g. | X | ____ | The job openings identified in the employment portion of the licensee's and its station's 1997 Annual Station Activities Survey were filled in accordance with Federal Communications Commission's regulations concerning equal employment opportunity (47 C.F.R. 73.2080). If the job openings were not filled in accordance with such regulations, a statement of the reasons for not filling the positions in accordance with such regulations must be submitted to CPB with this Certification of Eligibility. |

Figure 9.3 *Continued*

FY98 TV Certification of Eligibility   2

h. __X__ _____   The station and its licensee comply in full with the following sections of the Communications Act of 1934, 47 U.S.C. 390, et. seq.:

OPEN MEETINGS, OPEN RECORDS AND COMMUNITY ADVISORY BOARD

Section 396(k)(4) - Requiring all meetings of the governing body of the recipient, any committee of such governing body, and any advisory body of the recipient to be open, preceded by reasonable notice to the public to the extent that the deliberations of those bodies relate to public broadcasting. Exceptions to this provision are listed in Section 396(k)(4) and Section 397(5) of the Communications Act.

Section 396(k)(5) - Requiring that copies of the recipient's annual financial and audit reports, and other information regarding finances submitted to CPB, be made available by the recipient for public inspection.

Section 396(k)(8) - Requiring the establishment and maintenance of a community advisory board for certain licensees as described in this section of the law.

Section 396(k)(11) - Requiring, that the statistical report described in Section 12 of the "Fiscal Year 1998 Community Service Grant - Television General Provisions" be made available to the public at the central office of the station and at every location where more than five full-time employees are regularly assigned to work.

NETWORKS AND OTHER DUAL OPERATIONS:

A. Television "networks" consist of at least two television stations licensed in dual operations (multiple stations with the same licensee). Their operations will be consolidated to earn a single base grant over a three year period beginning in FY 1997.

B. Television stations in dual operations (multiple stations with the same licensee) that are located in the same city of license may consolidate operations to benefit directly from the Television CSG under the following conditions:

   1. Each station must be managed by and programmed by the professional staff assigned to the co-licensed CSG-supported station.

   2. Each station must provide a separate and distinct program service for the community of license.

   3. Each station must adhere to the programming policies contained in this document.

   4. Stations that are closed circuit, low power, student managed, and/or that provide in-service training type programming to licensee employees, clients, and/or representatives are not eligible.

List your dual licensed stations that meet the requirements set forth in A or B above.

Call Letters	Channel	Location

Figure 9.3   *Continued*

CERTIFICATION:

THE UNDERSIGNED ATTEST AND AFFIRM THAT THE INFORMATION PROVIDED THROUGHOUT THIS DOCUMENT IS ACCURATE AND VERIFIABLE.

THE UNDERSIGNED UNDERSTAND AND AGREE THAT THE LICENSEE WILL INFORM CPB IMMEDIATELY IN WRITING UPON FAILURE TO MAINTAIN ANY OF THE FOREGOING CRITERIA AND REQUIREMENTS.

Signatures of two different individuals are required: (1) an authorized official <u>of the licensee</u> responsible for signing grants/contracts for the licensee and who has knowledge and authority to certify that the licensee and its station meet or exceed each of the eligibility criteria set forth above and to certify the accuracy of all of the data and information above (e.g. chairman, treasurer or secretary of the board of directors, university vice president for finance, president of the school board, etc.) and (2) the chief executive officer in charge <u>of the operation</u> of the station (e.g. president, general manager, or station manager).

(1) For the Licensee: <u>Barney E Cansler, Treasurer</u>
                                                    (Name and Title)

Barney E Cansler   10/7/97
                                                    (Signature and Date)

(2) For the Station: Don Checots, President & General Manager
                                                    (Name and Title)

                                                    10/06/97
                                                    (Signature and Date)

Please return to:

System and Station Development
Corporation for Public Broadcasting
901 E Street NW
Washington, DC 20004-2037
1-800-527-2272

The CPB also disburses other, specialized funds. The principal separate funds, or pools, are:

Future Funds Pool: This is money set aside by the CPB to stimulate revenue development for public broadcasting in the future.

Transition Grant Pool: This money is used to assist those public television stations whose nonfederal annual funding is less than $2 million.

Overlap Pool: This pool provides additional support for those public TV stations that have signal overlap in metro markets. These stations compete with other public stations offering essentially the same product to some of the same viewers. The overlaps complicate membership drives and other funding components for these stations.

Stations may also apply to the National Telecommunications and Information Administration (NTIA) for support in purchasing equipment.[8] In this case, a formal grant application must be submitted to the NTIA, and the station must be able to raise matching funds from nonfederal sources. The CPB may exclude any nonfederal funds raised for equipment purchases supported by the NTIA from the calculation of $650,000 of nonfederal funds required to support the qualification for a Community Service Grant.

State and Local Governments　States may fund local licensees directly, as in the case of universities and community corporations, or indirectly, as when states fund agencies or commissions that operate state networks. In some states, the funding is calculated by using the CSG factor. Local governmental entities fund public school stations. Whatever the type of licensee, public station management must comply with the appropriate state or local procedures in a timely manner to ensure continued financial support.

Audience　No matter what level of viewer financial support a public station enjoys today, it is certain that all categories of licensees will have a greater need for it in the future. Historically, community stations, out of necessity, have better developed this method of raising funds than the other types of public television licensees. However, with traditional funding sources retrenching, many stations are discovering audience support.

For the novice fund-raiser, there are tried and proven methods to be employed, and there is outside assistance available. PBS has a division in its development department called Station Independence Program (SIP). It is user-supported and offers fund-raising assistance to stations, particularly in local pledge drives or auctions. One of its significant functions is to provide stations with programs that perform well as fund-raisers.

The principal fund-raising activities for most television stations are pledge or membership drives, usually built around a PBS-sponsored fund-raising activity commonly called "Festival," which is supported with national promotion and programming. It is conducted three times a year, and stations may participate in all, some, or none. Many stations take part more than once a year. However, multiple annual fund-raisers do cause a fatigue factor in the audience. As a result, some stations are experimenting with a plan that drops one of the extended on-the-air drives in favor of spot announcements emphasizing the value of public station programming and the need for public support. If a station chooses to be involved in only one, it is usually the multiday winter event. To tie in with "Festival," a station builds a set and structures a group of fund-raising appeals to be used during breaks in the specially selected programming. Timing, structure, and copy for the breaks are art forms in themselves.[9] The use of local celebrities is recommended, either to make appeals for funds or to take phoned-in pledges on camera. In areas without access to celebrities, videotapes of personalities making appeals are available from PBS. Stations may also offer premiums or gifts to viewers who call in pledges, with the value of the premium depending upon the amount of the pledge. Some stations, such as KETC-TV in St. Louis, have offered as a premium a gold membership card, which entitles members to discounts at local providers of goods and services. Like a membership magazine, the card offers members an ongoing reminder of the sustaining value of their public station commitment.

Another established fund-raising activity is the auction. Very simply, goods and services donated by area businesses and organizations are auctioned on the air to the highest bidder. Many stations also offer items donated by sports figures or celebrities. Auctions are expensive to produce and cause the preemption of regularly scheduled programs. However, they are an important source of funds. Some licensees are experimenting with concepts like four-day weekend auctions to lessen the negative impact on programming. Others are studying the possibility of doing half-hour to one-hour auctions regularly throughout the year. Still others conduct auctions as nonbroadcast community events.

Special events are an additional source of funds. One example is the annual wine-and-cheese party conducted by KETC at a major downtown hotel. This event is open to the public, with special discount admission available to members who have previously contributed in pledge drives. Another event type involves bringing in PBS talent, such as Jim Lehrer or William F. Buckley, Jr., for a local appearance. Funds are raised through admission prices or donations that enable participation in cocktail parties or dinners attended by the talent. There is literally no limit, save the lack of imagination, to the kinds of events that might be carried out. Contact with other PBS members and station executives is a good way to collect information on fund-raising ideas that work.

Underwriting   Underwriting is a mechanism used to develop or present programs by securing grants from foundations, corporations, or businesses.

Stations that are also production centers, such as those in Pittsburgh and Boston, may seek underwriting from major corporations or foundations to develop programs. The objective for the station and the underwriter is to have the production selected for distribution by PBS and use by other stations. For the funding sources, this provides visibility and enhances image. Achieving the objective does the same for the producing station.

Stations also obtain underwriting to present programs of local origination or programs obtained from other sources. The underwriter, in effect, sponsors the programs.

This type of local underwriting raises day-to-day operating funds for the station. It is also the kind of local revenue development that is most similar to the sale of spot announcements by commercial stations. However, public stations are somewhat restricted in what can be shown or said in an underwriting credit (i.e., identification of the funding source or sources), due to their essential noncommercial nature.

The pricing of underwriting credits is critical. Some public stations have written guidelines, similar to a commercial broadcaster's rate card. Whatever structure is employed, a public television broadcaster should market a program without limiting the underwriting announcement cost to that of the program itself. Stations that are hard-pressed for support are learning to ask for the value the marketplace puts on the program offered. Such value may well be in excess of the cost.

The Public Broadcasting Service regularly issues revised guidelines on the permissible limits in underwriting announcements. The underwriting rules were "enhanced," or made more flexible, by the Federal Communications Commission in 1982,[10] following a failed eighteen-month experiment allowing certain public stations to sell advertising. Current rules allow the presentation in donor underwriting credits of the following:

- logograms or slogans that identify and do not promote
- location
- value-neutral descriptions of product line or service listing[11]
- brand and trade names and product or service listings

The underwriting guidelines are a serious matter, and the FCC has shown an increasing willingness to entertain complaints brought against public stations alleged to have exceeded the limits.

Like audience support, underwriting must be developed for public television to survive. However, the noncommercial aspect is one of the appeals of public television, and this type of support could ultimately become counterproductive if the audience begins to perceive excessive commercialism.

Other Public television stations of the 1990s have had to become more than program purveyors to survive in the multimedia world. Stations are offering, or are learning to offer, a range of services beyond the traditional broadcast program model to remain competitive.

Some of these services generate support to augment that provided by government and the audience. One example is "for-profit" commercial production. Some stations, particularly community corporation licensees in large markets, have developed this alternative service into a significant revenue item. Entities engaging in this activity should organize a for-profit subsidiary

Figure 9.4 *Support elements for KPTS-TV, a community corporation licensee in Wichita, Kansas. (Used with permission.)*

Kansas Public Telecommunications Services, Inc.

FY99 BUDGET

Revenues	$	%
Member Contribution	1,141,500	51.3%
Donations	2,000	0.1%
Underwriting	325,000	14.6%
Production Contracts/Leasing	94,000	4.2%
Other Grants	9,666	0.4%
Government Support/State	251,487	11.3%
Government Support/Federal	395,000	17.8%
Other Income	6,500	0.3%
Total Revenue	**2,225,153**	**100.0%**

corporation to avoid charges of unfair competition from their commercial counterparts.

Other possible ancillary revenue sources include the sale of advertising in the membership publication. Selling editorial space to other community arts and educational organizations should be explored, especially with those organizations that are unable to support financially an independent publication.

Some public television stations rent tower space or equipment. USIV-TV in Carbondale, Illinois, generates revenue through rental of an uplink truck to a variety of users, including the traditional commercial over-the-air networks. In sum, management should always be alert to the development of potential revenue-generating opportunities in our expanding multimedia world.

Figure 9.4 illustrates the mix and significance of the support components that make up the total support package of a community corporation television licensee.

For public television, the budget battle will continue. New funding sources need to be identified and developed as old ones fade out. It is necessary for the public electronic media manager to stay abreast of trends.

One way to monitor developments is by reviewing the quarterly and annual revenue reports distributed by the Station Independence Program. Another, as mentioned earlier, is ongoing communication with associates in the industry.

Financial: Expenses   Expense control is a critical management function. Because of operational variables resulting from the different types of licensees and market sizes, it is difficult here to make more than general statements about expenses. However, specific comparative information is available from the Corporation for Public Broadcasting and the Association of America's Public Television Stations (APTS).[12] Utilization of the CPB and APTS data makes it possible for the station manager to compare local expense results with those of other public stations of similar type and size around the country. Judgments can then be made about the appropriateness of expense levels at the local station.

The largest single expense item for public television stations is programming. Prices of all programming are increasing, and competition for popular commercial syndicated product, in particular, has made its cost almost prohibitive for the budget-pressed public station. Cable networks — such as A&E and The Discovery Channel — are also competing for programming that was previously the exclusive prerogative of PBS and individual public stations.

Local origination is so expensive that most stations do little of it. Stations operated by universities have an edge here by utilizing qualified students, but at most universities this resource has not been fully developed. With more viewing choices available to audiences than ever before, local identity demands some local origination, and the problem will have to be dealt with. Some local origination is also necessary to satisfy FCC license obligations.

Personnel costs are always a pressure point, particularly in stations largely dependent upon governmental support. Many stations are unionized. To some degree, that impacts management's efforts to deal with the budget. Elected officials who make funding decisions for many public stations are susceptible to pressure applied by employees and their representatives.

The low inflation trend of the late 1980s has continued into the late 1990s. When those inflation patterns begin to rise — as they inevitably will — labor costs will surely rise with them, further straining already stretched resources.

Another major expense item is development. Development is responsible for generating audience financial support, securing underwriting, and conducting auctions and other events. As government support becomes more problematic and operating costs continue to rise, development costs will also grow.

Capital costs are a continuing problem. Technology developments are escalating rapidly. Government requirements, such as those associated with DTV, noted above, threaten to exacerbate capital demands. Some public stations have been successful at fully funding annual depreciation. Others are exploring the possibilities of capital-giving campaigns to remain competitive and develop the teleplex concept.

For an example of the distribution spread of a community corporation public station's expense dollar, see Figure 9.5.

Figure 9.5 *Expense dollar distribution for KPTS-TV, a community corporation licensee in Wichita, Kansas. (Used with permission.)*

Kansas Public Telecommunications Services, Inc.

FY99 BUDGET

Expenditures by Cost Center		
General & Administration	502,913	22.8%
Engineering	350,791	15.9%
Production/Public Affairs	249,949	11.3%
Programming & Educational Services	723,790	32.8%
Development		
Membership	331,488	15.0%
Underwriting	49,630	2.2%
Total Expenses	2,208,561	100.0%

Programming   Programming is a critical area of management responsibility. It is an axiom in public television that "without audience there is no support, and without support there is no audience." In this era of deregulation and fragmented audiences, management must focus on the three essential programming elements: *strategy*, *acquisition*, and *scheduling*. Only through a masterful management of all three can a public television station build the cumulative audience required for success.

Strategy   Most public television stations have program directors or managers who must develop the program strategy in conjunction with senior management. Program strategy is determined by the nature of the licensee, the needs and interests of the community, the requirements for fund-raising from the audience and, increasingly, by ratings. Public television executives for years have dismissed ratings as a game the commercial stations play. Since, so the reasoning went, public TV had a superior product for an audience other than the "lowest common denominator," there was no reason to be concerned about audience shares. However, increasingly, public stations must have significant audience financial support to survive. And so the quantity and frequency of viewers may, in the end, matter after all to public television.

The basic direction of program strategy depends upon the type of licensee. A community licensee puts emphasis on presenting entertainment and cultural programs. The university, public school, and state networks may have as their thrust more instructional or educational programs. Instructional programs were important in keeping public stations on cable systems before the return of the must-carry rule requiring cable carriage of local television stations. It was resurrected by the Cable Television Consumer Protection and Competition Act of 1992 and has now survived a Supreme Court challenge. Aside from its possible value as a cable carriage mechanism, however, instructional programming is also a revenue source. Eighty-three percent of public television stations carry some in-school, instructional programs.[13]

Paying attention to community needs and interests distinguishes a local public station from the many choices, including other public stations, now available to the viewer through cable. Identifying those needs and interests is treated later in the chapter.

Another factor in program strategy is the need to generate viewer financial support. Again, that varies with the type of licensee and location. Stations licensed to community corporations depend primarily on audience support. However, in these days of reduced governmental funding, all stations must rely increasingly on it. Hand-in-hand with this factor is the reality that, to some extent, public broadcasting has succeeded because it is unique. It presents something that the public cannot obtain elsewhere. Public television must remain unique, even though the wide range of viewing options available to audiences makes that a difficult objective.

Obviously, however, the amount of financial support required today cannot be supplied by a minuscule core of loyal viewers. Public television's audience base must be broadened. Ratings may not mean mass program numbers, as required in commercial television, but they do mean weekly cumulative household totals. To some extent, this need for larger ratings may be in conflict with the need to remain unique. A balance between ratings and uniqueness is a goal for management to achieve.

To the extent that ratings expectations play a role in program strategy, some general observations are in order:

1. A weekly cumulative audience of 30 percent of the television households in the market in prime time is a good goal or target.

2. Component numbers to achieve that goal depend upon individual program performance. Certain categories of programs produce predictable ranges of cumulative audience, as follows:
   - nature and science: 5 to 10 percent
   - drama: 4 to 5 percent
   - concerts: 3 to 4 percent
   - public affairs documentaries: 2 to 4 percent[14]

Acquisition   Having determined program strategy, management must next identify sources from which to secure the desired programming. There are five major sources. Together, they account for almost 95 percent of a public television station's total broadcast hours:

- Public Broadcasting Service: 63.9 percent
- regional networks: 14.0 percent
- instructional: 6.1 percent
- commercial syndication: 4.4 percent
- local origination: 6.4 percent[15]

Public Broadcasting Service   On the average, public stations obtain 64 percent of their programming from PBS. It can be acquired in one of two ways. The first method is *full-service*. Under this plan, the station pays a program assessment and is entitled to all of the programming that PBS provides. This includes the popular children's programs, such as *Barney* and *Sesame Street*, and the news and public affairs offerings, like *The Newshour with Jim Lehrer* and *Washington Week in Review*. It also includes other programming, such as *Mystery, Masterpiece Theater*, and *Nova*. Concerts, specials, and documentaries developed by PBS are also part of the plan. Program assessment payments by PBS member stations equal approximately $88 million per year.[16]

The second method is called the *low use discount* (LUD). Here, the member station pays a reduced fee, but receives only 15 percent of the PBS lineup. For additional monies, LUD stations can pick up to 50 percent of the entire schedule. Stations under financial pressure or those concerned with PBS's rising program costs may consider the LUD method. It may be attractive, also, to those stations that operate in markets with multiple public licensees. Most industry professionals, however, feel it would be very difficult to program a public station using the LUD alternative. And, in fact, experience has validated that judgment.

PBS now operates under the "chief program executive model." In other words, programs are commissioned and selected by one PBS executive, resulting in greater flexibility and freedom than was possible under the committee approach used formerly.

Regional Networks   As a second major program source, stations have four regional networks: Eastern Educational Television Network (EEN), Central Educational Network (CEN), Southern Educational Telecommunications Association (SECA), and Pacific Mountain Network (PMN). An example of a regional program is William F. Buckley, Jr.'s *Firing Line*. Most stations belong to at least one regional network. The EEN has spawned a spin-off, known as the American Program Service (APS), which offers how-to programs and some programs from the United Kingdom. It also produces the popular *Nightly Business Report*.

Instructional   Instructional programming plays a role in public television. How much of the schedule it occupies depends upon the type of licensee. Among the many sources for instructional programming are Western Instructional Television, TV Ontario, Central Educational Network, the Agency for Instructional Television (AIT), and Great Plains National (GPN).

Commercial Syndication Budget constraints and program strategy considerations formerly resulted in the infrequent use by public television stations of product supplied by commercial syndicators. In recent years, however, efforts to broaden the membership base have led to its increased use. Some large-market community stations have programmed off-network series successfully. Highly regarded offerings, such as *St. Elsewhere* and *Hill Street Blues*, have been purchased. PBS itself has resorted to this tactic. In 1993, it acquired *I'll Fly Away* for prime-time broadcast. Commercial syndicators, like Wolper Productions and Granada TV, have become regular sources for public television stations.

Local Origination The level of local origination depends upon the type of licensee and the location. Community stations in large cities do more than the other types of stations. Local programming is expensive, but it does provide identity and distinguishes public television stations from their commercial competitors and one another. To control the costs associated with local origination, some stations have experimented with hiring independent contractors on a per-program basis. Such arrangements avoid the expense of maintaining a large, on-site staff for local program production.

Scheduling Management can have a good program strategy and acquire excellent programming, but fail on scheduling. If the program schedule is not built properly, the desired goals will not be achieved.

There are as many opinions on how to schedule as there are stations in the country. While there is no absolute right or wrong, there are some general guidelines. Most public television stations observe the 1979 nonbinding Common Carriage Agreement, which has as its objective the airing by local stations of the PBS core schedule on the night and in the order fed during prime time (see Figure 9.6). This common carriage is important to program underwriters, to promotional efforts, and to establishment of a ratings position.

After making a decision on the core schedule, management should examine its commitment to, or requirement for, instructional programming. These programs are usually aired in daytime and may be a source of revenue. In many instances, stations now deliver instructional programming overnight via broadcast on a batch basis for later classroom use. This development frees up more daytime hours for programming.

With the two "must" parts of the schedule in place, allocation of the rest of the time is somewhat discretionary. Public stations do have constituencies that must be considered, including minorities and special interest groups. To those must be added the needs and interests of the community as a whole and the demands to raise financial support from the audience.

Whatever program choices are made, for whatever reasons, scheduling decisions must also be guided by the principles of audience flow and counter-programming. As noted in Chapter 4, "Broadcast Programming," audience flow is simply the movement of the audience from one program to the next and results from the placement of similar type programs back to back. Whenever possible, dissimilar programs should be separated. Counter-

Figure 9.6   *PBS Winter/Spring 1999 schedule.*

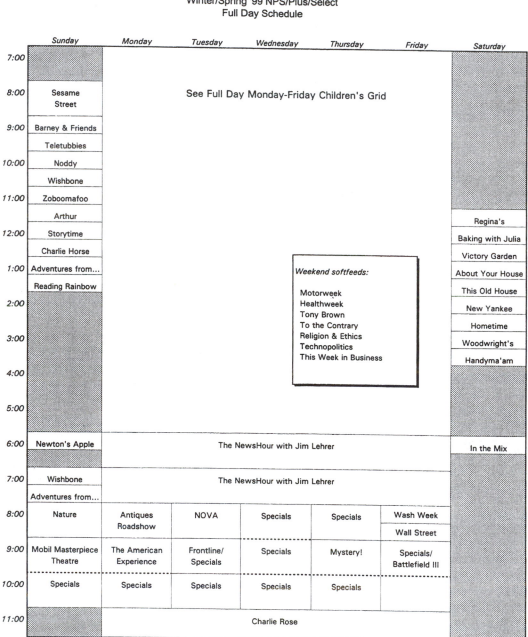

Winter/Spring '99 NPS/Plus/Select
Full Day Schedule

	Sunday	Monday	Tuesday	Wednesday	Thursday	Friday	Saturday
7:00							
8:00	Sesame Street			See Full Day Monday-Friday Children's Grid			
9:00	Barney & Friends						
	Teletubbies						
10:00	Noddy						
	Wishbone						
11:00	Zoboomafoo						
	Arthur						Regina's
12:00	Storytime						Baking with Julia
	Charlie Horse						Victory Garden
1:00	Adventures from...						About Your House
	Reading Rainbow						This Old House
2:00							New Yankee
3:00							Hometime
							Woodwright's
4:00							Handyma'am
5:00							
6:00	Newton's Apple			The NewsHour with Jim Lehrer			In the Mix
7:00	Wishbone			The NewsHour with Jim Lehrer			
	Adventures from...						
8:00	Nature	Antiques Roadshow	NOVA	Specials	Specials	Wash Week	
						Wall Street	
9:00	Mobil Masterpiece Theatre	The American Experience	Frontline/ Specials	Specials	Mystery!	Specials/ Battlefield III	
10:00	Specials	Specials	Specials	Specials	Specials		
11:00				Charlie Rose			

Weekend softfeeds:

Motorweek
Healthweek
Tony Brown
To the Contrary
Religion & Ethics
Technopolitics
This Week in Business

programming, as indicated earlier, is scheduling against the competition a program that will serve a segment of the audience whose interests or needs are not being met. Difference is the key to counter-programming, whereas similarity is encouraged for audience flow.

Special scheduling considerations come into play during fund-raising when, for example, emotional or special appeal programs produce the best results. Different considerations also may be a factor during ratings periods. Such periods are increasingly important, and the competition stacks the schedule with their best product at those times. Local licensee philosophy may prohibit ratings period schedule strategy, but management needs to consider it, at least.

Promotion   Historically, the role of promotion in public television has been neglected. Perhaps that resulted from the erroneous belief that ratings were not important, or possibly promotion was thought not to be important because public programming was unique and would sell itself. Whatever the reason, there is an increased awareness of its significance, and many public stations spend 5 percent or more of their budget on promotional activities.

There are many ways to promote, but the cheapest and most available is the station's own air. However, it has its limitations. The average household has the television set turned on more than seven hours a day, but that set is tuned to public television only one-to-two hours per week.[17] Therefore, the task is complicated. On-the-air promotion must be effective. That means that it causes the viewers of one program to sample other programs offered by the station. A viewer who watches *The Newshour with Jim Lehrer* is a candidate for *Washington Week in Review.* On-the-air promos for a program should be run during similar programs that are likely to attract the same audience. A *Firing Line* audience is probably not given to watching *Sesame Street.* It is a truism of audiences today that they watch programs and not stations. Accordingly, it makes good sense to promote in the program being aired other programs that that audience is likely to view.

On-the-air promotion must also be well produced. Promo production is an art form in the commercial world and needs to become such in public television. Promos should be attention-getting and not stereotyped. Station IDs should be alive and colorful. Public stations gradually have begun to recognize the importance of creative promos, and that trend must continue. Too often, management overlooks the role of effective, well-produced, and properly placed program and station promos.

On-the-air promotion reaches only the audience the station already has. So, too, does a station's monthly program guide (see Figure 9.7). For this reason, the program guide is a limited promotional vehicle. Typically, it is an in-house publication that is circulated to viewers pledging financial support and carries listings of regular and special programs. Stations that depend solely on on-the-air promotion and program guides limit their opportunities to broaden their audience and increase their financial support.

New viewers must be attracted. The most commonly used method of broadening the public television audience has been newspapers, especially Sunday

Figure 9.7 *Monthly program guide published by KPTS-TV, Wichita, Kansas. (Used with permission.)*

television sections, which may be more widely consulted than *TV Guide*. Newspapers are valuable for promoting image, news, and special series. However, their readership is declining, and newspaper demographics are older than the target audience public television needs to attract. Hence, newspapers should not be relied upon to the exclusion of other media choices available.

Radio can be used to supplement other promotion. It is economical and can be targeted to the desired audience. For example, *The Newshour with Jim Lehrer* can be promoted on news and talk stations. *Masterpiece Theater* and *Mystery!* spots can be run on adult contemporary stations.

Another potential promotional tool is cable television. While cable presents a financial and audience challenge to public television, it can be used effectively. Cable systems have local advertising time available in national, advertiser-supported networks. Cable spots are relatively inexpensive, often cheaper than radio, and certainly less expensive than commercial television. In addition, they can be targeted toward a specific audience. More and more stations are dedicating cash to the purchase of ad time in local system availabilities on basic cable networks. These campaigns are designed to attract viewers aged 25 to 44 and to change perceptions about public television.[18] The networks used include A&E, ESPN, CNN, TNT, USA, MTV, Lifetime, and Nickelodeon.

Periodicals such as *TV Guide* and local market life and leisure-type publications should also be considered as promotional vehicles. Other possibilities are outdoor, transit, and taxicab advertising.

In recent years, an exciting new promotional vehicle has emerged for public stations: the Internet. Stations can now display their programming on Websites and promote to an audience which, in large part, consists of the demographics public television needs to attract. This audience also can quite possibly be reached by the more traditional forms of promotion, like newspapers.

For the promotion-minded public broadcast executive, budget will be a problem. However, in this multiple-choice viewing world, promotion is essential. Management must know what promotion options are available and how to use them. The promotion function in public television now is of critical importance and, in many stations, is combined with the fund-raising function. For that reason, the promotion manager is typically called the *development director*.

Research   Research provides the road map for a station's programming and promotional strategies. Its importance cannot be over-emphasized. Research provides insights into what genre of programs should be considered for airing and into program placement in the schedule and in relation to other programs. It also provides guidance on what programs should be promoted to the public, both on the air and in outside media.

Research can be developed from routinely available sources or can be specially commissioned. The former include standard quarterly ratings reports provided to subscribing stations by Nielsen and containing valuable information on individual program performance and cumulative audience. In addition, specialized reports can be ordered. One example is the county coverage survey, which provides management with details of the relative strengths and weaknesses of a station in each county of the survey area.

Additional ratings information is available to PBS members in the *Station Audience Report*, issued at the end of each sweep period in November, February, May, and July. PBS also issues annual Designated Market Area (DMA) profiles. These research reports provide household demographic characteristics, sex/age demographics, and general market information for each of Nielsen's DMAs. Individual markets may have characteristics that require special consideration in programming and promotion. The *DMA Market Profile* is one source of such data.

The Pacific Mountain Network provides a ratings service to participating stations called "TV Ratings Analysis Coalition" (TRAC). Included in its reports are overnight ratings, monthly ratings, and a local station's top-25 performing programs.

Station management may utilize other methods of obtaining research information. One technique is to place a questionnaire in the monthly program guide, seeking the program preferences and attitudes of the audience, which presumably consists of confirmed viewers. Such input is important because of the necessity of satisfying this financially supportive core audience. Program guide surveys are augmented by mail and telephone calls to the station, usually from committed viewers.

To broaden its information base, a public station may commission special research among viewers in the market who may not be part of its current audience. In-depth special research may suggest program and promotional changes that could result in a broadening of the station's viewership.

There are many private companies that provide such services. For example, The Gallup Organization in Lincoln, Nebraska,[19] will work with a station to design a questionnaire, complete the field research, and issue a report. Companies charge a fee, and, for some stations, the cost is prohibitive. An alternative is to commission a local college or university to undertake the work. Public broadcast stations operated by university licensees are particularly well positioned to avail themselves of that opportunity.

Fund-raising efforts also are a research tool. Programs that produce the largest viewer pledges often are a good indication of what the audience wants. Comments made by viewers while calling in pledges during fund-raising also provide useful insights.

Stations also collect research information when they call viewers. Outside the on-air campaigns, many stations conduct telemarketing membership renewal campaigns, during which they compile audience program preference data.

To complement this local information, management should determine audience strategies that have worked well in other markets. Maintaining contacts with other public station managers can provide valuable data.

In the current fragmented, competitive viewer market, research is an important and ongoing function of the public television station executive.

Cable Relations   The emergence of the cable industry initially was a favorable development for public television. Many stations operate on UHF channels and experience coverage and signal-quality problems. Cable systems enhanced their coverage area and improved the reception quality for many viewers. Because public television relies heavily on viewers for financial support, the benefits to be derived from cable carriage are obvious.

It was noted in Chapter 8, "Managing the Cable Television System," that, in the mid-1980s, court decisions eliminated the FCC must-carry rule requiring cable systems to carry local broadcast stations.[20] The rule was restored by the Cable Television Consumer Protection and Competition Act of 1992 and upheld by the United States Supreme Court.[21] Under this law, a system's obligation to carry noncommercial educational stations depends on its channel capacity. Systems with twelve or fewer channels must carry one local noncommercial station. Those with thirteen to thirty-six channels must carry all local noncommercial educational stations up to a maximum of three, while systems with more than thirty-six channels must carry all local noncommercial educational stations.[22] If a system operates in a market with no noncommercial educational stations, it must import one.

Good relations with cable systems in the station's DMA are important. Public station managers must appreciate the need to maintain contact with cable systems to lobby for the uniqueness of their product. A growing number of stations designate a person to handle cable relations. The cable operator must be told of specials and schedule changes. If the station will be off the air for any reason, the cable system must be informed, since service interruptions result in telephone calls to the system. If adequately advised, cable operators may be able to avoid the calls by displaying information pertaining to the schedule change or transmission difficulties.

Problems with cable systems should be reported to the Washington-based Association of America's Public Television Stations, which works with policy makers on questions of vital concern to the public television industry. Cable regulation is certainly one.

Community Relations   Any entity that relies on governmental support as much as public television needs to be image-conscious and to maintain good community relations. Station and staff involvement in community life through participation in local activities and organizations can be helpful.

Beyond that, a very effective way to promote community relations is through on-the-air public service announcements and community events calendars. Requests for this kind of publicity assistance are frequent and, whenever possible, should be accommodated.

The concept of community relations also should be kept in mind when planning local origination of programs of a continuing nature, such as news or public affairs.

A final consideration is license renewal. Every television station must apply for renewal every eight years. If citizens or citizen groups do not believe that the station has been operated in the public interest, they can file a petition to deny renewal. This has happened to some public stations, most often because of the station's failure to address the needs of some constituency, such as an ethnic group.[23] Good community relations can identify a problem like this before it matures to a denial petition.

Engineering   Equipment must be purchased and maintained. Even the best programming is not worth much if the audience cannot receive a quality signal, but quality costs money. Capital costs are a significant ongoing expense. Most managers do not have engineering backgrounds and cannot evaluate technical options properly. However, it is important to devote the time required to stay abreast of these matters. The on-the-air look and sound are critical to the station's success.

As noted earlier in the chapter, the expense of equipment acquisition may be offset by grants from the National Telecommunications and Information Administration. However, the station applicant must support the purchase with some of its own funds, usually up to 50 percent of the total amount. DTV will be the magic engineering challenge in the early years of the twenty-first century.

Administration   Having identified the component parts of public television, let us now turn to the administrative function. Quite simply, it involves integrating the parts into a smoothly operating station that delivers the desired product to an aware audience. Among other things, administration is managing employee benefits, relations, and conflicts. It is negotiating — for acquisition of program product, for equipment, and union contracts. It also involves the presentation for approval of the operating budget to the supervising authority, be it a board, official, commission, or agency. It is paperwork, such as the preparation of grant applications, CPB Certifications of Eligibility, and program schedules for *TV Guide*, newspapers, and ratings services. In reality, administration is managing people and deadlines.

Administration is the management function where a lot of executives fail. If attention to detail is missing, the component parts, as good as they may be, will not matter. It is the least inspiring but most important aspect of public electronic media management. For it is here that it all does, or does not, come together.

RADIO

Two thousand noncommercial radio stations operate in the United States.[24] Among those, 362 licensees meet Corporation for Public Broadcasting criteria and may receive CPB grants.[25] Like public television stations, public radio stations are divided into four licensee categories:

- community (133)
- university (194)
- local authority (27)
- state (8)[26]

Organization and Personnel

The staff size and organizational structure of a public radio station depend on the market, type of licensee, and format. Normally, a station has a general

Figure 9.8   *Organizational chart, KMUW-FM, Wichita, Kansas. (Used with permission.)*

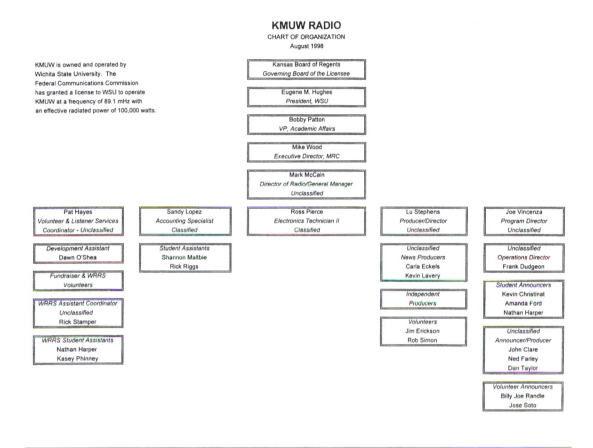

manager or station manager, who reports to a supervising authority. As in public television, the composition of the upper-level governing authority depends on the type of licensee.

Under the general manager or station manager are various departments. Structures and titles vary widely. Figure 9.8 presents the organizational chart of a 100,000-watt public station licensed to a community corporation in Wichita, Kansas. It broadcasts classical music, jazz, and news, and is affiliated with National Public Radio and Public Radio International (PRI).

Management Tasks

Public radio managers exercise responsibilities over seven principal station activities. A review of each of these management tasks will reveal the evolving nature of public radio and the problems it faces in the current fragmented, competitive marketplace. It will also allow an examination of the management tools and techniques to meet the challenges and an opportunity to contrast public radio with its commercial brethren. The tasks are as follows:

- financial
- programming
- promotion
- research
- community relations
- engineering
- administration

Financial: Revenues   Many of the comments about public television budgets made earlier in this chapter also apply to radio.

Formerly, program production was concentrated at the national level. Today, CPB radio programming funds are paid directly to qualified stations. In addition, National Public Radio has "unbundled" its programming. In other words, member stations now may take all or part of the NPR program offerings. These changes obviously have had an impact on the financial management of public stations.

Public radio is noncommercial. Unlike commercial radio, it does not have advertisers as a principal source of operating funds. Therefore, it has looked to alternative funding sources. The four principal sources are

- federal government
- state government
- audience
- underwriting

Federal Government   Public radio relies upon two principal kinds of federal funding, both of which emanate from the Corporation for Public Broadcasting. The first is Community Service Grants. To apply, a station must file an annual Certification of Eligibility with the Corporation for Public Broadcasting (see Figure 9.9). The certification must demonstrate that the station has adequate power to provide a minimum designated signal over the station's city of license, that it has at least five full-time employees, and that it operates a minimum of eighteen hours per day on a minimum nonfederal income of $182,500.

The station must also file a Station Activities Survey, financial report, and an Offer and Acceptance to receive the CPB grants. They usually cover two-year periods and, because a station files annually, there is an overlap.

CPB's second method of distributing federal funds is via National Program Production and Acquisition Grants. They are a result of the 1987 CPB decision to fund program production at the local station level rather than through NPR. Requisite documentation is an Offer and Acceptance, which the station submits annually (see Figure 9.10).

Neither the CPB's Community Service Grants nor the National Program Production and Acquisition Grants require any local-station matching funds. However, CPB does provide grants for many local station activities, some of which do require such funds.

Figure 9.9 *Radio Community Service Grant Certification of Eligibility, KMUW-FM, Wichita, Kansas. (Used with permission.)*

Code R02900	**Station**	KMUW-FM
City/State Wichita, Kansas		
Licensee Name	Wichita State University	

 CORPORATION FOR PUBLIC BROADCASTING

FISCAL YEAR 1998 RADIO COMMUNITY SERVICE GRANT CERTIFICATION OF ELIGIBILITY

NOTE: This document requires two different signatures: one for the licensee and one for the station. See bottom of this form for clarification.

To help determine the station's eligibility for a Fiscal Year 1998 CSG, review the items below and check "Yes" or "No" for each criterion.

CRITERIA FOR GRANT ELIGIBILITY

The station and licensee specified above currently meets or exceeds the following criteria:

    Yes   **No**

1.   _X_ _____ The station is licensed by the FCC as a noncommercial, educational radio station.

2.   _X_ _____ The station has an operating power of 250 watts or greater in the case of an AM radio station, or an effective radiated power of 100 watts or greater in the case of an FM radio station.

3a. _____ _X_ The station serves a coverage area population of 25,000 **or less** and employs a minimum of two full-time employees plus two full-time equivalent employees on an annual (12-month) basis. At least two full-time staff members are employed in a managerial and/or programming position. Minimum staff are not paid with CSG funds.

3b. _X_ _____ The station serves a coverage area population of 25,000 **or more** and employs a minimum of three full-time employees plus two full-time equivalent employees on an annual (12-month) basis. At least two full-time staff members are employed in a managerial and/or programming position. Minimum staff are not paid with CSG funds.

    Minority controlled and operated stations that have a mission to provide service primarily designed to meet the needs and interests of specific ethnic populations may count full-time equivalent staff toward the full-time staffing requirement. The term "full-time equivalent" will be understood to mean combined employment equal to the number of hours that constitute the normal full-time work week at each institution or station.

    (Full-time, professional, radio station staff includes permanent personnel with demonstrated skill and expertise in the management, programming, production, promotion, development or engineering areas of radio station operation, paid no less than the minimum federal hourly wage plus regular health benefits, whose terms of employment require the exercise of full-time duties in one or more of these areas. Clerical and custodial staff, students whose student status is a condition of employment, interns and trainees, do not meet the definition of this criterion, nor do personnel teaching or holding academic duties in excess of the equivalent of one three-hour credit course per quarter or semester. The term "full-time" will be understood to be the number of hours that constitute the normal work week at each institution or station. Persons employed on a nonpermanent basis, such as those on a public service employment training grant or those funded by the CSG or any type of restricted short-term grant, cannot be considered full-time, professional radio station staff to meet this criterion.)

Figure 9.9 *Continued*

2   FY98 Radio Certification of Eligibility

4. _X_ _____   Sufficient office space is provided. The station also has sufficient, professionally equipped on-air and production facilities to allow for broadcast of programming of high technical quality, including the capability for simultaneous local production and origination.

5. _X_ _____   The station's minimum operational schedule is 18 hours per day, 365 days per year. **(Should your station be an AM FCC- limited, please indicate.)** Shared time stations do not meet this criterion.

6. _X_ _____   The station's daily broadcast schedule is devoted primarily to programming of good quality that serves demonstrated community needs of an educational, informational and cultural nature within its primary signal area. Such programming is intended for a general audience.

●A program schedule designated to further the principles of particular political or religious philosophies does not meet the definition of this criterion.
●A program schedule designed primarily for in-school or professional in-service audiences does not meet the definition of this criterion. A campus station managed and operated by and for students does not meet the definition of this criterion.
●New applicants in areas already served by a CPB-supported station must propose a substantially different program service from the existing CPB-supported station(s) in the area, and clearly identify the unduplicated audience to be served.
●Stations licensed to political organizations do not meet the definition of this criterion.

7. _X_ _____   Station originates a significant, locally produced program service designed to serve its community of license.

8. _X_ _____   Station had a total annual nonfederal financial support of at least $177,700 during FY 97.

9. _X_ _____   The station and its licensee comply in full with the Federal Communications Commission's regulations concerning equal employment opportunity (47 C.F.R. 73.2080).

10. _X_ _____   The job openings identified in the employment portion of the licensee's and its station's 1997 Annual Station Activities Survey were filled in accordance with Federal Communications Commission's regulations concerning equal employment opportunity (47 C.F.R. 73.2080). If the job openings were not filled in accordance with such regulations, a statement of the reasons for not filling the positions in accordance with such regulations must be submitted to CPB with this Certification of Eligibility.

11. _X_ _____   The station and its licensee comply in full with the following sections of the Communications Act of 1934, 47 U.S.C 390, et seq.:

OPEN MEETINGS, OPEN RECORDS AND COMMUNITY ADVISORY BOARD

Section 396(k)(4)-Requiring all meetings of the governing body, any committee of such governing body, and any advisory body of the recipient to be open, preceded by reasonable notice to the public to the extent that the deliberations of those bodies relate to public broadcasting. Exceptions to this provision are listed in Section 396(k)(4) and Section 397(5) of the Communications Act.

Section 396(k)(5)-Requiring that copies of the recipient's annual financial and audit reports, and other information regarding finances submitted to CPB, be made available by the recipient for public inspection.

Section 396(k)(8)-Requiring the establishment and maintenance of a community advisory board for certain licensees as described in this section of the law.

Figure 9.9 *Continued*

---

3   FY98 Radio Certification of Eligibility

Section 396(k)(11) - Requiring that the statistical report described in Section 13 of the "Fiscal Year 1998 Radio CSG and NPPAG General Provisions" be made available to the public at the central office of the station and at every location where more than five full-time employees are regularly assigned to work.

FULL-TIME AND FULL-TIME EQUIVALENT STAFF

Number of full-time professional staff meeting the minimum staffing criterion specified in 3 above. **Exclude staff funded by CSG, or any other restricted, short-term grant.** ____7____

Identify full-time and full-time equivalent professional staff meeting the minimum staffing criterion:

NAME	TITLE	SOURCE OF FUNDS FOR SALARIES
Mark E McCain	General Manager	State Funds
Patricia Hayes	Volunteer/Listener Service Coordinator	State Funds
Frank Dudgeon	Operations Director	State Funds
Ross Pierce	Electronics Technician	State Funds/Gifts
Joseph Vincenza	Program Director	State Funds/Gifts

NETWORKS AND OTHER DUAL OPERATIONS:

A licensee must qualify overlapping stations as a single entity when the licensee operates two or more stations whose signals overlap by 50 percent or more.

A. Radio "networks" consist of at least two radio stations licensed in dual operations (multiple stations with the same licensee). Their operations may be consolidated to earn a single radio CSG under the following conditions:

   1. The stations (transmitters) serve separate communities.
   2. A minimum of 50% of the broadcast schedule for each station originates from a central network source.

B. Radio stations in dual operations (multiple stations with the same licensee) that are located in the same city of license may consolidate operations to benefit directly from the radio CSG under the following conditions:

   1. Each station must be managed and programmed by the professional staff assigned to the co-licensed CSG-eligible station.
   2. Each station must provide a separate and distinct program service for the community of license.
   3. Each station must adhere to the programming policies contained in this document.
   4. Stations that are closed circuit, low power, student managed, and/or that provide in-service training type programming to licensee employees, clients, and/or representatives are not eligible.

List your dual licensed stations that meet the requirements set forth in A or B above.

Call Letters	Channel	Location

Figure 9.9 *Continued*

4   FY98 Radio Certification of Eligibility

CERTIFICATION:

THE UNDERSIGNED ATTEST AND AFFIRM THAT THE INFORMATION PROVIDED THROUGHOUT THIS DOCUMENT IS ACCURATE AND VERIFIABLE.

THE UNDERSIGNED UNDERSTAND AND AGREE THAT THE LICENSEE WILL INFORM CPB IMMEDIATELY IN WRITING UPON FAILURE TO MAINTAIN ANY OF THE FOREGOING CRITERIA AND REQUIREMENTS.

Signatures of two different individuals are required: (1) an authorized official of the licensee responsible for signing grants/contracts for the licensee and who has knowledge and authority to certify that the licensee and its station meet or exceed each of the eligibility criteria set forth above and to certify the accuracy of all of the data and information above (e.g. chairman, treasurer or secretary of the board of directors, university vice president for finance, president of the school board, etc.) and (2) the chief executive officer in charge of the operation of the station (e.g. president, general manager, or station manager).

(1) For the Licensee: Eugene M. Hughes, President
                          (Name and Title)

                          Eugene M Hughes   10/8/97
                          (Signature and Date)

(2) For the Station: Mark E. McCain, General Manager
                          (Name and Title)

                          Mark McCain   10/13/97
                          (Signature and Date)

Approved as to Legal Form   GENERAL COUNSEL

Please return to:

System and Station Development
Corporation for Public Broadcasting
901 E Street NW
Washington, DC 20004-2037
1-800-527-2272

It is important for management to know the many kinds of available grants and how to obtain them. Some of them will be discussed later in the chapter.

Equipment purchase support is available through the National Telecommunications and Information Administration. To qualify for NTIA funds, stations must submit a detailed written proposal and be able to generate matching funds.

Figure 9.10 *National Program Production and Acquisition Grant Offer and Acceptance, KMUW-FM, Wichita, Kansas. (Used with permission.)*

Station Code	R02900	Station	KMUW-FM
City	Wichita	State	KS

cpb CORPORATION FOR PUBLIC BROADCASTING

FISCAL YEAR 1998
RADIO NATIONAL PROGRAM PRODUCTION AND ACQUISITION GRANT
OFFER
CPB No. 7480-30018

Wichita State University
(Licensee Name)

The Corporation for Public Broadcasting (CPB), relying on representations made by the applicant in the Application for a Radio Community Service Grant and National Program Production and Acquisition Grant, and the certifications and relevant data and information contained in all of the related documents and forms and in the CPB Annual Financial Report for Fiscal Year 1996 submitted by applicant, hereby offers applicant a Fiscal Year 1998 Radio National Program Production and Acquisition Grant (NPPAG) in the amount below. The amount of this grant has been computed pursuant to the NPPAG formula adopted by the CPB Board of Directors.

Amount Offered: $34,128

This offer is contingent upon CPB's receipt of its full authorized appropriation for Fiscal Year 1998 ($250.0 million), and is subject to decreases.

This offer is subject to acceptance by the applicant, which acceptance shall constitute an agreement by the applicant to comply with all of the terms and conditions set forth in the "Fiscal Year 1998 Radio Community Service Grant and National Program Production and Acquisition Grant - General Provisions" which are expressly made a part of this Offer.

CORPORATION FOR PUBLIC BROADCASTING

[signature]   09/05/97
(Signature)

ACCEPTANCE OF A RADIO NATIONAL PROGRAM PRODUCTION AND ACQUISITION GRANT

Applicant hereby accepts the Fiscal Year 1998 Radio National Program Production and Acquisition Grant offered above, and agrees to comply with all of the terms and conditions set forth in the "Fiscal Year 1998 Radio Community Service Grant and National Program Production and Acquisition Grant - General Provisions" which are expressly made a part of this Acceptance.

Applicant agrees that CPB shall pay no more than the amount here offered.

Applicant warrants the present accuracy of data and information contained in its Application for a Fiscal Year 1998 Radio Community Service Grant and National Program Production and Acquisition Grant and its response to the CPB Annual Financial Report for Fiscal Year 1996; agrees to report any subsequently discovered inaccuracies to CPB; and further agrees to downward adjustments that accurate data might require, whether reported by applicant or discovered during the course of an audit conducted pursuant to Section 8 of the "Fiscal Year 1998 Radio Community Service Grant and National Program Production and Acquisition Grant General Provisions."

Applicant certifies and warrants: (1) that it currently meets or exceeds each of the eligibility criteria set forth in the "Fiscal Year 1998 Radio Community Service Grant Certification of Eligibility"; and (2) the present accuracy of all of the data and information that it has provided in that Certification of Eligibility. Applicant agrees to inform CPB immediately in writing of any failures to maintain all such eligibility criteria, and any subsequently discovered inaccuracies or changes in the data or information provided.

Please return to:

System and Station Development
Corporation for Public Broadcasting
901 E Street NW
Washington, DC 20004-2037
1-800-527-2272

Approved As To
Legal Form *[signature]* 10/8/97
GENERAL COUNSEL

Wichita State University
(Licensee Name)

[signature]   10/8/97
(Signature of Authorized Official of Licensee)   (Date)

Eugene M. Hughes, President
(Name and Title of Authorized Official of Licensee)

Federal funding is the financial foundation of local public radio. Attention to the details and procedures necessary to ensure the station's continuing qualification is a management priority task.

State Government   A second key ingredient in public radio finances is the support of state governments. States may fund some licensees directly through annual appropriation, as in the case of public radio stations operated by universities. Some states operate statewide public radio networks that are funded in part by the state legislatures.

The future public radio manager should simply be aware that significant state financial resources are available and that complying with state procedures and deadlines is a major management function.

Audience   All public radio stations rely to some degree upon their audiences to meet their budgets. Generally, this audience outreach takes the form of one or more on-the-air pledge or membership drives. Spring and fall are favored times of the year for such activities.

Memberships are available at various levels. The higher the dollar amount, the better the premium that accompanies the pledge. For example, KMUW-FM, in Wichita, has four membership categories. The station has two eight-day drives each year, and members generate 30 percent of the station's total support.

The design of the fund-raising drive is in the hands of the local station. There is also a national fund-raising framework. Special versions of popular programs are presented.

Most stations prefer not to break the existing format during fund drives. Instead, special editions or encore presentations of programs are presented in their regular time periods. During fund-raising, a station might use a Garrison Keillor special, for example. Such programming is then interspersed with on-the-air appeals to the audience. Premiums might be anything, but the more successful ones are books, such as *Go Public*, which features coverage maps and format information on public radio stations across the country, and coffee mugs displaying the names of popular programs. Phone-in pledges are taken by volunteers, usually comprised of community leaders and members of community organizations. Where possible, involvement of local sports or entertainment celebrities is desirable.

Public radio stations do engage in other kinds of fund-raising. Some organize auctions. However, this technique is difficult because radio lacks the visual element. Special events with personalities from national programs carried by the station are another type. Some public stations mount concerts as revenue generators. Generally, the artists secured are those who are featured in the format. Other fund-raising activities might include sales of recordings.

New methods of audience fund-raising are developing and evolving. It is important to be aware of ideas and success stories from stations around the country. This can be done by direct contact with other public stations or by membership in selected organizations, such as The Development Exchange of Arlington, Virginia.[27] It circulates fund-raising information and sponsors workshops to enhance local stations' fund-raising abilities. The annual subscription cost for participation in the exchange is well worth the investment. Other development information is available on the Internet.[28]

Underwriting   This revenue source is used either to develop or present programs. As a rule, public radio stations are more active than television stations in program development. Stations involved in program production may submit grant applications to large corporations or foundations to secure development funds.

Stations not engaged in program development may still rely on underwriting to defray some of the costs of presenting programs. To secure presentation underwriting, a representative of the station offers a local business sponsorship identification during the program in exchange for a monetary contribution. To preserve noncommercial integrity, close attention must be paid to the preparation of underwriting copy.

Product identification is acceptable. Price information, product comparisons, and customer motivational language are not. Comments made earlier in this chapter about the similarity of this activity to commercial station spot sales and the dangers of not adhering to underwriting guidelines are relevant here.

Since underwriting is one of the few realistic revenue sources available to public radio, management should provide sufficient personnel and support to develop it.

Financial: Expenses

In these times of decreased resources and increased competition, expense control for public radio management is as important as revenue enhancement.

The largest public radio expense items are programming and staff. Public radio stations tend to originate more programming than public television stations. Many stations also maintain a local news presence, and that is expensive.

Purchased programming is also expensive. The unbundling of NPR programming has not led to the predicted cost reduction for stations. As a result, many member stations have defected and spent their money with competitors, like Public Radio International. Loss of member dollars for NPR programming only further increases the cost for those who use it.

Public radio is not as equipment-intensive as public television. However, the quality of on-the-air product and signal is affected by technological developments and their accompanying expense. Digital audio broadcasting (DAB) is an example of a likely future expense in this category. It is not as immediate as DTV, however.

Promotion is becoming a greater expense item. Deregulation has led to an increased number of radio stations with more varied formats. As a result, the public station will have to spend more on promotion to stay positioned as an attractive media alternative.

Specific expense comparisons can be made with similar public radio stations in other markets by consulting annual expense data compiled by the Corporation for Public Broadcasting. Management should examine such data as part of the continuing effort to allocate and control expense dollars.

Programming

The measurement of a successful program strategy in public television is cumulative audience. In public radio, however, it is time spent listening (TSL), or how long listeners are tuned in, and that requires a different program approach. The goal is to select a format that will retain the audience for extended periods of time. Usually, a public radio station plays to one constituency, whereas a public television station plays to many in order to build audience.

Public radio is format-based. In that respect, its programming is similar to its commercial counterparts. However, public formats are specialized, with narrower audience appeal. For that reason, most of them would not be commercially viable. Public stations provide an important function by servicing what would otherwise be unserved portions of the radio audience.

Format Selection   To succeed in public radio today, a niche in the fragmented radio spectrum must be identified and a format developed to fill it. Historically, management has had six recognized formats from which to select:

Classical and fine arts consists of recorded music and, at times, live concerts. Additional programming to support this format is available from NPR and other sources.

Jazz is mainly recorded music and live concerts. Supplemental programming is obtainable from NPR.

News and public affairs is a format that can be partly local and partly national. National programming support is available from NPR and from PRI, which carries the BBC World Service.

Community service and public access is primarily a locally originated format designed to provide information to, and a forum for, those who may be neglected by the programming of other radio stations in the market.

Eclectic is the format used by most stations. It offers something for everyone, but does not generate the high TSL now considered desirable.

Dual format is a program concept featuring news and a certain type of music, usually classical or jazz.[29]

In addition to these six recognized formats, a new public radio format has been evolving. Currently, it is known as the *Adult Acoustic Alternative* (AAA). This experimental concept represents an attempt to attract younger demographics by offering contemporary music, and it appears to be having some success.

Like public television, public radio has had to rely more on audience support due to decreased government support. Commercial services to assist public radio in increasing its audience have been developed. An example is "Classical 24," a service that selects classical music that will appeal to the NPR news listener.[30]

The format ultimately selected will be dictated by the type of licensee operating the station, the needs and interests of the community, and the positioning of other radio alternatives in the market.

National Affiliation   Having selected a basic format, the public radio program director must now decide how to augment it with a national service or services. At present, two primary services are available.

The oldest, and best known, is National Public Radio, a private, non-profit membership corporation that produces and distributes programs.

NPR has more than 300 members, and the programming it provides can be purchased in its entirety or in units. In recent years, NPR has tended to make more individual programs available. Major program blocks include the Morning News Service, the Afternoon News Service, and Performance Programming.

The morning service features a program called *Morning Edition*, and the afternoon service's main offering is *All Things Considered*. Both have weekend editions. Performance programming comprises a variety of content, including music (classical, jazz, and folk), drama, and comedy. Popular features are *Car Talk* and *Talk of the Nation*. NPR also offers as a major feed *Performance Today*, which includes occasional features in a classical music context.

NPR members pay for the programming they use and for transmission costs, as well as the basic station membership fee. As a result of the CPB's transfer of program grants from NPR to local stations and the withdrawal of some important member stations from NPR, these costs have risen sharply.

In addition to its programming services, NPR also provides program-producing stations with distribution services. The Extended Program Service enables local stations to send their programs to other stations via the Public Radio Satellite System, which maintains uplinks and downlinks throughout the country.

The other national service is Public Radio International. Originated in 1982, this nonprofit corporation provides an alternative to NPR, and many stations subscribe to both. Instead of membership fees, public stations pay affiliation fees, the amount of which depends on market size.

PRI's programs originate with local stations and independent producers. Funding for program acquisition is provided by foundations, corporations, and station program fees.

Initially, Public Radio International did not offer as full a range of programs as NPR. However, since its inception, its program offerings have expanded considerably. It distributes news and special programs, some of which, like *Prairie Home Companion* and *Whad'ya Know?*, have enjoyed significant popularity. As noted earlier, PRI also carries the BBC World Service.

Unlike NPR, PRI does provide some programming for the basic affiliation fee. It is an important program source for public radio directors, and affiliation with it does not preclude association with other sources.

National Public Radio's program pricing policies, coupled with its loss of significant member stations, has led to the rise of independent program producers seeking to capitalize on the programming void and develop a new market for their products.

Some major market public radio stations also have become program producers. Examples are WGBH, Boston, and WCLV, Cleveland, which operates as Seaway Productions. WFMT, Chicago, operates the Fine Arts Network. The final example is the Longhorn Network, which distributes the audio track of William F. Buckley, Jr.'s *Firing Line*.

Public radio program directors have an ever-increasing selection of program sources (see Figure 9.11). To stay in touch with what is happening, the local program director should consider membership in the Public

Figure 9.11   *Programming sources for KMUW-FM, Wichita, Kansas. (Used with permission.)*

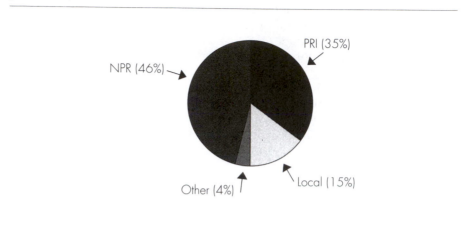

Radio Program Directors' Association (PRPD),[31] which makes information available to its members through a newsletter. Staying current is a continuing challenge for public radio management, and industry associations are one way to do it.

Promotion   Radio is more competitive and fragmented than ever. As more stations go on the air, as more are allowed to upgrade their power, and as contour overlap is reduced, the situation will intensify. In this climate, public radio management must promote. Gone are the days when programming promoted itself through its uniqueness. The number one way to promote is on your own air. The goal here is to get existing listeners to tune into some of your other programs and to extend the TSL.

Outside promotion in public radio is done in a variety of ways. The most traditional has been the program guide, which appears in all shapes and sizes, from simple one-sheets to elaborate magazine-style monthly publications, such as Minnesota Public Radio's *Minnesota Monthly*. Figure 9.12 illustrates the cover page of a guide that falls between the two extremes, a four-page publication.

Newspaper has also been a traditional public radio promotional vehicle. It is suitable for image promotion and can be employed to promote news, programs, and series.

There is a realization in public radio that promotion methods must change to adapt to the new competitive environment. While research shows that public radio listeners are above-average newspaper readers, many development directors now utilize television. Television is expensive and may be cost-prohibitive. However, some public radio stations have been successful at playing TV spots as public service announcements on commercial TV stations. While broadcast TV is expensive, cable TV is not. Local spots in national, advertiser-supported cable networks carried by local cable systems are affordable and effective. Announcements on CNN, A&E, The Discovery Channel, and The Weather Channel are examples.

Figure 9.12 *KMUW-FM, Wichita, Kansas, monthly program guide. (Used with permission.)*

3317 E. 17TH   WICHITA, KANSAS 67208   (316) 978-6789   kmuw@twsu.edu   www.kmuw.org   OCTOBER, 1998

KMUW's Fall Festival '98
October 23-31...$130,000 Goal

Because you're a listener and a contributor to KMUW, you've received a letter from General Manager Mark McCain reminding you to renew your financial support for the "programming you can't get anywhere other than public radio." Your support enables us to continue to provide you with some of the best programming you'll hear anywhere in the world.

If you'd like to volunteer to answer pledge phones during our Fall Festival just give us a call— 978-6789 and we'll schedule your arrival time. And, if you want to issue a challenge or matching grant to encourage others to

give, please let us know. There are lots of ways you can support your public radio station, and they're all important.

So, we're dusting off the cobwebs in pledge center in anticipation of your imminent visit. Remember, when you come by to pay your pledge in person, and pick up your special KMUW premium (which saves us postage), you'll also receive a copy of *Spotlight on Wichita '99* and a luncheon certificate from our good friends at The Spice Merchant. We look forward to seeing or hearing from you soon!

"Remembering Slavery"
a two-part special series

"Remembering Slavery" brings clarity and authenticity to our understanding of a tumultuous period in American history. In this two-part documentary, listeners hear former slaves describing their lives — in bondage, after emancipation, through the turn of the century.

Hosted by Tonea Stewart, each riveting hour-long episode presents restored recordings of interviews with Fountain Hughes, Laura Smalley, Harriet Smith, and several other former slaves. Their narratives are supplemented by dramatic readings of written interview transcripts read by noted actors such as James Earl Jones, Debbie Allen, Clifton Davis, Lou Gossett, Jr., Esther Rolle, and Melba Moore.

•Part One October 9th, 9 a.m. – "We were slaves. We belonged to people. They'd sell us like they sell horses and cows and hogs." These are the words of Fountain Hughes whose grandfather belonged to Thomas Jefferson. His stories and others re-construct life in bondage — slave auctions, life on the

Continued on page 2

It was a dog-gone difficult decision....

KMUW would like to thank everyone who took time to enter our 2nd annual "Dog Days of Summer" photo contest. Just like last year, we received lots of entries, and making the choices was not an easy task. However, our judges are happy to announce the winners.

The winner in the **Cutest Canine** category was "Harrison" and his person Sher Unruh-Friesen of Newton. Harrison sent us a great picture of himself enjoying the summertime, portable phone and sunscreen at the ready (too cute, really!).

In the **Finest Fido** category, we tip our collective hats to "Max" and his person Mark Kozubowski of Lindsborg. We even got a Haiku from Max & Mark:

"Top Dog" panting, tail dragging Max personifies dog days. Still runs to greet me.

He's a mighty fine looking dog indeed.

In the **Best of Breed** (BOB) category, we honor "Oscar" the Basset Hound, and his people Dee & Linda Starkey of Wichita. Oscar sent us a Christmas photo, wearing his "Santa's Helper" hat. We suppose he could be mistaken for a reindeer, only from the side though. Oscar is pure breed perfection.

And now (drum roll please) our **All Around Top Dog** award goes to "Daisy" a blue eyed

Siberian Husky, and her person Bill Hendry of Wichita. Looking glamorous and poised, we know that Daisy will accept her honors with grace and wear her title as **Top Dog** with pride for the next year.

Again, we thank everyone who entered the contest. You can see photos of all of our winners on the KMUW home page: **www.kmuw.org**

The winner of KMUW's 2nd annual "Dog Days" contest, Daisy poses proudly to demonstrate why she is the All Around Top Dog.

October Program Notes

We know that many of you enjoy listening to WORLD CAFE Sunday through Wednesday evenings here on KMUW. So, why not enjoy a little more of a good thing? Beginning this month, WORLD CAFE can also be heard on Thursday evenings at 10 p.m. here at FM 89.

Perhaps you were a fan of the AUDIOASIS program, formerly heard on Thursday evenings. Fear not! You can now enjoy Joe V's strange and stylish mix of music and humor on Saturday afternoons at 12:30. "What about the Cowboys" you say? Not to worry. RIDERS RADIO THEATER can be heard at its new time, Saturday at noon, right after Michael Feldman's WHAD' YA KNOW.

Then on Sunday, we invite you to join us at 2 p.m. for two new programs on KMUW. THIS AMERICAN LIFE, a program built around the innovative, personal vision of host

Continued on page 2

New forms of outside promotion for public radio are emerging. Borders, a national bookstore chain, promotes public radio with in-store kiosks. NPR and many of its member stations maintain Websites. (For an example of a station Website, see www.kmuw.org.) The Internet allows the station to display its program scheduling, features, and special events, and even to attempt to recruit new members.[32]

The Corporation for Public Broadcasting has recognized the importance of promotion and makes available to local stations promotional Tune In Grants. In order to qualify, stations must apply for them, but they are fairly automatic. There is a matching funds requirement, as well as a requirement to file a final report once the promotion campaign is over.

National Public Radio also develops promotions for its news programs, and promotional ideas are found in the NPR monthly memo to managers.

The Development Exchange, referred to earlier, is also a source for promotional ideas. Among the exchange's publications is the *Tune in Advertising/ Market Handbook*. Publications like this should be in every public radio station's promotion library.

Another idea source is the Public Radio Association of Development Officers (PRADO).[33] Peer contact is always valuable for insights into promotional concepts that have worked for others.

While some promotional techniques of commercial radio are inappropriate for public radio, there are many that can be used. Among those are bumper stickers, T-shirts, and some kinds of contests. On-the-air contests do build quarter-hour audience and do increase critical time spent listening. On-the-air promotion is an element of the total promotion concept.

Development directors for public radio are also frequently the promotion managers. The promotion aspect of the job should be given as high a priority as the fund-raising aspect.

Research   Public radio management must regularly identify the constantly changing program needs and interests of the audience. A good place to begin is with a review of reports provided to subscribing stations by the national rating service, Arbitron. The frequency of the report depends on the size of the market. Because public radio stations do not have access to the kind of ratings information provided by PBS to television stations, management should consider subscribing to a service that is available and affordable.

As an alternative, a public radio station may choose to develop its own data through specially commissioned research. Many public stations operated by colleges or universities are in a unique position to undertake audience research.

Other useful information comes from mail and telephone calls to the station. Talk shows featured on many public radio stations are an effective means of sampling audience attitudes. Station fund-raising also often yields valuable insights into listener likes and dislikes.

Finally, through the Corporation for Public Broadcasting, it is possible for a public radio station to secure financial assistance for research. CPB offers

Audience Building Grants for research development. Stations must submit detailed written proposals to qualify. Competition is quite intense, but the effort may prove worthwhile.

Community Relations   Community relations are as critical to public radio stations as they are to public television stations. The paramount reasons are the level of governmental support and the license renewal, which occurs every eight years. Over the years, there have been occasional cases in which the licenses of some public radio stations have not been renewed. Often, the reason lay in offenses to community sensibilities by the stations.[34]

To enhance community relations, a public radio station can, of course, utilize public service announcements and involve itself in local civic and charitable activities. Depending on the format, the station may have legitimate visible personalities. Talk shows have become America's town meetings. Stations with host talent should consider instituting a speakers' bureau to provide guest speakers for civic organizations, charities, and schools. Similarly, invitations to community leaders to appear on local radio interview programs will assist in maintaining good community relations.

There is more local programming in public radio than in public television. Hence, there are more opportunities to develop community relations.

Engineering   Observations made earlier about the importance of engineering in public television are equally applicable to public radio. Equipment must be bought and maintained to provide the quality signal necessary to retain and build audience. As already noted, management should be aware of the grant assistance available from NTIA for equipment acquisition. DAB is on the horizon and will be an engineering challenge.

Administration   Most of the comments made earlier in this chapter about public television administration also pertain to public radio. However, some additional comments are necessary.

Because radio budgets are tighter, fund-raising more difficult, and staff sizes smaller, public radio managers are under more pressure to administer expertly their more limited resources. Employing personnel who can perform multiple functions well is a real management challenge. Local program origination is a bigger factor than in television, and that poses its own problems. Coupled with that is the need for adequate supervision of on-the-air programming and talent. As discussed earlier, some public stations have offended public sensibilities with programs, music, or comments by on-the-air talent. Regulatory officials and lawmakers are taking a tougher, more rigid position on indecency and obscenity, as evidenced by the promulgation and implementation of the 1987 Federal Communications Commission's indecency standards. Public managers and program executives need to be vigilant. Apart from the equities of a case, the cost of defending an FCC indecency complaint can destroy the budget of even the best financially positioned station.

Public radio stations that belong to NPR do have some administrative assistance. NPR has representation and distribution divisions. The representation division attempts to protect the position of public stations on critical issues before various governmental bodies. It also acts as a mediator in disputes between NPR and member stations. The responsibility of the distribution division is the NPR satellite system, which is important to many stations that produce programs. NPR also provides a monthly memo that keeps management abreast of current issues and opportunities.

Management should also maintain contact with management at other stations for advice and ideas. A listing of stations and executives can be found in the *Public Broadcasting Directory*, published annually by the Corporation for Public Broadcasting.

WHAT'S AHEAD?

The fight for the soul of public broadcasting will continue. Some who work in it and consider it unique will have difficulty adjusting to the fragmentation of audiences. Purists in the audience will be offended by the increased number of underwriting credits and the growing amount of mainstream, entertaining programming.

Public broadcasting does account for a significant number of stations and jobs. It is a rewarding career field for many.

In the future, it will become more performance-driven to survive. In that respect, it will not be unlike its commercial counterparts. Local origination will probably decline due to cost. University licensees may be an exception, since they can receive assistance from students in exchange for academic credit. Syndicated programming will become more dominant in both radio and television.

The Congress and public broadcasting are in a truce over funding at the moment. A robust economy and the first national budget surplus since 1969 have reduced the pressure to do something immediate about public broadcasting.

But soon the issue will be faced again as the deadlines for the transition to DTV arrive. Public TV stations must have their DTV allocation built out by 2006, and failure to do so will result in a loss of authorization. It is estimated that the per-station conversion cost, in today's dollars, will be between $6 and $8 million. Few stations will have the resources to build DTV, and the federal government will have to determine whether or not to put up the requisite money. This could cost billions of dollars, and, even in these days of budget surplus, it is hard to imagine that such large amounts will not occasion another national debate over public broadcasting. Even if Congress agrees to put up part of the money, there is the question, as in the case of NTIA grants, of where local stations would get matching funds for the HDTV transition.

The role of the Internet in the future of public broadcasting must also be considered. A marriage of television and the Internet will occur and lead to a situation where viewers watch programs selected from a menu. Established delivery systems, such as the current over-the-air commercial and noncommercial networks, might be a thing of the past.

It will be important for the future that those aspiring to a public broadcasting career keep upgrading their professional qualifications through on-the-job experience and continuing education.

Events in the new century will move at a rapid pace, and the places and types of employment will probably be significantly different from those of the 1990s.

SUMMARY

Noncommercial broadcasting evolved into public broadcasting with the passage of the Public Broadcasting Act of 1967. A three-tiered structure now exists: (1) local stations funded in part by (2) the Corporation for Public Broadcasting, with program distribution provided by (3) nonprofit membership corporations — the Public Broadcasting Service (PBS) for television and National Public Radio (NPR) for radio.

The 368 public television stations are operated by four types of licensees: community, university, local authority, and state. Organization of the local station depends to some extent on licensee type. Some stations are more active in programming for general audiences and others in instructional television.

Absent any specialized activity, the major management tasks in public television stations can be classified fairly uniformly into eight categories: financial, programming, promotion, research, cable relations, community relations, engineering, and administration. Budget considerations have become paramount, because continued significant governmental funding is no longer assured. As a result of the necessity of raising nongovernmental funds, public television has become more ratings-conscious and pays special attention to weekly audience cumulative numbers, as opposed to program numbers. Increased competition from many sources has led to a need to attach more importance to programming concepts and promotion. The reality of cable television must also be dealt with, particularly since many stations depend on cable's reach to deliver viewing to areas not covered by their own signals.

The future will be demanding for public television. Management will have to refine and develop skills to contend with the opportunities and problems of the evolving competitive marketplace.

While there are 2,000 noncommercial radio stations in the United States today, only 362 licensees meet the eligibility requirements for funding by the Corporation for Public Broadcasting and thus are classified as "public." National Public Radio provides programming and distribution services for these stations. However, the growth in recent years of alternative program sources has decreased the reliance that stations once had on NPR.

Basically, public radio management has seven major functions: financial, programming, promotion, research, community relations, engineering, and administration.

Public radio also has had to make fund-raising a priority. Developing ratings is, therefore, important. Ratings in public radio mean time spent listening

(TSL), not cumulative audience. Fragmented markets have also led to a new emphasis on promotion.

Most stations use one of seven recognized and evolving formats: classical, jazz, news, access, eclectic, dual, and adult acoustic alternative (AAA). Many produce programs for distribution to other stations.

Strategy for the new century requires the public radio manager to achieve results in a more crowded marketplace and with fewer resources.

CASE STUDY: TELEVISION

KDOG-TV is a full-power public television station. It is licensed to a medium-sized market in the South, between two much larger markets about 100 miles away from "The Dog." It carries the full PBS schedule.

PBS member stations derive a significant proportion of their annual support from viewer memberships, generally over 30 percent. KDOG-TV gets just 10 percent of its support from memberships. It conducts one membership drive per year. For a membership fee of $50, viewers receive the station's photocopied program schedule.

Funding for KDOG-TV is well under $2 million, but in excess of the $650,000 required for a Community Service Grant.

The PBS stations in the nearby major markets are both imported into KDOG's market via the local cable system. Cable penetration is 90 percent.

KDOG-TV's home kennel has a substantial university with a credible electronic media program. However, the station is not licensed to the university and is not part of it.

Last year, the staff revolted against budget cuts engaged in by management in an attempt to keep the station on the air. A new manager has been hired to improve funding and programming and to restore morale and community confidence.

Exercises

1. Can the new manager access any additional federal funding in order to restore financial stability? Be specific in your recommendations and KDOG's qualifications.

2. What programming initiative could KDOG-TV take with PBS to sustain an acceptable level of program costs?

3. What other programming initiatives might KDOG-TV take, and how could the manager staff them?

4. What other sources of local nongovernment funding might be developed? Be specific.

CASE STUDY: RADIO

WREK-FM is a noncommercial public broadcasting FM station licensed to a university in the Midwest. While it has a class C with 100,000 watts of power, it is only on a 300-foot tower. The commercial stations in the community are also 100,000 watts, but most are on tall towers.

WREK-FM is an NPR member. It takes all the NPR programs which, in turn, take most of its budget.

Non-NPR hours are devoted to "breaking" new classical music from Europe. Public radio stations licensed to universities within 50 miles (also class Cs) compete for listeners in WREK-FM's market.

"The WREK" gets 10 percent of its support from memberships. It has no funds for staff, local origination, alternative program suppliers, or promotions. WREK does have one annual, four-day membership drive.

The university, with its own budget problems, has considered cutting WREK's hours or shutting down the station. Management is now locked in a debate over what viable alternatives there might be.

Exercises

1. Can anything be done about, or with, NPR to free up some funds and program time?

2. If the answer to the above question is "yes," what might some other program alternatives be?

3. Outside promotion does cost money. What are some things WREK-FM could do to promote that would not necessarily cost money?

4. How could the station make its classical music more relevant to its base NPR audience and stimulate memberships?

5. WREK-FM needs new equipment and has no obvious funding source. What funds might be available to assist, and what would the station have to do to access them?

NOTES

1. "By the Numbers," *Broadcasting & Cable*, November 16, 1998, p. 66.

2. *Ibid.*

3. *The Public Broadcasting Service: An Overview.* Alexandria, VA: Public Broadcasting Service, 1998.

4. *Ibid.*

5. "Funding Scramble is 'Nature' of Public TV," *Broadcasting & Cable*, January 31, 1994, p. 22.

6. *Corporation for Public Broadcasting Annual Report, 1997.* Washington, DC: Corporation for Public Broadcasting.

7. 1998 financial nonfederal funds qualifications required by the Corporation for Public Broadcasting.

8. The NTIA is part of the Department of Commerce and is the telecommunications policy office for the executive branch of government.

9. For what to do and what not to do in membership drive break structuring, see Susan T. Eastman and Robert Klein, *Promotion and Marketing for Broadcasting and Cable*, 2nd ed., pp. 249–279.

10. T. Barton Carter, Marc A. Franklin, and Jay B. Wright, *The First Amendment and the Fifth Estate: Regulation of Electronic Mass Media*, 4th ed., p. 352.

11. *Ibid.*

12. Public stations file annual financial reports with the Corporation for Public Broadcasting, which issues station revenue and expense profiles. The data are categorized according to the type of licensee and the size of the operating budget. Comparative financial data are also available through the Association of America's Public Television Stations, 1350 Connecticut Avenue, N.W., Washington, D.C. 20036.

13. Susan Tyler Eastman, *Broadcast/Cable Programming: Strategies and Practices*, 4th ed., p. 506.

14. *Ibid.*, p. 488.

15. *Ibid.*, p. 501.

16. "Funding Scramble is 'Nature' of Public TV," *Broadcasting & Cable*, January 31, 1994, p. 22.

17. Eastman and Klein, *op. cit.*, p. 254.

18. "Public Station Launches Commercial Campaign," *Broadcasting & Cable*, March 29, 1993, p. 46.

19. The Gallup Organization, 301 S. 68th Street Place, Lincoln, NE 68510.

20. Quincy Cable TV, Inc. v. Federal Communications Commission, 768 F2d, 1434, 1985; Century Communications Corporation v. Federal Communications Commission, 835 F2d, 292, 1987.

21. Turner Broadcasting System, Inc. v. Federal Communications Commission, 114 S. Ct. 2445.

22. 47 *USC* 535.

23. Alabama Educational Television Commission, 50 FCC 2d 461.

24. "By the Numbers," *Broadcasting & Cable*, November 16, 1998, p. 66.

25. *FAQ Brochure, 1997.* 901 East Street, N.W., Washington, D.C.

26. *Ibid.*

27. Development Exchange, Inc. (DEI), 1911 Fort Meyer Drive, Suite 906, Arlington, VA 22209.

28. See www.aranet.com.

29. Eastman, *op. cit.*, p. 514.

30. "Classical 24: Classical Music Service from Public Radio International," 100 North Sixth Street, Suite 900A, Minneapolis, MN 55403.

31. Public Radio Program Directors' Association (PRPD), P.O. Box 988, Olney, MD 20830.

32. "Pubcasting on the Web, Three Years Later," *Current*, September 14, 1998, p. 1.

33. Public Radio Association of Development Officers (PRADO), P.O. Box 21090, Washington, D.C. 20009.

34. In Trustees of the University of Pennsylvania, 69 FCC 2d 1394.

ADDITIONAL READINGS

Current. Washington D.C.: Educational Broadcasting Corporation.

DMA Market Profile. Washington, D.C.: Public Broadcasting Service.

i.e.development. Washington, D.C.: Development Exchange.

Keith, Michael C. *Radio Programming: Consultancy and Formatics.* Boston: Focal Press, 1987.

Keith, Michael C., and Joseph M. Krause. *The Radio Station,* 3rd ed. Boston: Focal Press, 1993.

Liebold, Linda, and Regina Sokas. *The Public Television Advantage.* Washington, D.C.: Public Broadcasting Service, 1984.

O'Donnell, Lewis B., Carl Hausman, and Philip Benoit. *Radio Station Operations: Management and Employee Perspectives.* Belmont, CA: Wadsworth, 1989.

Program Catalogue. Washington, DC: National Public Radio (published annually).

Public Broadcasting Directory. Washington, D.C.: Corporation for Public Broadcasting (published annually).

Public Radio Program Director's Handbook. Olney, MD: Public Radio Program Directors' Association, 1989.

Public Trust, A: The Report of the Carnegie Commission on the Future of Public Broadcasting. New York: Bantam Books, 1979.

Station Audience Report. Washington, D.C.: Public Broadcasting Service (published quarterly).

10

ENTRY INTO THE ELECTRONIC MEDIA BUSINESS

This chapter examines the methods of attaining management or ownership by focusing on

☐ how to identify and secure employment in a managerial capacity or a capacity that may lead to management

☐ how to buy an existing station, by exploring methods of finding the property, financing the acquisition, and following legal and other procedures to consummate the transaction

☐ how to build a new station or cable system, by identifying methods of locating open frequencies and franchises, obtaining financing, and complying with governmental requirements

Many college and university students pursuing the electronic media curriculum have as their ultimate goal either station management or ownership. Some use the first as a stepping-stone to the second. However, as noted in Chapter 1, "Broadcast Station Management," managers operate at various levels, and the aspirations of some students may stop short of those goals.

There is no precise formula for reaching management or ownership status, but almost eighty years of broadcast history and experience provide road maps to the promised land. The purpose of this chapter is to journey down that road and point out the landmarks along the way. This chapter is, in fact, a skeleton of some of the methods and procedures utilized by successful broadcasters. All the detail required to put flesh on the skeleton would require at least one volume, maybe more.

Students wishing to pursue the ownership option, in particular, are encouraged to take other courses to augment their broadcast education while they are still undergraduates. Prominent among those courses that might be suggested are basic introductions to business financing and accounting. Some understanding of the complexities and terminology of finance and accounting is critical to the realization of a person's ownership goals. This is even more important since the Telecommunications Act of 1996, because the places, numbers, and kinds of existing stations available for purchase have changed significantly.

EMPLOYMENT

Employment is the most traditional and common means of entering the electronic media business. Those professionals who have no present ownership goals may view increasingly challenging managerial positions as ends in themselves. Individuals with ownership aspirations also generally work in the industry for some time, because some personal resources are necessary, and because lenders and investors simply do not finance new owners without some demonstrable track record, which means experience. Even those few and fortunate individuals possessing extensive funds are better served by a working apprenticeship in the industry, given the competitive, specialized nature of media markets.

In all but rare cases, students enter the industry through employment. Despite possession of a degree, most college graduates will start on their career journey at the bottom, in an entry-level position.

Even at that level, competition for jobs is intense. Hundreds of colleges and universities graduate thousands of electronic media students annually. The edge will go to those who have used their college years wisely. That means high academic performance. It also means participation in relevant activities outside the classroom and laboratory. Internships completed and a demonstrated ability to write are especially helpful. The importance of such pursuits should not be minimized, since taking the first step is the most challenging part of the career journey. Academic achievement combined with professionally related experience are what most employers expect. Students who are serious about employment will not disappoint them.

There are several ways of accumulating experience before graduation. Volunteer or paid employment often is available to those who enroll in colleges and universities that operate radio or television stations or provide programming for cable television systems. Internships offer the chance to develop firsthand experience in commercial and noncommercial stations, cable systems, and allied operations, such as recording studios, production houses, commercial radio and television networks, advertising and public relations departments and agencies, and station representative companies. These opportunities have an added advantage: They provide interns with a valuable means of displaying their abilities to those engaged in the hiring of personnel. More and more schools have organized internship programs, in part through the efforts of alumni working in the industry. The Department of Radio and Television at Southern Illinois University, for example, has such programs in Hollywood and Chicago. Internships are becoming a significant employment source as more and more companies hire interns for starting positions. Many employers also seek out part-time employees, especially for weekend and vacation work.

Some new graduates set their sights on entry-level positions in large markets. That is probably unrealistic, and it is not necessarily the wisest course, since the level of competition is likely to be extremely high. In addition, it is too easy to become pigeonholed or lost in the crowd, both of which may prove to be impediments to advancement.

Small markets, on the other hand, offer several advantages. Competition for jobs is not as keen. Opportunities are more numerous. There are fewer unions. Most significantly, perhaps, employees are expected to perform a broader range of responsibilities. While the immediate reaction may be one of shock at the volume and variety of work required, such feelings will turn to appreciation later, with the realization of the wealth of knowledge and experience acquired.

The details of many of the managerial functions performed in the electronic media were discussed in earlier chapters. However, it may be useful here to identify examples of typical paths to career advancement.

A beginning position in radio as a disc jockey may lead to promotion to music director or production director and, ultimately, to program director. In time, a reporter may assume greater responsibility as public affairs director, en route to a news director's slot. The aspiring general sales manager may start out as a sales trainee and move in stages from small to larger accounts and into the local sales manager's chair before attaining the ultimate goal. From program director, promotion and marketing director, news director, or general sales manager, a step up to general manager may be the next move. Promotion to GM typically requires significant sales experience, however.

A starting camera operator in a television station may advance to a management position as program director, production director, or operations manager by achieving success, in turn, as a floor manager, production assistant, assistant producer/director, and producer/director. A general assignment reporter may progress to a beat reporter before advancing to assignment editor, news producer, assistant news director, and, finally, news director. Initial employment as an assistant in traffic, continuity, or promotion and marketing may pave the way for an upward move to traffic, continuity, or promotion and marketing director. Again, if the desired destination is a general manager's post, the final step may be taken comfortably from one of several department head positions.

A beginning producer/director in a cable television system may be advanced to director of local origination, a sales representative to sales manager, and then to marketing director. A technician may progress to chief technician or chief engineer, and a customer service representative to office manager and, subsequently, to accountant or bookkeeper and business manager. The top management position as system manager may result after advancement through the ranks to head of marketing, engineering, or business.

Upward movement in all electronic media careers often occurs through promotion in a station, system, or group. In such cases, identifying appropriate vacancies presents no problem, since they are publicized to existing employees. However, if advancement is possible only through a move to another station in the market or to another market, the search for positions is more challenging. A similar challenge faces those who are about to embark on a career.

Probably the best sources for locating positions are *Broadcasting & Cable, Electronic Media, Radio and Records (R&R), Inside Radio,* and the *M Street Journal.* Another would be *Radio Business Reports.* Some of these publications appear weekly and others monthly. They list openings in markets of all sizes and in all areas of commercial and noncommercial station activity, from entry level to general management (see Figures 10.1, 10.2, and 10.3). Those with a special interest in public broadcasting will find *Current* magazine helpful, while a publication such as *Multichannel News* will provide useful information on cable television openings.

There are several commercial publications, such as *Entertainment Employment Journal* and *Media Grapevine,* that list positions in all fields and at all levels. (For contact information, see the Additional Readings section at the end of the chapter.) Related national and state or regional professional associations also provide information on job openings in their publications.

Several organizations, including the National Association of Broadcasters and Promotion and Marketing Executives in the Electronic Media, operate clearinghouses.[1]

National station representative firms, such as Blair Television and Katz Radio, are often asked by client stations to identify candidates, especially for management positions. Many trade publications run "situations wanted" ads, and associations do likewise in their newsletters. Some, like the Radio-Television News Directors Association (RTNDA), maintain a telephone line dedicated to job openings. The fee for use of the service is nominal.[2]

Another method of taking the initiative in the job search is through registration with specialized employment placement firms, more commonly known as "head hunters." Many companies provide such services, and a partial listing can be found in the "Professional Services" section of *Broadcasting & Cable Yearbook.*[3] Typically, an applicant files a résumé with the firm, which attempts to match qualifications with the needs of an electronic media employer. Fees sometimes are paid by the employer.

The final method worthy of mention is networking. There is an old adage that it is not what you know but who you know that counts. Relationships

Figure 10.1 *Example of broadcast television help wanted classified ads displayed in* Broadcasting & Cable. *(Used with permission.)*

Classifieds

SYSTEMS ENGINEERS

FRONTLINE
Communications Corporation

Frontline Communications needs Broadcast Systems Engineers with experience designing and testing Audio, Video, Satellite Uplink and Microwave Systems used in Television Broadcast Vehicles. The position requires working directly with clients. Fluency with AutoCAD is a must. Send or FAX resume to the attention of , Personnel at Frontline Communications, 12725 Automobile Blvd., Clearwater, FL 33762; FAX: 813-573-1135. Frontline offers competitive salary, health and dental insurance, 401K.

EOE. Drug Free Work Place.

Chief Engineer. Progressive intermountain network affiliate has an immediate opening for a Chief Engineer. Hands on operation will require knowledge of transmitter/studio and computer technologies. Personnel skills and a strong management team approach are a must. FCC General or SBE Certification required. Please send resume to: Kelly Sugai, General Manager, KIVI Television, 1866 East Chisholm Drive, Nampa, Idaho 83687.

Air Operations Master Control Operator. NBC12 (WWBT-TV), Jefferson-Pilot Communications in Richmond, VA has an immediate opening for an experienced Air Operations Master Control Operator. Send current resume to Judy Gibson, Human Resources Director, NBC12, PO Box 12, Richmond, VA 23218. No calls. EOE MFD.

HELP WANTED NEWS

REPORTER

Must demonstrate skill in writing conversational broadcast copy, incorporating appropriate visual elements under daily deadline pressure. Must have above average typing skills and possess the ability to learn to use the newsroom's computer system. College degree and a minimum of 2 years experience as a news reporter for a commercial television station preferred. Must be able to work all hours and shifts.

VIDEO TAPE EDITOR

Must demonstrate skill in video tape editing under daily deadline pressure. Must have at least two years experience as a news tape editor in a news department of a commercial television station. Must be able to work all hours and shifts.

WRITER/VIDEO TAPE EDITOR

Must demonstrate skill in writing conversational broadcast copy, incorporating appropriate visual elements under daily deadline pressure. College degree preferred. Must be able to work all hours and shifts.

PRODUCER

Must demonstrate skill in producing feature segments. College degree and a minimum of 2 years experience in television news preferred. Must be able to work all hours and shifts.

For consideration, forward resume and letter to: KTVI/FOX 2, Human Resources Director, 5915 Berthold Avenue, St. Louis, MO 63110. Job Line: 314-644-7414. No phone calls, no faxes please. KTVI offers an academic credit internship program for registered college students.

WISC-TV has a full time opening for a News Photographer/Editor. A proficiency in television news photography and videotape editing is required. Knowledge of microwave and satellite truck operations and non-linear editing would be helpful. You should be creative, responsible and a quick learner. Must have an excellent driving record. Resumes accepted until May 4, 1998. Please send videotape/resumes to Mike Van Susteren, News Operations Mgr, WISC-TV, 7025 Raymond Rd, PO Box 44965, Madison, Wisconsin 53744-4965. EOE, M-F.

Assistant News Director - This person also functions as our E-P who plans and supervises special projects; develops research-based strategy and helps to oversee the daily newsroom operation. Qualifications: Degree in Journalism or equivalent; 5-10 years experience (3 years as a news manager). Individual must be computer savvy (NewStar experience very helpful) and must know what it takes to keep a top-rated, dynamic newsroom moving forward. Please submit resume, references, salary requirements and news philosophy to: Bruce Whiteaker, News Director, KXAN-TV, 908 W. MLK Blvd., Austin, TX 78701. whiteaker@kxan.com KXAN-TV is an Equal Opportunity Employer

WISC-TV, Madison, Wisconsin has an immediate opening for a Weekend Producer/Weekday Reporter. Duties include setting up coverage for weekend shows and producing four weekend newscasts; general assignment reporting during the week. Two years experience is preferred; applicants should have prior producing experience. Send non-returnable tape and resume to: Carmelyn Daley, WISC-TV, 7025 Raymond Rd, PO Box 44965, Madison, Wisconsin 53744-4965. EOE/M-F. Applications accepted until April 24th.

News Expansion. Want to join the fastest growing news team in Charlotte? Want to make your home in the south's most livable city? Want to work for a company that puts journalism first? A.H. Belo's NBC6 is searching for an assignment editor, producer, traffic reporter, meteorologist, (2) morning anchor/reporters and (2) videotape editors to join our growing news operation. We are expanding our weekday morning newscasts and are looking for high energy, hard working, extremely motivated journalists. If you are the best in your newsroom and are looking for the coaching and creative environment to be even better - send your resume, resume tape (if applicable) and salary history to: (No phone calls, please): NBC6, Human Resources Department, 1001 Wood Ridge Center Drive, Charlotte, NC 28217. EOE/M/F/V/H.

Producer/Reporter

We seek a freelance News Producer/Reporter with experience in producing medical or health related news programming. Most work will be in the NY Metro area, however some travel may be required. **Send resume and VHS tape to Ben at: University News, 83 Cromwell Avenue, Staten Island, N.Y. 10304**

TV News Photographer. WAVY-TV, a top 40 market TV station, is looking for an experienced, creative photojournalist to shoot local TV news. Must be a fan of photo essays and packages with lots of natural sound. We are in the Hampton Roads, Virginia area, which includes Norfolk, Virginia Beach and Williamsburg...about 3 hours south of Washington, DC. If you think you can catch the viewers attention by consistently shooting creative, upbeat stories, send tape and resume to Jeff Myers, Chief News Photographer, WAVY-TV, 300 Wavy Street, Portsmouth, VA 23704. *No phone calls.* EOE.

Weekend Anchor/Reporter: New FOX affiliate in Virginia Beach. Employee will report during the day and anchor the station's 10pm weekend news. The ideal candidate will have two years experience as an anchor. Strong writing and editorial judgement is critical. No beginners. Send VHS tape, resume and news philosophy to David Strickland, News Director, WVBT FOX 43 News, 300 Wavy Street, Portsmouth, VA 23704. *WVBT is an Equal Opportunity Employer. No phone calls!*

WWTV, Northern Michigan's News Leader, seeks to fill the following positions: *Anchor.* We want an experienced journalist for our one hour 5:00 pm newscast. We need a strong writer with solid news judgement and on-air ability. 2-5 years experience. No phone calls. *Reporter.* Looking for excellent story teller, conversational writer and team player. Minimum one year experience needed. No phone calls. *Producer.* Northern Michigan's number one news station needs a producer with strong writing skills. We discourage predictability. We want a creative story teller who keeps viewers interested from beginning to end. Phone calls accepted. *Photojournalist.* The top rated news station in Northern Michigan wants a photojournalist who takes pride in their work. We are building our news department with N.P.P.A. quality photojournalists. We shoot on Beta SP, and have two new microwave trucks and a loaded SNG rig. For all positions, Please send resume and tape to Jon-Michial Carter, Director of News and Operations, 9&10 News, P.O. Box 627, Cadillac, MI, 49601. Producers or Photojournalists may call 616-775-2478 #3300.

Television General Assignment Reporter. WZZM 13, the Gannett-owned ABC affiliate in Grand Rapids, Michigan is looking for a Reporter. We need someone who can work a beat and bring a lead story idea to the table every day. At least 2 years of broadcast television experience required. No phone calls please. Send your Beta or VHS tape immediately to: Bill Dallman, News Director, WZZM 13, 645 - Three Mile Road NW, Grand Rapids, MI 49544. EOE

Producer: WICS-TV, the NBC affiliate in Springfield, Illinois, is looking for a 10PM producer. We want someone with excellent writing skills and good news judgement. You must be able to craft a locally driven, highly produced newscast. At least one year producing experience and college degree required. Send non-returnable tape and resume to: Sue Stephens, News Director, WICS-TV, 2680 East Cook Street, Springfield, IL 62703. EOE. Women and minorities are encouraged to apply. WICS is an Equal Opportunity Employer and a division of Guy Gannett Communications.

Figure 10.2 *Example of cable television help wanted classified ads displayed in* Broadcasting & Cable. *(Used with permission.)*

Figure 10.3 *Example of radio help wanted classified ads displayed in* Inside Radio. *(Used with permission.)*

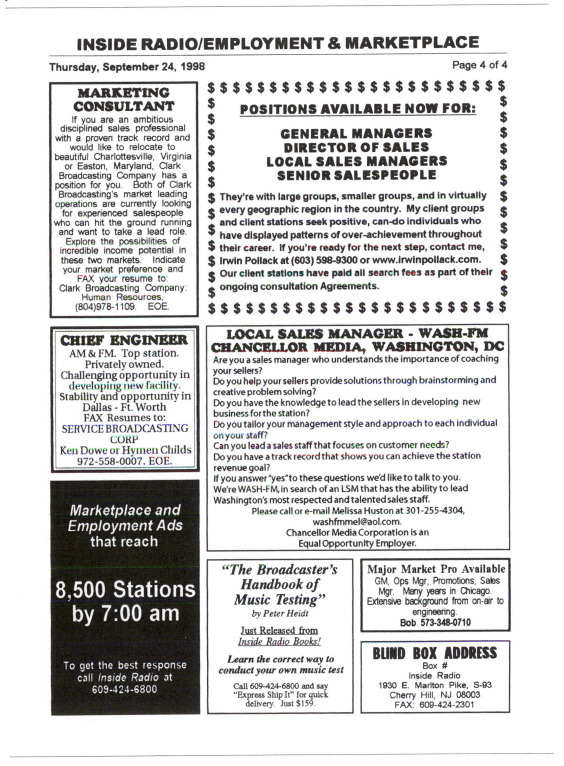

should be developed with industry professionals during internships. Most colleges and universities maintain active contact with their electronic media alumni. Many students belong to national organizations with local chapters, like Alpha Epsilon Rho, The National Broadcasting Society, which is more than fifty years old and has many distinguished alumni.[4] Each year, it has a national convention that affords a unique networking opportunity for participating students from around the country. Of special interest to minority students is Howard University's Annual Communication Job Fair in Washington, D.C. Representatives of many of the most important electronic media companies in the United States attend to meet and interview students who are seeking employment.

Job seekers looking for their first full-time position or advancement must convince employers of their skills and potential contributions. To that end, a letter of application must be accompanied by a résumé and, where appropriate, an audiotape or videotape. Tapes are not just for on-the-air positions. They may also demonstrate other skills, such as production, promotion, and copywriting. The résumé should include details of the broadcasting courses taken by the applicant. There was a time when broadcasters were skeptical of the relevance of a broadcast education, but in this age of fragmented audiences and increased competition, electronic media executives have come to appreciate the need for a formal education in the field. Consequently, it may be beneficial to highlight the management, programming, sales, promotion and marketing, and audience research courses completed in college. Information on related courses and "hands-on" experience also should be set forth. In some instances, it can be beneficial to list equipment competence, such as the AVID.

If the ultimate goal is ownership rather than management, the employment search may be conducted somewhat differently. There is no "best way" to go about it, but there are some tips and techniques that are often productive.

First, the market in which there is an interest in ownership must be identified, and stations and/or cable systems serving the market noted. A listing of stations may be compiled from *Broadcasting & Cable Yearbook*, which contains information on station ownership, management, formats, technical facilities, addresses, and telephone numbers.

To evaluate station desirability within a market, ratings and revenue information on each station may be acquired by reviewing material published by Duncan's American Radio.[5] Additional sources of information on ratings, market revenue, and growth are *Investing in Television* and *Investing in Radio*.[6]

After completing this audition process of markets and stations, it is time to address letters or telephone calls to the management at the target stations. If a group owner is preferred over an individual station, the group offices should be contacted.[7] With the relaxation of the three-year ownership rule and the expansion of the limits on multiple ownership, group operators account for an increasing percentage of station licensees.

Should there be an interest in cable, *Television and Cable Factbook*[8] provides telephone numbers, addresses, ownership, management, and system information. Data on multiple system operators (MSOs) and cable networks, such as HBO, USA, and CNN, are also included.

There is no right or wrong way to identify and secure employment. However, any approach must begin with facts. The information provided in this section should be adequate to initiate the process.

OWNERSHIP

The second method of entry into the electronic media business is through ownership, which can be accomplished in one of two ways: (1) purchase of an existing facility, or (2) construction of a new facility.

Purchase of an Existing Facility

In the United States today, there are about 10,000 commercial radio stations, approximately 1,200 commercial television stations, 11,500 cable systems, and permits outstanding to build additional radio and television stations.[9] The decision to purchase an existing facility will provide a far greater number of choices in more varied locations than are available when constructing a new facility. Purchase offers the additional advantage of being able to examine the performance record of a facility already operating. The job of financing the purchase of an existing station is substantially less difficult than that of a new build or start-up. The disadvantage of purchasing is that attractive existing operations are in demand.

Through the late 1990s, market demand for existing facilities was especially strong. The market hangover of the late 1980s and early 1990s — caused by the FCC's liberal licensing policies of the 1980s, station debt defaults due to exorbitant prices of that decade, and the 1989–1993 recession — came to an end. In addition to the removal of these three negative factors, two positive factors occurred.

The first positive factor was the 1996 Telecommunications Act. As noted in Chapter 7, "Broadcast Regulations," it eliminated national ownership limits for radio and reduced them for television. The law, implemented by the FCC, also allowed companies or persons to own up to eight radio stations in a single market. Duopoly of television stations still is not permitted. The relaxation or, in some instances, elimination of ownership rules occurred in the most favorable economic climate in this country in over a generation, and maybe since the postwar boom of the 1950s. In New York, the stock markets posted double-digit annual growth. Electronic media companies had record sales in the high employment, high consumer-confidence economy. Existing media companies and some new ones were quick to seize the opportunities offered by liberalized ownership rules and a surging stock market and economy.

All this created substantial demand for existing facilities. As a result, cash-flow multiples began to rise again from their 1991 lows. It was noted in Chapter 2, "Financial Management," that cash flow, or the amount of cash generated, determines the value of an electronic media property. Large-market radio multiples ranged from 14 to 20 (i.e., stations were valued at 14 to 20 times their cash flow). In middle markets, the range was 10 to 14 and in smaller markets, 8 to 10. Television multiples averaged 8 to 8.5. The dollar value of all sales of existing radio and television facilities shot up from the 1992 level of $1 billion.

Prices paid for groups went into the hundreds of millions of dollars. Chancellor, the largest holder of radio stations in the United States (472 stations), paid approximately $400 million to purchase group radio owner Shamrock. To see what consolidation has done to existing radio station ownership concentration, see Figure 10.4 for a listing of the top-fifty radio groups and their holdings. These numbers have changed almost weekly since the 1996 Telecommunications Act became effective.

Midway through 1998, existing radio and television station sales were approximately $6.8 billion.[10] Since many stations have been consolidated since 1996, the dollar pace is slowing and multiples are easing slightly. Price easing should be favorable for the aspiring owner. Unfortunately, however, there is a negative factor also at work. The pool of potentially available stations has been diminished substantially.

The market interest in existing operations also extended to cable systems. Cable rates, as noted in Chapter 8, "Managing the Cable Television System," were reregulated in 1992, and the 1996 Telecommunications Act proposed to end cable rate regulation. That outcome is still not certain. But rate regulation plagued cable market valuation until 1996. Cable systems also sell on multiples of cash flow, typically 11 to 12. However, most are priced on a per-subscriber basis. Prices vary, but the typical system sale may be in the range of $2,000 to $2,200 per subscriber.

While the rate regulation impact on cable valuation seems to have lessened, now there is the looming Direct Broadcast Satellite (DBS) challenge. For example, DBS added 494,000 subscribers in the first quarter of 1998 alone.[11] It is only four years old as an industry. Cable, on the other hand, is fifty years old and passes about 97 percent of the 98 million TV households in the country. Its future growth will have to come from other sources than new subscribers.

Some large cable operators are now exchanging systems to achieve geographical efficiencies. Others, such as Tele-Communications, Inc. (TCI), are seeking new marketing opportunities through mergers with companies like AT&T.

The basic consolidation now going on in radio and TV occurred in the cable industry years ago. The major trading activity tends to be mergers, like TCI-AT&T, or in the stock market for MSO shares. There are still small systems held by companies and individuals.

Finding the Station or System   What is for sale, and how does one locate it? Finding a station or cable system to purchase can be accomplished in two principal ways: (1) through direct contact with the station or system owner, and (2) through the use of an intermediary, most often a media broker.

Direct Contact   One way to initiate direct contact is to select markets that are of interest and then list the stations in the markets. A good source for this data is *Broadcasting & Cable Yearbook*. This publication gives the ownership of each station, which may be an individual, a partnership, a corporation, or a broadcast group. Owners sometimes operate stations, but often are nonoperating investors.

Figure 10.4   *Who owns what: top groups by stations. (Source:* Inside Radio. *Used with permission.)*

As of Monday, September 21, 1998

Top Groups by Stations

This Week	Last Week	Groups	No. of Stations
1	1	Chancellor	472
2	3	Jacor	215
3	2	Clear Channel	211
4	4	Cumulus	194
5	5	Infinity Broadcasting	161
6	6	Citadel	100
7	7	Cox	58
8	8	Sinclair	50
9	9	Marathon Media	48
10	10	Salem	44
11	11	Saga	42
12	12	Entercom	41
13	13	ABC Radio	37
		Forever	37
		Heftel	37
16	16	Journal	36
17	17	Broadcasting Ptnrs Hldgs	35
		Root	35
19	19	Regent	34
		Willis	34
21	21	Texas Eagle	32
22	22	Connoisseur	31
		Zimmer	31
24	24	Z Spanish	30
25	25	Beasley	28
	26	Commonwealth	28
27	27	Morris Comm	24
28	28	Mid-West Family	23
		Susquehanna	23
30	30	Crawford	22
		Roberts Radio	22
32	32	American General Media	19
		Metropolitan	19
		Mortenson Bcastg	19
		Sunbrook	19
		Sunburst Media	19
		Three Eagles	19
		Withers	19
39	39	Hall	18
		Pinnacle	18
		Simmons Family	18
42	42	Bloomington	17
		Buckley	17
		Cromwell Group	17
		EXCL	17
		Jefferson-Pilot	17
		Key	17
		Multicultural Radio Bcastg	17
		Renda	17
		WICKS	17

Owners and managers are very sensitive to sale rumors and inquiries, because these are disruptive and destabilizing for stations. For that reason, inquiry to a station owner should be discreet and direct, not through secretaries or other employees. Because of the sensitivity of the subject, an owner, even when properly contacted by someone unknown, may not want to confirm the availability of the property for sale. Occasionally, an owner may tell an unknown inquiring party outright that the station is for sale. A more likely answer is, "No, it is not for sale," or, in some cases, "Anything is for sale for the right price."

For these reasons, the direct approach may be time-consuming and, in the end, unproductive. If successful, however, it is probably going to be cheaper than other methods of purchasing a property.

Use of a Media Broker   The most efficient and productive search for a property is conducted through the use of a media broker, who generates income by listing stations or systems for sale and then locating qualified buyers for the properties. Brokers are known to media owners and are sensitive to their concerns about confidentiality. Media brokers compete actively among themselves to obtain listings.

When obtained, the listings may be *exclusive* or *nonexclusive*. Exclusive means that only one broker has a listing for a station for a designated period, while nonexclusive means that more than one broker has the same listing. The kind of listing may become important to the prospective buyer. For example, a would-be purchaser, who is about to make an offer on a station after expenditure of time and money to investigate, may be shocked to learn that the broker had a nonexclusive listing and that another broker has completed the deal. Accordingly, the broker should be asked exactly what kind of listing it is. For an illustration of an exclusive listing agreement, see Figure 10.5.

As mentioned earlier, brokers are paid for what they do. Fees vary, but a standard fee is 5 percent on the first $3 million or less, 2 percent on the next $7 million, and 1 percent on amounts over $10 million. Fees on very large transactions usually are negotiated and generally are not calculated by this formula. Whatever the fee, it does add to the price of the station, and the buyer will pay it through a higher price or through a direct agreement to pay some or all of it.

Despite the negatives, use of a media broker probably is the best way to proceed in acquiring a station or system. A listing of media brokers can be found in the "Professional Services" section of *Broadcasting & Cable Yearbook* and in the "Brokerage and Financing" section of *Television and Cable Factbook*. Brokers also run ads in trade publications and issue press releases and announcements on transactions they have completed or stations they have listed. An example appears in Figure 10.6.

Brokers may be national in scope, such as Media Services Group, Inc. and Blackburn and Company, or regional, like New England Media and William A. Exline, Inc. Some brokers provide more than sales assistance. Media Services Group, Inc., for instance, also offers financing help.

Figure 10.5 *Exclusive listing agreement used by Media Services Group, Inc., Richmond, Virginia. (Used with permission.)*

MEDIA SERVICES GROUP, INC.
ACQUISITIONS ● VALUATIONS ● FINANCING ● CONSULTATION

STATION MARKETING AGREEMENT

Seller: _____

Address: _____

hereby employs Media Services Group, Inc. ("MSG") with the exclusive right for the period of 180 days to sell the following:

Business: _____ Location: _____

Asking price shall be: S_____with a down payment of: S _____

and the balance payable over _____ years at _____ % interest, or at such other price and terms as Seller states in writing that it is willing to accept. Seller agrees to refer all inquiries to MSG, to cooperate with MSG in selling the Business and/or its assets, to have MSG serve as Escrow Agent, and to pay MSG according to the schedule below.

A commission is due according to the schedule below if any of the following occur after this the agreement is signed by Seller and MSG:

A contract for the sale of the Business is signed by Seller and any buyer solicited by MSG at any price; an offer is made by an able and willing buyer solicited by MSG at a price and terms that Seller has stated in writing that it was willing to accept, but such offer is declined by Seller; or a contract for a sale of the Business at any price is signed by Seller and any buyer solicited by MSG, within one year after this agreement is terminated by either Seller or MSG.

If Seller opts to enter into a Local Marketing Agreement ("LMA"), Time Brokerage or similar agreement instead of the sale of the Business to a prospect solicited by MSG, Seller agrees to make quarterly payments to MSG of 5% of the quarterly amount paid to Seller for such agreement.

COMMISSION SCHEDULE

Over one million dollars total consideration	Under one million dollars total consideration
5% on the first three million dollars, and 2% on the next seven million dollars, and 1% on amounts over ten million dollars.	10% on the first hundred thousand, and 5% of the balance up to one million dollars, with a maximum commission of $50,000, and a minimum of $25,000.

Figure 10.5   *Continued*

DEFINITIONS

A Sale. Includes a sale of all or part of the Business to any party of the stock, partnership shares, assets or a subsidiary of the Business to any buyer, including co-owners, affiliates, or employees.

Declination. An offer will be deemed to have been declined and the listed compensation due where the Seller fails to: 1) provide information reasonably requested by an able prospective buyer; 2) negotiate material terms of sale with such a prospective buyer in good faith; or 3) execute documents or take other action needed to complete the sale of the Business to such buyer.

Total Consideration. Includes all monies payable by a buyer, whether in cash, promissory notes or assumed obligations, whether for the purchase of assets, stock, partnership shares, LMAs, time brokerage or other similar agreements, covenants and/or consulting agreements.

MISCELLANEOUS TERMS

Exclusive Broker. MSG will be the exclusive broker for the sale of the Business unless either party elects to terminate such status upon 30 days written notice to the other party. Such notice may not be given less than 180 days after this agreement is signed by both parties.

When Payment Due. The commission set forth above is payable at the closing of the sale of the Business. If the commission is owed because a contract for sale was signed with a buyer solicited by MSG or because an LMA or similar agreement was reached, it is payable when the contract for sale is signed or the LMA or similar agreement begins to operate. In the case of a declination, the commission is due upon such declination. Forfeited monies are due upon forfeiture. Any earnest money deposit shall first be applied at closing or upon forfeiture to the payment of any commission or the portion of any forfeiture owed to MSG. Option or earnest money forfeited by any prospective buyer is to be divided equally between MSG and Seller. All sums due from Seller to MSG shall be made payable to "MEDIA SERVICES GROUP, INC." Seller agrees to include in any agreement for the sale of the Business a provision that sets forth its duty to pay MSG's commission in full.

Collection. In the event it is necessary to collect commissions or forfeitures unpaid by Seller through an attorney, Seller agrees to pay all costs of collection, including reasonable attorneys' fees, whether suit is brought or not. Seller also agrees to pay a charge of 1% per month on the unpaid balance of the commission or forfeiture owed to MSG, computed from its due date. Seller hereby consents to the jurisdiction of the Circuit Court for the City of Richmond, Virginia over any suit brought against it by MSG for the collection of payments due and agrees that venue there is proper.

Seller's Warranty and Indemnification. Seller warrants that all information provided to Media Services Group, Inc. and its representatives concerning the Business is true and correct to the best of its knowledge and belief. Seller agrees to indemnify and hold MSG harmless for any claim, loss or damage, including the expense of defending against any suit in law or equity arising from any incorrect information provided to MSG or from any material fact not disclosed by Seller.

Due Diligence. MSG does not guarantee the creditworthiness of any buyer and encourages Seller to investigate prospective buyers as required by the standards of due diligence.

Representation Of Others In Market Area. Seller agrees that MSG may represent other sellers and buyers in Seller's market area. Concurrent sales of two or more stations from a single seller to one buyer are considered to be one sale for the purpose of computing the commission due.

Final Agreement. This agreement supersedes any prior oral or written agreement between the parties and includes all terms agreed upon by them. This agreement may not be altered or amended except in a written document signed by the party against whom it is to be enforced.

OTHER PROVISIONS: _____

_____

AGREED, SELLER: _____

	Title	Date

RECOMMENDED BY: _____

	Title	Date

AGREED, MEDIA SERVICES GROUP, INC. _____

	Title	Date

Figure 10.6 *Media broker announcement of a completed transaction. (Source: Media Services Group, Inc., Richmond, Virginia. Used with permission.)*

SOLD!

WKIX-FM
Raleigh, North Carolina

$16.0 Million

Alchemy Communications
Limited Partnership No. 1

to

Curtis Media
Group

George Reed of Media Services Group, Inc.
represented the buyer in this transaction.
(904) 285-3239

MEDIA SERVICES GROUP, INC.
Acquisitions • Valuations • Financing • Consultation
San Francisco • Philadelphia • Washington • Kansas City • Providence • Salt Lake City • Jacksonville • Richmond

Having identified a broker, the prospective purchaser must choose the method of working with the broker. One way is to register by completing the broker's buyer information form. The data facilitate the matching of the buyer's geographical interest, the type of facility desired (AM, FM, TV, or cable), and the financial capability with the broker's listings. The buyer will be contacted by the broker as ownership opportunities develop. This procedure enables the broker to preclear the client as a qualified buyer so that immediate action can be taken when an especially good property comes along.

A second way of working with a media broker is to respond to a specific ad about a station or cable system. This amounts to a case-by-case use of a broker's services and does not necessarily lead to the close working relationship that could make one a favored client who is called first on that very special deal.

The receipt of information on available properties leads to the next stage of the acquisition process — station evaluation.

Station Evaluation   Once the acquisition candidate has been identified, it must be analyzed. Before analyzing the reasonableness of the price, the buyer should review the status of the market and its competition. Finance sources will expect the buyer to be fully versed on these topics. Rarely does a good price cure a bad market. Analyzing the market will be a key element in analyzing price.

Analyzing Market and Competition   Cash flow and capital appreciation of a station will depend in no small way upon the condition of the market and the number of existing and potential competitors. Market data can be obtained from local chambers of commerce or from Standard Rate and Data Service, which provides information on rates, facilities, and the market. Significant market and competition data can also be found in Duncan's American Radio publications and in Broadcast Investment Analysts' (BIA) *Investing in Radio* and *Investing in Television*. Statistics to analyze include population, retail sales, and employment trends. Is there explosive growth, stable growth, or no growth? Markets with no upside or, worse yet, with only a downside should only be considered if the price is substantially discounted or if some major economic development is scheduled for the area.

Market size determines the number of national advertising dollars spent in the market. The top-100 markets command more of those dollars than the 100+ markets. Whether or not a market is about to move into or out of the top 100 is a significant valuation consideration.

Retail sales also are important, because they are a reliable predictor of electronic media revenue available in a market. Generally, electronic media dollars equate to between 1 percent and 2 percent of retail sales, with television getting the larger share. To determine radio revenue, a good rule of thumb is to multiply retail sales by .0035. *Duncan's Radio Market Guide* provides estimates of electronic media market revenue as a percentage of such sales. Comparisons can be made to other markets to evaluate the relative strength of electronic media overall and the vitality of a market's radio and television components. For markets not covered by Duncan, *Investing in Radio*, or *Investing in Television*, prospective buyers can make their own calculations.

If a station has a high percentage of total revenue available, it may have peaked, which means it has no upside revenue potential. Another market evaluation benchmark is data on employment. Who are the largest employers and in what businesses are they engaged? The departure or closing of a large employer can depress a market. State governments, insurance companies, universities, and federal facilities are normally stable. Some caution is advised in the case of military bases and defense plants in the post-Cold War period. The Pentagon maintains a base closure list, which should be consulted if the target market has a military installation. Are any major plants about to be constructed or expanded? The market's employment base and stability should be examined.

After checking the vital signs of the market, the prospective buyer should examine the competition. Some markets have too many stations. It is not just the signals licensed to the community, but also those from outside the market that get in, that are competitive factors. Data on competition can be gathered from sources like *Investing in Radio* and *Investing in Television* and from national ratings services, such as Arbitron for radio and Nielsen for television. Determine how much of the audience is attributable to "below the line" or outside-the-market stations. The broker or station owner should provide the rating service's reports.

Not all the competition information may be readily apparent. In the 1980s, the Federal Communications Commission aggressively authorized new stations in a proceeding known as Docket 80–90[12] and permitted the upgrade of existing stations to new tower heights and power. In still other cases, commission rules allowed stations licensed to small communities to "move in" to larger ones. Any one of these developments could immediately diminish the attractiveness of a proposed investment. Communications attorneys stay current on these developments, as do consulting engineers. Analysis of the competitive environment is not complete until the status of potential new or modified signals that might affect the market is known.

Review of competition should not be limited merely to the number of stations. Station comparisons should also be made of power and antenna heights. Selection of a station with inadequate transmission capabilities when compared with the competition might lead to the purchase of a permanent, second-class station. Such purchase errors are difficult, if not impossible, to correct.

The competitive analysis should not be confined to a comparison of technical facilities. A prospective purchaser also should examine competitors' formats. The best discovery would be that a significant format was not being offered in the market at all. The presence of a "niche" opening satisfies an important investment criterion. If, however, there are no obvious format holes, research may reveal that a competitor already in the market with an established format is not executing it well. That may present enough of an opportunity, assuming everything else checks out, to justify going ahead. However, prospective purchasers must remember that the cost of head-to-head competition is always more. Even if success is achieved in such a battle, the return on investment will be less than can be achieved in markets where an open niche exists.

In television acquisition, it is wise to pay attention to network affiliation. Obviously, an affiliate with a strong network may command a better price than one with a weak network. Those stations that have an underperforming network parent have to do more locally to maintain market position. Probably, that will mean higher operating costs for programming, promotion, and personnel, especially news talent. Higher costs mean lower cash flow and lower valuation. Translated, that means the upside may be limited.

Television stations with no affiliation, or independents, are to be left to the sophisticated television investor. With the success of Fox, UPN, and The WB, those remaining true independents will have a very hard time making ends meet.

Assuming that the evaluation of the market and the competition is satisfactory, it is now time to evaluate the price.

Analyzing Price Stations and cable systems are usually offered for sale at a price rather than on a "best offer" basis. That price can be firm, which means that the seller will not take less, or an asking price, which is negotiable.

The reasonableness of the price must be evaluated. The most common and generally accepted criteria for judging prices are multiples of *cash flow*. Cash flow is a station's operating income before charges for depreciation, interest, amortization, and taxes. Stated another way, it is net revenue minus operating expenses, that is, general and administrative, program, sales, and technical. In some situations, cash flow may be increased by adding back on a pro forma basis certain expenses the current owner has that the new owner will not. Examples are extraordinary legal, telephone, or travel, or even an excessive compensation arrangement. How cash flow is defined is important, because it is the base number from which price computations emanate. Some lenders and investment bankers also use the term *trailing cash flow*, which means simply the cash flow as previously defined for the most recent twelve-month period available. This is a different concept from that of calendar year or fiscal year. Trailing cash flow analysis ensures that the financial performance of the station used to determine price will reflect the most current cash flow, along with any positive or negative trends that might be at work.

Once cash flow is determined, multiples are applied to calculate price. As noted earlier in the chapter, the late 1990s were marked by a resurgence of station and system trading activity. Multiples paid for radio stations depend on the market size. In larger markets or those where consolidation trading is under way, FM multiples range between 14 and 20. In middle markets, the range is between 10 and 14. Like FM radio, television multiples are related to cash flow, and they are in the 8 to 8.5 range. Except for AM radio, multiples in the late 1990s were in an upward trend. Multiples in this consolidation age have now exceeded the last trading frenzy of the pre-1989 period.

Prices paid for cable television systems are commonly calculated on a per-subscriber basis, with current levels fluctuating between $2,000 and $2,200 per subscriber. As in broadcasting, an alternate method of cable system valuation depends on multiples of cash flow. In the late 1990s, cable cash flow multiples ranged between 11 and 12. However, as mentioned earlier in the chapter, the effects of cable reregulation and the termination of the TCI-Bell Atlantic merger will likely see a softening of prevailing yardsticks.

Standard multiples are not absolute, however. Adjustments to the multiple depend on the size of the market and the station's place in it. Small markets do not justify the full multiple, nor do markets with depressed economies. Stations with declining sales and audience do not bring full price. Network affiliate prices have declined because of the erosion of audience shares and concerns about prospects for the future. The large number of bankruptcies of true independent stations in recent times depressed prices for those stations. AM stations rarely bring the full multiple today, due to declining listenership. (The National Association of Broadcasters [NAB] has buying, building, and valuation publications.)[13]

There are situations where multiples do not apply at all. A station may have no earnings and, in that instance, a determination has to be made on what a license in that market is worth. Some guidance can be found in calculating the property's probable revenues by applying a multiple to the retail sales in the area. One method applies a multiple to retail sales in the market to derive the electronic media revenue for the market, and then divides that figure by the number of stations in the market. That number yields possible station revenue and provides a basis to predict cash flow. Buying a station with no earnings is an art form and should be reserved for the sophisticated buyer.

Financing   At this point, the prospective buyer has evaluated the market and the station and has decided to make an offer. However, before the offer is submitted, the financing to complete the transaction must be in place. There are numerous sources of financing, depending upon the buyer's circumstances. Among the principal sources are these:

- banks
- venture capital
- investment banks
- funds for minority acquisition
- seller financing
- governmental agencies

Banks   The most traditional source of funds is the commercial bank. Banks have established criteria for lending that must be met. For example, they require the applicant to have some money of their own to invest, which means that a percentage of the purchase price and operating funds required comes from the applicant's own resources. There is no fixed rule, but a minimum of 20 percent is not uncommon. Banks also closely examine the operating statements of the facility to be purchased and will lend a multiple of the operating cash flow for the most recent twelve-month period. In the late 1990s, banks used a multiple between 5 and 6 times trailing broadcast cash flow to determine what they will land. They also will want statements of historical financial results and projections of future performance of up to five years. A pro forma balance sheet will also be required. The multiple will vary depending on the bank and is different for AM, FM, affiliate television, independent television, and cable. The multiple applied by a bank for loan purposes is less than the multiple used to evaluate the price of a station. Most banks have no standard for independent television and AM radio, because they do not view them as desirable lending opportunities. Cable systems command a multiple of 7 to 8 times trailing cash flow with large banks and are viewed as utilities. For FM and affiliate television, the multiple now used by most money center banks is 5 times trailing cash flow. To illustrate, consider the purchase for $8 million of an FM station cash flowing $800,000 per year. To establish the loan amount, the bank multiplies trailing cash flow ($800,000) by 5, resulting in a $4 million loan for the purchase. The down payment and working capital would have to be provided by the buyer. In this example, the equity required would equal 50 percent of the purchase price.

For the first-time buyer without significant personal funds or a substantial partner, bank financing is difficult to achieve. Banks will require experience in the business, as well as equity.

Another limitation with banks is that electronic media lending is an area of specialization, and many do not feel that they have the expertise to evaluate such transactions. Consequently, it may be difficult to find the right bank. Examples of commercial banks active in electronic media lending are Bankers Trust in New York and Society in Cleveland.[14] Note, however, that large money center banks consider only multimillion dollar, multistation transactions. For small, single-station purchases, banks in local communities likely will be the best source if one can be found that is willing to commit itself. If a station has no profit history, bank financing will not be available without a substantial personal guarantee.

Venture Capital   There are venture capital firms that assist and, in effect, become partners with the prospective entrepreneur to acquire a property. Unlike banks, venture capital firms are high-risk lenders. Such companies often will invest in stations or management that have potential but no proven track record. For example, there may be a station with good facilities that has never made any money. A venture capital firm might take a chance if it becomes convinced that a new format and new management can turn the station around. Most banks would never do a "turn around" without guarantees from investors with substantial capital. Similarly, a venture capital firm might invest with a manager who was successful for an owner but who has not yet been an owner, or who does not have adequate personal capital to become an owner.

Venture capital companies are often called "vulture capital companies." The name is derived from the price one has to pay to become a partner with one of these firms. While the venture capital fund may provide all or part of the necessary financing, the firm usually demands a significant ownership — often a majority position — in the acquired property. These investors will back proven management with capital, with the expectation of making money on increased value over time of that station and any additional stations that may be acquired. In most such arrangements, the buyer will be giving up control of the enterprise to the venture capital firm, and performance will have to satisfy the provider of the funds.

Examples of venture capital firms are McPartnes of Boston and Bain Capital, also of Boston.

Investment Banks   Many institutions have been very active in raising funds for the electronic media industry in recent times. Typically, an investment bank will agree to raise funds from public or private sources for a purchase. Their activities may be *guaranteed* or on a *best efforts basis*. Guaranteed means that on the day it is time to pay for the purchase, the investment banker will be there with the funds. Best effort means that the firm will attempt to raise the money, but it is not committed to the buyer if it does not.

For their services, investment bankers charge a fee, which is usually a percentage of the money raised. These companies prefer multimillion dollar transactions involving multiple stations and, normally, are not a source for a first-time buyer. Investment bankers are most often employed by small, intermediate, or large companies seeking to grow larger by acquisition or merger.

Morgan Stanley and Company in New York is an example of an investment bank. A regional investment banker would be Legacy, in Atlanta and Memphis.

Funds for Minority Acquisition   Government policy has attempted to encourage the development of minority ownership in the electronic media. Consequently, there are specialized financing sources available to minority buyers. Perhaps the most prominent of these is Broadcap, which is funded by the National Association of Broadcasters and whose offices are located at NAB headquarters in Washington, D.C.

Seller Financing   Sometimes, the seller becomes the financing source. To facilitate a sale or to avoid immediate tax consequences, a seller may extend terms to the buyer. The seller in effect becomes the lender and "carries the paper." Seller financing arrangements are attractive, because they might require less equity or down payment than a bank or other source. The seller might also be willing to have the debt bear a fixed rate of interest, as opposed to the floating rate over prime that most commercial banks use. Where this type of financing does occur, the seller takes a collateral position in the assets of the station. However, this interest of the seller in the station means the buyer cannot use the assets to secure any additional borrowing without the seller's permission. Seller financing is a good approach for the first-time buyer. However, due to the consolidation occasioned by the Telecommunications Act of 1996, most deals today are cash or publicly traded stock.

Governmental Agencies   Principal in this category is the Small Business Administration (SBA). For qualified applicants, this federal agency will guarantee up to 90 percent of a loan at a commercial participating bank, or it may make a loan directly from its own funds. As a threshold requirement, the applicant must demonstrate in writing rejections by at least two commercial banks. The negative in this case is the time it takes to get such a loan approved. It may be difficult to persuade a seller to wait for an extended period during which there is no guarantee of success. In addition, these are times of reduced circumstances for government spending, and there are concerns about the availability of such fund guarantees and even the future of the SBA.

In conclusion, there is more qualified assistance available for prospective purchasers than there was before the dawn of the deregulation decade in 1979. Most media brokers now provide financing services and can help select a source and assist in the written presentation. Fees are charged for such services, and they vary, depending upon whether the broker secures equity, senior debt, or junior debt. However, media brokers do know where electronic media financing is, and they have a substantial interest in securing it for their clients, since they do not collect the commission for the sale of a property unless the financing for the buyer is complete.

Among the publications available to introduce the novice to financial concepts and methods is the NAB's *Understanding Broadcast and Cable Finance: A Handbook for the Non-Financial Manager.*[15]

Submitting an Offer   With the financing in place, it is now time to formalize the offer, which must be submitted in writing for consideration by the seller. The media broker, if one is being utilized, will prepare a written offer (Figure 10.7) for the prospective buyer to review carefully and sign. It is wise at this stage to hire an attorney to examine the offer, since it is a legally binding document. Terms and conditions must be clearly written to avoid misunderstanding and even litigation. Attached to the offer should be a check for the deposit. Again, deposit amounts vary, but 5 percent of the total purchase price is the norm. This deposit assures the seller that the buyer is serious and will forfeit the deposit if the buyer does not complete the transaction as agreed. The offer should be written to expire at a certain time — 72 hours, for example. This will prevent the seller from shopping the offer in an attempt to get a higher price from another purchaser.

The offer may provide for an inspection period (most often thirty days) during which the buyer may examine facilities and financial records. If the inspection is unsatisfactory, the buyer may withdraw without penalty. However, with the expiration of the inspection period, all contingencies are removed and the transaction is firm. Risk has now been attached. That is, the buyer must now appear at the closing with funds in hand. Should that not happen, the escrow deposit will be lost. In other words, risk of losing the deposit by failure to close in a timely manner has now attached to the offer.

Letter of Intent, Contract, Transfer Application   Following acceptance of the offer by the seller, attorneys for both sides set to work on more formal documents. The offer may be succeeded by a letter of intent, which is a more complete legal recitation of the principal terms and responsibilities of both parties. Major topics in the letter are price, method of payment (which means cash or terms), and assets to be sold. The prorating of expenses is also often covered. This category includes the responsibility for accrued vacation time of employees and adjustments for annual expenses already paid, such as insurance and taxes. Parties must also provide for the payment of the accounts receivable owned by the station. Are they, too, included in the purchase price, or will they be collected by the buyer and remitted to the seller after a period of time, usually ninety days? Often stations have balances of air time owed to clients who provided goods or services. As noted earlier, these transactions are known in the industry as trade or barter, and adjustments to the accounts of buyer and seller may be in order here.

Parties may elect to bypass the letter of intent and to go directly to a formal purchase contract, which is a complete legal document that addresses all

Figure 10.7   *Offer letter. (Source: Blackburn and Company, Inc., Alexandria, Virginia. Used with permission.)*

DATE

Blackburn & Company, Inc.
Suite 340
201 N. Union Street
Alexandria, VA   22314

Gentlemen:

Subject to agreement on a formal contract, an inspection of the station, and subject to FCC approval, _____ hereby offer to purchase the fixed assets of _____ on the following terms and conditions:

1.   We will pay a total purchase price of $_____ as follows:

    (a) $_____ in cash at closing, of which $_____ will be placed in escrow at the time of signing a formal contract.

    (b)   Balance in the form of a first mortgage on the assets payable in equal _____ installments of principal and interest at _____ percent over _____ years. The payments, however, will be calculated on a _____-year basis with remaining principal paid in a lump sum at the end of _____ years. Buyer reserves the right to prepay this note in whole or in part at any time without penalty.

2.   It is understood that all of the assets owned by the Seller both real and physical, and used or useful in the operation of said station, will be delivered free and clear of all liens and encumbrances. An inventory of the assets to be delivered will be prepared and will become a part of the formal contract.

3.   _____ agree to assume all contractual obligations of the station which are usual and normal to its operation, such as music licensing agreements, news service contracts, studio and transmitter site leases, and the like, provided that all such contracts, agreements and leases are made available to us for our inspection and approval prior to the execution of a formal contract. A schedule of all such agreements to be assumed will be prepared and will become an exhibit to the formal contract.

Figure 10.7   *Continued*

Blackburn & Company, Inc.
Page 2

4.   It is understood and agreed that current assets, suc
     cash and accounts receivable, are not among the asset
     be delivered, but will remain the property of Sel
     However, all accounts receivable on the books at f
     closing are to be turned over to _____
     collection only for a period of _____ days, at the
     of which period _____ will pay to Seller all m
     collected against said accounts and will return to Se
     any such accounts remaining uncollected at that tim

5.   It is understood and agreed that all filing and g
     fees charged by the FCC in connection with
     transaction, if any, will be paid half by the Buyer
     half by the Seller.

6.   Both parties recognize Blackburn & Company, Inc.
     exclusive broker in this transaction. Seller agree
     pay Blackburn a brokerage commission in connection
     this transaction, as agreed on between Seller
     Blackburn, and to hold us harmless from any obliga
     for such commission to Blackburn.

As evidence of _____ good faith, ____ attach herewith a chec
the amount of $_____, made payable to Blackburn & Comp
Inc. If this offer is accepted and a formal contract agreed
this amount will become a part of the escrow payment menti
above. If this offer is not accepted, or if a formal contrac
not agreed to, this check is to be returned to _____ without
obligation.

This offer is being made on behalf of a corporation, eithe
existence or to be formed, in which the undersigned will
stockholder, and shall expire _____ days from the above date.

If this offer is accepted, both parties agree to cooperate prom
in the preparation of a formal contract and all other documents
applications required for filing with the FCC in order to ef
this transaction.

                         By: _____

              AGREED

                         By: _____

Received check for $ _____
BLACKBURN & COMPANY, INC.

By: _____

aspects of the transaction, major and minor. The contract outlines responsibilities, timetables, and place and time of the closing. It provides for everything, from transfer of title to real estate to accrued vacation time of employees, and may even provide a mechanism for dealing with disputes. Questions frequently arise over handling of accounts receivable and accounts payable, for example. Once executed, the purchase contract must be filed with the Federal Communications Commission within thirty days.

Subsequent to the filing of the purchase document, a transfer application, FCC Form 314 (Figure 10.8), must be filed with the commission. It requests the FCC to assign the license for the station from the selling to the acquiring entity.

The Federal Communications Commission or, to be specific, the commission's Mass Media Bureau, may not act on the transfer application until thirty days after it has been accepted for filing. In this thirty-day period, notices of the impending transaction are run on the air of the station and in the local newspaper. The purpose of this public notice is to give members of the community an opportunity to comment on the proposed transaction. Assuming no objections, and assuming the seller is in good standing with the FCC, the transfer will be approved.

The time required for commission approval depends upon the volume of transfers pending. Once approved, the FCC transfer order does not become final for forty days. In that forty-day period, the proposed transfer is still susceptible to challenge. However, at this advanced stage, it is only the Federal Communications Commission itself that can initiate the action. During this time, information may come to the FCC's attention reflecting on the character of, or on the integrity of the filing representations made by, parties seeking the assignment. Problems rarely occur in this "waiting period," but occasionally they do.

The procedure for acquisition of a cable system is much the same: offer, deposit, letter of intent, and contract. However, notification to, and approval by, the regulatory body is another matter. There is no central federal regulatory body for licenses of cable as there is for broadcast. Cable franchising, or licensing, authority has been specifically reserved for local governments by federal law.

However, even though franchising has been left to local governments, the federal government may still impose franchise requirements. For example, the Cable Television Consumer Protection and Competition Act of 1992 requires that once an existing system is acquired in a purchase, it must be held by the purchaser for three years before it can be sold again.[16] Most often, franchising authorities are cities, but some states have cable commissions. Consequently, each cable system has its own licensing authority which, in turn, has its own procedures. It is impossible to generalize such requirements, except to say that most franchise agreements have some language about notification to the governmental body of a sale. The proposed buyer must obtain competent advice on the local procedures and comply with them.

The parties now meet a final time for the closing. Documents are signed and funds transferred. The seller goes to Bermuda, and the buyer goes to work.

Figure 10.8   *Excerpt from FCC Form 314.*

Approved by OMB
3060-0031
Expires 08/31/98

FEDERAL COMMUNICATIONS COMMISSION
WASHINGTON, D.C. 20554

FCC 314

APPLICATION FOR CONSENT TO
ASSIGNMENT OF BROADCAST STATION
CONSTRUCTION PERMIT OR LICENSE

(Please read instructions before completing this form.)

FOR
FCC
USE
ONLY

FOR MASS MEDIA BUREAU USE ONLY

FILE NO.

Section I - GENERAL INFORMATION

1. APPLICANT NAME

MAILING ADDRESS (Line 1) (Maximum 35 characters)

MAILING ADDRESS (Line 2) (if required) (Maximum 35 characters)

CITY

STATE OR COUNTRY (if foreign address)

ZIP CODE

TELEPHONE NUMBER (include area code)

CALL LETTERS

OTHER FCC IDENTIFIER (IF APPLICABLE)

FOR MAILING THIS APPLICATION, SEE INSTRUCTIONS FOR SECTION I

2. A. Is a fee submitted with this application?   ☐ Yes   ☐ No

   B. If No, select the appropriate box to indicate reason for fee exemption (see 47 C.F.R. Section 1.1112) or reason a fee is not applicable and go to Question 3.

   ☐ Governmental Entity   ☐ Noncommercial educational licensee   ☐ Other (Please explain):

   C. If item 2.A. is Yes, provide the following information:

Enter in Column (A) the correct Fee Type Code for the service you are applying for. Fee Type Codes may be found in the "Mass Media Services Fee Filing Guide." Column (B) lists the Fee Multiple applicable for this application. Enter in Column (C) the result obtained from multiplying the value of the Fee Type Code in Column (A) by the number listed in Column (B).

(A)	(B)	(C)	
FEE TYPE CODE	**FEE MULTIPLE** (if required)	**FEE DUE FOR FEE TYPE CODE IN COLUMN (A)** $	FOR FCC USE ONLY

To be used only when you are requesting concurrent actions which result in a requirement to list more than one Fee Type Code.

(A)	(B)	(C)	FOR FCC USE ONLY
		$	

ADD ALL AMOUNTS SHOWN IN COLUMN C, LINES (1) THROUGH (2), AND ENTER THE TOTAL HERE. THIS AMOUNT SHOULD EQUAL YOUR ENCLOSED REMITTANCE.

TOTAL AMOUNT REMITTED WITH THIS APPLICATION
$

FOR FCC USE ONLY

August 1992 Edition Usable

Figure 10.8 *Continued*

SECTION I (Page 2)
PART I - Assignor

1. Name of Assignor	Street Address		
	City	State	ZIP Code
	Telephone Number (include area code)		

2. Authorization which is proposed to be assigned

   (a) Call letters_____ Location _____

   (b) Has the station commenced its initial program tests within the past twelve months?   ☐ Yes   ☐ No

    If Yes, was the initial construction permit granted after comparative hearing?   ☐ Yes   ☐ No

                                    Exhibit No.

    If Yes, attach as an Exhibit the showing required by 47 C.F.R. Section 73.3597.

   (c) Has the license for the station been acquired through the Commission's Minority Ownership Policy?   ☐ Yes   ☐ No

    If Yes, has the station been operated on-air for less than the past twelve months?   ☐ Yes   ☐ No

                                      Exhibit No.

    If Yes, attach as an Exhibit the showing required by 47 C.F.R. Section 73.3597.

3. Call letters of any SCA, FM or TV booster station, or associated auxiliary service stations (e.g., remote pickup, STL, inter-city relay) which are to be assigned:

4. Attach as an Exhibit a copy of the contract or agreement to assign the property and facilities of the station. If there is only an oral agreement, reduce the terms to writing and attach.   Exhibit No.

5. If this application is for assignment of a construction permit for an unbuilt station, submit as an Exhibit the detailed showings and declarations of the applicants required by 47 C.F.R. Section 73.3597 regarding the assignor's legitimate and prudent out-of-pocket expenditures and the retention, if any, of any interest in the station.   Exhibit No.

6. State in an Exhibit whether the assignor, or any party to the assignor: Exhibit No.

   (a) has any interest in or connection with an AM, FM or television broadcast station; or a broadcast application pending before the FCC; or

   (b) has had any interest in or connection with any dismissed and/or denied application; or any FCC license which has been revoked.

    The Exhibit should include the following information:

    (1) name of party with such interest;
    (2) nature of interest or connection, giving dates;
    (3) call letters or file number of application; or docket number; and
    (4) location.

7. Since the filing of the assignor's last renewal application for the authorization being assigned or other application, has an adverse finding been made or an adverse final action taken by any court or administrative body with respect to the applicant or parties to this application in a civil or criminal proceeding, brought under the provisions of any law related to the following: any felony; mass media related antitrust or unfair competition; fraudulent statements to another governmental unit; or discrimination?   ☐ Yes   ☐ No

                                        Exhibit No.

    If Yes, attach as an Exhibit a full description of the persons and matter involved, including an identification of the court or administrative body and the proceeding (by dates and file numbers) and the disposition of the litigation.

FCC 314 (Page 2)
August 1995

Figure 10.9 *List of FM allocations available for application. (Source: Fisher Wayland Cooper Leader & Zaragoza, Washington, D.C. Used with permission.)*

Community	Channel	Deadline
Frederiksted, VI	269B1	May 15, 1997
Greensboro, AL	256A	May 15, 1997
Zapata, TX	228A	May 22, 1997
Huron, CA	252A	May 22, 1997
Alexandria, LA	295A	May 29, 1997
Ball, LA	288A	May 29, 1997
Albion, NY	238A	May 29, 1997
Goochland, VA	263A	June 5, 1997
Battle Mountain, NV	253A	June 5, 1997
Cawker City, KS	242C3	June 19, 1997
Clear Lake, SD	296C3	June 27, 1997
Amargosa Valley, NV	266A	July 2, 1997
Wake Village, TX	223A	July 2, 1997
Humboldt, KS	232C3	July 10, 1997
Poplar Bluff, MO	223A	July 10, 1997

Construction of a New Facility

As an alternative to acquisition, entry into electronic media ownership may be achieved by construction of a new facility, or a start-up. Of the two possible means of ownership entry, this alternative is cheaper, riskier, and more difficult to finance. New builds also limit the range of choices as to type of station and location. However, on the plus side, the entrepreneur is not paying an excessive price based upon the goodwill of an existing station.

Locating a Frequency or Franchise   To build a facility, one must first identify an open, or vacant, frequency or franchise. Depending on the type of broadcasting, this procedure varies.

AM   In broadcast AM, the Federal Communications Commission does not assign frequencies to designated geographical areas. Instead, the prospective applicant must conduct a frequency search to identify what is available where. Most people are not in a position to do this unassisted, and the services of a consulting engineer must be obtained. Information on these consultants can be found in the "Technical Consultants" section of *Broadcasting & Cable Yearbook*. It is wise to get several quotes from these specialty firms on the cost of conducting a search.

FM and Television   In the case of FM and television, there is information readily available on what frequencies or channels are available where. The

Federal Communications Commission regularly updates this information, and it can be obtained from the agency directly. It may also be available through attorneys who specialize in FCC practice. Such data identify the frequency or channel, power, location, and the dates for filing of applications by interested parties. These filing dates are called windows and are usually thirty-day periods (Figure 10.9).

Cable   Cable systems are licensed by local governmental bodies, most often cities or counties, and such licenses are called franchises. In the case of a new service, the local governmental body usually authorizes the proposed new cable services by an ordinance that outlines the specifications an applicant will have to include in a proposal. Local governments have not been bashful in setting out their service and financial requirements. The list of items to be supplied spans the spectrum from local access channels to mandatory support of city services or donation of facilities. Inordinate franchising demands in no small way prompted passage of the Cable Communications Policy Act of 1984 and the prohibition on the award of exclusive franchises contained in the Cable Television Consumer Protection and Competition Act of 1992.[17] Following the ordinance, the local body will request proposals from interested parties. These proposal requests are called RFPs (requests for proposals). Existence of these new service opportunities can be found by reading cable trade publications, through cable brokers such as Communications Equity Associates, or by a review of legal notices in papers of general circulation in communities in which there is an interest. There are, of course, other methods. A call to a state cable television association, for example, may uncover a new build opportunity.

New Service: Application, Construction, and License   Once the vacancy has been identified, an application must be filed with the appropriate governmental body, the new facility must be constructed, and a license or franchise must be obtained.

Broadcast   For broadcasting, the procedure is to file an application with the Federal Communications Commission on FCC Form 301 (Figure 10.10). Note that the form is entitled Application for Construction Permit for Commercial Broadcast Station. This means that the prospective applicant must be qualified for, and receive, a construction permit prior to the issuance of a license for the proposed facility. Assistance of counsel in preparing this application is desirable, but not essential. Most successful applicants do use communications attorneys, a list of whom can be found in the "Professional Services" section of *Broadcasting & Cable Yearbook.* Many of these attorneys are located in Washington, D.C., where the FCC has its offices.

The applicant must satisfy certain basic qualification requirements. Among these are legal, technical, financial, and character rules, as set out in the Communications Act of 1934.[18] For example, the act precludes ownership of licenses by aliens or persons who have had a previous license revoked for antitrust violations. In addition, the proposed new service must not interfere

Figure 10.10   *Excerpt from FCC Form 301.*

Federal Communications Commission
Washington, D. C. 20554

Approved by OMB
3060-0027
Expires 06/30/98

FOR
FCC
USE
ONLY

FCC 301

APPLICATION FOR CONSTRUCTION PERMIT
FOR COMMERCIAL BROADCAST STATION

FOR COMMISSION USE ONLY
FILE NO.

Section I - GENERAL INFORMATION

1. APPLICANT NAME (Last, First, Middle Initial)		
MAILING ADDRESS (Line 1) (Maximum 35 characters)		
MAILING ADDRESS (Line 2) (Maximum 35 characters)		
CITY	STATE OR COUNTRY (if foreign address)	ZIP CODE
TELEPHONE NUMBER (include area code)	CALL LETTERS	OTHER FCC IDENTIFIER (IF APPLICABLE)

2. A. Is a fee submitted with this application?   ☐ Yes   ☐ No

    B. If No, indicate reason for fee exemption (see 47 C.F.R. Section 1.1113) and go to Question 3.

    ☐ Governmental Entity   ☐ Noncommercial educational licensee   ☐ Other (Please explain):

    C. If Yes, provide the following information:

Enter in Column (A) the correct Fee Type Code for the service you are applying for. Fee Type Codes may be found in the "Mass Media Services Fee Filing Guide." Column (B) lists the Fee Multiple applicable for this application. Enter in Column (C) the result obtained from multiplying the value of the Fee Type Code in Column (A) by the number listed in Column (B).

(1)	(A) FEE TYPE CODE	(B) FEE MULTIPLE (if required)	(C) FEE DUE FOR FEE TYPE CODE IN COLUMN (A) $	FOR FCC USE ONLY

To be used only when you are requesting concurrent actions which result in a requirement to list more than one Fee Type Code.

(2)	(A)	(B)	(C) $	FOR FCC USE ONLY

ADD ALL AMOUNTS SHOWN IN COLUMN C, LINES (1) THROUGH (2), AND ENTER THE TOTAL HERE. THIS AMOUNT SHOULD EQUAL YOUR ENCLOSED REMITTANCE.	TOTAL AMOUNT REMITTED WITH THIS APPLICATION $	FOR FCC USE ONLY

Figure 10.10 *Continued*

Section I - GENERAL INFORMATION (Page 2)

3. This application is for: (check one box)   ☐ AM   ☐ FM   ☐ TV

(b) Channel No. or Frequency	(b) Principal Community	City	State

(c) Check one of the following boxes:

☐   Application for NEW station

☐   MAJOR change in licensed facilities; call sign: .... _____

☐   MINOR change in licensed facilities; call sign: .... _____

☐   MAJOR modification of construction permit; call sign: .... _____

     File No. of construction permit; call sign: .... _____

☐   MINOR modification of construction permit; call sign:........................... _____

     File No. of construction permit; call sign: .... _____

☐   AMENDMENT to pending application: Application File Number: .... _____

NOTE: It is not necessary to use this form to amend a previously filed application. Should you do so, however, please submit only Section I and those other portions of the form that contain the amended information.

4. Is this application mutually exclusive with a renewal application?   ☐ Yes   ☐ No

    If Yes, state:

Call letters	Community of License	
	City	State

with any existing service. This means that the applicant must affix an engineering exhibit identifying the tower site, height, power, and coverage area. The assistance of a consulting engineer is normally required to prepare the exhibit. The height and location of the tower may necessitate the filing of an application with the Federal Aviation Administration (FAA). The consulting engineer who prepares the engineering exhibit will be able to advise how to satisfy this requirement.

The applicant must also demonstrate the financial ability to complete the project. This requires a showing that the prospective licensee can construct the station and operate for three months without any revenue.

The final area of examination is character. The FCC looks at three main character questions: (1) Has the prospective applicant engaged in conduct that violated the 1934 act or FCC rules? (2) Has the applicant been guilty of misrepresentation or lack of candor before the commission? (3) Has the applicant aired fraudulent programming? The FCC has broadened its character review to include certain applicant felony and misdemeanor convictions that are not broadcast-related. Drug convictions are a specific problem. All of these threshold basic qualifications must be satisfied.

In filing an application for new FM service, the applicant should be aware that the FCC does grant preference for current owners of AM stations. Preferences also exist for minority applicants.

When complete, the application is filed with the Mass Media Bureau of the Federal Communications Commission. If there are no other applicants and the licensing requirements of the 1934 act have been met, the commission issues a construction permit, known as a "CP." The new station then must be constructed within a designated period or the permit will lapse. Extensions may be granted, depending upon circumstances.

If, however, more than one application is filed for the same frequency, the FCC, under the 1996 Telecommunications Act, will conduct an auction among qualified applicants, as opposed to a comparative hearing among them as was the case in past years.

With the issuance of the construction permit and the construction of the station, the process is almost over. Once constructed, the new facility is tested to determine conformity with the technical outlines set forth in the applicant's FCC Form 301. Assuming the results are positive, the applicant now files an FCC Form 302 to obtain the license.

Cable   The procedure for processing a cable application requires that the franchise proposals be submitted by a certain date. Multiple applications are compared for conformity with the bid requirements in the RFP. Additional consideration might be the extent of local ownership, and the expertise and financial capability of each applicant. Public hearings may or may not be required. Legal appeals by dissatisfied applicants are possible, but at some point the franchise will be granted and construction will begin. Often the franchise grant contains specific requirements as to what parts of the system will be built when.

A final note on cable is necessary. It is a capital-intensive business. Everything from the headend, or origination source, to miles of cable is very costly. It is significantly more difficult to construct a new cable system than a new broadcast station. Coupled with the front-end capital costs is the likelihood that it will be years before revenue exceeds cost and debt service. Usually, it takes six years to break even on a cable start-up. For this reason, cable construction often falls to large companies already in the business that have adequate capital and that can realize the tax benefits accruing from interest and depreciation.

This is not an enterprise to be embarked upon with anything less than full knowledge and substantial funding. However, the financial markets tend to view cable very favorably, which enhances the prospects of successfully undertaking the new system project.

As discussed earlier, this construction alternative for ownership entry is generally much cheaper than the purchase of an existing property, but it is not without risk and danger. It is, however, an attractive option to the purchase of an existing facility.

WHAT'S AHEAD?

As a consequence of the station consolidation that followed the Telecommunications Act of 1996, the number of individual owners has declined. So, too, has the number of opportunities for individuals with ownership aspirations.

For today's student, the road to ownership will be difficult. The markets and the quality of available stations will not be as good as in the pre-1996 period. Financing for the single owner will probably be harder to get.

The best opportunities may now arise through competing for new allocations that the FCC will authorize from time to time. However, even here there is a new reality. Competing applications will be decided by auction. Again, that puts an emphasis on financial resources.

Financing will depend on demonstrated success in earlier employment. Management experience and professional and financial acumen will be even more important than in past years.

There will still be ownership opportunities, institutions willing to finance, and even sellers willing to take seller paper. But it all will be very different from earlier years. And the reduced number of opportunities will go only to those who have demonstrated their command of the ownership prerequisites.

SUMMARY

Entry into the electronic media business can be achieved either by employment or ownership. Since experience may be required to secure financing to own, employment is often the first step. It is a necessary first step for those who aspire to management.

Typically, initial employment is in an entry-level position in a station or cable system. Small-market stations provide the greatest number of openings and offer opportunities to develop a depth of knowledge and breadth of experience. Advancement comes as a result of promotion within a station, system, or group, or through a move to another station or market. Job vacancies may be identified through trade and association publications. Clearinghouses and specialized employment firms also are used to locate positions.

Ownership is accomplished through buying or building a station. The purchase of a property begins with the identification of stations for sale. This can be done directly or indirectly through a media broker. Once identified, the purchase candidate must be evaluated as to market, competition, and price. Price evaluation begins with standard multiples.

Prior to making an offer, the prospective purchaser must have a financing commitment to complete the transaction. There are six traditional financing sources from which to select, depending upon circumstances: banks, venture capital, investment banks, funds for minority acquisition, seller financing, and governmental agencies. Once the offer is accepted by the seller, contracts are prepared, and an application to transfer the license or franchise is made to the appropriate governmental authority. Subsequent to transfer approval, the transaction is completed when the buyer pays the seller.

Construction of a new station or cable system is an alternative to purchase. Information on available frequencies or franchises can be obtained in a variety of ways and may require the services of a consulting engineer. Once the opportunity has been located, application for the new service will have to be made to the FCC for broadcast or to the local governmental authority for cable. The length and outcome of the application process will depend on whether competing applications have been filed. Once the application evaluation has been completed, the appropriate body will issue a construction permit or franchise. At this point, construction commences, and it must be completed in a timely manner. In broadcast, the licensing follows completion of construction and operational tests. A cable franchise precedes construction.

Construction of a new facility is a riskier venture than the purchase of an existing operation, though it is also less expensive.

CASE STUDY: ACQUISITION

KASH-FM is a stand-alone 50,000-watt class B FM in a small, unrated market with six other FMs, all 100,000 watts. It programs Country & Western (C&W), as does one of its competitors.

No radio revenue information on the market is available from the traditional sources, like BIA or Duncan. What is known about the market is that retail sales in its trade area are $50 million.

The economy is diverse — everything from a large grain elevator, which exports to Asia, to a 25,000 uniformed personnel Air Force base. The base is home to B-1s, B-2s, and certain missiles.

Overall, this is a blue-collar community that favors the C&W format and buys American. Efforts are under way to attract refugees from Silicon Valley to a new industrial high-tech park near the air base.

KASH-FM is owned by the man who put it on the air under FCC Docket #80–90 in 1983. He is now 70 years old and wants continuing income for his expected life span, as reflected in the mortality tables used by The Mutual of Omaha company.

The station's net billing has been flat for the last three calendar years, about $500,000. Expenses, including the owner's $250,000 salary, are $400,000. Other market managers make about $25,000. Stated cash flow is approximately $100,000, also flat. This year, eight months of which have passed, cash flow is down about $50,000 from the comparable period one year earlier. Last year, it averaged about $8,000 per month.

"Mr. KASH" is asking $2 million for his station. He plans to retain ownership of the tower and studio office building, which he will lease to a new owner for $2,000 per month. In order to expedite the sale, the owner has retained Media Services Group, Inc. on a nonexclusive basis to find a qualified buyer.

Exercises

1. What should a proper price for this station be, based upon prevailing industry standards as discussed in this chapter?

2. Should the price, once determined, be adjusted for any market or competitive situation in this example? Be specific.

3. Calculate a pro forma trailing cash flow for KASH-FM using information provided in this case study.

4. What total amount of bank financing might an aspiring purchaser hope to achieve?

5. What are some realistic alternatives to bank financing in this situation?

CASE STUDY: NEW BUILD

Prevailing market conditions in the consolidation age seem to make the purchase of existing properties impossible for many first-time buyers. Mr. Owner Wannabe seeks an alternative and thinks that perhaps he should just build a new radio station, rather than pay excess dollars to buy someone else's profit and goodwill.

Due to his uncle's bad driving, he has a trust fund of $1 million, which is designated to set up the deceased's nephew in a business of his choice.

Exercises

1. How does the nephew identify a potential AM frequency?

2. How does he identify a potential FM frequency?

3. Once a potential frequency has been located, how does he apply for it?

4. If there is more than one applicant for the same vacant frequency, what procedure is used to award it to one of the multiple competing applicants?

5. Does the applicant have any alternative to using his own funds to finance this project?

NOTES

1. National Association of Broadcasters, 1771 N Street, N.W., Washington, D.C. 20036; Promotion and Marketing Executives in the Electronic Media, 6255 Sunset Boulevard, Suite 624, Los Angeles, CA 90028.

2. RTNDA Job Service, Radio-Television News Directors Association, 1000 Connecticut Avenue, N.W., Suite 615, Washington, D.C. 20036. The service's telephone number is (202) 659–6510, and the fax is (202) 223–4007.

3. *Broadcasting & Cable Yearbook*. New Providence, N.J.: R.R. Bowker.

4. Alpha Epsilon Rho, The National Broadcasting Society, College of Journalism, University of South Carolina, Columbia, SC 29208.

5. *Duncan's Radio Market Guide*. Indianapolis, Ind.: Duncan's American Radio, Inc.

6. Available from Broadcast Investment Analysts (BIA), Inc., Box 17307, Washington, D.C. 20041.

7. Relevant information may be found in *Broadcasting & Cable Yearbook*.

8. *Television and Cable Factbook*. Washington, D.C.: Warren Publishing, Inc.

9. "By The Numbers," *Broadcasting & Cable*, November 16, 1998, p. 66.

10. "Changing Hands," *Broadcasting & Cable*, June 22, 1998, p. 64.

11. "DBS, Cable's Ambitious Competitor," *Broadcasting & Cable*, April 20, 1998, p. 46.

12. 47 *CFR* 73.202.

13. Examples include *Buying or Building a Broadcast Station in the '90s*, 3rd ed., and *Fair Market Value of Radio Stations: A Buyer's Guide*, 2nd ed.

14. For a more complete listing of financial institutions with electronic media expertise, see the "Professional Services" section of *Broadcasting & Cable Yearbook*.

15. Available from the National Association of Broadcasters.

16. 47 *USC* 537.

17. 47 *USC* 541.

18. 47 *USC* 308(b), 310(b), 313.

ADDITIONAL READINGS

Cable Yellow Pages. Torrance, CA: CYP, Inc. (published annually).

Cablevision. New York: Cahners Business Information (published 19 times annually).

Entertainment Employment Journal. Van Nuys, CA: Entertainment Employment Journal, Inc. (published 22 times annually).

Media Grapevine. Tucson, AZ: Morven Communications, Inc. (P.O. Box 12693, Tucson, AZ 85732-2693).

Predicting Radio Station and Market Revenues. Washington, DC: National Association of Broadcasters, 1992.

Radio & Records (R&R). Los Angeles, CA: Radio & Records, Inc. (published weekly).

Radio Financing: A Guide for Lenders and Investors. Washington, DC: National Association of Broadcasters, 1990.

APPENDIX A
TV PARENTAL GUIDELINES

TV PARENTAL GUIDELINES

For Programs Designed Solely for Children

TV-Y   (All Children — *This program is designed to be appropriate for all children.*) Whether animated or live-action, the themes and elements in this program are specifically designed for a very young audience, including children from ages 2 to 6. This program is not expected to frighten younger children.

TV-Y7   (Directed to Older Children — *This program is designed for children age 7 and above.*) It may be more appropriate for children who have acquired the developmental skills needed to distinguish between make-believe and reality. Themes and elements in this program may include mild fantasy or comedic violence, or may frighten children under the age of 7. Therefore, parents may wish to consider the suitability of this program for their very young children. Note: For those programs where fantasy violence may be more intense or more combative than other programs in this category, such programs will be designated TV-Y7-FV.

For Programs Designed for the Entire Audience

TV-G   (General Audience — *Most parents would find this program suitable for all ages.*) Although this rating does not signify a program designed specifically for children, most parents may let younger children watch this program unattended. It contains little or no violence, no strong language, and little or no sexual dialogue or situations.

TV-PG   (Parental Guidance Suggested — *This program may contain material that parents may find unsuitable for younger children.*) Many parents may want to watch it with their younger children. The theme itself may call for parental guidance and/or the program contains one or more of the following: moderate violence (V), some sexual situations (S), infrequent coarse language (L), or some suggestive dialogue (D).

TV-14   (Parents Strongly Cautioned — *This program contains some material that many parents would find unsuitable for children under 14 years of age.*) Parents are strongly urged to exercise greater care in monitoring this program and are cautioned against letting children under the age of 14 watch unattended. This program contains one or more of the following: intense violence (V), intense sexual situations (S), strong coarse language (L), or intensely suggestive dialogue (D).

TV-MA   (Mature Audience Only — *This program is specifically designed to be viewed by adults and therefore may be unsuitable for children under 17.*) This program contains one or more of the following: graphic violence (V), explicit sexual activity (S), or crude indecent language (L).

APPENDIX B
RADIO STATION
MANAGER'S GUIDE:

SOME BASICS OF THE FCC'S RULES AND POLICIES

Source: Arter & Hadden, Washington, D.C. Used with permission.

We have prepared this guide to some of the basic FCC rules and policies applicable to commercial radio stations to familiarize the reader with most of the day-to-day and periodic operating and reporting requirements the FCC imposes on broadcast stations and their owners. It is divided into four topic areas: (1) Fundamentals; (2) Daily Operating Requirements; (3) Other General Operating Requirements, which is divided into Programming and Technical/Engineering Matters; and (4) Periodic FCC Filing and Reporting Requirements.

This guide is not intended as a complete explanation of the subjects and rules discussed: in the interest of simplicity, details are omitted that could affect the application of a rule to any given station's situation. References are made in some cases to memoranda that we have prepared previously or articles in our monthly newsletter, *Arter & Hadden Antenna,* which provide additional information about some of these subjects. If you would like a copy of any of these memoranda or articles, please contact us. We also recommend that you obtain a copy of the FCC's rules and keep them on hand for future reference.

I. FUNDAMENTALS

A. *Main Studio Requirements*

Recent Rule Change: In August 1998 the FCC adopted changes to its main studio and public file rules. The FCC is expected to issue a public notice sometime in October 1998 indicating that the new rules have become effective. Because the current main studio and public file rules will remain effective for only another month or so, this guide discusses the requirements adopted in the *new* rules. Where appropriate, references are made to the current requirements to place the new rules in perspective. Questions will no doubt arise as to how the FCC intends to implement or enforce the new rules. If you have such questions, you should contact the FCC or legal counsel.

1. Each station's main studio must be located within the principal community contour of any station, of any service (*e.g.,* AM, FM, or TV), licensed to the same community of license (the principal community contour is defined as the 5.0 mV/m daytime contour for AM stations; 3.16 mV/m contour for FM stations; 74 dBu for TV Channels 2–6; 77 dBu for TV Channels 7–13; and 80 dBu for TV Channels 14–69),[1] or no more than 25 miles from the reference coordinates of the station's community of license. If a station has an FCC granted waiver of the previous main studio rule allowing operation from a primary main studio that serves one or more satellite stations, the waiver will remain in effect under the new rule.

2. The FCC requires that each broadcast station maintain a "meaningful management and staff presence" at its main studio. This means that a station must employ at least one full-time management level person and one full-time staff person to be present at its main studio during regular business hours. The management level person must report to work at the main studio on a daily basis, spend a substantial

amount of time there, and use the station as a "home base." As long as the station remains attended during normal business hours, the staff person may also take on responsibilities for another organization. For example, the staff person may be a receptionist for more than one organization.

3. The main studio must have the capability to originate programming.

4. Each station must maintain a local or toll-free telephone number in its community of license.

B. *Public Inspection File*

Recent Rule Change. The following discussion concerns the FCC's revised but not yet effective public file rule. See comment under Main Studio Requirements.

1. *Location.* Every station must maintain a public inspection file at its main studio, wherever the studio is located. This is a change from the current rule that requires the public file to be maintained at an accessible location within the station's community of license. The new rule applies even if a licensee has a waiver of the main studio rule allowing operation of a station from a studio located a significant distance from the community of license. (Note: Although the text of the FCC's Report and Order seems quite clear on allowing the public file to be maintained at the remote studio location where a main studio waiver exists, and makes specific accommodation for the relaxation of the rule as discussed in the next paragraph, the FCC's staff has questioned informally whether this is, in fact, what the Commission intended. However, absent further clarification from the FCC to the contrary, stations should be able to rely on the explicit language contained in the FCC's Report and Order that allows for the remote location of public files.)

2. *Availability.* While the new rule allows for the maintenance of the public file at the main studio, it imposes additional requirements for making the public file available. Under the current rule, the public file must be available during normal business hours to all members of the public who request to see it; stations must allow those inspecting the public file to make copies of any material in the file; stations may charge a reasonable photocopying fee; and, if there is no photocopying equipment where the public file is located, the station must supply the requested copies within seven days of a request. A station may request those inspecting the file to provide their name and address, but it may not ask the reason for the inspection, the reason a particular document is requested, or the name of the organization with which a person is affiliated. While these requirements remain, the new rule imposes the additional requirement that stations make photocopies of public file documents available by mail upon receiving a telephone request for such documents. A station may require the person requesting the documents to pay reasonable photocopying expenses (before the documents are sent), but the station must pay the postage. An exception to this is the revised edition of "The Public and Broadcasting," which stations must make available free of charge

to callers requesting it. Stations must also assist callers seeking information about the public file, including providing information about the file's contents. (Note: The FCC has stayed the effective date of the new rule until November 4, 1998, only as it applies to responding to telephone inquiries concerning the political file component of a station's public file; all other aspects of the new rule are expected to become effective in mid-October.)

3. *Contents.* Generally, under the new rule, the public file must contain in an orderly and organized manner the following documents: a station's current authorization and any modifications or conditions on the authorization (new requirement); applications filed with the FCC and related amendments and correspondence; the most recent and complete ownership report and a copy or list of contracts filed with the FCC (if only a list is maintained in the public file, copies of the contracts must be available upon request); requests for time from candidates for political office and a report on how the station responded to the requests; annual employment reports filed with the FCC and related exhibits and correspondence; the station's quarterly programs/issues lists; a copy of all written comments and suggestions received from the public, including e-mail communications, regarding the station's operation; a copy of each time brokerage agreement related to the licensee's station or involving programming of another station in the same market by the licensee; a certification that the required public notices were broadcast on the station before and after the filing of the station's license renewal application; the FCC's revised procedure manual "The Public and Broadcasting"; a copy of any current service contour maps submitted with any application filed with the FCC, and other information in the application showing service contours and the locations of the main studio and transmitter site (new requirement); and material that has a substantial bearing on a matter that is the subject of an FCC investigation or a complaint to the FCC about which the station has received notice (new).

4. *Electronic Public File.* The new rule gives stations the option of maintaining all or part of their public file in computer databases. A station that elects this option must make a computer terminal available for public review of the file and must provide paper copies of public file materials upon request. With specific reference to the e-mail communications from the public required to be maintained as noted in paragraph 3, stations may retain these communications in a paper file or a computer file. If a computer file is used, stations have the option of making the e-mail communications available to the public on a computer diskette or via a computer terminal where the messages can be reviewed. If a station maintains its entire public file in computer databases, the applicable requirements will satisfy the separate requirements applicable to maintaining copies of e-mail communications.

A more detailed explanation of the new public file rule appears in the special Mid-August issue of *Arter & Hadden Antenna.*

C. *Posting Station Licenses*

The FCC requires all stations to post in a conspicuous place at the principal control point all licenses and other instruments of authorization. This includes the FCC license, license renewal authorizations, FCC acknowledgment of receipt of renewal applications, construction permits, FCC consents to an assignment of license or transfer of control, experimental authorizations, special temporary authorizations, any FCC grant of a waiver, and any other official FCC document specifying the station's operation. In lieu of posting the licenses on a wall, you may keep them in a binder or folder at the posting location. For more information on the posting of station licenses, please see the attached article from the June, 1997 *Arter & Hadden Antenna.*

D. *Chief Operator*

1. *Written Designation.* Each AM, FM and TV station must designate a person to serve as the station's chief operator. The licensee must also designate another person as the acting chief operator on a temporary basis when the chief operator is unavailable or unable to act *(e.g.,* vacations, sickness). The designation of the chief operator must be in writing with a copy of the designation posted with the station's license. Any agreements with a chief operator hired on a contract basis (see below) must also be in writing and kept in the station's files.

2. *Employee/Contract Requirement.* Whether a chief operator must be a station employee or can be hired on a contract basis depends on the type of station. For an AM station using a directional antenna or operating with greater than 10 kW authorized power, the chief operator must be an employee. For a nondirectional AM station operating with authorized power not exceeding 10 kW, or for an FM station, the chief operator may be either an employee *or* hired on a contract basis.

3. *Duty Hours.* The chief operator must be on duty for whatever number of hours per week the licensee determines is necessary to keep the station's technical operation in compliance with the FCC's rules and the terms of the station's authorization.

4. *Duties.* The chief operator's primary duties include: inspection, calibration, repair and adjustment of the transmission system, required monitors, and metering and control systems; periodic AM field monitoring and equipment performance measurements; review of the station's records at least once each week to determine if required entries are made correctly; verification that the station is operating as required under the FCC's rules and the station's license; and making required entries in the station's log.

E. *Station Logs and Records*

1. *General.* Every station must have a station log that is kept by station employees competent to do so who have actual knowledge of the facts required. All log entries must accurately reflect a station's operation and be signed by the employee making the entry. The log must be kept in an orderly and legible manner. No portion of a log may be

erased, obliterated, or destroyed during the applicable retention period. Changes or corrections to the log are permitted only under specified conditions. The station log is *not* part of the station's public file, but must be available to the FCC upon request.

2. *Contents.* Station logs must contain entries regarding equipment status, equipment calibration, tests and activation of the Emergency Alert System, tower light outages (note that daily inspections of tower lights or an automatic indicator that registers outages, or use of an automatic alarm system to detect a lighting failure is required but need not be recorded in the log), AM directional field strength measurements, and any other matters required in the station's authorization. Entries may be made manually or automatically but must include the time of the observation. Entries regarding operating parameters must be made prior to any adjustments to the equipment. Adjustments to equipment and the nature of corrective action taken, if any deviation was beyond a prescribed tolerance, must also be logged. A directional AM station without an FCC approved antenna sampling system must make a number of entries specifically related to its operation.

3. *Storage Format.* Station logs may be retained on microfiche, microfilm, or other data storage systems subject to certain conditions, including the availability of viewing devices and full-size reproductions.

4. *Retention Period.* Station logs must be retained for a period of two years unless the logs involve communications incident to a disaster, or incident to or in connection with an investigation by the FCC, in which case the logs are retained until the station is specifically notified by the FCC that they may be destroyed. Logs incident to or involved in a claim or complaint should be retained until the claim or complaint is fully satisfied or it is barred under the applicable statute of limitations.

F. *Emergency Alert System (EAS)*

The EAS provides a means for national, state, and local government officials or their designated representatives to provide emergency communications to the public concerning national, state, or local emergencies. The EAS replaced the emergency broadcast system (EBS).

1. *EAS Handbook.* Stations must keep a copy of the EAS Operating Handbook at normal duty positions or at the EAS equipment location. This handbook is issued by the FCC and contains a summary of the actions station personnel must take upon receiving an Emergency Alert Notification (a national emergency), state or local area alert, and EAS tests. Stations must monitor the two EAS sources assigned pursuant to the monitoring priorities in the EAS Handbook. On September 3, 1998, the FCC issued a Public Notice stating that with the concurrence of the Federal Emergency Management Agency (FEMA) and the White House Communications Agency (WHCA), the FCC will no longer distribute Emergency Alert System authenticator lists (also known as the red envelopes), which previously had to be kept with the EAS Handbook.

2. *Equipment.* Generally, all stations must have operational EAS equipment that is certified by the FCC and is capable of sending and receiving EAS messages using the digital EAS protocol. This equipment may operate either manually or automatically, but must be operational during all hours of broadcast operations. Manually operated equipment must be located so that station staff at normal duty locations are alerted immediately when EAS messages are received and can initiate the EAS code and Attention Signal transmission. Co-owned and co-located stations that have a combined studio or control facility may use a single EAS monitor (decoder) and signal generator (encoder).

The FCC will consider requests for waivers of the EAS equipment requirement for satellite stations that are operated from and rebroadcast the signal of a primary station. If a waiver is granted, it will be conditioned on the continuation of the specific mode of operation described in the waiver request. If later changes occur regarding any factor that the FCC considered in granting the waiver, the waiver will terminate, although the licensee of the satellite station may reapply for a new waiver.

3. *Participation.* Unless specifically exempted by the FCC, all stations are categorized as Participating National (PN) sources and must remain on-the-air and provide necessary information during a national level Emergency Activation Notification (EAN). A Non-Participating station must go off-the-air during such a condition. Stations may choose whether to participate in state and local area EAS plans. However, all stations must monitor for state and local EAS activations. When a state or local level activation is received, participating stations must take action under the state or local plan and discontinue normal programming. The FCC must review and approve state and local EAS plans. Stations may activate the EAS at the state or local area at their discretion for day-to-day emergency situations that pose a threat to life and property.

4. *Tests.* All stations are required to participate in the weekly and monthly EAS tests. Weekly tests are conducted at random days and times. The monthly tests are conducted as coordinated by the Emergency Communications Committee for each state. The weekly test is optional during weeks the monthly test is conducted. If the monthly test is conducted in an odd-numbered month, it must occur between 8:30 A.M. and sunset, and during an even-numbered month, it must occur between local sunset and 8:30 A.M. *Note:* Since stations are required to monitor two EAS sources, each station should receive at least one weekly test from each of the two stations. The monthly test may result in only one test being received that week.

5. *Log.* All stations must keep a log, either manually or automatically, of all EAS tests that are received or initiated by the station. The EAS test data may be contained in the official station log or a separate log that is then considered part of the station log. The log also must contain

a description of why any test activation was not received, any corrective action taken, and the date and time defective equipment was removed from the station and restored to service.

6. *Defective Equipment.* A station may operate with defective EAS equipment for no more than 60 days. If the equipment cannot be restored within that time period due to circumstances beyond the licensee's control, the station must request an extension of the 60-day period from the FCC's District Director. The request for extension must contain the steps taken to repair or replace the defective equipment, the alternative procedures in use while the equipment is out of service, and an estimate of when the equipment will be repaired or replaced.

G. *Equal Employment Opportunities (EEO)*

Recent Court Ruling. In April 1998, a three-judge panel of the U.S. Court of Appeals issued a decision in *Lutheran Church-Missouri Synod v. FCC,* holding that the FCC's EEO program requirements are unconstitutional. Because the FCC requested the entire court to rehear the case, the three-judge panel's decision was not immediately effective. In September 1998, by a 6–4 vote, the court denied the FCC's request and refused to rehear the case. As a result, the Court's original decision holding the FCC's EEO program requirements unconstitutional became effective on September 23, 1998.

However, the scope of the Court's ruling is not entirely clear. In particular, it is uncertain whether it applies to all of the FCC's EEO requirements, or only the "EEO program requirements" as the Court stated (which is subsection (c) of the FCC's EEO rule). If the latter, then the FCC's general requirement (subsection (b) of the rule) that all stations establish, maintain, and carry out a continuing EEO program would remain. Further, the Court indicated that it was not ruling on the FCC's nondiscrimination requirement (subsection (a) of the rule), but instead remanded the case for the FCC to determine the scope of its authority to promulgate a nondiscrimination rule.

As of the writing of this guide, the FCC is in the process of determining how it will respond to the Court's ruling. Possible options include an appeal to the U.S. Supreme Court (which decision is not within the FCC's sole jurisdiction but also involves other U.S. agencies, departments, and the Solicitor General), or adopting new EEO requirements that the FCC believes address the Court's concerns (prior to the Court's decision, the FCC had initiated a rule-making proceeding that looked toward possibly modifying and simplifying its EEO requirements). It is also unclear as to the extent to which the FCC will enforce those portions of its EEO rules left intact after the Court's ruling. It is expected that the FCC will issue future public notices explaining how it intends to proceed and describing broadcasters' EEO responsibilities. This is a regulatory area in a state of flux, and all broadcasters should continue to monitor how the FCC responds. Broadcasters should also remember that the ruling discussed above does not affect any employment regulations that agencies other than the FCC (such as the federal EEOC or state law) may impose.

Despite the uncertain status of the FCC's EEO rules as of this writing, the following discussion summarizes the rules and FCC procedures that were the subject of the *Lutheran Church* case. As noted, the future of these requirements will ultimately depend on the scope of the Court's ruling, the FCC's response to that ruling, and possible further litigation before the Supreme Court.

1. *EEO Program.* Each station is required to establish, maintain, and carry out a continuing program of practices designed to ensure equal employment opportunities. The program should include defining each level of management's responsibility to implement and enforce the program; advising employees and employee organizations of the station's EEO policy and program and enlisting their cooperation; communicating the EEO policies and program and the station's employment needs to and requesting recruitment assistance from sources of qualified applicants without respect to race, color, religion, national origin, or sex; an ongoing program to exclude all illegal forms of prejudice or discrimination in personnel policies, practices, and working conditions; and an ongoing review of job structure and employment practices and the adoption of appropriate measures to ensure equal employment opportunity. For stations with five or more full-time employees, the EEO program is usually submitted to the FCC with an application for a new station or the acquisition of an existing station. The FCC does not require the hiring of any particular person, and does not require a station to give a hiring preference to any person or group of persons. It is assumed that having a diverse and qualified applicant pool will, absent discrimination, result in a diverse station workforce.

2. *Recruiting.* A station must follow its EEO program whenever a job opening occurs (part-time or full-time). That is, for each employment position that becomes available, a station should contact each recruiting source listed in its EEO program seeking qualified applicants. All station personnel involved in the hiring process should be aware of the station's EEO program and follow its procedures.

3. *Documentation.* A station must keep adequate records to document the performance of its EEO program. Generally, this means a record of the gender, minority status, and referral source of job applicants and the persons interviewed for each position. The failure to maintain adequate records is an area where broadcasters have received fines and admonishments from the FCC. A station may receive numerous referrals from its recruiting sources, but if it does not have records that reflect those results, it may have difficulty documenting the performance of its EEO program if questions arise.

4. *Self-Assessment.* A station must review the performance of its EEO program on a continuing basis to assess whether it is working effectively to produce a qualified and diverse applicant pool. If not, a station should modify its program and expand or change its recruiting sources to improve the program.

5. *FCC Enforcement.* The FCC generally reviews a station's EEO performance when it is also reviewing a station's license renewal application, although it can also review EEO matters in the context of a station sale or transfer of control. The FCC's primary emphasis in enforcing the EEO rules is station efforts. This means recruiting for job openings using the referral sources in a station's EEO program whenever job openings occur, monitoring and assessing the results of those recruitment efforts on an ongoing basis, and modifying an EEO program that is not working effectively. Even if a station has a diverse workforce, it must continue to implement its EEO program. The FCC can impose a variety of penalties against a station that fails to adhere to the EEO rules, including a monetary fine (forfeiture), reporting conditions, and a short-term license renewal. If there is evidence of discrimination or extremely serious EEO violations, the FCC may designate a license renewal application for hearing to determine whether renewal is warranted (it was in such a context that the *Lutheran Church-Missouri Synod* case arose).

In February 1998, the FCC announced a modification of its enforcement of the EEO rules with respect to religious broadcasters. The FCC stated that religious broadcasters may establish for all employees a religious belief or affiliation job qualification. The FCC did not intend this as a blanket exemption from the EEO rules, and does not permit religious broadcasters to engage in discrimination against women or minorities. The requirement to engage in active recruitment still applies without regard to race, color, national origin, or gender among those who share the relevant religious affiliation or belief.

In addition to the foregoing, the FCC has a working arrangement with the federal EEOC whereby the two agencies will share information concerning complaints of discrimination. Generally, if there is a discrimination complaint against a broadcaster pending before the EEOC when the FCC considers a station's license renewal application, the FCC may condition any action on the renewal on the final outcome of the EEOC discrimination complaint. The FCC may also undertake its own investigation independent of the EEOC.

II. DAILY OPERATING REQUIREMENTS

A. *Attended or Unattended Operation*

1. *General.* A broadcast station's transmission system may be operated in either an attended or unattended mode. Whichever mode of operation is employed, licensees must employ procedures that will ensure compliance with the rules governing the Emergency Alert System (EAS).

2. *Attended Operation:* A designated person is responsible for the proper operation of the transmitting apparatus either at the transmitter site, a remote control point, or an automatic transmission system control point. Supervision may be by automated equipment that is configured to contact a designated person. A person must be on duty at a fixed location during all hours of broadcast operation to control the transmitter and monitor the station operating parameters, or to be contacted by automated equipment. The transmitter must be turned off within three hours of a technical malfunction that can cause interference that cannot be corrected within that three-hour period.

3. *Unattended Operation.* Unattended operation is permitted when highly stable equipment or automated monitoring of the station's operating parameters is used. Automated equipment must be configured to take the station off the air within three hours of any technical malfunction that is capable of causing interference. No prior FCC approval is required for unattended operation.

B. *Station Identification*

All stations are required to broadcast an identification announcement at the beginning and end of each time of operation and hourly during a natural break in programming, as close to the "top of the hour" as possible. The announcement must contain the station's call letters followed immediately by the station's community of license. A station may insert the licensee's name, or the frequency or channel number between the call letters and community of license, but nothing else. However, at the end of the announcement (*i.e.,* after the name of the station's community of license) a station may include any additional communities.

C. *Sponsorship Identification*

Any material broadcast in exchange for money, services, or other valuable consideration paid to a broadcast station, directly or indirectly, must be accompanied by a sponsorship identification announcement that identifies the matter as sponsored, paid for, or furnished, and fully and fairly discloses who paid or on whose behalf the consideration was paid. For commercial products or services advertisements, an announcement that states the sponsor's corporate or trade name, or the name of the sponsor's product, if the announcement clearly constitutes a sponsorship identification, is sufficient to meet the requirement. Certain additional requirements apply to political matter, including candidate and issue advertisements, which are not discussed here in detail. The sponsorship identification requirement also relates to rules and policies governing "payola" and "plugola," which are discussed separately in Part III.

D. *Tower Registration. Marking and Lighting*

1. *Registration.* Owners of tower structures over 200 feet must register the tower with the FCC. All proposed and altered antenna structures over 200 feet must be registered with the FCC prior to building or modifying the structure. The tower registration number must be displayed prominently so that it is visible near the base of the tower. It should be placed on the gate or fence leading to the tower if the tower is not easily seen from outside of the property where the tower is located.

2. *Tower Marking.* All broadcast towers must be painted and lighted in accordance with the specifications shown on the station's authorization or as required in the FAA's determination of "no hazard" for the tower. If the tower owner is unable to maintain the appropriate

marking and lighting, each tenant licensee must undertake efforts to maintain the painting and lighting. If a licensee believes the structure is not properly marked or lit, it must notify the owner, the site management company (if applicable), and the FCC, and make a diligent effort to ensure that the antenna structure is brought into compliance. If no painting or lighting is required, then the station's authorization will specify "NONE" or "NONE REQUIRED." The FCC requires all towers to be cleaned or repainted as required to maintain good visibility for aircraft.

3. *Lighting Check.* The lighting on tower structures should be observed at least once in every 24-hour period by either physical observation, an automatic indicating device, or an automatic alarm system. All automatic or mechanical monitoring devices must be inspected at least every three months.

4. *FAA Notification.* A tower owner must notify the nearest FAA Flight Service Station within 30 minutes of learning of an improperly functioning or extinguished top steady burning light or flashing obstruction light regardless of its position on the tower, with a follow-up notification when the lights are restored to the proper function. Notification is not required if steady burning side intermediate lights are improperly functioning, but their function must be restored as soon as possible.

5. *Log Entries.* The owner of a tower with lighting specifications must enter in the station's log any observed or known lighting malfunction of any tower light regardless of its position on the tower, including the nature of the malfunction, the date and time the malfunction was observed or otherwise noted, and the date, time, and nature of the adjustments, repairs, or replacements made.

6. *Fencing.* AM stations using antenna towers with RF potential at the base of the tower (series fed, folded unipole, and insulated base antennas) must enclose such towers within an effective locked fence or other enclosure, unless the tower is enclosed within a protective property fence. Fencing must be capable of preventing access by small children and livestock. Ready access must be provided to each tower for meter reading and maintenance purposes. Fencing around other towers is recommended to prevent unauthorized access.

III. OTHER GENERAL OPERATING REQUIREMENTS

A. *Programming Matters*

1. *Quarterly Issues/Programs List*

All stations must prepare a list of approximately five to ten issues of importance to the station's community of license and the nonentertainment programming broadcast on the station responsive to those issues. The list should enumerate the programs that provided the station's most "significant treatment" of the listed issues during the three months covered. There is no specific requirement as to how a station ascertains which issues are of importance in its community. The intent is that a station will use the ascertained issues to determine its nonentertainment programming that addresses community needs and issues. The list must be placed in the station's public inspection file by the tenth day following the close of each calendar quarter (January 10, April 10, July 10, and October 10). For more information concerning the quarterly issues/programs list requirements, see the article in the October 1995 *Arter & Hadden Antenna* entitled "Quarterly Issues/Programs Lists."

2. *Broadcasts of Telephone Conversations*

A licensee must inform any party to a telephone conversation that it intends to broadcast the conversation or record it for broadcast *before* actually broadcasting or recording the conversation. It is a violation of the rule if a station calls a party during a broadcast and immediately informs them that they are on the air, or if a station records a conversation and informs the called party prior to the broadcast, but after the conversation is recorded, that it will be broadcast. An exception applies when the other party is aware or may be presumed to be aware from the circumstances of the conversation that it is being or likely will be broadcast. Such awareness is presumed to exist when the other party is associated with the station, or originated the call, and it is obvious that it is in connection with a program in which the station regularly broadcasts telephone conversations.

3. *Broadcast of Lottery Information*

Subject to various exceptions, a station may not broadcast any material that concerns a lottery. A lottery has three elements — prize, chance, and consideration — and includes such activities as bingo and casino gambling. Whether a particular broadcast is prohibited depends on the facts of each case and, if a lottery is involved, whether one of the exceptions applies. The exceptions include lotteries conducted by a state or a not-for-profit organization, Indian gaming activities if certain requirements are met, and promotions by commercial organizations that are occasional and ancillary to the organization's primary business. For these exceptions to apply various conditions must be met, which often include issues of state law. If you have questions whether a broadcast involves a lottery or is prohibited, please call us before broadcasting the material.

4. *Broadcasts of Promotions and Contests*

A contest includes any scheme in which a prize is offered or awarded to the public based upon chance, diligence, knowledge, or skill. A contest differs from a lottery in that at least one of the three elements required for a lottery does not exist (*i.e.*, prize, chance, or consideration). A licensee that broadcasts or advertises information about a contest that it conducts must accurately describe the contest so that no description is false, misleading, or deceptive with respect to any material term. A station must disclose the material terms of the contest in a reasonable number of announcements in all dayparts and must conduct the contest substantially as announced or advertised. Stations must announce the material terms when describing the conditions or terms of the contest, but not when the station simply promotes the contest.

Note: While this is not an FCC requirement, you should be aware that when a station sponsors or conducts a contest in which a prize worth $600 or more is awarded, or an individual wins several prizes with an aggregate value of $600 or more, the station must file federal tax Forms 1099 and 1096 MISC.

5. *Broadcasts of Hoaxes*

A station may not broadcast false information concerning a crime or catastrophe if it knows the information is false and it is foreseeable that broadcast of the information will cause substantial public harm. Programming accompanied by a disclaimer is presumed not to pose foreseeable harm if the disclaimer characterizes the program as fiction and is presented in a manner that is reasonable under the circumstances. The rule is not intended to restrict "harmless pranks."

6. *Political Broadcasts*

a. *General.* The FCC's rules governing political broadcasts apply to legally qualified candidates for public office. These rules are summarized briefly below. The rules are complex, particularly those pertaining to the lowest unit rate that must be charged to candidates (see (c) and (d) below). Failure to comply with these rules can result in lengthy and costly legal proceedings before the FCC, and potential forfeitures and refunds if a violation is found. We recommend that prior to an election year station managers and sales managers refamiliarize themselves and all affected station personnel with the political rules and establish a uniform procedure for handling candidate advertising. We suggest that you contact us if any questions arise about the application of these rules in a particular situation.

b. *Equal Opportunities.* If a licensee allows a legally qualified candidate for office to use its station, it must give an equal opportunity to that candidate's opponents to use the station. This rule does not apply if a candidate's appearance is during a bona fide newscast, bona fide news interview, bona fide news documentary (if the candidate's appearance is incidental to the subject of the documentary), or on-the-spot coverage of a bona fide news event.

c. *Lowest Unit Rate.* Stations may charge candidates for the use of the station in connection with a campaign. In general, a station must treat candidates the same as it treats commercial advertisers, except that during prescribed periods prior to a primary election (45 days) and general election (60 days), candidates may be charged no more than the lowest unit rate for the class and type of time (spot) purchased.

d. *Disclosure Requirements.* If time is sold to a candidate, a station must disclose to that candidate information about the station's rates, terms, conditions, and any value-enhancing discounts offered to commercial advertisers. The disclosure must include information about: (1) the classes of time available; (2) the lowest unit charge and related privileges for each class of time; (3) how the station sells preemptible time; (4) the approximate likelihood of preemption for each class of preemptible time; and (5) an explanation of any station sales policies based on audience delivery.

e. *Political File.* Stations must keep and permit public inspection of a political file that contains records of all requests for broadcast time by candidates for public office, the schedule of the time purchased, and the station's disposition of the request, including whether free time was provided, the rates charged, when spots or candidate uses actually aired, and the classes of time purchased. This information must be placed in the file promptly.

Although the political file requirements remain unchanged, the new public file rule could impact how candidates obtain or meet the requirements for obtaining their equal opportunity rights. Under the new rule, if a candidate requests that a station mail information from the station's political file as to the candidate's opponent's use of the station, the station would have seven days in which to respond. Thus, the information might arrive too late for the candidate to review the material and assert any applicable equal opportunity rights within the required seven days of the initial candidate use that triggers those rights. Candidates can avoid this problem by requesting a station to provide the relevant information over the phone, or as was the case prior to the rule change, reviewing the political file in person. The FCC has not addressed directly this potential issue, although as discussed previously, it has stayed the effective date of the requirement to provide a telephonic or mailed response to a request for information from the political file until November 4, 1998.

f. *Reasonable Access.* Stations are required to provide candidates for federal elective office (*i.e.*, President, Vice President, and Congress) reasonable access to broadcast time. This does not apply to candidates for state or local office; *i.e.*, a station may decide not to allow the use of a station by any candidate for a state or local office. However, in determining whether to provide access to state or local candidates, stations should consider the significance of the particular election and their general public interest obligation to provide programming responsive to significant issues of local concern. Stations should also remember that if one state or local candidate is permitted to use the station, equal opportunity rights will then apply to all legally qualified opposing candidates.

g. *Political Editorials.* If a station endorses or opposes a legally qualified candidate in an editorial, within 24 hours of the broadcast the licensee must transmit to the other qualified candidates for the same office or to the candidate opposed in the editorial, (i) notification of the date and time of the editorial, (ii) a tape or script of the editorial, and (iii) an offer of a reasonable opportunity for the candidate to respond over the licensee's facilities.

7. *Payola and Plugola.*

a. *Payola.* Payola is the unreported receipt or payment of money or other valuable consideration in exchange for the broadcast of any programming. Any person who has paid, accepted, or agreed to pay or accept consideration for the broadcast of programming must report that fact to the station's licensee before the programming in question is broadcast. The failure to report such payments or consideration is a violation of the Communications Act and could subject both the licensee and the persons involved to criminal prosecution.

b. *Plugola.* Plugola occurs if a station employee promotes over-the-air an activity or matter in which he or she has a direct or indirect interest. The FCC views plugola as a conflict of interest and violation of the sponsorship identification requirements if the interest is not disclosed and the proper announcements are not made.

c. *Licensee Responsibility.* Licensees are required to use reasonable diligence on a continuing basis to obtain from station employees and other persons with whom a station deals sufficient information to ensure that the station complies with the prohibitions against payola and plugola. We recommend that stations routinely remind employees in writing of the prohibitions and obtain, particularly from on-air personnel, affidavits attesting that the employee has neither received nor paid consideration for the broadcast of any programming and has not promoted any activity or matter in which the employee has an interest. We can provide you with a form of affidavit if you do not already have one.

8. *Obscene and Indecent Programming.*

a. *General.* Obscene programming and indecent programming are not legally the same. Obscene programming is prohibited at all times and is not constitutionally protected. Indecent programming is constitutionally protected and may be broadcast during the hours of 10:00 P.M. to 6:00 A.M. If you have a question whether program material is obscene or indecent, you should not broadcast the material between 6:00 A.M. and 10:00 P.M., and we recommend that you consult with counsel to determine whether that the material is obscene and therefore strictly prohibited.

b. *Indecency.* Program material is indecent if "it describes, in terms patently offensive as measured by contemporary community standards for the broadcast medium, sexual or excretory activities and organs, at times of the day when there is a reasonable risk that children may be in the audience."

c. *Obscenity.* Program matter is obscene if it meets the following three-part test:

(i) the average person, applying contemporary community standards, would find that the material appeals to the prurient interest;

(ii) the material describes or depicts sexual conduct in a patently offensive manner; and

(iii) taken as a whole, the material lacks serious literary, artistic, political, or scientific value.

9. *Advertising of Alcoholic Beverages*

There are no FCC or other federal prohibitions currently in effect on broadcast advertising for alcoholic beverages. However, state laws may exist that restrict the advertising of alcoholic beverages in some respects. Although proposed new laws governing the advertising of alcoholic beverages on broadcast stations frequently arise in Congress, no such laws have passed to date.

10. *Advertising of Tobacco Products*

The advertising of cigarettes, little cigars, and smokeless tobacco products (such as chewing tobacco and snuff) on broadcast stations is prohibited under federal law. Pipe tobacco and cigars (not subject to the definition of little cigars) are not covered under this prohibition. The incidental mention of a cigarette product as part of a program title (*e.g.*, Winston Cup Racing, Virginia Slims Tennis Tournament, etc.) is generally assumed to be permitted as long as it does not constitute a commercial for the product, but it is recommended that a station minimize the mentions of the name of the cigarette product. The Justice Department, rather than the FCC, has jurisdiction for enforcing the prohibition against tobacco advertising.

11. *False or Deceptive Advertising*

Although the FCC no longer has a rule that prohibits false and deceptive advertising, stations still have a responsibility under their general public interest obligations not to broadcast advertising that is known to be false or misleading. If a broadcaster participates in a scheme or promotion that is ultimately found to be illegal and is convicted, the FCC may take this into consideration in determining whether a licensee is qualified or should have its license canceled or revoked.

B. *Technical/Engineering Matters*

1. *Transmission System Inspections and Equipment Performance Measurements*

a. *Inspections.* All stations are required to conduct periodic inspections of their transmitting systems and all required monitors to ensure that stations are operating properly. Licensees have discretion to make these inspections as they deem appropriate to ensure proper station operation.

b. *Performance Measurements.* Licensees are required to make equipment performance measurements for each main transmitter that a station has at certain specified times, including the initial installation of a new or replacement main transmitter, modification of a transmitter as permitted under the FCC's rules, and annually for AM stations (with not more than fourteen months between measurements). The specific technical data required in conducting the tests, and a description of the equipment and procedure used in making the measurements, signed and dated by a qualified person making the measurements, must be kept on file at the transmitter or remote control point for a period of two years and be made available to the FCC upon request.

2. *Minimum Operating Schedule*

   a. *Minimum Requirements.* All radio stations are required to operate for a minimum number of hours each day of the week except Sunday, as follows:

   (i) For AM and FM stations other than daytime-only stations, at least eight hours between 6 A.M. and 6 P.M., and four hours between 6 P.M. and midnight.

   (ii) For daytime-only stations, a minimum of two-thirds of the total hours the station is authorized to operate between 6 A.M. and 6 P.M., and two-thirds of the total hours it is authorized to operate between 6 P.M. and midnight.

   b. *Off-Air Procedures.* Stations that are unable to meet the minimum operating schedule or to continue operating may limit or discontinue their operation for no more than 30 days without FCC authority. However, the station must notify the FCC of its status no later than the tenth day of limited or discontinued operation. During this period, the station's tower must remain lighted as specified in the station's license. If normal operation is resumed prior to the end of the 30-day period, the licensee must notify the FCC of the date normal operations resumed. If it is not possible to resume normal operation before the end of the 30-day period, then an informal request to the FCC for authority to remain off-the-air for longer than 30 days must be filed.

   c. *Automatic License Termination.* If a station fails to operate for twelve consecutive months, its license is automatically terminated at the end of that 12-month period.

3. *Modification of Station Transmission Systems*

   a. *General.* There are three categories of station modifications: (1) those that require prior FCC approval; (2) those that a licensee may do on its own and then file a license application with the FCC; and (3) those that a licensee may do on its own and then simply notify the FCC of the change. Before making any change in a station's facilities, a licensee should check with counsel to determine in which of these categories a particular modification falls.

   b. *Prior FCC Approval.* Changes that require prior FCC approval include construction of a new tower (except for the replacement of an existing tower with a new tower having the same height and geographic coordinates), a change in the geographic coordinates of a tower including coordinate corrections, relocation of a directional FM antenna to a different tower even with the same coordinates, certain changes in directional antennas, and certain increases and decreases in power.

c. *Modification by License Application.* There are a number of different types of modifications that a licensee may make without prior FCC approval conditioned on the filing of a license application within 10 days of beginning operation with the modified facilities. These include replacing an omnidirectional antenna if the antenna radiation center is no more than two meters higher or four meters lower than is authorized, replacing a directional FM antenna if certain conditions are met, and certain power increases and decreases for FM stations.

d. *Modification Upon Notification.* A station may change its main studio location within its principal community contour, begin remote control operation, or modify an AM directional antenna sampling system without prior FCC approval, provided the changes are made in compliance with the FCC's rules and the FCC is notified of the changes.

IV. PERIODIC FCC FILING AND REPORTING REQUIREMENTS

A. *Employment Reports*

Every station is required to file with the FCC an annual employment report. Those stations with five or more full-time employees must identify the total number of employees at the station, both full- and part-time, and the race, gender, and job category for each employee (the employees need not be identified). Beginning in 1998, the annual employment report must be filed no later than September 30. Previously, the FCC required the filing of these reports no later than May 31. Copies of the annual employment reports must be kept in the station's public file. Note: Following the Court of Appeals' decision in *Lutheran Church-Missouri Synod* (discussed previously), some have questioned whether the FCC may continue to require broadcasters to file annual employment reports. However, this rule was not at issue in the court proceeding, and until such time as the FCC says otherwise, broadcasters should continue to file the report.

B. *Ownership Reports*

Every licensee that is not a sole proprietorship is required to file with the FCC an annual ownership report. If no changes have occurred since the filing of the licensee's previous ownership report, a licensee may file a certification to that effect in lieu of the annual report. The due date for the annual ownership filing varies by state and falls on the anniversary of the date of filing for a station's license renewal application. Licensees are also required to file an ownership report after the grant of an initial construction permit for a new station, concurrent with a license application for a new station, and following the consummation of an assignment of a station's license or a transfer of control. A $45 filing fee must accompany the annual ownership filing, but not any of the other ownership filings. Copies of all ownership reports or certifications and related exhibits and correspondence to or from the FCC must be kept in the station's public file.

C. *Regulatory Fees*

All stations are required to pay an annual regulatory fee. The payment is made in September, with the specific due date and amount of the payment usually determined in a rule-making proceeding that the FCC conducts earlier in the year. The amount of the regulatory fee depends on the type and class of station, as well as the station's market size. Holders of construction permits for new stations are also required to pay annual regulatory fees. Regulatory fees also apply to all FCC authorizations a licensee holds, including broadcast auxiliary facilities (*e.g.*, STL, intercity relay, remotes) and other microwave facilities or business radio licenses.

D. *License Renewal*

1. *License Term.* Broadcast station licenses are now granted for a period of eight years (prior to 1996, radio licenses were granted for seven years and television licenses for five years). The license periods for broadcast stations are staggered over several years and different months based on the state in which a station is located (*e.g.*, all radio licenses for stations located in New York expired June 1, 1998, while licenses for television stations in New York expire June 1, 1999).

2. *License Renewal Application.* Four months prior to the expiration of a station's license, the licensee must file an application for license renewal. The FCC usually mails to each licensee a booklet containing the relevant applications and forms that must be filed as part of the license renewal application, and other information and instructions relevant to the renewal process. Among other things, a licensee must certify that it has filed all required reports with the FCC, that its public file is complete and all required documents were placed in the public file in a timely manner (*e.g.*, the quarterly problems-programs lists), whether the station is operating, and that the station is in compliance with the FCC's standards for limiting public and occupational exposure to RF (radio frequency) radiation.

3. *EEO Report.* With the renewal application licensees must file a report (Form 396) on the performance of their EEO program during the preceding year, including the recruitment sources contacted, the number of minority and female applicant referrals obtained from those sources, the number of job hires and promotions the station made over the past year, both overall and among minorities and women, any complaints of employment discrimination against the station, and any other information relevant to the station's EEO program. Note: In light of the court's decision in *Luther Church-Missouri Synod*, it is uncertain at this time whether the FCC may continue to require the filing of the EEO Report as part of the license renewal application. However, until

such time as the FCC says otherwise, it is recommended that licensees submit Form 396 with their renewal application.

4. *Public Notice Announcements.* The FCC requires stations to broadcast public notices announcing that they will soon file and then have filed their renewal applications. These public notices must be broadcast on the first and sixteenth days of the two months preceding the filing of the renewal application and the three months after the renewal application is filed. A certification attesting to the date and time these announcements were broadcast must be placed in a station's public file.

5. *FCC Review.* The FCC will grant a renewal application if it finds that: (1) the station has served the public interest, convenience, and necessity; (2) the licensee has not committed any serious violations of the Communications Act or the FCC's rules and regulations; and (3) the licensee has not committed any other violations of the Communications Act or the FCC's rules and policies that taken together would constitute a pattern of abuse. If a licensee fails to meet this standard, the FCC may grant the renewal but assess a monetary forfeiture against the licensee, grant the renewal for a shorter term than the normal eight years, or in the most serious cases, designate the renewal application for a hearing to determine whether license renewal is warranted. In 1996, Congress amended the Communications Act to preclude the filing of any other applications that conflict with a license renewal application.

V. CONCLUSION

It is important to remember that this memorandum provides only a brief overview of each of the rules and regulatory requirements discussed. The FCC periodically reviews its existing rules and adopts new rules that affect the requirements discussed in this memorandum or which may impose new requirements. It is the responsibility of every licensee to understand and comply with all of the FCC's rules and policies. It is therefore important that stations have in place appropriate procedures to assure that they are aware of and in compliance with, and that station personnel fulfill their responsibilities under, the FCC's rules and policies. If you would like assistance in developing station systems and procedures to comply with the FCC's rules and policies, or have any questions concerning matters discussed in this memorandum, please contact us.

Arter & Hadden LLP
September 1998

NOTE

1. Note that the relevant television contours listed are for the current analog NTSC service, not the new DTV service.

GLOSSARY

Acceptable use policy (AUP): policy to govern employee use of company computers.

Accounts payable ledger: an account book that reflects amounts owed to the providers of goods and services.

Accounts receivable ledger: an account book that records amounts owed to a broadcast station by its clients or to a cable system by its clients and subscribers.

Administrative management: a managerial approach emphasizing the effectiveness and efficiency of the total organization.

Affiliation contract: an agreement governing the relationship between a network and an affiliated station.

Age Discrimination in Employment Act: legislation that forbids employers with twenty or more employees from discriminating in employment practices against any person 40 years of age or older.

Americans with Disabilities Act: legislation that prohibits employers with fifteen or more employees from discriminating in employment practices against qualified individuals with disabilities.

Amortization: the systematic reduction or writing off of an amount over a specific number of time periods, usually years.

Asset: an object, right, or claim that is expected to provide benefits to its owners.

Audience flow: the movement of an audience from one television program to another on the same channel.

Auditorium testing: a radio station research method that seeks reactions to short excerpts from recordings played to several dozen people gathered in a large room or auditorium.

Average quarter-hour (AQH) audience: average number of persons listening or viewing for at least five minutes in a fifteen-minute period.

Balance sheet: a periodic financial statement that reports a company's assets, liabilities, and net worth.

Barter: a transaction involving the exchange of advertising time for goods or services. Also called a *trade-out.*

Barter-plus-cash programming: a station acquires a syndicated program for a fee and also surrenders to the syndicator some of the commercial inventory.

Barter programming: a syndicator provides a program to a station at no cost, but retains for sale some of the commercial inventory.

Basic cable: the minimum number of cable channels a subscriber may receive for a monthly fee.

Behavioral school of management: a school of management thought that emphasizes employee needs and their role in motivation.

Block programming: scheduling several television programs of similar kind or with similar audience appeal back-to-back. Also called *vertical programming.*

Bonus spots: spots given to an advertiser at no cost as a consideration for buying other spots. Also called *spins.*

Budget: a financial plan showing estimated or planned revenues and expenses.

Bureaucratic management: an approach to management that pays special attention to the structure of the organization and its impact on efficiency.

Call-out research: a radio station research method that seeks reactions to recordings by playing over the telephone short excerpts or "hooks."

Cash disbursements journal: a transaction record of all funds disbursed by a company.

Cash flow: operating income before charges for depreciation, interest, amortization, and taxes.

Cash receipts journal: a transaction record of all funds received by a company from any source.

Checkerboard programming: scheduling a different TV program series in the same time period daily.

Churn: the turnover in cable television subscribers.

Civil Rights Act: legislation that prohibits discrimination in employment practices based on race, color, religion, sex, or national origin.

Classical school of management: a school of management thought that embraces administrative, bureaucratic, and scientific approaches to management.

Community Service Grant (CSG): a grant from the Corporation for Public Broadcasting to public radio and television stations for operating costs and program purchases.

Compact disc (CD): a recording whose content is encoded in digital form and read by a laser beam.

Contingency theory: a management approach that takes into account the particular circumstances in reaching decisions and undertaking actions.

Contract: a formal legal document containing all the terms of a proposed transaction between buyer and seller, and accompanied by exhibits reflecting details of all assets to be conveyed and all liabilities to be assumed.

Co-op advertising: the cost of the retailer's advertising is shared, usually between the retailer and the manufacturer. An abbreviation for *cooperative advertising*.

Core programming: FCC term to describe television programming designed primarily to meet the educational and informational needs of children 16 years old or younger.

Cost-per-rating point (CPP): the cost of a spot divided by the rating for the program or period in which it is broadcast.

Cost-per-thousand (CPM): the cost of reaching 1,000 targeted households or persons with a commercial.

Counter-programming: scheduling a TV program that appeals to a different audience from that sought by the competition in the same time period.

Cume: an abbreviation for *cumulative audience*—an estimate of the number of different households or persons viewing or listening for at least five minutes in a specified period.

Current asset: an asset expected to be sold, used, or converted into cash within one year.

Current liability: amounts, taxes, and commissions payable in the near future, usually within one year.

Current ratio: the relationship of total current assets to total current liabilities.

DAB: digital audio broadcasting.

Debt-equity ratio: the relationship of total long-term liabilities to stockholders' equity.

Depreciation: the systematic reduction in value of long-lived assets due to use or obsolescence.

Designated market area (DMA): Nielsen's term for the geographic area in which television stations in the survey market receive a preponderance of viewing.

Diary: an audience measurement method in which a sample of people record their listening or viewing activity in a small booklet.

Direct broadcast satellite (DBS): the transmission of a television signal by satellite to a small receiving dish.

Domain name: an Internet address.

Duopoly: a situation in which two radio stations in the same service (i.e., AM or FM) in the same market are licensed to a single person or entity.

Equal Employment Opportunity Commission (EEOC): the governmental agency that ensures compliance with laws prohibiting discrimination in employment practices.

Equal Pay Act: legislation that prohibits wage discrimination between male and female employees.

Expenses: costs of services and facilities used in the production of current revenue.

Fair Labor Standards Act: legislation that sets forth requirements for minimum wage and overtime compensation.

Family and Medical Leave Act: legislation that requires employers with fifty or more employees to make available to them up to twelve weeks of unpaid leave during any twelve-month period for specified family or medical reasons.

Fiber optics: the conversion of electrical signals into light waves sent through glass fibers.

Financial interest and syndication rules: FCC rules that prohibited networks from ownership interest in, and syndication of, their prime-time entertainment programs. The rules were relaxed in the early 1990s to allow for network ownership interest in such programs.

First-run syndication: the sale to television stations or other outlets of programs produced expressly for syndication.

Fixed asset: an asset that will be held or used for a long term, usually more than one year.

Flipping: the use of a remote-control pad to switch from channel to channel within and between television programs.

Focus group: a research method in which a dozen or so people engage in a moderator-led discussion on a question of importance.

Format: a radio station's principal content element or sound.

Format search: a research method to determine if there is a need or place in a market for a radio format or for elements within a format.

Franchise: an agreement between a governmental body and a cable television company setting forth the conditions under which the company may operate.

Frequency: the number of times a home or person is exposed to a program or commercial.

General journal: an account book used to record "other" expenses, such as depreciation, amortization, and interest.

General ledger: the basic accounts book, in two sections: one records figures for assets, liabilities, and capital; the other, income and expense account figures.

Generic promo: a promotional announcement for a program series.

Goodwill: the term used to describe the intangible assets of a broadcast station, such as reputation, image in the market, and the value of the license.

Grazing: the continuous scanning of the TV dial with the use of a remote-control pad.

Grid card: reflects fluctuations in advertising rates according to supply and demand.

Gross impressions (GIs): the total number of exposures to a schedule of commercials.

Gross rating points (GRPs): the total of all rating points achieved for a schedule of commercials.

Hammocking: placing a new or untested television program between two popular programs.

Hawthorne Effect: despite a deterioration in working conditions, productivity is likely to increase when managers pay special attention to employees. Takes its name from Western Electric's plant in Hawthorne, Illinois, where the phenomenon was observed.

Head-to-head programming: a strategy whereby a television station competes directly against another station (or stations) by scheduling a similar program or one with similar audience appeal in the same time period.

Hierarchy of needs: Abraham Maslow's theory that human beings have certain basic needs that are organized in a hierarchy.

High-definition television (HDTV): a television system using more than 1,000 scan lines and an increased width-to-height ratio.

Hook: see *Call-out research.*

Horizontal programming: see *Strip programming.*

House accounts: accounts that require no selling or servicing and on which no commissions are paid.

Households using television (HUT): the percentage of all television households in a survey area with TV sets in operation at a particular time.

Hygiene factors: Frederick Herzberg's term to describe factors associated with conditions surrounding work, such as salary, benefits, and job security.

Image promotion: an attempt to establish, shift, or solidify public perceptions of a station.

Income statement: a periodic financial statement that reports a company's revenues, expenses, and resulting profit or loss. Also called an *operating statement* or *profit and loss (P and L) statement.*

Information superhighway: a term coined to describe the projected high-capacity networks and information services interconnecting every home and business in the country.

Internet: worldwide network of computer networks; also called *the Net.*

Internet Service Provider (ISP): a company that connects subscribers directly to the Internet. Also called *Internet Access Provider.*

Leased access channel: a cable television channel on which time may be purchased by individuals or groups for the transmission of programs.

Liability: an obligation to pay an amount or perform a service.

Local marketing agreement (LMA): a contractual agreement whereby a radio or a television station sells a block of air time to a third-party programmer, who uses the time to broadcast content, including commercials, over the station. May also be applied to a situation where the licensee sells only its commercial inventory to a third party and retains programming control.

Local origination channel: a cable television channel equipped and maintained by the cable system to provide locally originated programming.

Logo: a distinctive symbol that identifies a station and often incorporates its call letters and frequency or channel number.

Long-term liability: an obligation, such as bank debt, mortgages, and program contracts, to be paid over an extended period of time.

Loss: the excess of expenses over revenue.

Lottery: a contest containing the elements of prize, chance, and consideration.

Lower-level managers: those responsible for overseeing the day-to-day performance of employees.

Low-power television (LPTV): a television station that broadcasts to a limited geographical area, usually about ten to fifteen miles in radius.

Low use discount (LUD): an alternative to full membership in the Public Broadcasting Service (PBS) that allows a public television station to carry up to 15 percent of the PBS program schedule at a reduced rate.

Management: the process of planning, organizing, influencing, and controlling to accomplish organizational goals through the coordinated use of human and material resources.

Management by objectives (MBO): a management approach whereby all employees establish objectives designed to assist in the achievement of organizational goals, and the progress towards attaining them is reviewed periodically.

Management science: a school of management thought that uses mathematical models to simulate situations and to project the outcomes of different decisions.

Market perceptual study: a research method to determine target audience perceptions of a station.

Metro area: a geographical area generally corresponding to the metropolitan area defined by the U.S. Government's Office of Management and Budget.

Middle managers: those responsible for the coordination of activities designed to assist the organization in achieving its overall goals.

Motivators: the term coined by Frederick Herzberg to describe factors associated with job content, such as achievement, recognition, and advancement.

Multiple: a number by which the cash flow of a company is multiplied to determine the offering price.

Multiple system operator (MSO): a company that operates more than one cable television system.

Must carry: FCC rule providing that television stations may demand carriage on cable systems within their designated market area.

National Telecommunications and Information Administration (NTIA): the White House telecommunications policy office, located within the Department of Commerce.

Net loss: the excess of all expenses, including taxes, over revenue.

Net profit: the excess of revenue over all expenses, including taxes.

Net worth: the owners' equity in a company, reflecting the difference between total assets and total liabilities.

NSI area: Nielsen's term for a market's metro and designated market area counties, plus other counties necessary to account for approximately 95 percent of the average quarter-hour audience of stations in the market.

Occupational Safety and Health Act: legislation that requires employers to ensure that the workplace is free of hazards that could cause illness, injury, or death.

Occupational Safety and Health Administration (OSHA): the governmental agency that administers the Occupational Safety and Health Act.

Off-network syndication: the sale to stations or other outlets of programs formerly aired on a television network.

Operating expense: the expense of performing normal business activities as opposed to the expense of financing the business.

Operating loss: the excess of operating expenses over revenue.

Operating profit: the excess of revenue over operating expenses, excluding depreciation, amortization, interest, and taxes.

Operating statement: see *Income statement*.

Orientation: the process whereby new employees are introduced to other employees and the station.

"Other" expenses: nonoperating cash and noncash costs of a business, usually including depreciation, amortization, and interest.

Pay cable: channels added to basic cable offerings for which an extra subscriber fee is required.

Payola: the practice whereby recording company representatives secretly reward disc jockeys for playing or plugging certain recordings.

Pay-per-view (PPV): cable programming for which the subscriber pays on a per-program or per-event basis.

PEG channel: cable television channel allocated for public, educational, and governmental use.

People Meter: electronic metering system used by Nielsen to measure audiences for broadcast and cable networks and nationally distributed barter-syndicated programs.

Per-inquiry advertising: an advertiser pays a commercial rate based on the number of responses generated by the advertising.

Piracy: the unauthorized reception of a cable television signal.

Playlist: the list of recordings played by a radio station.

Plugola: the on-air promotion of goods and services in which someone responsible for selecting the material broadcast has a financial interest, without disclosing that fact to the audience.

Policy book: contains the philosophy and policies of a broadcast station and sets forth the responsibilities of individuals and departments.

Pregnancy Discrimination Act: legislation that forbids discrimination in employment practices based on pregnancy, childbirth, or related medical conditions.

Prepaid expense: an expense paid in advance of its occurrence.

Pretax loss: the excess of expenses, including depreciation, amortization, and interest, but excluding taxes, over revenue.

Pretax profit: the excess of revenue over expenses, including depreciation, amortization, and interest, but excluding taxes.

Prime-time access rule (PTAR): discontinued rule generally forbidding network-affiliated television stations in the top-fifty markets from airing more than three hours of network or off-network programming between 7:00 and 11:00 P.M. (ET).

Profit: the excess of revenue over expenses.

Profit and loss (P and L) statement: see *Income statement.*

Program promotion: the promotion of a station's content.

Promo: an announcement promoting a station and/or its content. An abbreviation for *promotional announcement.*

Public access channel: a cable television channel for which individual members of the public or groups provide content.

Rating: in television, the percentage of all television households or persons in a survey area viewing a particular station. In radio, the percentage of all persons in a survey area listening to a particular station.

RBOC: an abbreviation for a Regional Bell Operating Company, a Bell company serving a geographic region (e.g., BellSouth).

Reach: the number of different homes or persons exposed to a program or commercial.

Request for proposals (RFP): an invitation from a governmental body to submit a proposal for the establishment of a cable television system.

Retransmission consent: legislation that permits a station to waive its "must-carry" right in return for the right to require its consent before a cable system may carry its signal.

Revenue: the inflow of resources to a broadcast or cable business from the sale of time or the provision of services.

Rotation: the frequency with which a recording is played by a radio station.

Sales journal: a transaction record of billings to clients for commercials run over a certain period of time, usually a month.

Saturation schedule: a heavy commercial load aired when targeted homes or persons are tuned in.

Scientific management: a systematic approach to management with an emphasis on productivity.

SDARS: satellite digital audio radio services.

Share (of audience): in television, the percentage of households or persons using television tuned to a particular station. In radio, the percentage of all listeners tuned to a particular station.

Specific promo: a promotional announcement for one program in a series.

Spectrum plan: a moderate number of spots scheduled throughout the day.

Spins: see *Bonus spots.*

Spot schedule: a series of commercials aired in only one or two periods of the day.

Station rep: a company that represents a radio or television station in the sale of time to national and regional advertisers and advises the station on the purchase, scheduling, and promotion of programs.

Strip programming: scheduling a TV program series at the same time each day, usually Monday through Friday. Also called *horizontal programming.*

Superduopoly: a situation in which three or more radio stations in the same service (i.e., AM or FM) and in the same market are licensed to the same person or entity.

Syndicated program exclusivity rule (syndex): a rule protecting a local television station's syndicated programs against duplication from signals imported by a cable television system.

Syndicators: companies that sell programs or features to radio and television stations and other outlets.

Systems theory: a management approach that views an organization as a system of parts related to each other and to the external environment.

Telco: an abbreviation for a telephone company.

Television network: the FCC defines it as an entity providing more than fifteen hours per week of prime-time entertainment programming to interconnected affiliates on a regular basis. Such programming must reach at least 75 percent of the nation's television households.

Theory X: a philosophy of human nature, advanced by Douglas McGregor, suggesting that managers must coerce, control, and even threaten to motivate employees.

Theory Y: a philosophy of human nature, advanced by Douglas McGregor, suggesting that employees are capable of accepting responsibility and exercising self-direction.

Tier: a level of service offered by a cable television company.

Time spent listening (TSL): the time a person listens to a radio station during a specific period of the day.

Top managers: those who coordinate an organization's activities and provide its overall direction.

Total quality management (TQM): a management approach that focuses on the customer and emphasizes quality in everything the organization undertakes.

Trade-out: see *Barter.*

Trailing cash flow: a company's cash flow for the most recent twelve-month period, which may or may not correspond with the fiscal year.

Underwriting: the provision of funds by businesses for the production and airing of programs on public radio and television stations in exchange for announcements in the programs.

Union contract: an agreement governing relations between an employer and unionized employees.

Vendor support program: a method whereby a retailer obtains manufacturer dollars to cover advertising costs.

Venture capital: financing in which the company providing the funds receives an ownership interest in the facility to be acquired, as well as interest on the funds advanced.

Vertical programming: see *Block programming.*

Webcasting: carriage of a station's signal on the World Wide Web.

Web page: units of information on one or more computer screens, often with links to other pages or graphics.

Website: location of a computer called a server that contains the home pages for a company.

World Wide Web (WWW): a portion of the Internet formatted with hypertext links.

Zapping: using a remote-control pad to change TV channels to avoid commercials.

Zipping: the fast-forwarding of videocassette recorders through commercials in recorded programs.

BIBLIOGRAPHY

The first part of the bibliography lists works cited in the text and others that the student of electronic media management may find useful. The second part consists of selected periodicals.

WORKS CONSULTED

Accounting Manual for Broadcasters. Des Plaines, IL: Broadcast Financial Management Association, 1981.

Accounting Manual for Radio Stations. Washington, DC: National Association of Broadcasters, 1981.

Accounting Manual for Television Stations. Washington, DC: National Association of Broadcasters, 1990.

Albarran, Alan B. *Management of Electronic Media*. Belmont, CA: Wadsworth, 1997.

Americans with Disabilities Act, The: Questions and Answers. Washington, DC: U.S. Equal Employment Opportunity Commission and U.S. Department of Justice Civil Rights Division, 1992.

Avery, Robert K. (ed.). *Public Service Broadcasting in a Multichannel Environment*. White Plains, NY: Longman, 1993.

Baldwin, Thomas F., D. Stevens McVoy, and Charles Steinfield. *Convergence: Integrating Media, Information & Communication*. Thousand Oaks, CA: Sage, 1996.

Balon, Robert E. *Radio in the '90s: Audience Promotion and Marketing Strategies*. Washington, DC: National Association of Broadcasters, 1990.

Bartlett, Eugene. *Cable Communications: Building the Information Infrastructure*. New York: McGraw-Hill, 1995.

Benson, K.B. *HDTV: Advanced Television for the 1990s*. New York: Intertext/McGraw-Hill, 1991.

BIB Television Programming Source Books. Philadelphia: North American Publishing, published annually.

Block, Alex B. *Outfoxed: The Inside Story of America's Fourth Television Network*, updated ed. New York: St. Martin's Press, 1991.

Bone, Jan. *Opportunities in Cable Television.* Lincolnwood, IL: VGM Career Horizons, 1993.

Brady, Frank R., and J. Angel Vasquez. *Direct Response Television: The Authoritative Guide.* Lincolnwood, IL: NTC Publishing Group, 1995.

Brinkley, Joel. *Defining Vision: The Battle for the Future of Television.* New York: Harcourt Brace, 1997.

Broadcast and Cable Employment Trend Report. Washington, DC: Federal Communications Commission, published annually.

Broadcasting & Cable Yearbook. New Providence, NJ: R.R. Bowker, published annually.

Brown, James A., and Ward L. Quaal. *Radio-Television-Cable Management*, 3rd ed. New York: McGraw-Hill, 1998.

Buzzard, Karen. *Electronic Media Ratings.* Boston: Focal Press, 1992.

Cable Television Developments, Spring 1998. Washington, DC: National Cable Television Association, 1998.

Cable Yellow Pages. Torrance, CA: CYP, published annually.

Cablevision Blue Book, Vol. VII (Spring/Summer, 1998). New York: Cahners Business Information, 1998.

Carlisle, Howard M. *Management Essentials: Concepts for Productivity and Innovation*, 2nd ed. Chicago: Science Research Associates, 1987.

Carroll, Raymond L., and Donald M. Davis. *Electronic Media Programming: Strategies and Decision Making.* New York: McGraw-Hill, 1993.

Carter, T. Barton, Marc A. Franklin, and Jay B. Wright. *The First Amendment and the Fifth Estate: Regulation of Electronic Mass Media*, 3rd ed. Westbury, NY: Foundation Press, 1993.

Contests, Lotteries and Casino Gambling: What You Don't Know May Get You in Trouble. Washington, DC: National Association of Broadcasters, 1996.

Covington, William G., Jr. *Systems Theory Applied to Television Station Management in the Competitive Marketplace.* Lanham, MD: University Press of America, 1997.

Crandall, Robert W., and Harold Furchgott-Roth. *Cable TV: Regulation or Competition?* Washington, DC: Brookings Institution, 1996.

Creech, Kenneth C. *Electronic Media Law and Regulation.* Boston: Focal Press, 1993.

Czech-Beckerman, Elizabeth Shimer. *Managing Electronic Media.* Boston: Focal Press, 1991.

Day, Louis A. *Ethics in Media Communications: Cases and Controversies*, 2nd ed. Belmont, CA: Wadsworth, 1997.

DBS Revolution, The: Emerging Markets Bring New Competition. Washington, DC: National Association of Broadcasters, 1997.

DeSonne, Marcia L. *Advanced Broadcast/Media Technologies: Market Developments and Impacts in the '90s and Beyond.* Washington, DC: National Association of Broadcasters, 1992.

Devol, Kenneth S. (ed.). *Mass Media and the Supreme Court*, 4th ed. New York: Hastings House, 1987.

Dickey, Lew. *The Franchi$e: Building Radio Brands.* Washington, DC: National Association of Broadcasters, 1994.

Dipboye, Robert L. *Selection Interviews: Process Perspectives.* Cincinnati, OH: South-Western, 1992.

Ditingo, Vincent M. *The Remaking of Radio.* Boston: Focal Press, 1995.

DMA Market Profile. Washington, DC: Public Broadcasting Service, published annually.

Doyle, Marc. *The Future of Television: A Global Overview of Programming, Advertising, Technology and Growth.* Lincolnwood, IL: NTC Publishing Group, 1993.

Drucker, Peter F. *Management: Tasks, Responsibilities, Practices.* New York: Harper & Row, 1974.

Drucker, Peter F. *Managing in a Time of Great Change.* New York: Truman Talley Books/Dutton, 1995.

Drucker, Peter F. *The Practice of Management.* New York: Harper & Row, 1954.

Duncan, James H., Jr. *Duncan's Radio Market Guide.* Indianapolis, IN: Duncan's American Radio, published annually.

Eastman, Susan T., and Robert Klein. *Promotion and Marketing for Broadcasting and Cable,* 2nd ed. Prospect Heights, IL: Waveland Press, 1991.

Eastman, Susan Tyler, and Douglas A. Ferguson. *Broadcast/Cable Programming: Strategies and Practices,* 5th ed. Belmont, CA: Wadsworth, 1997.

Eicoff, Alvin, and Anne Knudsen. *Direct Marketing through Broadcast Media: TV, Radio, Cable, Infomercials, Home Shopping and More.* Lincolnwood, IL: NTC Publishing Group, 1995.

Equal Employment Opportunity Guidebook: How to Comply with the Requirements of the Federal Communications Commission. Washington, DC: National Association of Broadcasters, 1991.

Estes, Ralph. *Dictionary of Accounting.* Cambridge, MA: MIT Press, 1986.

Evans, Craig Robert. *Marketing Channels: Infomercials and the Future of Televised Marketing.* Englewood Cliffs, NJ: Prentice-Hall, 1994.

Farris, Linda Guess. *Television Careers: A Guide to Breaking and Entering.* Fairfax, CA: Buy the Book Enterprises, 1995.

Fayol, Henri. *General and Industrial Management.* Translated by Constance Storrs. London, England: Sir Isaac Pitman and Sons, 1965.

Fenneran, William B., and Richard E. Wiley (eds.). *The Cable Television Consumer Protection and Competition Act of 1992: What Does It Mean?* Englewood Cliffs, NJ: Prentice Hall, 1993.

Fidler, Roger. *Mediamorphosis: Understanding New Media.* Thousand Oaks, CA: Pine Forge Press, 1997.

Fuller, Linda K. *Community Television in the United States: A Sourcebook on Public, Educational, and Governmmental Access.* Westport, CT: Greenwood Press, 1994.

Greenwood, Ken. *High Performance Selling.* West Palm Beach: Streamline Press, 1995.

Guide to Disability Rights Laws, A. Washington, DC: U.S. Department of Justice Civil Rights Division, 1996.

Guidelines for Radio: Best of the Best Promotions—III. Washington, DC: National Association of Broadcasters, 1994.

Halper, Donna L. *Full-Service Radio: Programming for the Community*. Boston: Focal Press, 1991.

Halper, Donna L. *Radio Music Directing*. Boston: Focal Press, 1991.

Herweg, Ashley, and Godfrey Herweg. *Recruiting, Interviewing, Hiring and Developing Superior Salespeople*, 4th ed. Washington, DC: National Association of Broadcasters, 1993.

Herweg, Godfrey, and Ashley Herweg. *Making More Money: Selling Radio Advertising Without Numbers*, 2nd ed. Washington, DC: National Association of Broadcasters, 1995.

Herzberg, Frederick. *Work and the Nature of Man*. Cleveland, OH: World Publishing, 1967.

Herzberg, Frederick, Bernard Mausner, and Barbara Bloch Snyderman. *The Motivation to Work*, 2nd ed. New York: John Wiley, 1959.

Hilliard, Robert L. *The Federal Communications Commission: A Primer*. Boston: Focal Press, 1991.

Holsinger, Ralph L., and Jon Paul Dilts. *Media Law*, 3rd ed. New York: McGraw-Hill, 1994.

Howard, Herbert H., Michael S. Kievman, and Barbara A. Moore. *Radio, TV, and Cable Programming*, 2nd ed. Ames, IA: Iowa State University Press, 1994.

Hoynes, William. *Public Television for Sale: Media, the Market, and the Public Sphere*. Boulder, CO: Westview Press, 1994.

Jankowski, Gene F., and David C. Fuchs. *Television Today and Tomorrow: It Won't Be What You Think*. New York: Oxford University Press, 1995.

Johnson, Leland L. *Toward Competition in Cable Television*. Cambridge, MA: The MIT Press, and Washington, DC: The American Enterprise Institute for Public Policy Research, 1994.

Kahn, Frank J. (ed.). *Documents of American Broadcasting*, 4th ed. Englewood Cliffs, NJ: Prentice-Hall, 1984.

Keith, Michael C. *Radio Programming: Consultancy and Formatics*. Boston: Focal Press, 1987.

Keith, Michael C. *Selling Radio Direct*. Boston: Focal Press, 1992.

Keith, Michael C., and Joseph M. Krause. *The Radio Station*, 3rd ed. Boston: Focal Press, 1993.

Langevin, Michael J. *Basic Radio Programming Manual*. Washington, DC: National Association of Broadcasters, 1996.

Lashley, Marilyn. *Public Television: Panacea, Pork Barrel, or Public Trust?* New York: Greenwood Press, 1992.

Liebold, Linda, and Regina Sokas. *The Public Television Advantage*. Washington, DC: Public Broadcasting Service, 1984.

Limburg, Val E. *Electronic Media Ethics*. Boston: Focal Press, 1994.

Lotteries and Contests: A Broadcaster's Handbook. Washington, DC: National Association of Broadcasters, 1990.

MacDonald, Jack, and Curtis R. Holsopple. *Handbook of Radio Publicity and Promotion*, 3rd ed. Blue Ridge Summit, PA: TAB Books, 1990.

MacFarland, David T. *Future Radio Programming Strategies: Cultivating Listenership in the Digital Age*, 2nd ed. Mahwah, NJ: Lawrence Erlbaum, 1997.

Maney, Kevin. *Megamedia Shakeout: The Inside Story of the Leaders and the Losers in the Exploding Communications Industry*. New York: John Wiley, 1995.

Marsteller, William A. *Creative Management*. Lincolnwood, IL: NTC Business Books, 1992.

Marx, Steve, and Pierre Bouvard. *Radio Advertising's Missing Ingredient: The Optimum Effective Scheduling System*, 2nd ed. Washington, DC: National Association of Broadcasters, 1993.

Maslow, Abraham H. *Motivation and Personality*, 2nd ed. New York: Harper & Row, 1970.

Matelski, Marilyn J. *Daytime Television Programming*. Boston: Focal Press, 1991.

McGregor, Douglas. *The Human Side of Enterprise*. New York: McGraw-Hill, 1960.

Metcalf, Henry C., and L. Urwick (eds.). *Dynamic Administration: The Collected Papers of Mary Parker Follett*. London: Harper and Brothers, 1942.

Miles, Peggy. *Internet World Guide to Webcasting: The Complete Guide to Broadcasting on the Web*. New York: John Wiley, 1998.

Mintzberg, Henry. *The Nature of Managerial Work*. Englewood Cliffs, NJ: Prentice Hall, 1980.

Mirabito, Michael M.A., with contributions by Barbara L. Morgenstern. *The New Communications Technologies*, 3rd ed. Boston: Focal Press, 1997.

Mogel, Leonard. *Making It in Broadcasting: An Insider's Guide to Career Opportunities*. New York: Collier Books, 1994.

Mondy, R. Wayne, Robert E. Holmes, and Edwin B. Flippo. *Management: Concepts and Practices*, 2nd ed. Boston: Allyn & Bacon, 1983.

Money Makers II: Sales Promotions from the Hundred Plus Television Markets, 2nd ed. Washington, DC: National Association of Broadcasters, 1996.

NAB Legal Guide to Broadcast Law and Regulation, 3rd ed., and *1991 Supplement*. Washington, DC: National Association of Broadcasters, 1988 and 1991.

NAB Television Financial Report. Washington, DC: National Association of Broadcasters, published annually.

1998 Report on Television. New York: Nielsen Media Research, 1998.

Norberg, Eric G. *Radio Programming: Tactics and Strategy*. Boston: Focal Press, 1996.

O'Donnell, Lewis B., Carl Hausman, and Philip Benoit. *Radio Station Operations: Management and Employee Perspectives*. Belmont, CA: Wadsworth, 1989.

Ouchi, William G. *Theory Z: How American Business Can Meet the Japanese Challenge*. Reading, MA: Addison-Wesley, 1981.

Owen, Bruce M., and Steven S. Wildman. *Video Economics*. Cambridge, MA: Harvard University Press, 1992.

Parsons, Patrick R., and Robert M. Frieden. *The Cable and Satellite Television Industries*. Boston: Allyn & Bacon, 1998.

Pavlik, John V. *New Media Technology: Cultural and Commercial Perspectives*, 2nd ed. Boston: Allyn & Bacon, 1998.

Pember, Don R. *Mass Media Law*, 3rd ed. Dubuque, IA: William C. Brown, 1984.

Personnel/Human Resources Forms Guideline for Broadcasters. Des Plaines, IL: Broadcast Financial Management Association, 1984.

Phillips, John B., Jr. *Employment Law Desk Book*. Nashville, TN: M. Lee Smith, 1989.

Predicting Radio Station and Market Revenues. Washington, DC: National Association of Broadcasters, 1992.

Pricing and Rate Forecasting Using Broadcast Yield Management. Washington, DC: National Association of Broadcasters, 1992.

Pringle, Charles D., Daniel F. Jennings, and Justin G. Longenecker. *Managing Organizations: Functions and Behaviors.* Columbus, OH: Merrill, 1988.

Public Broadcasting and You. Washington, DC: Corporation for Public Broadcasting, 1993.

Public Radio Program Director's Handbook. Olney, MD: Public Radio Program Directors' Association, 1989.

Public Trust, A: The Report of the Carnegie Commission on the Future of Public Broadcasting. New York: Bantam Books, 1979.

Radio Data Broadcasting Technologies: Revenue Streams of the Future. Washington, DC: National Association of Broadcasters, 1995.

Radio Financing: A Guide for Lenders and Investors. Washington, DC: National Association of Broadcasters, 1990.

Radio Marketing Guide and Factbook for Advertisers, 1997–1998. New York: Radio Advertising Bureau, 1997.

Radio Today: How America Listens to Radio. New York: Arbitron, 1998.

Rauscher, David Grant. *The Broadcaster's Guide to the Internet and the World Wide Web.* Washington, DC: National Association of Broadcasters, 1996.

RDS Applications: Opportunities for Radio Broadcasters. Washington, DC: National Association of Broadcasters, 1995.

Reinsch, J. Leonard, and E.I. Ellis. *Radio Station Management,* 2nd ed. revised. New York: Harper and Brothers, 1960.

Robbins, Stephen P., and Mary Coulter. *Management,* 5th ed. Upper Saddle River, NJ: Prentice Hall, 1996.

Roberts, Ted E.F. *Practical Radio Promotions.* Boston: Focal Press, 1992.

Sashkin, Marshall, and Kenneth J. Kiser. *Putting Total Quality Management to Work: What TQM Means, How to Use It, and How to Sustain It Over the Long Run.* San Francisco: Berrett-Koehler, 1993.

Schoderbek, Peter P., Charles D. Schoderbek, and Asterios G. Kefalas. *Management Systems: Conceptual Considerations,* 3rd ed. revised. Plano, TX: Business Publications, 1985.

Schoderbek, Peter P., Richard A. Cosier, and John C. Aplin. *Management.* San Diego, CA: Harcourt Brace Jovanovich, 1988.

Schulberg, Pete. *Radio Advertising: The Authoritative Handbook,* 2nd ed. Lincolnwood, IL: NTC Publishing Group, 1996.

Seel, Peter B., and August E. Grant (eds.). *Broadcast Technology Update.* Boston: Focal Press, 1997.

Sherman, Barry L. *Telecommunications Management: Broadcasting/Cable and the New Technologies,* 2nd ed. New York: McGraw-Hill, 1995.

Small Market Television Manager's Guide — II, The. Washington, DC: National Association of Broadcasters, 1992.

Smith, Anthony. *The Age of Behemoths: The Globalization of Mass Media Firms.* New York: Priority Press, 1991.

Smith, F. Leslie, Milan Meeske, and John Wright. *Electronic Media and Government: The Regulation of Wireless and Wired Communication in the United States.* White Plains, NY: Longman, 1995.

Sound Solutions: Why Radio Can Help You Solve Your Toughest Marketing Problems. New York: Radio Advertising Bureau, n.d.

Station Audience Report. Washington, DC: Public Broadcasting Service, published four times annually.

Strategic Planning Handbook for Broadcasters. Washington, DC: National Association of Broadcasters, 1994.

Strong, William S. *The Copyright Book: A Practical Guide,* 4th ed. Cambridge, MA: MIT Press, 1992.

Successful Radio Compensation Strategies. Washington, DC: National Association of Broadcasters, 1994.

Teeter, Dwight L., Jr., and Don R. Le Duc. *Law of Mass Communications: Freedom and Control of Print and Broadcast Media,* 7th ed. Westbury, NY: Foundation Press, 1992.

Television and Cable Factbook. 2 vols. Washington, DC: Warren Publishing, published annually.

Television Data Broadcasting. Washington, DC: National Association of Broadcasters, 1997.

Television Employee Compensation and Fringe Benefits Report. Washington, DC: National Association of Broadcasters, published annually.

These Taxing Times: A Guide for Broadcasters. Washington, DC: National Association of Broadcasters, 1996.

Understanding Broadcast and Cable Finance: A Handbook for the Non-Financial Manager. Washington, DC: National Association of Broadcasters, 1994.

Understanding DAB: A Guide for Broadcast Managers and Engineers, 2nd ed. Washington, DC: National Association of Broadcasters, 1994.

Vane, Edwin T., and Lynne S. Gross. *Programming for TV, Radio, and Cable.* Boston: Focal Press, 1994.

Vaughn, Tom, and Associates. *Advanced Television Transmission: Planning Your Station's Transition.* Washington, DC: National Association of Broadcasters, 1995.

Wage and Hour Guide for Broadcasters, 2nd ed. Washington, DC: National Association of Broadcasters, 1991.

Walker, James R., and Douglas R. Ferguson. *The Broadcast Television Industry.* Upper Saddle River, NJ: Prentice-Hall, 1998.

Warner, Charles, and Joseph Buchman. *Broadcast and Cable Selling,* 2nd ed. updated. Belmont, CA: Wadsworth, 1993.

Weber, Max. *The Theory of Social and Economic Organization.* Translated by A.M. Henderson and Talcott Parsons. Edited with an introduction by Talcott Parsons. New York: The Free Press, 1947.

Webster, James G., and Lawrence W. Lichty. *Ratings Analysis: Theory and Practice.* Hillsdale, NJ: Lawrence Erlbaum, 1991.

Williams, Frederick. *The New Communications,* 3rd ed. Belmont, CA: Wadsworth, 1992.

Wimmer, Roger D., and Joseph R. Dominick. *Mass Media Research: An Introduction*, 5th ed. Belmont, CA: Wadsworth, 1997.

Zelezny, John D. *Communications Law: Liberties, Restraints, and the Modern Media.* Belmont, CA: Wadsworth, 1993.

PERIODICALS

Advertising Age. Chicago: Crain Communications. Weekly.

Billboard. New York: BPI Publications. Weekly.

Broadcast Engineering. Overland Park, KS: Intertec Publishing. Monthly.

Broadcast Investor. Carmel, CA: Paul Kagan Associates. Monthly.

Broadcasting and the Law. Miami, FL: Broadcasting and the Law. Monthly.

Broadcasting & Cable. Washington, DC: Cahners Publishing. Weekly.

Cable TV Advertising. Carmel, CA: Paul Kagan Associates. Monthly.

Cable TV Investor. Carmel, CA: Paul Kagan Associates. Monthly.

Cable TV Technology. Carmel, CA: Paul Kagan Associates. Monthly.

Cable World. Denver, CO: Cowles Business Media. Weekly.

Cablevision. New York: Cahners Business Information. Nineteen times annually.

Channels: The Business of Communications. New York: Act III Publishing. Semimonthly.

Columbia Journalism Review. New York: Graduate School of Journalism, Columbia University. Bimonthly.

Communications and the Law. Littleton, CO: Fred B. Rothman. Quarterly.

Communications Daily. Washington, DC: Warren Publishing. Weekdays.

Community Media Review. Washington, DC: Alliance for Community Media. Quarterly.

Current. Washington, DC: NAEB Current Publishing Committee. Biweekly.

Daily Variety. Los Angeles: Cahners Business Information. Weekdays.

Electronic Media. Chicago: Crain Communications. Weekly.

Entertainment Employment Journal. Van Nuys, CA: Entertainment Employment Journal. Twenty-two times annually.

Feedback. Washington, DC: Broadcast Education Association. Quarterly.

Financial Manager for the Media Professional. Des Plaines, IL: Broadcast Cable Financial Management Association. Bimonthly.

Inside Radio. Cherry Hill, NJ: Inside Radio. Weekdays.

Journal of Broadcasting and Electronic Media. Washington, DC: Broadcast Education Association. Quarterly.

Journal of Popular Film and Television. Washington, DC: Heldref Publications. Quarterly.

Journalism and Mass Communication Quarterly. Columbia, SC: Association for Education in Journalism and Mass Communication. Quarterly.

Media Studies Journal. New York: Media Studies Center. Quarterly.

Multichannel News. New York: Cahners Business Information. Weekly.

NRB Magazine. Manassas, VA: National Religious Broadcasters. Ten times annually.

Pay TV Newsletter. Carmel, CA: Paul Kagan Associates. Monthly.

Post. Port Washington, NY: Testa Communications. Monthly.

Private Cable & Wireless Cable. Torrance, CA: Bobit Publishing. Monthly.

Promax International. Los Angeles: Promotion and Marketing Executives in the Electronic Media. Quarterly.

Public Broadcasting Report. Washington, DC: Warren Publishing. Biweekly.

Radio & Records. Los Angeles: Radio & Records. Weekly.

Radio Business Report. Springfield, VA: Radio Business Report. Weekly.

Radio Only Magazine. Cherry Hill, NJ: Inside Radio. Monthly.

RTNDA Communicator. Washington, DC: Radio-Television News Directors Association. Monthly.

Satellite Communications. Atlanta, GA: Intertec Publishing. Monthly.

SMPTE Journal. White Plains, NY: Society of Motion Picture and Television Engineers. Monthly.

Television Digest with Consumer Electronics. Washington, DC: Warren Publishing. Weekly.

Television Quarterly. New York: National Academy of Television Arts and Sciences. Quarterly.

TV Guide. Radnor, PA: News America Publications. Weekly.

TV Technology. Falls Church, VA: Industrial Marketing Advisory Services. Biweekly.

Variety. New York: Cahners Publishing. Weekly.

Video Week. Washington, DC: Warren Publishing. Weekly.

INDEX